INNOVATION AND FIRM PERFORMANCE

Innovation and Firm Performance
Econometric Explorations of Survey Data

Edited by
Alfred Kleinknecht
and
Pierre Mohnen

palgrave

First published 2002 by
PALGRAVE
Houndmills, Basingstoke, Hampshire RG21 6XS and
175 Fifth Avenue, New York, N.Y. 10010
Companies and representatives throughout the world

PALGRAVE is the new global academic imprint of
St. Martin's Press LLC Scholarly and Reference Division and
Palgrave Publishers Ltd (formerly Macmillan Press Ltd).

ISBN 0-333-96109-9 ✓

This book is printed on paper suitable for recycling and
made from fully managed and sustained forest sources.

A catalogue record for this book is available
from the British Library.

Library of Congress Cataloging-in-Publication Data
    Innovation and firm performance: econometric explorations of survey
    data / edited by Alfred Kleinknecht and Pierre Mohnen.
        p.cm.
    Includes bibliographical references and index.
    ISBN 0-333-96109-9 (cloth)
        1. Research, Industrial—Economic aspects. 2. Technological
    innovations—Economic aspects. 3. Industrial productivity.
    I. Kleinknecht, Alfred, 1951 – II. Mohnen, Pierre A.
    HC79.R4 I56 2001
    338'.064—dc21   2001034816

10 9 8 7 6 5 4 3 2 1
11 10 09 08 07 06 05 04 03 02

Printed and bound in Great Britain by
Antony Rowe Ltd, Chippenham, Wiltshire

Contents

PART III   SPILLOVERS AND R&D COLLABORATION

PART IV   INNOVATION AND EXPORT PERFORMANCE

List of Tables

List of Figures

Notes on the Contributors

Spyros Arvanitis is a Senior Research Economist of KOF/ETH (Swiss Institute for Business Cycle Research, Swiss Federal Institute of Technology), Zurich. He is head of the Industrial Economics Research Group of this institute (together with Dr H. Hollenstein). Dr Arvanitis holds doctoral degrees from the University of Zurich (economics) and the Swiss Federal Institute of Technology (chemistry). He has published on economics of innovation, technology diffusion, firm performance and market dynamics.

John Baldwin is Director of the Micro-Economics Analysis Division of Statistics Canada. He has taught at Queen's University, the Canadian Centre for Management Development and was a senior research director at the Economic Council of Canada. His published work includes *The Dynamics of Industrial Competition* and more recently articles on technology and firm performance.

Erik Brouwer is manager at PricewaterhouseCoopers (PwC) at Amsterdam. From 1990 onwards he worked at the Foundation of Economic Research at the University of Amsterdam (SEO) where he received a PhD in 1997. His PhD concerned the use of new types of innovation indicators, determinants of innovation and knowledge transfer. Before joining PwC he worked for two years as a senior researcher at Dialogic, a consulting firm for innovation policy issues.

Alexandre Cabagnols is research assistant in the *Auguste et Léon Walras Research Centre* of the University Lyon 2 (France).

Marcel Dagenais (deceased) was Emeritus Professor at the University of Montreal, a Fellow at CIRANO and a member of the Royal Society of Canada. He was an associate editor and a Fellow of the *Journal of Econometrics*. He published in *Econometrica*, the *Journal of Econometrics*, the *Journal of the American Statistical Association*, the *Review of Economics and Statistics*, and the *Canadian Journal of Economics*.

Paul Diederen is Senior Researcher at the Agricultural Economics Research Institute (LEI) in The Netherlands. He previously held research positions at Maastricht University in The Netherlands and at Warwick

Business School in the UK. His work deals with science, technology and innovation policies. Together with Paul Stoneman, Otto Toivanen and Arjan Wolters, he wrote the book *Innovation and Research Policies: An International Comparative Analysis.*

Florent Favre is 'Attaché INSEE'. He works in SESSI, an institute that performs statistical studies, in particular in manufacturing enterprises, within the French Ministry of Industry. With his expertise in industrial statistics he has contributed to several industrial surveys (especially innovation surveys) in France.

Paul Geroski has been a Professor of Economics at the London Business School and currently serves as a deputy Chairman at the UK Competition Commission. He is a Fellow of the Centre for Economic Policy Research (CEPR) and sits on the Council of the Royal Economic Society.

Petr Hanel is Professor of Economics at the Université de Sherbrooke, Canada, and member of the Centre Inter-universitaire de Recherche sur la Science et la Technologie (CIRST). He is the author of *Technology and Export of Pulp and Paper Machinery* and several articles on the economics of technological change and in international economics. His new book (co-authored with John Baldwin) is *Innovation and Knowledge Creation in an Open Economy.*

Heinz Hollenstein is a Senior Research Economist of KOF/ETH (Swiss Institute for Business Cycle Research, Swiss Federal Institute of Technology), Zurich. He is head of the Industrial Economics Research Group of this institute (together with Dr S. Arvanitis) Dr Hollenstein holds degrees in economics from the University of Berne. He has published on international trade, foreign direct investment, economics of innovation, technology diffusion and firm performance.

Alfred Kleinknecht is Professor in the Economics of Innovation at Delft University of Technology (TU Delft). Previously he was Professor of Industrial Economics at Amsterdam. Since 1978 he was affiliated to the Berlin *Wissenschaftszentrum*, the University of Maastricht, and the two Amsterdam Universities.

José M. Labeaga is Associate Professor of Economics at the Department of Economics of UNED, Madrid. He previously taught at the Department of Economics of Universitat Autònoma of Barcelona and Universitat Pompeu Fabra. He has been member of the Editorial Board of

Investigaciones Económicas and is now member of the Editorial Board of
Revista de Economía Aplicada. His recent papers include 'A double-hurdle
rational addiction model with heterogeneity: estimating the demand for
tobacco', published in the *Journal of Econometrics*, and 'Autoregressive
Models with Sample Selectivity for Panel Data' (joint with M. Arellano
and O. Bover), published in C. Hsiao, K. Lahiri, Lung-Fei Lee y M. H.
Pesaran (eds), *Analysis of Panels and Limited Dependent Variable Models*.

Christian Le Bas is Professor in the Economics of Innovation and
Organisation at University Lyon 2 (France). He is former deputy director
of University Lyon 2. He carries out research in the field of evolutionary
economics and the applied economics of innovation in the *Auguste et Léon
Walras Research Centre*.

Elisabeth Lefebvre is Professor of Technology Management in the
Industrial Engineering Group at École Polytechnique de Montréal. She has
contributed with Pierre Mohnen and Louis Lefebvre to *Doing Business in
the Knowledge-Based Economy: Facts and Policy Challenges*.

Louis-André Lefebvre is Professor of Innovation Management in the
Industrial Engineering Group at École Polytechnique de Montréal, where
he also acts as Director of the research group ePoly. He has contributed
with Pierre Mohnen and Elisabeth Lefebvre to a recent work published
by *Economica* entitled 'La conduite des Affaires dans l 'Économie du
Savoir'.

Aija Leiponen is Assistant Professor of Applied Economics and
Management at Cornell University. She obtained her PhD from the
Helsinki School of Economics and Business Administration, and has previously worked at the Research Institute of the Finnish Economy (ETLA).
Her research concentrates on the organizational aspects of innovation.
Most recently she has examined knowledge creation in service industries,
particularly knowledge-intensive business services. The focus of this
research is on the organization of collaboration and knowledge exchange
among firms.

Nadine Mandran is statistician at the French National Institute of
Agronomic Research.

Vincent Mangematin is Senior Researcher at the French National
Institute of Agronomic Research since 1993. He studies innovation and
technology transfer in life sciences and biotechnology in particular.

Ester Martínez-Ros is Assistant Professor of Management at the Department of Business Administration at Universidad Carlos III, Madrid. She previously taught at the Department of Business Administration of Universitat Autonòma of Barcelona. Her recent papers have been published in the *Journal of High Technology Management Research* at the *Economics of Innovation and New Technology*.

Pierre Mohnen is Professor at the University of Quebec in Montreal, a Fellow at CIRANO, and a frequent visitor at foreign universities and research centres. He has published in the *European Economic Review*, the *International Journal of Economics*, the *Canadian Journal of Economics*, *Structural Change and Economic Dynamics*, and *Annales d'Économie et de Statistique*.

Syoum Negassi is Professor of Econometrics and Innovation Management at the West Indies University and he also acts as Consultant at the Ministry of Industry (SESSI) in Paris. His sphere of competence is official statistics and industry surveys on production, employment, tangible and intangible investment, firms' financial results and innovation.

Remco Oostendorp is Senior Researcher at the Economic and Social Institute of the Free University, Amsterdam. He is also a Fellow of the Amsterdam Institute for International Development and a Research Associate of the Centre for the Study of African Economies at the University of Oxford.

Etienne Pfister has a PhD from the University of Paris–Sorbonne. His fields of interests include intellectual property rights, technological spillovers and firms' innovative strategies. He is currently teaching macroeconomics, microeconomics and the economics of innovation at Sorbonne. His recent publications cover the pharmaceutical industry and the Trade-Related Intellectual Property Rights (TRIPS) agreement.

David Sabourin is a Senior Research Analyst at Statistics Canada and has worked extensively on technology and innovation. Recent work includes investigation of the impact of technology use on firm performance in Canadian manufacturing.

Hans van Meijl is Senior Researcher at the Agricultural Economics Research Institute (LEI) in The Netherlands. He previously held research positions at Maastricht University and MERIT (Maastricht Economic Research institute on Innovation and Technology) in The Netherlands.

He worked on innovation and international trade. He is the author of *Endogenous Technological Change: The Influence of Information Technology, Theoretical Considerations and Empirical Results.*

Hans van Ophem is Associate Professor of Econometrics of the University of Amsterdam. He has published in the *Review of Economics and Statistics, Econometric Theory, Journal of Business and Economic Statistics* and the *International Economic Review.*

John Van Reenen is a Professor at University College London, a Research Fellow at the Institute for Fiscal Studies and a partner in Lexecon Economics. He is an editor of the *Journal of Industrial Relations*, the *Review of Economic Studies* and the *European Economic Review.*

Chris Walters is a Senior Consultant with Lexecon – Europe's leading antitrust economics consulting firm. He was previously a faculty member in the Department of Economics at London Business School. His research interests include innovation and corporate growth. Recent publications include 'Are Differences in Firm Size Transitory or Permanent?' (*Journal of Applied Econometrics*), 'How Persistently do Firms Innovate?' (*Research Policy*) and 'Corporate Growth and Profitability' (*Journal of Industrial Economics*).

Arjan Wolters is Researcher at the Agricultural Economics Research Institute (LEI) in The Netherlands. He previously held a research position at MERIT (Maastricht Economic Research institute on Innovation and Technology) in The Netherlands. At MERIT his work was mainly concerned with the evaluation of regional innovation policy. At LEI he studies innovation among Dutch farmers. Together with Paul Diederen, Paul Stoneman and Otto Toivanen, he wrote *Innovation and Research Policies: An International Comparative Analysis.*

Table 1 Overview of data coverage in this book

Chapter	Country	Sector	Innovation data	Other data
1 Mohnen and Dagenais	Denmark; Ireland	Manufacturing	CIS 1, 1992 (in microaggregated form)	–
2 Geroski *et al.*	UK	Manufacturing	SPRU database; unbalanced panel of 640 firms, 1972–83	Data stream; US Patent Office
3 Van Ophem *et al.*	Netherlands	Manufacturing and services	Community Innovation Survey, 1992	Dutch Innovation Survey, 1988
4 Diederen *et al.*	Netherlands	Agriculture	Farm Innovation Survey, 1995–7	–
5 Baldwin *et al.*	Canada	Manufacturing	Survey of Innovation and Advanced Technology, 1993	–
6 Le Bas and Cabagnols	France	Manufacturing	French Innovation Surveys, 1991, 1993	Appropriability of Innovation Survey; Annual Enterprise Survey
7 Martínez-Ros and Labeaga	Spain	Manufacturing	Spanish Innovation Surveys, balanced panel, 1990–3	–
8 Mangematin and Mandran	France	Agro-food sector	French Innovation Survey, 1986–90	R&D survey; Annual Enterprise Survey
9 Favre *et al.*	France	Manufacturing	CIS survey, 1990–2; French Innovation Survey, 1994–6	Appropriability, R&D, Annual Enterprise Surveys DREE database
10 Arvanitis and Hollenstein	Switzerland	Manufacturing	Swiss Innovation Survey, 1990	R&D Survey, Patent Data, Enterprise Survey
11 Leiponen	Finland	Manufacturing	Finnish Innovation Survey, 1996	Labour Survey
12 Lefebvre and Lefebvre	Canada	Manufacturing	Longitudinal data of SME contractors, 1994, 1997	–
13 Kleinknecht and Oostendorp	Netherlands	Manufacturing, services, agriculture	National Enterprise Panel of the Organisation for Strategic Labour Market Research (OSA)	–

Introduction

Alfred Kleinknecht and Pierre Mohnen

The chapters in this volume are a selection of revised contributions presented at two workshops financed by the European Commission within the Targeted Socio-economic Research Program (TSER) entitled 'R&D, Innovation, and Productivity'. The first took place in Paris in June 1998, the second in Delft in February 1999. The common thread behind these contributions is that they all use innovation survey data to explore econometrically a wide range of topics on innovation, from measurement issues, to sources and effects of innovation.

THE DATA USED IN THE VARIOUS STUDIES

The data used span a broad spectrum of innovation data from ten different countries or regions. All studies are based on firm data, and most of the data are from manufacturing. Two studies focus on particular sectors: Diederen *et al.* on agriculture, and Mangematin and Mandran, on agro-food firms. Van Ophem *et al.* and Kleinknecht and Oostendorp, besides manufacturing, also have data on services. Most data are cross-sections from a single survey. Le Bas and Cabagnols and Lefebvre and Lefebvre contrast the results obtained from two cross-sections. Geroski *et al.*, van Ophem *et al.*, and Martínez-Ros and Labeaga estimate dynamic models with panel data. About half of the studies rely exclusively on the information contained in the innovation surveys, while the other half use complementary data from other surveys or patent statistics.

ORGANISATION OF THE BOOK

This volume is divided into four parts. The three studies in Part 1 deal mainly with innovation indicators. Mohnen and Dagenais, in Chapter 1 propose an innovation indicator constructed from innovation survey data. Their indicator is the conditional expected share in sales of innovative products, combining the estimated probability to innovate and the estimated percentage of sales resulting from new products. Geroski *et al.* (Chapter 2) examine the relationship between two indicators of innovative output: numbers of significant innovations and patent counts. They examine the causality between both of them and cash flow. Van Ophem *et al.* (Chapter 3) look into the interrelationship between patent counts and research and development (R&D) expenditures.

The four studies in Part 2 focus on the determinants of innovation in four different types of environment: Canadian, French and Spanish manufacturing firms, and farms in the Netherlands. The contributors Diederen *et al.* (Chapter 4), Baldwin *et al.* (Chapter 5), Le Bas and Cabagnols (Chapter 7), and Martínez-Ros and Labeaga (Chapter 8), examine the influence of firm size, market concentration, diversification, competition among innovators, vertical integration, firm age or experience, membership of a group or of a consortium, foreign ownership, capital intensity, export orientation, sources of knowledge, appropriability conditions, R&D intensity, research organization, and other firm strategies. The three studies on manufacturing data examine, in particular, the differential determinants of product and process innovation.

Part 3 is devoted to the study of R&D collaboration and knowledge spillovers, and indirectly on the appropriate private and public organization of knowledge. Mangematin and Mandran (Chapter 8) explore the presence of public research spillovers in the French agro-food sector. Favre *et al.* (Chapter 9), and Arvanitis and Hollenstein (Chapter 10) study the effects of domestic and international R&D spillovers in French and Swiss manufacturing firms respectively. In terms of R&D policy, Favre *et al.* compare the influence of subsidies from the European Union (EU) and from the French government on R&D and international R&D spillovers. Arvanitis and Hollenstein try to assess whether returns to knowledge (own, and spilled over from domestic and foreign sources) depend on appropriability and opportunity conditions, on the types of innovation costs incurred, on the objectives of innovation, on sources of knowledge, and on the degree of innovativeness. Leiponen (Chapter 11) examines possible complementarities between own R&D, collaboration with various partners (competitors, customers, suppliers and universities), R&D outsourcing, and product innovations.

The two studies in Part 4 examine innovation and export performance in Canadian and Dutch firms respectively. In the Lefebvre and Lefebvre study in Chapter 12, the accent is on the importance of technological and commercial capabilities on export performance. The Kleinknecht and Oostendorp study (Chapter 13) focuses rather on the direction of (mutual) causality between R&D and exports.

We have classified the studies into one of the four thematic groups, but this does not preclude their addressing some of the other topics. In an attempt to give credit to the contributions of each chapter, we now review them by contrasting their individual results.

EXECUTIVE SUMMARY OF RESULTS

We group and summarize the empirical findings of the various studies along major influential variables. Next to each result we mention the authors of the study, where the interested reader can find more details and qualifications about the result obtained. Some of these results may be country- or industry-specific, or even depend on the econometric treatment of the data. But we believe that this quick summary gives a flavour of what innovation survey data can reveal about determinants of innovation, of potential points of disagreement among researchers and the need for further investigation, and of yet unexplored topics.

The Relationship between Innovation Indicators

Mohnen and Dagenais use the observed binary responses to the question of whether a firm is innovative or not, and its reported share in sales of innovative products, to construct for each firm an expected share in sales conditional on firm and market characteristics. On the basis of this measure they compare the innovation performances of Denmark and Ireland. They conclude that, overall, Denmark is slightly more innovative than Ireland, but also that non-innovators have more or less the same potential to innovate in both countries, and that each country has some sectors where it is more innovative than the other country. Of the three variables related to R&D (R&D expenditures, continuous R&D programmes and R&D co-operation), only R&D done on a continuous basis has a significantly positive effect on the amount of innovation. Baldwin *et al.* find that R&D accounts for about 25 per cent of the probability of innovating. Both results come quite close to earlier findings by Brouwer and Kleinknecht (1996). Analysing CIS 1 (1992) data from the Netherlands, the latter also found that there is only a weak relationship between R&D input and innovative output, the relationship between inputs and outputs being moderated by numerous other factors (for example, technological trajectories, firm size, regional environment, and others). The finding that the nature of the R&D function (continuous R&D rather than occasional R&D) is highly significant for innovative output underlines the importance of the historical accumulation of knowledge.

Using a panel of patent and innovations counts, Geroski, Van Reenen and Walters find that patents (Granger) cause innovations, and not the reverse. Patents are more sensitive to supply-side factors, and innovations are more sensitive to variations in demand. Both have a strong history dependence (positive feedback) reflecting opportunity and appropriability conditions. Using a blunter measure of patents (for products, and of trade secrets for processes), namely a dummy variable indicating the use or non-use of these appropriability measures, Baldwin, Hanel and Sabourin reach a somewhat different conclusion. Innovators are more likely than non-innovators to use patents and trade secrets. More interesting, perhaps, is the absence of an effect of patents on innovations. The authors interpret this finding as an indication that past success does not necessarily breed future success. Perhaps the difference between the two studies is to be ascribed to the nature of the innovations considered. Geroski, Van Reenen and Walters use the Sussex database on 'significant' innovations in the UK, while Baldwin, Hanel and Sabourin use innovations in Canada that may be less significant. In any case, they emphasize that Canada has a fairly low R&D intensity. Both papers agree that is difficult to account for the episodic nature of innovation.

Regarding the link between patents and R&D, van Ophem, Brouwer, Kleinknecht and Mohnen find that patents affect R&D, but R&D does not affect patents. The evidence drawn from two innovation surveys in the Netherlands indicates that it is more likely that a patent leads to further development R&D than that R&D yields new patents in a kind of input–output relationship. This is easy to reconcile with the findings by Geroski, Van Reenen and Walters.

Determinants of Innovation

The various chapters report some sporadic evidence for the importance of factors such as subsidies for a firm's R&D investment (Favre *et al.*), or of foreign control that seems to play no significant role once consideration is given to size and R&D (Baldwin *et al.*), or of experience and firm age on innovativeness (for example, Diederen *et al.*). The main findings on determinants of innovation can be summarized around four topics: firm size; past demand growth; competition; and sources of knowledge and technical collaboration.

Firm Size

Diederen *et al.*, Baldwin *et al.*, and Leiponen conclude that the probability of being innovative increases with firm size. For Mohnen and Dagenais, the probability of innovating also increases with size, although in a non-linear way. Martínez-Ros and Labeaga also find indications of non-linearity. The latter report that size stimulates process innovation only for firms with more than 2000 employees. Certainly, these indications of non-linearity still merit further study, in which case the nature of a firm's technological trajectory is likely to play a role (see, for example, Vossen and Nooteboom, 1996). For the time being, we can conclude that, apart from the question whether the relationship is linear, the various studies conclude consistently that the probability of being innovative increases with firm size.

Besides the probability of innovation, Mohnen and Dagenais also offer information about the share of total sales taken by innovative products. This latter indicator can be interpreted in two different ways. A high share of innovative products in total sales can either mean that the firm has introduced a high number of new products, and/or it can mean that these products underwent a rapid diffusion. The former would be a measure of innovation intensity, while the latter would measure successful diffusion. Whatever interpretation we prefer, we can conclude from Mohnen and Dagenais that the share of innovative products in total sales is not related strongly to size. In other words, smaller firms definitely have a lower probability of being innovators; however, given that they innovate, the number of innovations introduced and/or the speed of diffusion is certainly not lower than in larger firms. This is consistent with earlier findings, some of which suggested that the innovation intensity of smaller innovators might be even higher than those of their larger counterparts (see several chapters in Kleinknecht, ed., 1996).

Past Demand Growth

Starting from Schmookler's (1966) classical study, the hypothesis that the flow of innovations is enhanced by (expected) growth of effective demand has been investigated several times. For example, Scherer (1982), and Kleinknecht and Verspagen (1990) found support for Schmookler's hypothesis, although the evidence was less striking than was suggested in Schmookler's original work. In a time series analysis of British innovation and patent data, Geroski and Walters (1995) found innovations being Granger-caused by demand, and in a recent panel analysis, Brouwer and Kleinknecht (1999) report that firm-level changes in R&D are sensitive to demand growth.

However, these positive findings about 'demand-pull' need an important qualification. Walsh (1984) reported evidence of a 'counter-Schmookler' pattern in a historical study of new chemical entities. Moreover, in the context of discussing Kondratieff long waves in long-run economic growth, evidence was found that fairly radical innovations ('basic innovations') move in a counter-cyclical ('counter-Schmookler') pattern (Kleinknecht, 1990). Following Schumpeter (1939), these radical innovations are supposed to cluster in the 'troughs' (and early recovery periods) of Kondratieff long waves, and initiate new growth industries. For simplicity, let us call them 'Schumpeterian' innovations. These earthshaking 'Schumpeterian' innovations may open up entirely new technological trajectories and initiate new growth industries, while (incremental) 'Schmooklerian' innovations occur within established technological trajectories and industries.

All the innovations indicators used in this book are 'Schmooklerian' rather than 'Schumpeterian'. Unfortunately, some of the chapters miss demand as a control variable. Clearly, the specification of models is still hampered by data availability. Mohnen and Dagenais find some evidence of demand-pull in their Irish (but not in their Danish) data, and Geroski *et al.* find some influence of cash flow on patents and (less so) on innovations, while past innovations have more influence on cash flow than patents. Obviously, innovation enhances demand and, in turn, demand enhances innovation. As we get more and better panel data, future studies will be able to explore more precisely what is the relative strength of causation in either direction.

Competition

The extensive literature on market structure and innovation is not really conclusive, and, whatever the outcome may be, the explanatory power of market structure for innovation is not very strong (see the survey by Scherer, 1992). There is some evidence in this book that market power is conducive to innovation. However, there is no consistent evidence about the nature of this relationship. Baldwin *et al.* argue that innovation seems to be most favoured by intermediate levels of competition (Baldwin *et al.*). In contrast, Martínez-Ros and Labeaga confirm the Schumpeter hypothesis (measured by the average gross-profit margin): monopoly stimulates innovation. However, they also find that the probability of innovating decreases with the degree of vertical integration (that is, the share of intermediate products). Le Bas and Cabagnols find that competition has a different impact on product and process innovations. Leiponen concludes that competition stimulates innovation, and that the Schumpeter effect (as captured by the proportion of small firms in the industry) is never significant.

Sources of Knowledge and Technological Collaboration

According to Leiponen, innovation in all its dimensions (the propensity to engage in R&D activities, the tendency to collaborate on R&D with outside partners, and innovative output) is depressed in technological regimes where competitors and suppliers are important sources of knowledge. However, innovation is thriving in regimes where customers and universities are important sources of information. Leiponen stresses the importance of technological regimes and competencies for innovation and R&D collaboration. Competencies matter for R&D, collaboration and innovation, apart from collaboration with competitors. Personnel with technical skills are more sought after than those holding a post-graduate degree, for instance, in collaborations with suppliers.

Leiponen obtains complementarities between internal R&D, R&D outsourcing, outside collaboration, and product innovation. Similarly, Favre *et al.* report that internal R&D, external R&D and inward foreign direct investment are complementary. Diederen *et al.* also observe significant complementarities: innovative firms are also active in marketing, organizational changes, integration and horizontal co-operation.

Determinants of Product versus Process Innovation

Product and process innovations have different determinants: firm size, competition, sources of knowledge, diversification, and complementarity between product and process innovations.

Firm Size

Firm size enhances process innovations more than product innovations (Le Bas and Cabagnols, Baldwin *et al.*, and Martínez-Ros and Labeaga). Baldwin *et al.* obtain a monotonic relationship between size and innovation, while Martínez-Ros and Labeaga find a U-shaped relationship.

Competition

For Le Bas and Cabagnols, economic competition (measured by the inverse of the Herfindahl index of sectoral concentration, or the inverse market share) favours process innovations, whereas technological competition (the percentage of innovators in the same sector) stimulates more product innovations. Martínez-Ros and Labeaga's findings that the disciplining effect from foreign ownership and the retarding effect from recession only apply to process innovations is consistent with the Le Bas and Cabagnols finding.

Sources of Knowledge

Le Bas and Cabagnols find that process innovators tend to rely on upstream sources of knowledge and on consortium research, whereas product innovators source their knowledge from downward and horizontal links. Martínez-Ros and Labeaga also report insignificant R&D spillover effects from within the industry for process innovations, but negative effects for product innovations.

Diversification

Diversification (Le Bas and Cabagnols), laboratory research (Le Bas and Cabagnols), experience from past innovations (Martínez-Ros and Labeaga), and high capital intensity (Martínez-Ros and Labeaga) favour product over process innovations.

Complementarity between Product and Process Innovations

Martínez-Ros and Labeaga report that, after controlling for the lagged own dependent variable, the significance of the other indicator vanishes. Hence, apparently, there is no complementarity between product and process innovations. By contrast, Le Bas and Cabagnols report that past innovators are more likely to innovate in both products and processes simultaneously, a result they interpret as a tendency for those firms to develop a widening profile of innovation. They also find that firms that pursue a cost-reduction strategy favour not so much process over product innovations, but rather joint product and process innovations over product innovations alone.

Spillovers

Geroski *et al.* report that user-industry output growth stimulates innovations but not patents. There is little sign of innovation or patent spillovers from other firms in the main operating industry. Mangematin and Mandran find, first, no sign of geographic R&D spillovers in the French agro-food industry. Second, the presence of academic labs influences the probability of firms innovating, but not their innovation intensity. Third, academic research affects all agro-food firms, not just the R&D-intensive ones. Fourth, firms with an R&D facility are more likely to realize radical than incremental innovations. Arvanitis and Hollenstein also report important spillovers, domestic and foreign, that enhance total factor productivity in Swiss firms. Intersectoral spillovers dominate intra-industry spillovers.

Returns to Innovation

Diederen *et al.* report that innovative farms show higher profits and grow faster. Similar results are reported by Favre *et al.* They find that factors such as a firm's R&D intensity, market share and concentration have a positive impact on profits. The same holds for national R&D spillovers, but the impact of international R&D spillovers on profits is larger (Favre *et al.*). Arvanitis and Hollenstein report that the productivity of knowledge capital increases with the use of external knowledge sources, with technological opportunity, and the degree of innovativeness. Among innovation inputs, development activities have the highest effect on productivity. The return to patents increases with higher appropriability conditions, and with the deliberate pursuit of certain objectives, such as the creation of new markets.

Co-operation

In Dutch farming, Diederen *et al.* report that innovators develop ideas themselves. They collaborate to implement them, but do not benefit from being member of a club, and do not protect their innovation. Favre *et al.* find that external R&D and inward foreign direct investment are complementary to international R&D co-operation, and that subsidies from the French government or the European Union have a positive effect on R&D dedicated to international co-operation. R&D collaboration increases with firm size (Leiponen).

Innovation and Export Performance

Lefebvre and Lefebvre report that firm size, firm age, and type of firm (contractor or subcontractor) influence exports positively. Moreover, technological characteristics such as R&D, the level of automation, knowledge intensity, unique know-how, quality norms, and commercial capabilities such as trademarks, networking, distribution access, manufacturing agents and import activities play a positive role. In high-tech industries, technological capabilities dominate. The presence of trade unions, the degree of modernization of equipment, and technical norms other than ISO-certification turn out not to be significant. Kleinknecht and Oostendorp find that a firm's export intensity exerts a positive influence on its probability of being an R&D performer. At the same time, R&D intensity increases the probability of being an exporter. In terms of intensities, export intensity influences R&D intensity, but not vice versa. Moreover, Kleinknecht and Oostendorp find that the share of employment with higher education enhances both R&D and export performance. This latter finding is consistent with the emphasis on competences for export performance by Lefebvre and Lefebvre.

Econometric Discussion

Innovation survey data have peculiar characteristics, which require some special econometric techniques and invite us to be modest regarding the results obtained. If researchers have to rely entirely on the data from these surveys and cannot merge them with other data sets, the number of explanatory variables for innovation is rather limited. In particular, it is not easy to discriminate between innovators and non-innovators from innovation survey data alone. As indicated in Table 1, some of the studies in this volume resort to more than one source of data. Some innovation surveys are more complete than others and allow more questions to be examined.

Because of the way the standard survey questionnaires are set up, most of the information and explanatory variables are available for innovators only. There is thus a problem of selection bias, which has to be corrected for. This is done by using tobit or generalized tobit models (see Mohnen and Dagenais, Lefebvre and Lefebvre, and Kleinknecht and Oostendorp). Many variables in the surveys are qualitative in nature (binary responses, ordinal responses, or count data) and require the application of dependent variable techniques. A number of these techniques have been used in the papers here assembled: the univariate probit model (Lefebvre and Lefebvre), the univariate logit model (Martínez-Ros and Labeaga), the bivariate probit model (Baldwin *et al.*), the trivariate probit model (Leiponen), count data models (Geroski *et al.*, van Ophem *et al.*), and the multinomial logit model (Le Bas and Cabagnols, Mangematin and Madran), using maximum likelihood or pseudo-maximum likelihood techniques.

To date, few innovation surveys are available in most countries, preventing the analysis of dynamic models and the use of panel data techniques, which both require longitudinal data. Yet, after controlling for experience effects (lagged values of the same variable) and unobserved heterogeneity, the picture regarding determinants of innovation can be quite different. For example, complementarities between product and process innovations (captured by cross-effects) disappear in Martínez-Ros and Labeaga's analysis when lagged effects are included. Only the chapters by Geroski *et al.* and Martínez-Ros and Labeaga estimate panel data and dynamic effects. Geroski *et al.* estimate a three-equation linear feedback model with fixed effects. Martínez-Ros and Labeaga compare the estimates from a pooled logit model assuming no unobserved heterogeneity, a random effects logit model, and the Chamberlain two-step method to handle unobserved heterogeneity, all with dynamic effects. Favre *et al.* compare the within, between and random coefficients panel data techniques.

A serious problem with innovation survey data is the handling of simultaneity. It is hard to exclude a priori the absence of simultaneity between innovation, exports, R&D, patents, investments and so on. A firm that innovates is also likely to incur R&D expenditures, to invest in new equipment and to patent, with common explanatory variables for each of these variables. New products are likely to be sold domestically as well as abroad, and therefore lead to more exports and increase in size. But exports and size may also in themselves provide better conditions for innovating. Careful consideration of simultaneity is given in the papers by Baldwin *et al.*, Geroski *et al.*, Favre *et al.*, and Kleinknecht and Oostendorp.

References

ARVANITIS, S. and HOLLENSTEIN, H. (1996) 'Industrial innovation in Switzerland', in A. Kleinknecht (ed.), *Determinants of Innovation*. London: Macmillan, pp. 13–62.

BROUWER, E. and KLEINKNECHT, A. (1996) 'Determinants of innovation: A micro-econometric analysis of three alternative innovation output indicators', in A. Kleinknecht (ed.), *Determinants of Innovation*. London: Macmillan, pp. 99–124.

BROUWER, E. and KLEINKNECHT, A. (1999) 'Keynes-plus? Effective Demand and Changes in Firm-level R&D: An Empirical Note', *Cambridge Journal of Economics*, vol. 23, pp. 385–91.

GEROSKI, P. A. and WALTERS, C. F. (1995) 'Innovative Activity over the Business Cycle', *Economic Journal*, vol. 105, pp. 916–28.

KLEINKNECHT, A. (1990) 'Are there Schumpeterian waves of innovation?', *Cambridge Journal of Economics*, vol. 14, pp. 81–92.

KLEINKNECHT, A. and VERSPAGEN, B. (1990) 'Demand and Innovation: Schmookler Re-examined', *Research Policy*, vol. 19, pp. 287–394.

SCHERER, F. M. (1982) 'Demand-pull and Technological Innovation: Schmookler Reconsidered', *Journal of Industrial Economics*, vol. 30, pp. 225–37.

SCHERER, F. M. (1992) 'Schumpeter and Plausible Capitalism', *Journal of Economic Literature*, vol. 30, pp. 1416–33.

SCHMOOKLER, J. (1966) *Invention and Economic Growth*. Cambridge, Mass.: Harvard University Press.

SCHUMPETER, J. A. (1939) *Business Cycles*, New York: McGraw-Hill (2 vols).

VOSSEN, R. W. and NOOTEBOOM, B. (1996) 'Firm Size and Participation in R&D', in A. Kleinknecht (ed.), *Determinants of Innovation*. London: Macmillan, pp. 155–66.

WALSH, V. (1984) 'Invention and Innovation in the Chemical Industry: Demand-pull or Discovery-push?', *Research Policy*, vol. 13, pp. 211–34.

Part I
Comparing Innovation Indicators

1 Towards an Innovation Intensity Index: The Case of CIS 1 in Denmark and Ireland

Pierre Mohnen and Marcel Dagenais *

1.1 INTRODUCTION

Under the guidelines set out in the Oslo Manual (OECD, 1992) and under the co-ordination of Eurostat, various European countries conducted an innovation survey in the year 1992. The Oslo Manual and the Community Innovation Surveys (CIS) grew out of a concern to capture: (a) a wider range of innovation activities than R&D expenditures, such as the acquisition of patents and licences, product design, personnel training, trial production, and market analysis; (b) indicators of innovation output other than patents, such as the introduction of new products, processes and organizational changes, the percentage of sales arising from new products, the percentage of sales arising from products new to the industry, and the share of products at various stages of the product life-cycle; and (c) information about the way innovation proceeds, such as the sources of knowledge, the reasons for innovating, the perceived obstacles to innovation, the perceived strength of various appropriability mechanisms, and the recourse to research cooperation.

The purpose of this chapter is to propose a composite innovation indicator derived from an econometric prediction of the likelihood of innovating, and of the amount of innovation performed by a particular firm, given information on its characteristics and on the environment in which it operates. The indicator is constructed from various pieces of information contained in the Community Innovation Surveys. It combines qualitative and quantitative data. It allows for the comparison of innovativeness across industries or classes of firms in a particular country. To the extent that the national innovation surveys are sufficiently homogeneous, it also allows comparisons across countries. As more surveys become available, we can proceed to a comparison of innovation over time. This chapter applies the proposed indicator to the CIS 1 data for Denmark and Ireland. The composite indicator is compared to various partial indicators contained directly in the innovation surveys.

The chapter is organized as follows. In Section 1.2 we go over the various partial innovation indicators available in CIS 1, and use them to compare innovation records in Denmark and Ireland. In Section 1.3 we discuss the possibility of constructing a single composite innovation indicator. In Section 1.4 we present the model underlying our proposed composite indicator. In Section 1.5 we present the estimation results of our model and compare our composite innovation indicator with the partial innovation indicators. We summarize the main points of the chapter in the concluding section.

1.2   VARIOUS PARTIAL INNOVATION INDICATORS

The CIS 1 dataset contains a rich amount of data on the input, the output, and the modalities of innovative activities. Some of these data are quantitative, some are dichotomous (yes/no responses), and some are polychotomous, categorically ordered, data (on a scale of 1 to 5, the so-called Likert scale). On the input side, we have quantitative data on R&D expenditures, and on current and capital expenditures on innovation, and dichotomous data on whether firms have engaged or not in R&D, in R&D collaboration or in acquisition of technology. On the output side, we have the declaration of whether an enterprise has introduced a new product or process, the percentage of sales with respect to incrementally or significantly changed products, the percentage of sales at various stages of the product life-cycle, the sales share of innovative products new to the enterprise/group, and the sales share of innovative products new to the industry.[1] Innovation and R&D expenditures are further broken down into products and processes, and sales figures are split into domestic sales and exports.[2] On the modalities of innovation, we have dichotomous data on whether R&D was done on a continuous basis, and in co-operation with others, and categorical data on information for innovation, the reasons for innovating, the perceived obstacles to innovation, and the perceived strength of various appropriability mechanisms.[3]

Do these various indicators coincide? There are good reasons to think that input and output indicators might differ. First of all, not all firms are equally efficient in turning research efforts into sales, productivity or profits. Secondly, firms may have different ways of innovating. Some rely on their own research, while others rely more on research networks or on the outright purchase of ideas. Different structures in the current expenditures on innovation can therefore coexist, just as firms can have different technologies of production. Therefore, reliance on R&D expenditures alone might give a false impression of the comparative innovation efforts or capacities.

These points are illustrated in the following two studies. Baldwin and Gellatly (2000) show that the ranking of Canadian newly-born firms in terms of innovation capacity depends on whether the emphasis is placed on technological competencies (for example, computer-controlled production; use of information technology), innovative competencies (for example, R&D; the introduction of new products) or human capital skills (for example, training; skilled personnel). All new firms are strong somewhere. Crépon *et al.* (1996) report that only 20 per cent of the 9871 French manufacturing firms in their sample that did some research in 1989 innovated between 1986 and 1990, whereas only 74 per cent of all innovators performed some R&D. These numbers show very clearly the difference between R&D and innovation.

In spite of this, various studies show that the alternative measures of innovation are correlated to some extent. Crépon *et al.* (1996) use the French Innovation Surveys, which cover the period 1986–90, and compare four indicators of innovation: the amount of R&D, the number of patents, the dichotomous variable indicating whether or not a firm made a radical innovation, and the share in sales of new products. They find similar sectoral and firm-specific determinants for the four innovation measures, although the explanation is stronger for R&D than for the share in sales of new products. The four indicators are therefore likely to be correlated. A similar exercise has been done on the Dutch Innovation Survey data by Brouwer and Kleinknecht (1996). They compare the determinants of new product announcements, of the shares in sales of products new to the firm but not to the industry (imitations), and of the shares in sales of products new to the industry (genuine innovations). They estimate a generalized tobit model and find that R&D is correlated with the probability of innovation, whatever the measure of innovation, but not with the level of it, except for imitations. They also find a similar estimated 'innovation production model' on the three sets of data. Crépon *et al.* (1998) relate the share of products less than five years old to the stock of R&D. They estimate an elasticity of the former with respect to the latter of 0.3 on French innovation data.

Before comparing various partial innovation indicators from CIS 1, we want to make a few remarks about the data they contain.

1. We should bear in mind that the data we are working with have been micro-aggregated by Eurostat for reasons of confidentiality (Eurostat (1996) explains the micro-aggregation procedure used). On the basis of statistical criteria (such as sample distributions by deciles, variance, Pearson correlation coefficients) Eurostat (1996) concludes that the quality of the micro-aggregation is quite good. However, it admits that the quality is not the same for all variables (because the response rates are higher for some variables than others), and that the comparability between the original and the micro-aggregated variables deteriorates in the tails of the distributions. In the remainder of the report we shall treat each observation as pertaining to a particular firm.

2. We should also be aware of the inherent limitations of the data. As discussed at great length in Archibugi *et al.* (1994), the first round of the Community Innovation Surveys has a number of deficiencies: the national surveys differ regarding sample units, coverage, cut-off points in the number of employees, actual data collection, and sampling design. The questionnaire was perceived to be too long, which could explain the low response rates as well as the bad quality of, and inconsistency in, some of the responses. In particular, many non-responses were observed for the items 'expenditures on innovation', 'sales according to life cycle' and 'sales from new or improved products'. The international comparability of the CIS data is therefore hazardous. The data are probably better suited for cross-industry comparisons within countries than for cross-country comparisons.

3. There is little information in the dataset regarding non-innovators. Firms are first asked some general questions on their identity, such as their total sales (broken down into domestic sales and exports), their number of employees, their industry affiliation, and their possible belonging to a conglomerate. Then come the three central questions: whether or not they have introduced a new or a changed product; whether they have introduced a new process; and whether they intend to do either of these in the near future. If they respond 'no' to the three questions, they are only asked for their perception of a list of obstacles to innovation. And that completes the questionnaire. There is thus very little information in the CIS 1 database to discriminate between innovators and non-innovators. In some countries, subject to data accessibility, innovation surveys can be merged with other surveys on the same business units. Access to these data then allows a deeper analysis of the innovation potential for non-innovative firms, and a correction for selectivity bias in econometric analyses on quantitative data characterizing innovative firms.

We have cleaned the data for outliers, missing values, and inconsistencies. We have eliminated all enterprises with fewer than twenty employees, with missing industry affiliation, with sales growth from 1990 to 1992 lower than −40 per cent and higher than 250 per cent, with R&D/sales ratios positive but lower than 0.1 per cent or higher than 50 per cent, or with current expenditures on innovations positive but lower than 0.1 per cent or higher than 100 per cent of their sales. Table 1.1 summarizes the outcome of this cleaning exercice.

The first way to ascertain the innovation performance is by way of count data. We can count the percentage of innovating firms, the percentage of innovators with products new to the industry, the percentage of R&D performers, the percentage of continuous R&D performers, and so on. Table 1.2 presents some of those count indicators. Of the total number of manufacturing firms in the restricted sample, 65 per cent of them have innovated in Denmark against 77 per cent in Ireland.[4] Two-thirds of the innovators (or 42.6 per cent of all firms in the sample) have introduced a product new to the industry in Denmark. No information on this variable exists for Ireland. Of all innovating firms in Denmark (Ireland), 82 per cent (67 per cent) are R&D performers. Because of the way the questionnaire has been formulated, there is unfortunately no information on the number of R&D performers who have not innovated. The proportion of innovating firms is generally higher in Ireland than in Denmark. The notable exception is the amalgam of industries 23 and 24 (refined petroleum and chemicals – see Appendix Table A1.1).

A simple count of the number of innovators has, however, a range of drawbacks. First, it does not truly reflect the importance of those innovations. Some are minor product improvements, others relate to a whole new product line. There is not, as patent citations are for patents, a measure that

Table 1.1   Data selection: criteria and outcome, CIS 1 micro-aggregated data, 1992

Criteria	Denmark	Ireland
Original number of observations	674	999
Minus small enterprises	644	762
Minus missing industry affiliation	638	762
Minus very high and small growth rates	578	718
Minus too high and small R&D/sales and innovations/sales	559	692

Table 1.2   Partial innovation indicators: count measures, Denmark and Ireland, CIS 1 micro-aggregated data, 1992

Industry abbreviations	Number of firms	Industry distribution of firms (%)	Percentage of innovating firms	Percentage of firms with products new to industry	Percentage of R&D performers
Denmark					
Food	72	12.9	50.0	30.6	43.0
Textile	24	4.3	50.0	25.0	33.3
Wood	69	12.3	44.9	15.9	20.3
Chem	32	5.7	84.4	65.6	78.1
Plastic	32	5.7	65.6	37.5	62.5
Non-met	28	5.0	67.9	50.0	57.1
Metals	78	14.0	61.5	43.6	48.7
M&E	97	17.4	72.2	55.7	64.9
Electric	64	11.4	82.8	67.2	78.1
Vehic	27	4.8	63.0	44.4	63.0
Nec	36	6.4	38.9	25.0	25.0
Total	559	100.0	62.3	42.8	52.1
Ireland					
Food	101	14.6	63.4	–	59.4
Textile	68	9.8	76.5	–	64.7
Wood	84	12.1	45.2	–	41.7
Chem	80	11.6	73.8	–	68.7
Plastic	52	7.5	71.2	–	57.7
Non-met	31	4.5	64.5	–	61.3
Metals	69	10.0	62.3	–	56.5
M&E	50	7.2	70.0	–	62.0
Electric	108	15.6	83.3	–	74.1
Vehic	16	2.3	62.5	–	43.7
Nec	33	4.8	69.7	–	60.6
Total	692	100.0	68.1	–	60.7

one could use to attach weights to innovations. Some of the responses to the innovation are subjective, based not on a company's accounting data but on the respondent's own judgement (for example, drastic versus incremental innovation). What is considered to be an innovation for a small firm might not qualify as such for a large firm. Product innovations might be declared more often than process innovations. Second, a cross-sectional comparison of innovation counts is not very meaningful if the industry concentration (the number of firms per industry), the statistical definition of a firm, and the sample coverage differ.

A second way of measuring innovation is by way of quantitative data on innovation inputs. We have selected two measures: the traditional R&D expenditures, and the more encompassing concept of current expenditures on innovation. R&D, as defined in the Frascati manual, is a concept that firms should be familiar with, since R&D surveys have been conducted for many years now. Current expenditures on innovation is a new concept, which, as we shall see, firms have evidently not grasped well. It comprises expenditures related to R&D, acquisition of patents and licences, product design, trial production, training and tooling-up, market analysis, and others not elsewhere classified.[5] Few firms, however, keep accounts relating to innovation expenditures, whereas they often do for R&D expenditures, if only for claiming tax deductions. The new variable is thus badly measured, with questions regarding it often being left unanswered.[6]

A third way of measuring innovation is to resort to quantitative data on the output of the innovation process, the sales arising from new products. These can be decomposed into sales of incrementally changed, and of significantly changed or newly introduced products. We have regrouped the two categories and exploited instead the distinction between sales of products new to the firm but known to the industry, and sales of products new to the industry. The former can be assimilated with imitations, the latter with drastic innovations. Two innovations can be of unequal value in terms of sales, exports or profits. Therefore, it would be best to weight them differently according to their impact on the variable one is interested in. In a way, that is what the share-in-sales indicator does. If an innovation is very successful, it generates a high percentage of sales from new products. A high share may, however, also imply that many new products have been introduced in recent years, with some being more successful than others. Strictly speaking, the two output measures pertain to product innovation. We have no measure of the impact of process innovation. However, the firms that declare themselves to be product innovators most of the time also declare themselves to be process innovators.[7] Auzeby (1994) noticed the same with the French innovation survey. It can indeed be argued that a new product generally requires a new production method, while new processes are difficult to introduce without changing the products.

In Table 1.3 we compare the four quantitative indicators (R&D, current expenditures on innovation, sales resulting from changed or new products, and sales of products new to the industry), expressed as percentages of total sales, at the industry level. The figures are sales-weighted averages of individual figures. A better way to aggregate the individual indicators

Table 1.3   Partial innovation indicators: quantitative measures, Denmark and Ireland, CIS 1, micro-aggregated data, 1992 (percentages)

Industry abbreviation	Expenditures of R&D/total sales		Current Innovation expenditures/ total sales		Sales of new products/total sales		Sales of products new of industry/ total sales	
	All firms	Innova-tors	All firms	Innova-tors	All firms	Innova-tors	All firms	Innova-tors
Denmark								
Food	1.3	2.5	0.5	0.9	12.1	22.6	4.4	8.1
Textile	1.0	1.9	1.2	2.3	41.8	79.2	18.2	34.5
Wood	0.4	0.5	1.2	1.6	26.2	35.9	3.8	5.2
Chem	7.4	8.8	4.5	5.4	43.9	53.3	19.2	23.3
Plastic	2.0	2.8	2.8	3.8	21.5	29.9	3.2	4.5
Non-met	0.9	1.1	1.7	2.1	13.7	16.9	3.3	4.0
Metals	2.4	3.2	1.9	2.6	26.3	35.8	3.7	5.0
M&E	5.9	6.5	2.7	3.0	60.2	66.7	14.9	16.5
Electric	7.8	8.4	7.5	8.0	45.0	48.1	18.1	19.4
Vehic	3.5	3.7	3.8	4.0	80.3	84.0	46.5	48.7
Nec	1.2	2.1	1.4	2.6	25.9	47.1	5.1	9.4
Total	3.5	4.7	2.5	3.3	35.5	47.6	12.7	16.9
Small firms*	2.0	3.2	2.4	4.0	24.5	39.7	6.8	11.1
Ireland								
Food	0.7	1.0	0.6	0.8	21.1	32.1	–	–
Textile	1.1	1.3	1.6	2.0	30.3	37.3	–	–
Wood	1.2	1.6	2.5	2.7	21.8	35.1	–	–
Chem	2.5	3.1	3.7	4.6	27.8	36.0	–	–
Plastic	1.3	1.5	2.7	3.1	44.7	51.2	–	–
Non-Met	0.4	0.4	1.2	1.2	37.5	38.1	–	–
Metals	1.4	2.6	2.3	3.2	31.2	51.1	–	–
M&E	0.8	0.9	3.5	3.8	64.5	74.0	–	–
Electric	2.3	2.6	5.5	6.1	49.6	55.4	–	–
Vehic	1.2	1.4	2.5	3.1	21.1	28.4	–	–
Nec	0.7	0.9	2.0	2.6	24.4	33.6	–	–
Total	1.3	1.6	2.2	2.8	31.5	41.0	–	–
Small firms*	2.2	3.0	3.9	5.3	29.4	39.2	–	–

Note: * Small firms are defined as those with sales below the median sales figure for the whole sample.

would have been to use value added as weights, value added reflecting more accurately the importance of firms in total activity. Value added is, however, not available from CIS.[8] The conclusions we draw are not very different if we use employment weights instead of sales weights.

The first thing to notice is the high intensity of R&D in the innovation sample. An R&D/sales ratio (even lower than the R&D/value-added ratio) of 3.5 per cent for Denmark is inconsistent with the OECD-reported Danish ratio of gross expenditures of business enterprise R&D over disposable income of 1.3 per cent. Either the innovation sample is biased towards innovators, or the respondents declared more R&D in the innovation survey than in the R&D survey. The difference is somewhat less pronounced in Ireland.

There is a striking incoherence between the ratio of R&D over current innovation expenditures that can be computed from the two separate items in the questionnaire, and the ratio that is directly reported by the respondents when asked about the R&D composition of their current expenditures on innovation. In Denmark, the computed ratio is 1.41 for all innovators, and the weighted average of the declared ratios is 0.48. The fact that the former is greater than 1 clearly shows the misunderstanding regarding the definition of the current innovation expenditures. In Ireland, the inconsistency is not so strong, the computed ratio being 0.56, and the declared ratio 0.29. One possible explanation for this incoherence is that current innovation expenditures and their components were interpreted by the respondents as pertaining only to the costs of current innovations – those that materialized in new products or processes declared elsewhere in the questionnaire – whereas the question on R&D was understood as pertaining to R&D as an investment, whether or not it led to immediate innovations. In some instances, it was crystal-clear that the question was interpreted as asking what innovation costs were incurred besides R&D expenses (although the questionnaire clearly defined innovation costs as *including* R&D expenses). Moreover, innovation expenditures sometimes referred to product innovations only, sometimes to both product and process innovations, and, for some countries, it was not even clear which definition was indicated. Current expenditures on innovation is thus not a very reliable indicator.

We report the quantitative indicators once with respect to all firms, once with respect to innovating firms only – that is, the numerators remain the same, and only the denominators differ. For all firms in the sample, sales of changed or new products account for 35.5 per cent of total sales in Denmark and for 31.5 per cent in Ireland. The figure climbs to a sizeable 47.6 per cent and 41.0 per cent respectively for the subsample of innovating firms. The proportion of sales arising from products new to the industry represents 12.7 per cent, in Denmark, roughly a third of innovative sales. For Ireland, this information is not available in CIS 1.The innovation ratios with respect to overall industry sales reflect both the intensity of innovation for innovating firms and the percentage of innovating firms. For example, in textiles and leather (industries 17–19) Danish innovating firms are very innovative in terms of the percentage sales in new products (79.2 per cent).

If we correct for the fact that only 50 per cent of the respondents declare themselves as innovators, the indicator drops to 41.8 per cent. The Irish firms in this industry only have 37.3 per cent of their sales in new products, but given that a high percentage (80.9 per cent) of the respondents declare themselves as innovators, the industry-wide sales percentage of the new products indicator drops to only 30.3 per cent. We also report statistics on small firms, defined as firms with sales below the median sales figure for the whole sample. Smaller firms are less innovative on almost all counts in Denmark, while in Ireland they score higher in R&D/output and innovation expenditures/output ratios.

Table 1.3 illustrates the difficulty of choosing a single innovation indicator, and the advantage of using the input and output indicators separately. The two output indicators achieve the highest score for the motor vehicle and other transportation equipment industry (industries 34–35) in Denmark, and for the manufacture of machinery and equipment in Ireland (industry 29), but this is not reflected at all in the input indicators. Both countries achieve the highest R&D intensity as well as the highest intensity in current expenditures on innovation despite the inconsistency, in petroleum refining and chemicals (industries 23–24) and in electrical and electronic machinery and equipment (industries 30–33). Danish firms are more R&D-intensive than Irish firms. Only in wood, paper and printing is Ireland ahead of Denmark. However, Irish firms declare a higher percentage of sales in new or improved products than Danish firms in six out of the eleven industries.

In Table 1.4 we examine the pairwise correlations between the four quantitative innovation measures. The two input indicators and two output

Table 1.4   Correlations between partial innovation indicators for innovating firms, Denmark and Ireland, CIS 1, micro-aggregated data, 1992

	Current innovation expenditures/total sales		Sales of new products/total sales		Sales of products new to industry/total sales	
	Denmark	*Ireland*	*Denmark*	*Ireland*	*Denmark*	*Ireland*
R&D/total sales	0.63	0.68	0.06	0.09	0.08	–
Current innovation expenditure/ total sales			0.08	0.01	0.09	–
Sales of new products/ total sales					0.47	–

indicators are highly correlated, which is normal, since one is a component of the other. Moreover, there is probably a time lag between the inputs and the outputs of innovation which, given the cross-sectional nature of our data, we are unable to take into account.

The main conclusions we can draw from the analysis of the partial indicators of the Danish and Irish CIS 1 data can be summarized as follows:

(i) Current expenditures on innovation is a variable of dubious quality.
(ii) There is more to innovation expenditure than R&D, but the two measures are highly correlated. The correlations are around 0.65 at the firm level.
(iii) There is more correlation between R&D and current expenditures on innovation, or between sales of new products and sales of products new to the industry, than there is between any of the two input and any of the two output indicators of innovation.
(iv) Each country has its own pattern of sectoral specialization in innovations.

In view of this, it might be advisable to consider a range of innovation indicators. It is, for example, useful to look at both the input and the output indicators, because they reveal different types of information. The input indicators are predictors of future innovations, whereas the output indicators reflect past innovation efforts. One is forward-looking and the other backward-looking. The output indicators have the advantage over the input indicators in measuring the success of innovation; that is, indirectly to give more weight to innovation efforts that turn out to be successful. Alternatively, one could consider devising a global innovation indicator taking these various dimensions of innovation into account and aggregrating them some way in one index. This is the approach we shall now pursue.

1.3   A COMPOSITE INNOVATION INDICATOR

A weighted index of the various measures could be constructed if, a priori, one was ready to put more weight on some pieces of information than on others. For instance, an innovation would be worth more if it corresponded to a product new to the industry than if it was merely new to the firm but not to the industry; or an incremental innovation would be worth less than a drastic innovation. Of course, these weights are subjective.

A more objective way of aggregating the various partial indicators is to perform a principal component analysis on them to extract combinations of variables which best summarize the total variation in the indexes.[9] A global index of innovation intensity can then be obtained by taking the first principal component, or the sum of the first two or three principal components. The ranking of firms by principal components could be compared to the ranking according to individual responses. The drawback of this analysis is the absence of a model. In a way, one lets the data speak. It is therefore difficult to interpret the resulting principal components, or the resulting global innovation index. Usually, the principal components are named after the variables with the highest factor loadings. By using a varimax rotation – that is, a transformation of the factor loadings – in order to produce a simple loading structure, one can venture to give a more clear-cut interpretation to each factor. Moreover, all information is treated as being equally important, whereas we know a priori that some variables are better measured or more informative than others. For example, Crépon *et al.* (1996) find unbelievable results using the dichotomous variable of innovation, which are incompatible with the results obtained using the variable 'shares of sales from new products'. They suspect a large measurement error in the former variable, thinking that small firms may be more inclined to report innovations which larger ones would not regard as such.

Hollenstein (1996) has performed such a factor analysis on Swiss innovation survey data. The technical dimension of the data (R&D and technical assessment of innovation) and the market orientation (share in sales of new products) are the two factors singled out for product innovation, and the input and the output side of the innovation process (R&D and technological and economic assessment of innovation) are the two factors identifying process innovations. Hollenstein (1996) relates his factor-based innovation measures to explanatory variables of innovation by way of a canonical correlation analysis. He finds that the composite indicator is more correlated to the set of explanatory variables (demand expectation, market structure, knowledge appropriability, technological opportunities) than any partial indicator. A potential drawback of his analysis is that he examines only innovating firms.

Baldwin and Johnson (1996) define innovative firms as those above the median value in the ranking on the first principal component from nineteen variables pertaining to innovations (p. 791, Table 1). From the 'Growing Small and Medium-Sized Enterprise Survey', conducted in 1989 on Canadian firms, they use the responses of 820 firms to questions relating to the activities of the firms (for example, export performance, sources of financing, training, marketing, intensity of R&D), to their characteristics profile (region of operation, ownership structure, country of control, size, occupational distribution, involvment in mergers and acquisitions), and to their strategies (regarding marketing, inputs, technology acquisition, management techniques, human-resource). They find that innovative firms differ from non-innovative firms in many respects (using the non-parametric Wilcoxon rank sum test): they value human resources more highly; they place greater emphasis on the importance of marketing; they strive for efficiency; they rely more on outside sources of financing, such as venture capital, public equity, and parents and affiliates, and less heavily on suppliers and financial institutions; they value general government programs; and they view management skills as a key to success. While the authors distinguish innovating from non-innovating firms, they fall short of providing an index of innovativeness.

The other way of constructing a composite innovation indicator is the econometric prediction of the conditional expectation of innovation from an estimated explanatory model. Porter and Stern (1999) have constructed such an innovation capacity index. They estimate a national innovation capacity equation for seventeen OECD countries and the period from 1973 to 1993 by regressing international patenting per head on a number of variables deemed to capture the basic determinants of innovation: factor conditions (human resources, basic research infrastructure, information infrastructure, and the supply of risk capital), supporting environment (competition, innovation incentives, presence of clusters, and local suppliers), and demand conditions (sophisticated customers, anticipated needs). Not all of these variables are available for all countries, or even easily measurable. Yet, on the basis of a certain number of explanatory variables, they estimate an index, which in their own words 'is the expected number of international patents per million persons given a country's current configuration of national policies and resource commitments'. This index can then be applied to other countries or future data to project their innovation capacities.

We shall, in spirit, follow their direction, but we shall depart from their work in three respects. First, we shall estimate a somewhat more structured model, taking into account the qualitative nature of some of the data available in the CIS surveys. Second, we shall base the index directly on firm data. Third, we shall extract information from both innovators and non-innovators.

1.4   MODEL

The main objective of this chapter is to construct a composite indicator of innovation from the variables contained in the Community Innovation Surveys. The survey first identifies innovators and non-innovators. After giving some general information about their enterprise, respondents are required to answer 'yes' or 'no' to the question 'Have you introduced a new product or a new process, or do you plan to do so in the near future?' If the answer is yes, they are asked to give some figures about the amount of innovation input and output.

As already mentioned above, quantitative data on innovation (R&D expenditures, sales of new products) are available in CIS 1 only for those firms that introduced a new product or a new process between 1990 and 1992. Hence, exploiting only those data would restrict us to the universe of innovating firms. If we limited ourselves to qualitative data, we could compute an 'ability to innovate' index for all firms, but we would fail to exploit the information we have on the amount of their innovation. Therefore, we suggest the estimation of a generalized tobit model, with a separate structure for the probability of innovating and for the amount of innovation. The estimated model can be used to predict the probability of innovating and the amount of innovation, given a set of values for the conditional variables. Our index of innovation will then be defined as the conditional expectation of innovation, which can be evaluated at different levels of the conditioning variables. This procedure has the advantage of exploiting the dichotomous information available for all firms in the survey (not just the innovating ones), and the continuous variation contained in the quantitative data. Of course, only variables for which observations exist for all firms can enter the latent variable function. Given that certain variables are measured only for innovative firms, the difference in specification between the qualitative and the quantitative part of the generalized tobit is in part determined by the way the CIS 1 questionnaire was set up.

We thus model the determinants of innovation with two equations. The first explains what makes a firm innovative or not. The second determines the amount of innovation conditional on the fact that the firm is innovative. Formally, we assume that there is a latent variable y_{1i}^* for firm i generated by the first equation:

$$y_{1i}^* = x_{1i}b_1 + u_{1i}$$

where x_{1i} is a vector of explanatory variables, b_1 is a vector of coefficients to be estimated, and u_{i1} is an error term caused by unaccounted-for influences, such as the quality of the managers, organizational effectiveness, and the degree of intellectual property protection. If y_{1i}^* is positive, the firm has enough incentive to innovate, and the dichotomous variable takes the value of one (corresponding to 'Yes, I innovated'). We expect the incentive to innovate to be a function of technological opportunity conditions: it is easier to innovate in certain fields than in others. Since, by and large, opportunity conditions are industry-specific, they can be approximated by industry dummies. Industry dummies could also capture the effects of industry-targeted innovation policies. We also expect the incentive to innovate to depend on size. The size effect could reflect access to finance or scale economies. We have classified firms into six size classes: with a number of employees less than or equal to 49, between 50 and 99, between 100 and 249, between 250 and 499, between 500 and 999, and above 1000. Past growth can be a determining factor, as a predictor of future growth, as a demand-pull effect (see Brouwer and Kleinknecht, 1999), or as a signal of easy access to capital financing. The growth of sales between 1990 and 1992 is available in the dataset. Firms that are part of a group are expected to benefit from knowledge spillovers, internal access to finance, or synergies in marketing, distribution and so on, and to be more innovative because of this.

The only other variable available in the dataset, with observations for both innovative and non-innovative firms, that we could put forward to explain the probability of innovating is the degree of perception of the obstacles to innovation. We have not included this variable among the regressors, for two reasons. First, perceptions are subjective and we do not want to predict innovations on the basis of some subjective variable. Second, various authors have found that the obstacles to innovation are more obvious when firms try to innovate and face these obstacles than when they do not innovate, and hence do not encounter them (Baldwin and Lin, 2001; Mohnen and Rosa, 2001). The sign effect of this variable can thus go either way, and it is therefore a bad predictor of the readiness to innovate.

The amount of innovation is modelled by another latent variable, y_{2i}^*. If the firm is innovative, $y_{2i}^* = y_{2i}$, the latent variable is equal to the actual amount of innovation, otherwise the latent variable is equal to zero, or non-observable. Since the percentage of innovative sales is bounded by 0 and 1, the dependent variable in the second equation is specified in log-ratio form (for a discussion of tobit models with bounded dependent variables, see Cragg, 1971):

$$z_{2i}^* = \ln(y_{2i}^*/(1 - y_{2i}^*)) = x_{2i}b_2 + u_{2i}$$

where x_{2i} is a vector of explanatory variables, b_2 is a vector of coefficients to be estimated and u_{2i} is a stochastic error term reflecting omitted variables and other sources of heterogeneity. When $y_{2i}^* = 0, u_{2i} = -\infty$ and when $y_{2i}^* = 1, u_{2i} = \infty$. The explanatory variables in x_{2i} are in principle the same as those in x_{1i}. However, for innovating firms, we have more information to explain the amount of innovation. We shall add in x_{2i}, in addition to the variables already intoduced in x_{1i}, various dimensions of R&D: the dichotomous variable 'doing R&D on a continuous rather than occasional basis', the dichotomous variable indicating whether R&D is done in co-operation with partners or not, and the R&D/sales ratio. We have not included current expenditures on innovation as an innovation input, because, as documented in Section 1.2, this variable is badly measured. For the same reasons that we excluded the perceived obstacles to innovation, we have also excluded the perceived strength of appropriability conditions for product or for process innovations.

Since y_{2i}^{*} is only observed when $y_{1i}^{*} \geq 0$, u_{1i} and u_{2i} are likely to be correlated. We assume their joint distribution to be a bivariate normal distribution:

$$u_i \sim N(0, \Sigma)$$

where $u_i = [u_{1i} \, u_{2i}]'$, $\Sigma = [\sigma_1^2 \, \rho\sigma_1\sigma_2 | \rho\sigma_1\sigma_2 \, \sigma_2^2]$, and 0 is a 2×1 vector of zeros.

The generalized tobit model is estimated by maximum likelihood. We maximize the likelihood of observing the y_{1i} and y_{2i} in our sample. Since the dependent variable of the equation for the percentage of innovative sales has been transformed, a Jacobian has to be added to the log-likelihood function to correct for the transformation. The log-likelihood function is given by:

$$
\begin{aligned}
\ln L = {} & \sum_0 \ln[1 - \Phi(x_{1i}b_1/\sigma_1)] \\
& + \sum_1 \ln \Phi\left(\frac{x_{1i}b_1 + [\rho\sigma_1/\sigma_2][\ln(y_{2i}/(1 - y_{2i})) - x_{2i}b_2]}{\sigma_1\sqrt{1 - \rho^2}} \right) \\
& + \sum_1 \ln\left(1/\sigma_2[y_{2i}(1 - y_{2i})]^{-1} \phi[(y_{2i} - x_{2i}b_2)/\sigma_2] \right)
\end{aligned}
\tag{1}
$$

where the index 0 under the summation sign refers to non-innovators and the index 1 refers to innovators, Φ is the standard normal distribution function, and ϕ the standard normal density function. Since only b_1/σ_1 is identifiable, we shall put $\sigma_1 = 1$. Initial estimates are obtained from Heckman's two-step estimation: first, estimate the probit equation and compute from it the inverse Mills ratio; and, second, introduce this ratio as an additional regressor in the ordinary least squares regression of the second equation, run on positive values of y_{1i}. Estimates of ρ and σ_2 can be retrieved from these estimates (see Gouriéroux, 1989, p. 209). We assume the u_i error terms to be independently and identically distributed over all observations.

Our proposed index of innovation is then defined as the expected percentage of innovative sales for each enterprise, conditional on the values taken by the explanatory variables. The mean of y_{2i} conditional on the observed values for the explanatory variables x_{1i} and x_{2i} is equal to:

$$E(y_{2i}|x_{1i}, x_{2i}) = \int_{-x_{1i}b_1}^{\infty} \int_0^1 y_{2i} f(u_{1i}, y_{2i})\, du_{1i}\, dy_{2i}$$

After some manipulation, this expression can be shown to be retrieved from the area under a bivariate standard normal distribution function by the following formula:

$$E(y_{2i}|x_{1i}, x_{2i}) = \int_{-x_{1i}b_1}^{\infty} \int_{-\infty}^{\infty} \exp(x_{2i}b_2 + \sigma_2 u_{2i}^*)/(1 + \exp(x_{2i}b_2 + \sigma_2 u_{2i}^*))$$
$$\times f(u_{1i}^*, u_{2i}^*)\, du_{1i}^*\, du_{2i}^*$$

where $u_{2i}^* = u_{2i}/\sigma_2$, $u_{1i}^* = u_{1i}$, and $f(u_{2i}^*, u_{1i}^*)$ is the bivariate standard normal distribution with correlation coefficient ρ. This conditional mean is then evaluated at the estimated values of b_1, b_2, ρ and σ_2.[10]

1.5   RESULTS

As a measure of the amount of innovation y_{2i}, we take the share in sales of new, incrementally improved or significantly improved products, as no data are available in Ireland for the alternative, sharper measure of innovation, the share in sales of products new to the industry. Some enterprises declare they have introduced a new product or process, but report no share in sales arising from new products. There could be a time lag between the introduction of a new product to the market and the realization of sales from this new product. As we cannot account for any time lags, we attribute the value of 0 or 1 to y_{1i} according to whether y_{2i} is equal to zero, or takes a positive value. Missing data for y_{2i} are treated as zero responses. Missing data for R&D are also considered as zero responses.

Table 1.5 presents some descriptive statistics. There are 62 per cent of innovating firms in the Danish sample, and 68 per cent in the Irish sample. The unweighted average of the share in sales of innovative products is 26.6 per cent in Denmark, and 29.0 per cent in Ireland. In Table 1.3 we report economy-wide or sales-weighted average of 35.5 per cent and

Table 1.5 Summary statistics; Denmark and Ireland, CIS 1, micro-aggregated data, 1992 (sample mean with sample standard deviation in parenthesis for continuous variables)

Variable	Denmark	Ireland
Dummy for innovators	0.623	0.681
Percentage in sales of	0.266	0.290
innovative products	(0.294)	(0.308)
Dummy for 50–99 employees	0.242	0.249
Dummy for 100–249 employees	0.304	0.194
Dummy for 250–499 employees	0.141	0.090
Dummy for 500–999 employees	0.047	0.028
Dummy for >999 employees	0.032	0.007
Dummy for being part of a group	0.658	0.606
Sales growth (1990–2)	0.082	0.162
	(0.230)	(0.235)
R&D/sales	0.023	0.020
	(0.048)	(0.036)
Dummy for continuous R&D	0.340	0.464
Dummy for co-operative R&D	0.379	0.262

31.5 per cent, respectively. The Danish sample has somewhat bigger firms than the Irish sample. Indeed, when we look at the size distribution by the number of employees we notice that the mode of distribution is in the 100–249 category in Denmark, and in the 50–99 category in Ireland. As large firms innovate more often than small firms (as we shall see), it is normal that the weighted averages are larger than the unweighted averages. A larger percentage of the Danish firms belong to a group. The mean R&D intensity is similar in both countries, with the variance being somewhat greater in Denmark. Whereas more of the Danish firms co-operate on R&D, less of them, compared to the Irish, employ R&D on a continuous basis.

Tables 1.6 and 1.7 present the maximum likelihood estimates of the generalized tobit model for Denmark and Ireland, respectively. The reference group is the smallest size class (between 20 and 50 employees) of enterprises in the food, beverage and tobacco sector, with independent status, who do not engage in collaborative and continuous R&D. The continuous variables (number of employees, R&D/sales, and sales growth rate) have been normalized. In Denmark, the propensity to innovate is particularly high in the chemicals, machinery and equipment, electrical products, and vehicles sectors. Innovative sales are high in these sectors, plus textiles. In Ireland, the highly innovative sectors, both in the percentage of innovative firms and

Table 1.6   Maximum likelihood estimates of a generalized tobit model of innovative sales, Denmark, CIS 1, micro-aggregated data, 1992

Variables	Propensity to innovate	Asymptotic t-value	Intensity of innovation	Asymptotic t-value
Constant	−0.631	−3.28	−2.550	−6.92
Textile	0.395	1.32	1.751	3.18
Wood	0.098	0.44	−0.192	−0.46
Chem	0.848	2.85	0.882	1.82
Plastic	0.314	1.15	0.242	0.51
Non-met	0.495	1.71	−0.522	−1.04
Metals	0.365	1.63	−0.041	−0.10
M&E	0.763	3.64	1.169	3.20
Electric	0.865	3.60	1.307	3.19
Vehic	0.805	2.73	1.378	2.73
Nec	−0.041	−0.14	0.463	0.85
50–99 employees	1.311	1.10	–	–
100–249 employees	0.219	1.75	–	–
250–499 employees	0.564	3.25	–	–
500–999 employees	0.350	1.41	–	–
>999 employees	1.431	3.01	–	–
Number of employees	–	–	0.076	0.98
Part of a group	0.459	3.79	0.541	2.62
Sales growth rate: 1990–2	0.027	0.47	0.010	0.11
R&D/sales	–	–	0.019	0.26
R&D on a continuous basis	–	–	0.345	2.17
Co-operative R&D	–	–	0.209	1.31
Estimated standard error of error term	1 (assumed)	–	1.885	18.90
Correlation coefficient ρ	–	–	0.921	1.24

in the sales share in innovative products, are textiles, machinery and equipment, and electrical products. Firms of greater size have a higher probability of innovation, but the relationship between size and the probability of innovating is non-linear. In both countries, the share in sales of innovative products is not strongly related to firm size.

Danish firms which belong to a larger consortium have a significantly higher probability of innovation, as well as a higher share in sales of innovative products. In Ireland, this variable hardly matters. Exactly the opposite holds for past growth in sales. It has no effect on innovation in Denmark, whereas in Ireland it increases significantly both dimensions of

Table 1.7   Maximum likelihood estimates of a generalized tobit model of innovative sales, Ireland, CIS 1, micro-aggregated data, 1992

Variables	Propensity to innovate	Asymptotic t-value	Intensity of innovation	Asymptotic t-value
Constant	0.540	0.41	−2.343	−7.78
Textile	0.560	2.92	1.438	3.75
Wood	−0.357	−2.02	−0.165	−0.42
Chem	0.231	1.28	0.365	0.99
Plastic	0.249	1.21	0.557	1.32
Non-met	0.206	0.86	0.031	0.07
Metals	0.263	1.35	0.178	0.45
M&E	0.401	1.93	1.73	4.00
Electric	0.513	2.94	1.176	3.42
Vehic	0.061	0.18	0.435	0.62
Nec	0.449	1.84	0.664	1.34
50–99 employees	0.197	2.22	–	–
100–249 employees	0.039	0.40	–	–
250–499 employees	0.361	2.37	–	–
500–999 employees	1.189	4.05	–	–
>999 employees	0.441	0.79	–	–
Number of employees	–	–	0.108	1.21
Part of a group	0.132	1.20	0.018	0.08
Sales growth rate: 1990–2	0.092	1.84	0.338	3.34
R&D/sales	–	–	0.107	1.64
R&D on a continuous basis	–	–	0.340	2.17
Co-operative R&D	–	–	0.153	0.97
Estimated standard error of error term.	1 (assumed)		2.32	23.43
Correlation coefficient ρ	–	–	0.96	1.28

innovation. Regarding R&D, the input into the innovation process, only the property of being a continuous R&D performer exerts a significantly positive effect on the share in sales of innovative products in both countries. In Ireland, the R&D/sales coefficient is marginally significant. In both countries, collaborative R&D does not in itself increase innovative sales. The correlation coefficient ρ between the error terms u_{1i} and u_{2i} is high, but imprecisely estimated, in both countries.

From these estimates of the qualitative and quantitative information of innovation contained in the CIS 1 data, we can compute for each observation in the sample the mean expected share in sales of innovative products conditional on the observed values of the explanatory variables. This expectation is computed from the joint probability distribution of the error terms in both equations, the estimated threshold above which an enterprise becomes innovative, and the estimated regression line of the share of innovative sales. In Table 1.8 we report the weighted averages by industry of the

Table 1.8   Composite innovation indicator, Denmark and Ireland, CIS 1, micro-aggregated data, 1992

Industry	Share in sales of new products		
	Predicted conditional mean (weighted average) (%)	*Observed weighted average (%)*	*Correlation between observed and predicted*
Denmark			
All firms	32.3	35.5	0.84
Innovators	35.6	47.5	0.88
Non-innovators	22.8	0.0	–
NACE:			
Food	23.5	12.1	0.13
Textile	39.9	41.4	0.68
Wood	18.2	26.2	0.88
Chem	41.0	43.9	0.91
Plastic	26.7	21.5	0.65
Non-met	19.4	13.7	0.70
Metals	22.6	26.3	0.79
M&E	46.8	60.2	0.98
Electric	41.9	44.8	0.77
Vehic	46.8	79.9	0.98
Nec	22.5	25.9	0.70
Ireland			
All firms	31.1	31.4	0.64
Innovators	31.6	41.0	0.79
Non-innovators	24.4	0.0	–
NACE:			
Food	28.5	21.1	0.46
Textile	38.5	30.2	0.68
Wood	21.4	21.8	0.43
Chem	28.7	27.8	0.56
Plastic	29.5	44.4	0.98
Non-Met	25.6	37.5	0.94
Metals	24.9	31.2	0.58
M&E	45.4	64.5	0.99
Electric	42.0	49.6	0.92
Vehic	23.9	21.1	0.87
Nec	30.7	24.4	0.52

expected conditional shares of innovative sales and of the observed shares of innovative sales, over all enterprises (innovative or not). The difference between the two averages arises from the fact that in the former we use the probability of innovating, which lies between zero and one, and the predicted amount of innovation conditional on being above the innovative threshold, and in the latter we use the actual amount of innovative sales for innovators and zero for non-innovators.

In Denmark, the expected conditional average share in sales of innovative products for all firms is 35.2 per cent, not too far from the observed average of 35.6 per cent. In Ireland, the two figures are even closer, 31.1 per cent versus 31.5 per cent. The correlation between the observed and predicted innovation performances, weighted by the respective sales, is 0.84 for all firms in Denmark and 0.64 in Ireland. It means that in eight out of ten cases (six out of ten resp.) when the actual figure is high (above its mean) the expected is high as well, or both of them are low. The correlations are even higher for actual innovators. The conditional expectations are substantially below the actual performance for innovators: 35.6 per cent against 47.6 per cent for Denmark, and 31.6 per cent versus 41.0 per cent for Ireland. However, for actual non-innovators we predict a substantially higher share in sales of innovative products: 22.8 per cent in Denmark, and 24.4 per cent in Ireland. At the industry level, the correlations between the expected conditional shares and the actual shares are most of the time above 0.5 and often even above 0.7. The industrial rankings in terms of expected percentages of innovative sales are different from the rankings on the basis of the observed percentages. The top innovative sectors are machinery and equipment, vehicles, electrical products, chemicals, and textiles in Denmark, and machinery and equipment, electrical products, and textiles in Ireland. In both countries the food industry is predicted to be much more innovative, controlling for size, sector, group and R&D, than actual figures make it appear. The greatest difference between our measure and the actual statistics on the percentages of innovative sales regards the non-innovators. Even non-innovators have a capacity to innovate, given the innovation determinants we have taken into account. But their expected innovation record is lower than for actual innovators.

If we want to compare Denmark and Ireland, we must have a common structure. The figures in Table 1.9 are not comparable because they are derived from two sets of estimates. One solution would be to estimate a common structure for the data generation process; and the other solution would be to compare their respective performance, taking one of the two estimated structures. The latter is what Table 1.9 reports. In the first two columns the expected conditional means are computed, using the estimated

Table 1.9 Comparison of innovativeness in Denmark and Ireland; predicted conditional means of the share in sales of new products, CIS 1, micro-aggregated data, 1992

	Predicted conditional means with estimates from Denmark		Predicted conditional means with estimates from Ireland	
	Denmark	Ireland	Denmark	Ireland
All firms	32.3	30.4	33.3	31.1
Innovators	35.6	31.8	35.9	31.6
Non-innovators	22.8	25.8	25.4	24.4
NACE:				
Food	23.5	26.0	28.0	28.5
Textile	39.9	42.8	40.2	38.5
Wood	18.2	18.8	18.2	21.4
Chem	41.0	36.1	35.8	28.7
Plastic	26.7	24.7	30.1	29.5
Non-Met	19.4	21.1	24.6	25.6
Metals	22.6	19.8	26.1	24.9
M&E	46.8	37.9	53.7	45.4
Electric	41.9	43.6	40.2	42.0
Vehic	46.8	39.6	33.7	23.9
Nec	22.5	23.4	29.1	30.7

Danish model; and in the last two columns the estimated Irish model is used. By analysing Table 1.9, we can draw four conclusions. First, the conditional predictions obtained with both estimates are pretty close. Second, except for one industry, the bilateral rankings between the two countries in terms of their expected shares of innovative sales are identical. Third, Denmark seems slightly more innovative than Ireland, except perhaps for those firms that did not innovate between 1990 and 1992. Fourth, if we disregard the textiles sector, where the two estimates do not pick the same winner, our results find Denmark to be more innovative than Ireland in the production of petroleum and chemical products, rubber and plastics, basic and fabricated metals, machinery and equipment, and motor vehicles and transportation equipment, but Ireland is more innovative in the manufacture of wood, food, non-metallic minerals, and electrical products.

1.6 CONCLUSION

The Community Innovation Survey data contain a lot of information to construct an innovation index, innovation being more encompassing than

R&D. It contains quantitative, dichotomous and polychotomous variables, and information about the input, the output and the modalities of innovation. We suggest the construction of a composite indicator of innovation, taking many of these variables into account. Innovation is measured as the expected mean share of sales resulting from new or improved products conditional on the innovation input, the way innovation is organized, and some characteristics of the firm and its environment. The indicator is based on a generalized tobit model which models the propensity to innovate, and the amount of innovation in case of innovation. It combines the quantitative and qualitative variables contained in the database. The former are richer in content than zero/one or categorical variables, as they are measurable on a continuous rather than on just a discrete basis. However, they only pertain to innovating firms. They are supplemented by constructing aptitudes of innovation for all firms, transforming a dichotomous variable into a continuous one.

An exploratory application of this measure to Danish and Irish innovation data from CIS 1 shows that it can be applied, even within the limited set of data available in CIS 1. It allows comparison between countries, industries, firms in different size classes, innovators and non-innovators. By providing an explanation for the propensity to innovate and the intensity of innovation, it explains indirectly what makes a firm innovative. Counter-factual experiments can then be run, applying the characteristics of one firm to another, to compare innovation performances.

Our analysis leads us to conclude that the CIS 1 data indicate that Denmark is slightly more innovative than Ireland, but not to a great extent. The potential to innovate for actual non-innovators is much the same in both countries. Size has a positive influence on the ability to innovate but not on the amount of innovation. Belonging to a consortium matters in Denmark but not in Ireland, while the opposite holds for the influence of past growth. R&D increases the share in sales of innovative products, but the only significant effect comes from performing R&D on a continuous basis.

The indicator could be improved further, in several directions. First, if data on sales of products new to the industry were available for both countries, we could in a similar vein construct some type of true innovation indicator, but the above analysis was confined to imitators (products new to the firm but not to the industry). Second, if data from CIS surveys could be merged with other kinds of data for the same respondent, such as capital, patent or balance-sheet data, we would have a good chance of improving the predictive performance of our model, and construct more reliable innovation indicators. Third, the innovation indicators may not to be representative of

the entire population of firms in the various subsamples. We could expand
the data to cover the entire population, since the CIS survey provides rais-
ing factors. However, these factors should be specific to each variable, and
grossing up all variables by a common factor would not change the innovation ratios. Fourth, we could also estimate a common innovation structure by estimating the model on pooled data. Fifth, we could generalize the
model along the lines of Crépon, Duguet and Mairesse (1998) by allowing
for simultaneity between R&D, innovations and exports.

Appendix

Table A1.1   Industry definitions

Industry abbreviation	NACE code (rev.1)	Industry definition
Food	15–16	Manufacture of food, beverages and tobacco
Textile	17–19	Manufacture of textiles, wearing apparel, dressing and dyeing of fur, tannings and dressing of leather, luggage, handbags, saddlery, harness and footwear
Wood	20–22	Manufacture of wood and products of wood and cork, except furniture, manufacture of straw and plaiting materials, pulp, paper, and paper products, publishing, printing, and reproduction of recorded media
Chem	23–24	Manufacture of coke, refined petroleum products and nuclear fuel, manufacture of chemicals and chemical products
Plastic	25	Manufacture of rubber and plastics products
Non-met	26	Manufacture of other non-metallic mineral products
Metal	27–28	Manufacture of basic metals, fabricated metal products, except machinery and equipment
M&E	29	Manufacture of machinery and equipment NEC
Electric	30–33	Manufacture of office machinery and computers, electrical machinery and apparatus, radio, television and communication equipment and apparatus, medical, precision and optical instruments, watches and clocks
Vehic	34–35	Manufacture of motor vehicles, trailers, semi-trailers, and other transport equipment
Nec	36	Manufacture of furniture, manufacturing NEC

Notes

*   We thank Dominique Guellec for many stimulating discussions. Alfred
        Kleinknecht, Jacques Mairesse and José Labeaga provided helpful comments.
        We are also grateful for the comments we received when presenting this paper
        at WZB, CIRANO, OECD, a TSER conference in Delft, and a SESSI confer-
        ence in Paris. We thank Eurostat for giving us permission to use the micro-
        aggregated CIS 1 data. Financial support from OECD and the Social Science
        and Humanities Research Council of Canada is gratefully acknowledged.
        Finally, we wish to thank Julio Rosa for his dedicated research assistance.

1.   The various sales percentages are in principle data on a continuous scale
        between 0 and 1. They are, however, often reported in round figures. In the
        French survey, they are treated simply as a categorical variable.
2.   Other measures of innovation output, not contained in the CIS surveys, are
        the number of patents (used by Crépon *et al.*, 1996), the number of innova-
        tion counts (used by Albach *et al.*, 1996), and the number of new product
        announcements in trade journals (used by Brouwer and Kleinknecht, 1996).
        These three indicators are more objective than the self-assessment responses
        from the innovation surveys, but they suffer from a selection bias resulting
        from the firms' own propensity to patent, to declare an innovation, to pub-
        lish new findings in trade journals, and also from the patent officer's or the
        publisher's acceptance of the innovation as worthwhile. Moreover, these
        indicators do not convey any information on the success of an innovation.
3.   For a thorough discussion on the comparison among a number of innovation
        indicators (even beyond those contained in the CIS 1 surveys), see
        Kleinknecht (1999).
4.   As some firms declare that they have introduced or developed a technologi-
        cally changed product or process, but do not report any sales of new prod-
        ucts, we have been conservative and only considered as innovators those
        that actually report a share in sales resulting from new products.
5.   In the 1992 CIS for the Netherlands, for a sample of 8874 firms, Brouwer
        and Kleinknecht (1997) report that R&D accounts for 34 per cent of total
        innovation expenditures in manufacturing, and for 20 per cent in services. In
        Italy, R&D expenses amount to 20 per cent of innovation costs, in the
        Nordic countries to 50 per cent (Archibugi *et al.* (1994)).
6.   Brouwer and Kleinknecht (1997) have estimated that the probability of giv-
        ing accurate estimates increases with the R&D intensity, and with the ten-
        dency to do R&D on a continuous basis.
7.   In our sample, there is no occurrence of a Danish enterprise doing process
        innovation without also doing product innovation and only 5 firms do product
        innovation without doing process innovation. In Ireland, the figures are,
        respectively, 5 and 3.
8.   We have data on labour in the questionnaire, but no information of labour
        costs, which could have been used as a proxy for value-added, under the
        assumption of uniform wages within an industry.
9.   Alternatively, one could do a factor analysis. In a principal component analy-
        sis, the aim is to account for the maximum of the variance and covariance
        among the original variables (in this case the innovation indicators). In a

factor analysis, the goal is only to explain as much as possible the intercon-
nection between the variables (see Reyment and Jöreskog, 1993).
10. Brouwer and Kleinknecht (1996) have estimated a similar model based on
the Dutch CIS 1 data. They compared the determinants of the probability
and of the intensity of innovation using three types of indicator: the sales
share of innovative products; the sales share of imitative products; and the
number of new product and service announcements in journals. They estimated this model on manufacturing as well as on service data, and had
access to original enterprise data rather than micro-aggregated data. They
did not, however, use their estimates to predict innovation and compare it
across countries.

References

ALBACH, H., AUDRETSCH, D. B., FLEISCHER, M., GREB, R., HÖFS, E.,
RÖLLER, L.-H. and SCHULZ, I. (1996) 'Innovation in the European Chemical
Industry', *Wissenschaftszentrum Berlin, Discussion Paper FS* IV 96–26.
ARCHIBUGI, D., COHENDET, P., KRISTENSEN, A. and SCHÄFFER, K.-A.
(1994) *Evaluation of the Community Innovation Survey (CIS), Phase 1*, EIMS pub-
lication No. 11, Aalborg, Denmark: IKE Group, Department of Business Studies.
AUZEBY, F. (1994) 'Des innovations de produits plutôt que de procédés', in
Les Chiffres Clés. L'Innovation Technologique dans l'Industrie. Ministère de
l'Industrie, des Postes et Télécommunications et du Commerce Extérieur. Paris:
Dunod.
BALDWIN, J. R. and GELLATLY, G. (2000) 'A Firm-Based Approach to Industry
Classification: Identifying the Knowledge-Based Economy', in L.-A. Lefebvre,
E. Lefebvre and P. Mohnen (eds), *Doing Business in a Knowledge-Based Economy.
Facts and Policy Challenges*. Boston, Mass.: Kluwer Academic Publishers.
BALDWIN, J. R. and JOHNSON, J. (1996) 'Business Strategies in More- and
Less-Innovative Firms in Canada', *Research Policy*, vol. 25, pp. 785–804.
BALDWIN, J. and LIN, Z. (2001) 'Impediments to Advanced Technology Adoption
for Canadian Manufacturers', Mimeo, forthcoming in *Research Policy*.
BROUWER, E. and KLEINKNECHT, A. (1996) 'Determinants of Innovation:
A Micro Econometric Analysis of Three Alternative Innovative Output Indicators',
in A. H. Kleinknecht (ed.), *Determinants of Innovation. The Message from new
Indicators*. London: Macmillan, pp. 99–124.
BROUWER, E. and KLEINKNECHT, A. (1997) 'Measuring the Unmeasurable: A
Country's Non-R&D Expenditure on Product and Service Innovation', *Research
Policy*, vol. 25, pp. 1235–42.
BROUWER, E. and KLEINKNECHT, A. (1999) 'Keynes-plus? Effective Demand
and Changes in Firm-level R&D: An Empirical Note', *Cambridge Journal of
Economics*, vol. 23, pp. 385–91.
CRAGG, J. (1971) 'Some Statistical Models for Limited Dependent Variables with
Application to the Demand for Durable Goods', *Econometrica*, vol. 39, pp. 829–44.
CRÉPON, B., DUGUET, E. and KABLA, I. (1996) 'Schumpeterian Conjectures: A
Moderate Support from Various Innovation Measures', in A. Kleinknecht (ed.),
Determinants of Innovation. The Message from New Indicators. London: Macmillan.

CRÉPON, B., DUGUET, E. and MAIRESSE, J. (1998) 'Research and Development, Innovation and Productivity: An Econometric Analysis at the Firm Level', *Economics of Innovation and New Technology*, vol. 7, no. 2, pp. 115–58.

EUROSTAT (1996) *Manual on Disclosure Control Methods*. Luxembourg: Statistical Office of the European Communities.

FELDER, J., LICHT, G., NERLINGER, E. and STAHL, H. (1995) 'Appropriability, Opportunity, Firm Size and Innovation Activities. Empirical Results Using East and West German Firm Level Data', Mannheim: Centre for European Economic Research, Discussion Paper No. 95–21.

GOURIEROUX, C. (1989) *Econométrie des Variables Qualitatives*. Paris: Economica.

HOLLENSTEIN, H. (1996) 'A Composite Indicator of a Firm's Innovativeness. An Empirical Analysis Based on Survey Data for Swiss Manufacturing', *Research Policy*, vol. 25, pp. 633–45.

JOHNSTON, J. (1972) *Econometric Methods* (2nd edn). New York: McGraw-Hill.

KLEINKNECHT, A. (1999) 'Indicators of Manufacturing and Service Innovation: Their Strengths and Weaknesses', in J. S. Metcalf and I. Miles (eds, 2000): *Innovation Systems in the Service Economy*, Boston/Dordrecht/London: Kluwer, pp. 169–86.

KLEINKNECHT, A. H. (1993) 'Testing Innovation Indicators for Postal Surveys: Results from a Five-Country Comparison', in A. H. Kleinknecht and D. Bain (eds), *New Concepts in Innovation Output Measurement*. London: Macmillan, pp. 153–88.

MADDALA, G. S. (1983) *Limited-Dependent and Qualitative Variables in Econometrics*. Econometric Society Monographs in Quantitative Economics. Cambridge University Press.

MOHNEN, P. and ROSA J. (2001) 'Les obstacles à l'innovation dans les industries de service au Canada', *Actualité Economique*, forthcoming.

Organization for Economic Co-operation and Development (1992, 1996), *Oslo Manual*, (1st & 2nd edns). Paris, OECD.

PORTER, M. and STERN, S. (1999) *The New Challenge to America's Prosperity: Findings from an Innovation Index*. Washington DC: Council on Competitiveness.

REYMENT, R. and JÖRESKOG, K. G. (1993) *Applied Factor Analysis in the Natural Sciences*. Cambridge University Press.

VOLLE, M. (1985) *Analyse des données* (3rd edn). Paris: Economica, Collection ENSAE.

2 Innovations, Patents and Cash Flow

Paul Geroski, John Van Reenen and
*Chris Walters**

2.1 INTRODUCTION

Studies of the innovative activity of firms which focus on R&D spending generally conclude that relatively few firms engage in R&D, but that those who do display a relatively stable pattern of spending on R&D over time. Differences between firms in R&D spending (or in spending intensity) are typically much more important than variations in spending within firms over time. As a consequence, the interesting research question to be addressed in these studies is: 'Which firms do R&D?' By contrast, studies of innovative output using patents or counts of major innovations generally show that many of the firms who do produce an innovation do so only sporadically. Few firms put together multi-year spells of sustained patent or 'major' innovation production, and the timing of their innovative activities is episodic, idiosyncratic and relatively hard to predict. This adds a second interesting question to the research agenda, namely: 'When (if ever) do firms innovate?'

At a purely statistical level, answering this second question means finding exogenous variables that display the same kinds of variation as patents or 'major' innovation counts; that is, finding independent variables that display a high ratio of within to between variation, plus a tendency towards irregular bursts of sub- or supernormal activity. For economists interested in the determinants of innovative activity, this is likely to rule out factors such as 'technological opportunity', 'conditions of appropriability' or market structure (all of which tend to be different for different firms or industries, but stable over time). However, potential determinants of innovation, such as demand or the financial state of firms, are both interesting on theoretical grounds and potential candidates on purely statistical grounds.

The debate about the effect of demand on innovation is of long standing and reasonably familiar to most scholars.[1] The role of finance is, however, more controversial, and feeds directly into public policy debates about how best to support innovative activity. In particular, it is often argued that internal and external sources of capital are not perfect substitutes, and, as a consequence, that a 'financing hierarchy' exists which may affect real investment decisions. There are a variety of reasons why internal finance might be cheaper than external finance: high costs of small, new share issues, low taxes on capital gains relative to dividends, asymmetric information that creates a 'lemons premium', and various agency problems associated with debt. If these arguments are well-founded, then internal cash flow may affect investment spending, particularly for financially constrained firms (that is, those facing a large difference between the cost of internal and external finance), or for firms with very ambitious investment projects.[2] These arguments are particularly likely to apply to investment in intangibles and/or in particularly risky investments, such as those associated with new product or process innovations. However, cash flow is very sensitive to demand fluctuations (particularly when costs are fixed), meaning that, in practice, the effects of demand on innovative activity are likely to be hard to distinguish from those associated with a firm's financial state. Either way, though, cash flow seems, a priori, to be a potentially important determinant of the timing of innovative activity, and worth further exploration.

Our goal in this chapter is to explore the determinants of corporate innovative activity, concentrating as much on the 'when' question as on the 'who', by searching for systematic patterns of variation between measures of innovative output, cash flow and other factors. We do this by building a dynamic three-equation model linking counts of major innovations, counts of patents produced, and cash flow. We find that patents appear to 'cause' innovations (but not the reverse), that the production of innovations is more sensitive to demand pull pressures and less sensitive to supply push pressures (such as industry R&D spending) than patents and, finally, that while innovations and patents generate cash flow, cash flow itself has almost no short- or long-run effect on the numbers of innovations or patents produced, and only a modest effect on the timing of the production of new major innovations. The plan of the chapter is as follows. In Section 2.2, we describe the model that will be applied to the data. The data and regression results are examined in Section 2.3, while Section 2.4 concludes, with a summary of the results and a few speculative remarks on the design of technology policy.

2.2   THE EXPERIMENT

Our goal is to examine the relationship between the production of major innovations, patenting activity and variations in cash flow. In this section, we describe the procedures we have followed, and some of the issues that will arise in the interpretation of the results.

2.2.1 The Model

There are many ways to structure one's thinking about the innovation process, but we find it useful to think in terms of a three-step model with a feedback loop: firms make decisions to do R&D, the stock of knowledge built up by R&D spending leads to the production of innovations, and these innovations generate a stream of profits over time. Each of these steps is affected by various exogenous variables, including firm size, market power, technological opportunity, appropriability conditions, various types of public policy initiative, cash flow, demand and so on. The feedback loop that ties the model together is that the profit expectations that stimulate R&D ought to be based on rational conjectures about how many innovations will be produced, and how much profit each will generate.

Although there are many virtues to working with a structural model specified along these (or related) lines, our data are simply not rich enough to allow us to observe either R&D spending at the firm level (we can only observe industry totals), or the profits generated by particular innovations. Thus, we collapse the three-step model to focus on the middle stage: the production of innovations. The reduced form that emerges is, however, richer than appears at first sight. Since it is clear that 'innovative activity' produces a multiple of outputs, we use two indicators to measure innovative output: the production of 'major' innovations (denoted n_t) and the production of patents (denoted p_t). In the reduced form, they depend on all of the exogenous variables of the system and, in particular, on cash flow (denoted c_t). However, it may not be reasonable to take a firm's cash flow as being exogenous to the production of patents or innovations. We have therefore allowed current-period cash flow to be affected by current and recent past innovations and patents in much the same way that innovations and patents depend on current and recent-past cash flow.

These considerations lead to a three-equation system in n_t, p_t and c_t, which can be written as:

$$n_t = \theta_1(L)\, n_{t-1} + \theta_2(L)\, p_{t-1} + \beta_1(L)\, c_{t-1} + w^1_{t-1} \tag{1}$$

$$p_t = \theta_3(L)\, n_{t-1} + \theta_4(L)\, p_{t-1} + \beta_2(L)\, c_{t-1} + w^2_{t-1} \tag{2}$$

$$c_t = \theta_5(L)\, n_{t-1} + \theta_6(L)\, p_{t-1} + \beta_3(L)\, c_{t-1} + w^3_{t-1} \tag{3}$$

where $\theta_j(L)$ and $\beta_j(L)$ are polynomials in the lag operator L, and the $w^j(t)$ are vectors of lagged exogenous variables. As we are mainly interested in tracing the effects of cash flow, in practice we need only include other determinants of n_t and p_t that may be correlated with it. Since large, oligopolistic firms may have fewer financial constraints than smaller, specialized firms, we have included a number of market structure variables (including market share) in some experiments, and have explored differences in sensitivity to cash flow between large and small firms. We have also included other measures of corporate financial well-being in some experiments. Finally, we have included fixed effects (to correct for technological opportunities and conditions of appropriability) in all our experiments, and have allowed for technological spillovers between firms in some. Dummy variables for 1974 and 1979 have been included in all equations. The 1974 dummy captures the oil shock. The patents data presents a particular problem because of the cutbacks in the US Patent Office over this time period (see Griliches, 1990), and we include the ratio of patent applications over examiners as well as a 1979 dummy (the year when the cutback was particularly large) to control for this.

2.2.2   Interpreting the Model

The model in Equations (1)–(3) contains three sets of parameters of interest: $\theta_2(L)$ and $\theta_3(L)$, which describe the relationship between patents and innovations, $\theta_1(L)$ and $\theta_4(L)$, which describe the degree of history dependence of each, and the coefficients on the exogenous variables (including the $\beta_j(L)$ which link cash flow to innovative output).

There are at least two different ways to interpret any apparent 'causal' relations between n_t and p_t, depending on how one interprets what patents measure. The first is to think of patents as measures of input into the innovation process.[3] The idea here is that patents measure technological knowledge which, when combined with information about user needs, design and manufacturability, will produce output in the shape of major innovations. If technological knowledge (that is, patents) in period t is used to produce more technological knowledge (that is, more patents) in $t + 1$ and in the future and, further, if technological knowledge (that is, patents) produced at any time t has effects on innovative output (that is, major innovations) in $t + 1$ and in the future, then patents will appear to 'cause' innovations, but innovations will not appear to 'cause' patents. This pattern of association corresponds to a simplification of Equations (1)–(3) in which: $\theta_3(L) = 0$, generating a model with a recursive structure.[4] An alternative way to interpret the data is to think of patents as minor innovations, and to suppose that inputs of knowledge generate clusters of major and minor innovative activity. If innovations appear to 'cause' patents but not the reverse (that is if $\theta_2(L) = 0$ in Equations (1)–(2)), one might conclude that major innovations typically unleash a wave of minor innovations as firms explore newly-opened technological territory. If, on the other hand, patents are observed to 'cause' innovations but not the reverse (that is, if $\theta_3(L) = 0$), one might conclude that minor innovations typically pave the way for major breakthroughs.[5] Note that in this interpretation the sense in which one of these variables can be said to 'cause' the other refers only to the timing of their appearance: both are, in fact, caused by the input of knowledge which starts off the process of innovation.[6]

The second set of parameters of interest are $\theta_1(L)$ and $\theta_4(L)$. Distributed lags are a natural feature of any model in which R&D spending builds up a stock of technological knowledge capital that does not decay rapidly, and, therefore, which produces a stream of innovations over time. It is natural to think of $\theta_1(L)$ and $\theta_4(L)$ as measuring the (private) rate of depreciation of knowledge stocks. Alternatively and equivalently, they measure the degree to which exogenous shocks are magnified over time, meaning that they identify the degree (if any) to which innovative activity is subject to increasing returns (or cycles of positive feedback) over time.

The third set of parameters of interest are those on the exogenous variables. Of these, the parameters measuring the sensitivity of major innovations or patents to cash flow are of most interest (that is, the $\beta_j(L)$). If internal and external sources of funds are perfect substitutes, then real investment decisions are unlikely to be affected by financial measures. Hence, it is usually argued that a non-zero correlation between cash flow and measures of investment (or, in our case, innovative output) is consistent with the hypothesis that investment (or innovative) activities can be affected adversely in financially constrained firms.[7] The major problem with this inference procedure was noted earlier: namely, that when most costs are fixed, and payment schedules are exogenous or predetermined, changes in demand have an immediate and direct impact on cash flow (and profits), meaning that cash flow might act as no more than a proxy for current demand.[8] Thus, while a positive correlation between cash flow and innovation may reflect financial constraints or (possibly less clearly) demand, the absence of a correlation almost certainly means that financial factors do not have a major systematic effect on innovative activities.

2.2.3 Some Econometric Issues

To estimate Equations (1)–(3), we need to resolve (at least) three econometric difficulties. The first is that patents and innovation are both integer-valued ('count') variables. Standard linear estimating procedures applied to this kind of data may be inappropriate, because the distribution of the residuals is heteroscedastic and the predicted counts can be below zero. Count data models of the exponential family (such as Poisson models) are often used as solutions to this problem. In these models, the conditional expectation of the variable of interest has the general form:

$$E(Y_{it}|X_{it}) = \exp(X'_{it}\theta) \tag{4}$$

where $E(.)$ is the expectations operator, Y_{it} is the underlying stochastic variable with realisation Y_{it} (an integer valued count) and X_{it} are the observables. The exponential form in Equation (4) guarantees non-negativity but, unfortunately, dynamic count data models which recognize explicitly the feedback from past to present technological activity raise several difficulties, especially in the presence of fixed effects. In particular, allowing the lagged dependent variable to enter the **X** vector will, in general, lead to a model with poor stability properties over time (see Blundell *et al.*, 1995c). A natural alternative is the linear feedback model (LFM) where the dynamic process is characterized by:

$$E(Y_{it}|W_{it}) = \theta_1 y_{it-1} + \exp(W'_{it}\theta) \tag{5}$$

This is a member of the class of integer valued autoregressive processes, and can be generalized to allow for longer lags and other count variables. As we are relating two count processes together (patents and innovations), the link between them should be in levels if they are both distributed as Poisson variables.[9] These considerations lead us to rewrite Equations (3)–(5) as:

$$E(n_t|p_{t-k}, n_{t-k}, c_{t-k}, w_t^1) = \theta_1(L)n_{t-1} + \theta_2(L))p_{t-1} \\ + \exp\{\beta_1(L)c_{t-1} + w_{t-1}^1\} \tag{6}$$

$$E(p_t|.) = \theta_3(L)n_{t-1} + \theta_4(L)p_{t-1} + \exp\{\beta_2(L)c_{t-1} + w_{t-1}^2\} \tag{7}$$

$$E(c_t|.) = \theta_5(L)n_{t-1} + \theta_6(L)p_{t-1} + \beta_3(L)c_{t-1} + w_{t-1}^3 \tag{8}$$

In estimating Equations (6)–(8), we utilize a Pseudo-Maximum Likelihood technique that does not impose the Poisson assumption that the first and second moments are equal (see Gourieroux *et al.*, 1984). All equations are then fully corrected for arbitrary heteroscedasticity across cross-section units and autocorrelation over time (White, 1980).

The second econometric problem relates to fixed effects. The standard way to control for unobserved heterogeneity in panel data is to transform the data to eliminate the individual fixed effects. Consequently, we estimate the cash-flow equation in first differences. However, count data models are not linear, so simply differencing the data is not an option. To deal with fixed effects in the patents and innovations equation, we include variables to measure the firms' pre-sample 'knowledge stock' or the 'technological opportunities' that it faces (which are the unobservables that the fixed effects are trying to control for). In the innovations equation, we use the average number of innovations pre-sample (from 1945) and a dummy variable equal to one if the firm ever innovated pre-sample. This 'innovation stock' variable proxies the fixed effect so long as the underlying process generating innovations is stationary. We use a similar technique to construct a 'patents stock' (from 1969 to 1973) for the patents equation.[10]

A final econometric problem relates to the use of instruments to eliminate bias in dynamic panel data models. Since we use lagged values of all our control variables, simultaneity bias should not be a major problem. In the case of the cash-flow equation, however, taking first differences will generate a correlation automatically between the transformed error term and the lagged dependent variable. It is therefore necessary to instrument the lagged dependent variable. As instruments, we use lags dated at least $t - 3$ of cash flow and market share, using a GMM approach (see Arellano and Bond, 1991). The GMM approach allows us to use more instruments as the panel progresses through time. For example, in period $t = 4$ we can use cash flow in $t = 1$ as an instrument, while in $t = 5$ we can use cash flow in both $t = 2$ and $t = 1$, and so on. Needless to say, this yields efficiency gains relative to standard IV techniques. These instruments will be valid in the absence of serial correlation of memory longer than 1 period in the untransformed levels model (for example, MA(1) in the errors).

2.3 THE REGRESSION RESULTS

2.3.1 The Data

Our dataset is drawn from several data sources. The primary database is a panel of companies drawn from the DATASTREAM on-line service. Reliable accounts are available from 1972 for all firms listed on the UK stock market. To facilitate matching with industry data, we focused on companies whose principle operations were in manufacturing. Innovation counts drawn from the Science Policy Research Unit's (SPRU) database were then added into the data. The SPRU dataset contains information on more than 4300 technologically significant and commercially successful innovations in the UK economy between 1945 and 1983 (see Robson *et al.*, 1987 and/or Geroski, 1995 for a description of this data), but it has no information on patenting activity. To remedy this problem, we turned to the US Patent Office's databank of patents granted to UK companies between 1969 and 1988. US patents were chosen to screen out the large number of very low-value patents that cause huge heterogeneity in standard patent data. This left us with the number of innovations commercialized and patents granted for each of the firms in our sample. There is also a complete innovation history for each firm going back to 1945, and a patenting history for each firm back to 1969. After cleaning the data of outliers (see below), and insisting on at least six continuous time series observations for each firm, we were left with a sample of 640 firms observed between 1972 and 1983, 373 of whom were observed for the whole eleven years. The year 1983 was dropped because we were concerned that the sharp drop in innovative activity recorded in that year might be an artefact of how the data was collected.

The data have several properties of interest. Not surprisingly, the production of major innovations and patents is correlated positively: 71 per cent of the firms who innovated also patented (only 28 per cent of those who did not innovate patented), while 45 per cent of patenting (11 per cent of non-patenting) firms also innovated. There were 111 firms who both innovated and patented at some point. In fact, the total number of innovations and patents produced per firm in the sample is correlated positively (the correlation coefficient is 0.6). This said, the average number of innovations (patents) produced per firm per year is 0.05 (0.85). Since so few firms innovate or patent (only 17 per cent of the sample did both), it is interesting to ask whether innovators and patenters differ from non-innovators and non-patenters in any interesting ways. The major differences seem to be that firms who innovated or patented over the period 1972–82 are larger (however measured), have higher cash flows and are rather more likely to be located in industries with high R&D/sales ratios (but they are no more likely to be in highly concentrated, or unionized, or open, industries than non-innovators).

The low incidence of innovation and patent production arises because relatively few firms ever innovate or patent, and, more interestingly, because those who do only do so sporadically. Only 15 per cent of the firms in our sample produced an innovation over the period 1972–82 (only 25 per cent did over the much longer period 1945–82), and only 9 per cent produced more than one. Similarly, 35 per cent of the firms in our sample produced at least one patent, but only 16 per cent produced more than one.[11] Only one firm innovated in all eleven years of our panel (29 firms patented in every year), and only three (54) firms had a spell of innovating (patenting) which lasted at least five years. Trying to account for this pattern of variation is the main challenge in the data.

2.3.2 Baseline Regression Results

Table 2.1 contains OLS estimates of Equations (1)–(3). In the innovations equation, innovation stocks (which are controls for fixed effects) are highly significant (as one would expect), and many of the lagged innovations and patents terms are individually significant. More importantly, F-tests reveal that one cannot reject the hypothesis that the lagged patents variables jointly are significant predictors of innovation (with the strongest effects at $t - 2$ and $t - 3$), and that the lagged dependent variables jointly are significant. Patents also show strong history dependence, with estimated coefficients on the lags of the dependent variable being large and highly significant. What is different between columns (i) and (ii), however, is that the innovation terms jointly are insignificant in the patents equation, but the patents terms are significant in the innovations equation; that is patents appear to 'cause' innovations, but not vice versa. This finding is quite robust: it is a recurrent feature of virtually all versions of Equations (1)–(3) which we examined, including those estimated on a variety of subsamples (see below). The F-tests for the joint significance of lagged patents in the innovation equation are: 2.89 for the balanced subsample, 2.62 for the patenters-only subsample, and 2.32 for the innovators-only subsample. The equivalent F-tests for the joint significance of innovations in the patent equation are: 1.06, 1.02 and 0.78 respectively. The pattern of apparent 'causation' and history dependence shown in Table 2.1 is also robust to the estimation method used, as can be seen in Table 2.2, which shows the corresponding estimates of Equations (6)–(8).[12,13]

Both innovations and patents appear to have significant and positive effects in the cash-flow equation (see regression (iii) in Table 2.1), and it seems clear that variations in cash flow are very procyclical.[14] One problem with (iii) is that there are no controls for dynamics. Equation (vi) in Table 2.2 rectifies this by including two lags of cash flow, and using the GMM approach outlined in the previous section.[15] Taking dynamics into account reveals that the OLS results underestimate the effects of innovations on cash flow relative to patents. The short-run pay off of producing one more innovation on the producer's cash flow is close to £2m, compared to £357 000 for a typical patent. The effect of cash flow on innovation and patents, however, is a different story. Virtually none of the specifications that we estimated suggest that variations in cash flow have any appreciable (or precisely estimated) long-run effect. The OLS results in Table 2.1 contain a hint that

Table 2.1 Models of innovations, patents and cash-flow OLS

Method	Innovations OLS levels	Patents OLS levels	Cash flow OLS first differences
Mean (level)	**0.052**	**0.847**	**8.812**
	(i)	(ii)	(iii)
Patents$_{t-1}$	−0.0042	0.4637	0.4435
	0.0073	*(0.00624)*	*(0.1510)*
Patents$_{t-2}$	0.01188	0.2157	0.5666
	(0.0071)	*(0.0655)*	*(0.2565)*
Patents$_{t-3}$	0.0143	−0.05995	0.0051
	(0.0071)	*(0.0594)*	*(0.1886)*
Patents$_{t-4}$	−0.0054	0.0612	0.0808
	(0.0070)	*(0.2280)*	*(0.1724)*
Innovs$_{t-1}$	0.2206	0.2730	1.3462
	(0.0483)	*(0.2104)*	*(0.6712)*
Innovs$_{t-2}$	−0.018900	−0.2558	0.4724
	(0.0404)	*(0.2374)*	*(0.6988)*
Innovs$_{t-3}$	0.0215	−0.1483	−0.2880
	(0.04111)	*(0.2216)*	*(0.7148)*
Innovs$_{t-4}$	0.1023	−0.682	−0.5656
	(0.0486)	*(0.2288)*	*(0.6325)*
Cash flow$_{t-1}$	0.0031	−0.0093	–
	(0.0015)	*(0.0092)*	
Cash flow$_{t-2}$	−0.0028	0.01000	–
	(0.0016)	*(0.0099)*	
Industry R&D$_{t-1}$	0.0010	0.0342	0.1135
	(0.0024)	*(0.0129)*	*(0.1912)*
Stock of innovation	0.4491	−1.7628	–
	(0.1240)	*(0.6647)*	
Innovation stock >0	0.01562	0.2160	–
	(0.01568)	*(0.0822)*	
Stock of patents	−0.0048	0.2805	–
	(0.0070)	*(0.1109)*	
GDP growth$_{t-1}$	0.1377	−0.1964	14.3269
	(0.1644)	*(0.9642)*	*(2.4972)*
1974 dummy	−0.0211	0.1791	−2.5648
	(0.0157)	*(0.0969)*	*(0.3507)*
1979 dummy	0.0064	−0.2089	−0.4705
	(0.0150)	*(0.0662)*	*(0.1757)*
US patent examiners/ total patent applications$_{t-1}$	–	0.0383	–
		(0.1772)	
Constant	−0.0006	−0.0651	−0.1510
	(0.0041)	*(0.1761)*	*(0.0826)*

Table 2.1   Continued

Method	Innovations OLS levels	Patents OLS levels	Cash flow OLS first differences
R^2	0.334	0.846	0.0497
Joint Significance	2.61	23.80	3.10
(patents) p-value	0.034	0.000	0.015
Joint Significance	6.78	0.97	1.53
(innovs) p-value	0.000	0.425	0.189

Notes: The sample period is 1974–82, and the data includes 640 firms and 5358 observations. All standard errors are heteroscedastic consistent, and the joint significance test is an F-Test of the joint significance of either the four lags innovations or the four lags of patents. Its critical value at 5 per cent level of significance is 2.37.

there may be a short-run effect of cash flow in bringing forward the timing of an innovation, but the count data models in Table 2.2 (column (iv)) imply that there is no significant effect of cash flow on innovation, even in the short run. There is also some evidence in column (v), that cash flow has a significant effect on patenting behaviour, but it is rather weak.

It is sometimes argued that cash flow may affect investment because it is a proxy for current expectations of future demand. If, for some reason, past cash flow is used to form expectations about future profitable opportunities, then including a measure of market value should drive the cash-flow coefficients to zero. On the other hand, if cash flow sensitivity implies the existence of liquidity constraints, then the cash-flow variable should remain significant even after conditioning on market value. To pursue this, we collected data on market value from the LBS Share Price Database using the end of year value of the firm's equity. Lags of this variable were included in column (v). The variable was not available for all companies and so we were forced to drop the sample size to 4748 observations. The coefficient (standard error) on market value in $(t - 1)$ was -0.0334 *(0.0113)*, and on $t - 2$ it was 0.493 *(0.0139)*. Thus there is a positive long-run effect of market value on the probability of patenting, as one would expect (although the negative sign on the first lag is surprising). More interestingly, the coefficients on lagged cash flow were driven into insignificance by the inclusion of market value. The estimates for cash flow $(t - 1)$ and cash flow $(t - 2)$ respectively were 0.0038 *(0.0104)* and 0.0020 *(0.0079)*, compared to -0.0072 *(0.0101)* and 0.0170 *(0.0080)* in the baseline model (in this restricted sample of 4748 observations). Thus, the long-run effect of cash flow drops

Table 2.2 Alternative estimation techniques

Method	Innovations LFM	Patents LFM	Cash flow GMM first differences
Mean	**0.052**	**0.847**	**8.812**
	(iv)	(v)	(vi)
Patents$_{t-1}$	0.0012	0.3961	0.3506
	(0.0034)	(0.0300)	(0.1137)
Patents$_{t-2}$	0.0096	0.2581	0.4433
	(0.0039)	(0.0287)	(0.2570)
Patents$_{t-3}$	0.0042	0.1033	−0.0245
	(0.0034)	(0.0251)	(0.2160)
Patents$_{t-4}$	0.0028	0.1089	−0.1279
	(0.0037)	(0.0226)	(0.1434)
Innovs$_{t-1}$	0.1688	0.0301	1.9552
	(0.0371)	(0.0347)	(0.8774)
Innovs$_{t-2}$	0.0233	0.0340	0.2870
	(0.0186)	(0.0575)	(0.9902)
Innovs$_{t-3}$	0.0643	0.0498	−0.1137
	(0.0284)	(0.0448)	(0.8216)
Innovs$_{t-4}$	0.1734	0.0884	−0.4447
	(0.0374)	(0.0523)	(0.7591)
Cash flow$_{t-1}$	0.0083	−0.0072	0.2368
	(0.0189)	(0.0101)	(0.0627)
Cash flow$_{t-2}$	−0.0003	0.0170	−0.0723
	(0.0199)	(0.0080)	(0.1906)
Industry R&D$_{t-1}$	0.1486	0.0247	0.2435
	(0.0589)	(0.071)	(0.1490)
Innovations stock >0	2.5966	1.271	−
	(0.3667)	(0.287)	
Innovations stock	1.395	−5.845	−
	(0.3160)	(3.395)	
Patents stock	−0.0380	0.0908	−
	(0.0516)	(0.0148)	
GDP growth[a]$_{t-1}$	0.0352	−0.0705	0.1264
	(0.0848)	(0.0556)	(0.0323)
1974 dummy	−0.6083	0.3817[a]	−
	(0.8591)	(0.5107)	
1979 dummy	0.4871	−0.3835[a]	−1.7019
	(0.4662)	(0.4368)	(0.7376)
US patent examiners/ total patent applications$_{t-1}$	−	0.629[a]	−
Constant	−6.1492	−3.4727	0.2687
	(0.3593)	(1.0789)	(0.0984)
Number of observations	5358	5358	4658

Table 2.2 Continued

Method	Innovations LFM	Patents LFM	Cash flow GMM first differences
Time period	1974–82	1974–82	1975–82
Joint significance (patents) p-value	19.30 0.000	1448 0.000	10.86 0.028
Joint significance (innovs) p-value	46.73 0.000	6.2524 0.181	8.1665 0.086
Instruments (both $t-3$–$t-5$)	–	–	Cash flow & market share
First order serial correlation	–	–	–2.271
Second order serial correlation	–	1.245	

Notes: (a) Coefficients and standard errors divided by 100. (iv) and (v) are estimated by a linear feedback model where all the controls except innovations and patents are in the experimental (see text); (vi) is estimated in first differences by a GMM technique with standard errors robust to arbitrary heteroscedasticity and autocorrelation. Serial Correlation is a $N(0, 1)$ test for the presence of residual autocorrelation as described in Arellano and Bond (1991). Joint Significance is a Wald test of the joint significance of either patents or innovations.

by about half when we condition on market value. We conclude that some fraction of the 'cash flow effect' on patents may reflect expectations of future profitable opportunities rather than liquidity constraints. Market value and cash flow were, however, always insignificant in the innovations equation.

2.3.3 Robustness Checks

To check the robustness of our estimates, we conducted a range of experiments on (i)–(vi). First, we tried to measure demand effects more carefully, using industry level variables rather than the growth of GDP. The major problem here is that allocating firms to an industry by their main sales group may be misleading, since, it is demand emanating from the industry that is the main user of a firm's innovations that matters, and many of the SPRU innovations are first used in very different industries than the main producing industry (Robson *et al.*, 1988). Consequently, each firm was allocated up to three different 'innovating using industries' (at the two-digit level). Firms who did not innovate were allocated to their principle two-digit operating industry. A weighted average of real output growth in these 'innovation-using industries' was used to construct an index of the growth of user demand (where the weights were based on the historical proportion of innovations used by these industries). Adding this variable to (i)–(ii) showed that industry output growth has a positive effect on the probability of innovating, but not on patenting. Since industry and aggregate demand are highly correlated, it is no surprise to discover that excluding the insignificant GDP growth variable improved the precision with which industry demand effects are estimated, and they became (weakly) significant in the innovations equation (while remaining wholly insignificant in the patents equation). Dropping firms who did not innovate pre-sample revealed that the user-demand variable is much a stronger driver of innovation for pre-sample innovators than for the sample as a whole (the coefficient on user-demand rises from 0.056 to 0.38). Finally, it seems clear that cash flow picks up at least some demand growth effects: dropping the cash-flow variables increases the size of the estimated effects of demand on innovations and patents (for example, in the innovation equation, the coefficient rises from 0.056 to 0.084 when both cash flow and aggregate GDP growth are excluded). We conclude from this that demand affects innovation more than it affects patents, and that the results reported in (i)–(vi) both understate the size of these effects and exaggerate the imprecision with which they are measured.[16]

Second, we examined the effects of spillovers of innovations and patents by including several lags of the net number of innovations and patents produced in each firm's principal operating industry in (i)–(ii). The results of this exercise suggest that spillovers from innovations and patents are small and very imprecisely estimated, even for the subsample of innovating firms who might be most likely to benefit from spillovers. The weakness of the spillover effects in our regressions may arise because this way of measuring spillover effects is poor, or because the knowledge embodied in patents and innovations (unlike that measured by industry R&D intensity) is too use-specific to spill over very much or very far.[17]

Third, we included a number of size and market structure variables (market share, concentration, import penetration and union density) in all our regressions to ensure that estimates of the effects of cash flow are not conflated with the effects of firm size or market power. Although sometimes significant, the inclusion of these variables does nothing to alter the main tenor of the results. In particular, the pattern of 'causality' between innovation and patents is unaltered (the relevant F-tests are 3.12 for patents in the innovation equation, and 1.12 for innovations in the patent equation), and market share is correlated only weakly with cash flow. We also re-estimated the model on subsamples of 'large' and 'small' firms (those firms who were above and below median pre-sample period turnover). The strongest difference we observed is that small firms are more sensitive to cash flow than large firms, producing noticeably more patents (in the long run) for each unit increase in cash flow. Although these results are not inconsistent with the idea that financial constraints on small firms inhibit their innovative activity, the difference was not significant at conventional levels.

Fourth, we undertook a range of specification checks on the dynamics of the model. Data limitations required a parsimonious representation of the lag structure of cash flow (only available from 1972 onwards). However, allowing lags up to $t - 3$ and $t - 4$ produced insignificant coefficients, no substantive changes in other coefficients, and cost us two cross-sections of data. Longer lags on industry R&D, patents or innovation did not add significantly to the explanatory power of the regressions, they did not substantially change the other coefficient specifications, and they had no effect on the apparent causal relationship between patents and innovations.[18] Estimating (i)–(iii) on subsamples of firms from Engineering, Chemicals and Other industries did not change the main pattern of the results, although there was some evidence that the industry demand effects were stronger in Engineering than elsewhere (coefficient of 0.11 on user demand with a standard error of 0.06 in Engineering, but a negative and insignificant coefficient in the non-Engineering sectors). Similarly, the results were much the same when we re-estimated (i)–(iv) on subsamples of firms who only innovated or only patented, and using a balanced panel gave qualitatively similar results in all respects to the unbalanced one used here.

Fifth, we explored the effects of outliers on our results. The data used in (i)–(iv) were trimmed so that firms who patented more than seventy-eight times in any one year or innovated over eight times in any one year were removed (these thresholds were three standard deviations above the mean of the non-zero observations). This data-cleaning exercise removed two potentially important outliers: ICI (Imperial Chemical Industries) and GEC (The General Electric Company). ICI had a total of 1920 patents between 1974 and 1982, sixty times larger than the mean of the non-zero observations. GEC had eighty-two innovations over the same period (eight times the mean). The models in Table 2.1 were reasonably robust to the inclusion of GEC. The patterns of 'causality' were as before: patents were jointly significant (at the 10 per cent level) in the innovation equation, but innovations jointly insignificant in the patents equation (F-tests of 2.18 and 0.92, respectively). Pay-offs in the cash-flow equation were slightly higher, indicating that GEC has a relatively higher-than-average effect of innovations on cash flow. Unfortunately, the results were more sensitive to including ICI. Although the causal pattern in the patents equation were unaltered, in the innovations equation the patents terms were not significant (F-test 0.65). This is because ICI has such a huge number of patents relative to its number of innovations, so the patents terms effectively are driven to zero. We tried various experiments to make the model robust to the inclusion of ICI, but the bottom line is that our model structure is not well suited to this one particular, highly patent-intensive company.

2.3.4   Measuring Long-Run Effects

Equations (1)–(3) describe a fairly complex interaction over time between n_t, p_t and c_t, and it is difficult to get a sure feel for the very long-run response to exogenous shocks that is implied by the estimated coefficients. We have therefore simulated the short- and long-run response of innovations and patents to a one-off change in the firm's cash flow which might be caused by a public policy initiative designed to stimulate innovation. To motivate the experiment, we calculated that £500 m (in 1980 prices) could be used to increase cash flow per firm by £380 000 and, using these figures, we simulated the response of a representative firm's expected number of innovations and patents.[19] Firms are assumed to be in steady state in period $t = 0$, the shock hits at period $t = 1$, it is first felt in period $t = 2$ (since all our explanatory variables in the models were lagged at least one period), and the model then generates a series of simulated effects over about ten years. To get a feel for the value created by these policies, it is necessary to cumulate the expected number of innovations or patents over all the relevant population of firms, and then value the resulting volume. We do this for the population of UK quoted firms in 1980 (about 2000 in number), using valuations of innovations and patents reported in the literature.[20]

As one might have guessed from Tables 2.1 and 2.2, this policy initiative has no long-run effects on the number of innovations produced. Patents produced declined by one in the first five years after the tax cut, but rose to one net new patent produced after ten years. Rerunning the simulation on large and small firms separately (and using the estimates of (1)–(3) for each subsample) produced estimates of a slightly larger output of patents for smaller firms, and a slightly smaller output for larger firms. Estimates and simulations based on subsamples of innovative firms or firms in Engineering or in Chemicals (the big innovation-producing sectors) were very similar to those for the sample as a whole. To put these results in context, we undertook two complementary simulations, spending £500m to raise industry R&D intensity by 0.25 per cent and GDP growth by 0.0025 per cent.[21] R&D subsidies generated forty-eight extra patents and one innovation after five years, and fifty-seven patents and a total of two innovations after ten years.[22] Increasing GDP growth produced one more innovation and one fewer patent after five years, but induced no further changes. The conclusion would seem to be that cash flow has a positive but modest effect on innovation and patent production, particularly in small firms, and that this effect is bigger than that associated with GDP growth, but smaller than that occasioned by increasing non-discretionary R&D subsidies.

4.1 CONCLUSIONS

Our goal in this project has been to try to account for the episodic and idiosyncratic nature of the variation in innovative output produced by firms, and we have focused in particular on the relationship between innovative output and cash flow. The results are relatively easy to summarize. We have uncovered an apparent causal relationship running from patents to innovative activity, but not from the production of major innovations to patenting. Patents seem to be more sensitive to supply-side factors (such as R&D spending), while innovations seem to be more sensitive to variations in demand. Both variables have fairly large, precisely-estimated effects on cash flow, but neither are affected in any appreciable way by variations in cash flow. In the case of innovations, the (modest) effect of cash flow is to alter the timing rather more than the total number of innovations produced. For patents, mildly significant positive effects only materialize after a two-period lag (if then). Further, the effects running from cash flow to innovation and patents do not seem to be robust to the inclusion of a measure of current expectations of future profits, namely market value. Finally, the smaller firms in our sample appear to be somewhat more cash-flow sensitive than larger ones. It would seem reasonable to conclude from all of this that it is unlikely that the innovative activities of larger firms are severely or systematically financially constrained. For smaller firms, the conclusion is either that they are relatively more sensitive to demand fluctuations than large firms, or that they are often more financially constrained than larger firms (but not by much). Since we are fairly comfortable with how we have controlled for demand, we are (weakly) inclined to opt for the latter inference. The effects are not, however, large, and it is not clear that this adds up to impressive support for launching a major public policy initiative to alleviate the financial distress of small but potentially innovative firms.

More generally (and more speculatively), our impression of the data is technological opportunity and conditions of appropriability (as imperfectly captured by innovation and patent 'stocks', lagged dependent variables and industry R&D) are much more important than either cash flow or demand in identifying which firms innovate. By contrast, if cash flow has any effect, it is on the timing of innovations rather than on the total volume of innovations produced. Demand also seems to affect when firms innovate, and may be a more important driver of innovation than cash flow (although the effects of the two are difficult to disentangle). This said, there is no question that it is hard to account for the episodic nature of innovative activity, and our success has been modest. What also seems to be clear is that the production of 'major' innovations tends to follow the production of patents, and these, in turn, are sensitive to variations in industry (and presumably firm) R&D spending. It may be, then, that the true explanation of the episodic nature of the production of innovations by firms is to be found inside the innovation process itself, and not outside the firm in product or capital markets.

Appendix 2.1: Data Description

The data sources include:

(i)   Firm accounts from the DATASTREAM on-line service. This is basically the population of all firms listed on the London Stock Exchange. Firms who had fewer than six continuous time series observations, whose principal operating industry (defined by sales) was outside manufacturing, or who were involved in large-scale merger activity were removed from the sample.

(ii) The Science Policy Research Unit's innovations database. This consists of over 4378 major innovations defined as 'the successful commercial introduction of new or improved products, processes and materials introduced in Britain between 1945 and 1983'. The aggregate innovations data displays discernable peaks and troughs at roughly five-year intervals. There is a sharp fall in 1983, which appears to be because the survey was conducted mid-year (there were similar single-year drops in the previous two waves, in 1970 and 1980). Consequently, 1983 was dropped. The distribution of innovations across time appears broadly to be stable, with the bulk concentrated in four two-digit industries – mechanical engineering, electrical engineering, vehicles, and chemicals. They were identified by 'innovating unit', which was parented using Dun and Bradstreet's *Who Owns Whom* from various years. When matched to firm accounts we managed to capture about a third of all the innovations in the SPRU dataset over 1972–82. The reminder accrue mainly to smaller firms who are not listed on the Stock Exchange. Examples of innovations include turbomolecular pumps, an aphicide for pest control,

Interferon, solar glass windows, photochromatic glass, and superplastic furniture.

(iii) Patents granted to UK firms by the US Patent Office between 1969 and 1988. The decision to use US rather than UK patents was in order to screen out the numerous very low-value patents taken out each year. These were parented and matched in the same way as the innovations data using the company name.

One problem with the patents data is that they are listed by date granted rather than application date. Most patents granted are applied for within the previous three years, with the mode at $t - 3$. For example, in 1977, of the population of 2752 US patents granted to UK firms, 73 per cent were applied for in the previous three years: 1.7 per cent were applied for in 1976; 30 per cent were applied for in 1975; and 41 per cent were applied for in 1974. We are grateful to Sam Kortum, of Boston University, for the data underlying these calculations. A further problem is that the number of patents granted depends on the efficiency of the US Patent Office. For this reason we included the lagged ratio of examiners to patent applications in the US Patent Office in the previous year as an extra regressor.

After cleaning, we were left with 640 firms between 1972 and 1982. The balance of the full panel was as follows: 10 firms with 6 years of data; 6 firms with 7 years'; 35 with 8 years'; 45 with 9 years'; 171 with 10 years'; and 373 with 11 years'.

The variables used are:

Innovation (n_t)   Count of the number of innovations commercialized by a firm in a particular year. *Source*: SPRU dataset (mean = 0.0517, standard deviation = 0.3987).

Innovations stock (I_0)   Average number of SPRU innovations 1945–74 (0.0382, 0.1700).

Innovations stock > 0   Dummy variable equal to unity if firm innovated at least once during 1945–72 (0.2029, 0.4021).

Industry innovations used (IIU)   Number of innovations used in a firm's principle two-digit operating industry net of its own innovations (3.9053, 4.9221).

Patents (P_t)   Number of patents granted to firm by the US Patent Office in the year (0.8391, 3.5729).

Patent stock (P_0)   The average number of patents 1969–74 (0.9891, 4.0637).

Industry patents (IP)   Number of patents granted in firm's two-digit industry net of own patents. Aggregated from sample only (21.8692, 27.8758).

Cash flow (C_t)   Operating profits before tax, interest and preference dividends plus depreciation DATASTREAM items 137 + 136. In £m 1980 prices (8.7728, 22.5986).

Research and development   R&D expenditures as a proportion of sales in a firm's principle two-digit industry (1.1675, 1.9392). *Source: Business Monitor* M014, various years.

Capital (K)   We use the change in gross fixed assets totals to estimate the breakdown of investment, and the perpetual inventory formula to calculate the replacement cost of capital. Starting values were taken to be the historical value of the

50   *Innovations, Patents and Cash Flow*

capital stock in 1968 (see Bond and Meghir, 1994, for a full description) (8.4189, 23.4617), £m, 1980 prices. *Source*: DATASTREAM.

Industry demand growth   Growth of real output taken from Census of Production (data kindly provided by Ian Small). For innovating firms we could observe where the firm had seen its innovations used. We allowed each firm to have up to three 'principal innovating industries'. Demand growth in these upstream industries was weighted by the proportion of a firm's innovations taken out between 1960 and 1982. For non-innovators, we simply allocated to the principal operating industry (-0.0195, 0.0771).

US Patent Examiners/Patent Application   These were kindly supplied by Zvi Griliches, and calculated from US Patent Office data. (0.0097, 0.0011).
Real GDP growth.   *Source: Economic Trends*, various years (0.0089, 0.0216).

Notes

We would like to thank the Centre for Business Strategy, the Gatsby Foundation and the ESRC for financial assistance. We would also like to thank Richard Blundell, Paul David, Rachel Griffith, Zvi Griliches, Bronwyn Hall, Adam Jaffe, Alfred Kleinknecht, Sam Kortum, Jose Maria Labeaga, Steve Martin, Frank Windmeijer, two referees and participants at: the 1995 RES Conference at Kent, the 1994 NBER Summer School, the CEPR Workshop on R&D Spillovers in Lausanne, the ESRC Network of Industrial Economists meeting in Edinburgh, Dundee University, Newcastle University, Durham University, Harvard University, the Jerome Levy Institute at Bard College, the European University in Florence, the University Catholique de Louvain, the Athens University of Economics and Business and the 1999 TSER workshop on Innovation and Economic Change at Delft University of Technology who provided useful comments on early drafts of this work. The usual disclaimer applies.

1.   For recent work suggesting that demand may play a major role in affecting the timing or implementation of innovations, see Schliefer (1986). More generally, see the survey by Cohen and Levin (1989).
2.   For arguments and tests of the 'financing hierarchy' hypothesis and investment spending generally, see, *inter alia*, Fazzari *et al.* (1988), Chirinko (1997), and the careful critique by Kaplan and Zingales (1997). For a survey of work on R&D and finance, see Goodacre and Tonks (1994). Recent empirical work on finance and R&D includes Himmelberg and Peterson (1994), who find cash flow effects on R&D for small US firms in high-tech sectors, and Seaton and Walker (1997), who have observed that cash flow is an important determinant of firm-level R&D expenditures in the UK.
3.   The tradition of thinking of patents as a measure of (at least intermediate) inputs dates back at least to Schmookler (1966); for further discussion, see Griliches (1990).
4.   Consider a simple example of this argument. If patents in t are used to produce patents in $t + 1$ and in the future, then $p_t = \theta_4(L)p_{t-1} + w_t^2$ (say). That

patents are used to produce innovations now and in the future implies that patents contribute to a stock of knowledge, $k_t = \alpha_0 p_{t-1} + \alpha_1 p_{t-2}$, which, in turn, generates innovations now and in the future, $n_t = \beta_0 k_t + \beta_1 k_{t-1} + w_t^1$. This implies that $n_t = \beta_0 \alpha_0 p_{t-1} + \beta_0 \alpha_1 p_{t-1} + (\beta_1/\beta_0)n_{t-1} + w_t^1$, which is a simplification of Equation (1). This system differs from Equations (1) and (2) only in so far as $\theta_3(L) = 0$.

5. Jovanovic and Rob (1990) describe this kind of relationship between major and minor innovations in terms of 'extensive' and 'intensive' search.

6. Yet a third approach might model n_t and p_t as depending on a moving average in a pair of orthogonal unobservables (such as 'technological knowledge' and 'knowledge of user needs'). Inverting the moving averages yields Equations (1)–(2), and if (say) p_t depends on only one type of knowledge and n_t on both, this will induce a Granger causal relationship running from p_t to n_t. For the use of models of this type, see Pakes (1985), Lach and Shankerman (1989), Geroski (1991), Griliches *et al.* (1991) and others.

7. Some of the literature on real investment has gone further and argued that if one ranks firms by some measure of financial constraint (earnings retention, interest coverage, financial slack and so on), then more constrained firms should display more sensitivity to cash flow. Not only is this hard to accept as a prediction, but such tests are very sensitive to exactly how 'financially constrained' firms are identified (see Kaplan and Zingales, 1997).

8. In principle, this should not matter too much, partly because innovative activity should be driven by expected future, and not current, demand, and partly because current customers are not always the target group for innovations (and hence their current demand may not be pertinent). Further, it should be possible to control directly for demand. In practice, however, none of these arguments completely overwhelms one's sense that cash flow may be correlated highly with demand, and, hence, that it may be partly a proxy for product market demand as well as of capital market constraints.

9. This is one reason why the LFM is preferred to the exponential feedback model (EFM) considered by Blundell *et al.* (1995a). The LFM also has simpler dynamic properties than the EFM; see Blundell *et al.* (1995b) for more details, and, for a recent survey of work on modelling count data, see Winkelmann and Zimmermann (1995).

10. Chamberlain (1993) suggests a quasi-differencing GMM procedure for count data models. Unfortunately, our counts are characterized by a large number of zeros, which makes this strategy infeasible. Hausman *et al.* (1984) suggest using the total number of within sample patents to control for the fixed effect which, unfortunately, requires that all the regressors are strictly exogenous. Our method follows that suggested by Blundell *et al.* (1995a) and conditions on the pre-sample average.

11. These results are consistent with data on the skewness of R&D spending within industries reported by Cohen and Klepper (1992). For further work on the determinants of how persistently firms innovate or patent, see Geroski *et al.* (1997).

12. One potential explanation (in addition to those discussed earlier in the text) for the pattern of causality between patents and innovation is based on the observation that patents and innovations are noisy proxies of the same thing: economically useful knowledge. Innovation counts, may, however, measure this latent variable with greater error than patents. Thus, whereas patents are

reasonably good predictors of innovation, innovations are very poor predictors of patents, and, as a consequence, patents appear to 'cause' innovation, but not vice versa. This is a very difficult argument to counter in the absence of any instrumental variables to correct for the bias caused by measurement error. We have tried to minimize the danger by only estimating on the later years of the innovation dataset (it runs back to 1945) and using US patents, which screen out many of the lowest-value UK patents.

13. This pattern of causality between patents and innovations contrasts with that found by John Baldwin, Petr Hanel and David Sabourin in chapter 5 in this volume. For a sample of 1280 large Canadian manufacturing firms surveyed in 1993, they find a dummy variable indicating whether firms use patent protection has at best an unstable positive effect on innovation, and at worst none at all. They also find innovative activity affects use of patent protection in a robust, strong positive fashion. Leaving aside differences in estimation technique and measurement (our data are a panel, theirs' a cross-section; our innovations and patents data are integers, theirs' dichotomous), we believe this apparent contradiction can be resolved by considering the *type* of invention that the two respective patent variables measure. US patents are used in our sample to screen out the numerous minor patents which cause huge heterogeneity in domestic patent counts (as the US economy is roughly seven times the size of the UK's). This count of domestic patents is what Baldwin, Hanel and Sabourin's indicator variable captures. Thus we might expect, in line with our earlier discussion, that our 'major' US patent measure captures easily commercialized inventions which subsequently appear as innovative new products (that is, patents 'cause' innovations); whereas Canadian innovations typically unleash a wave of minor domestic patents (that is, innovations 'cause' patents). Interestingly, dividing their sample between World and Canada first innovations, and other innovations ('major' and 'minor' innovations), their results for major innovations look much more like our innovations equations in Tables 2.1 and 2.2 than their results for minor innovations do.

14. We included a measure of replacement value of the capital stock in (iii) to insure that the knowledge stock variables are not merely picking up a size effect. Capital was significant, but the coefficient on the technological variables were essentially unaltered.

15. Note that we have to lose a cross-section in order to generate extra instruments, so the sample period is 1975–82.

16. These results are consistent with aggregate time series data which suggest that innovations and patents vary pro-cyclically, and follow increases in demand. See Geroski and Walters (1995).

17. There is some question about exactly how spillovers ought to be measured (see, for example, Griliches, 1979), and it is not clear that the 'horizontal' method we have used has much to recommend it besides convenience (see Jaffe (1986) for an interesting alternative procedure). Most studies have revealed spillovers associated with R&D spending but not with innovations; see Geroski (1994) for a survey. That innovative firms are the only ones to benefit from spillovers is consistent with the idea of Cohen and Levinthal (1989) that spillovers are enjoyed primarily by firms who have invested in building up a research capacity.

18. It has been argued that the production of innovations is a long process, and that one or two lagged values of cash flow are insufficient to measure the effects

of financial constraints on innovation. similarly, to explain patents *granted* (as opposed to patent applications) more than two years' data on cash flow may be necessary. This may be so (in which case an experimental design involving a shortish panel may be flawed), although in the absence of data on the time pattern of cash consumption during innovation projects it is hard to be sure. Still, our conclusions about the weakness or absence of cash flow effects might be more accurately expressed in terms of 'short run cash effects'.

19.   Pre-tax gross profits were £6.2bn for all UK companies in 1980Q3 (*Economic Trends*, 1985). If 80 per cent of this is taxable (because of depreciation, tax allowances, etc) then a 9.5 per cent reduction in corporation tax should cost about £500m. Pre-tax profits were on average £4.044m in our sample, so this would lead to an increase in cash flow on the order of £380 000.

20.   These simulations are carried out using the regression results for the OLS innovations and patents equations, and the first difference GMM cash flow equation. The LFM innovations and patents equations do not change the main findings of their OLS equivalents, whereas the OLS cash flow equation gives misleading results. Simulations using the non-linear dynamic feedback models are prone to non-convergence problems.

21.   Assume GDP is £201bn (as it was in 1980). At a BERD/GDP ratio of approximately 1.5 per cent, this could raise the ratio to 1.75 per cent. If we assume that the spending translates directly to the R&D to sales ratio, then we are considering an increase of 0.25 in industry R&D intensity. This might be achieved either through grants or a well-designed tax credit. The second experiment assumes that the money could be used directly to stimulate GDP growth. If the spending goes straight into GDP (say, through an income tax cut) and ignoring any multiplier effects, this will mean an extra 0.0025 per cent in GDP growth. Finally, consider an increase in cash flow achieved, say, by a cut in corporation tax.

22.   If we assume patents are worth £2000 (slightly more than estimated by Shankerman and Pakes, 1986), then 57 patents generate about £114 000 in (undiscounted) value. Geroski *et al.* (1993) valued each innovation at about £2m, and this means that the total private value of the innovations and patents produced over ten years following a £500m R&D shock is likely to be about £5m. These results are consistent with much of the work that has examined the effects of R&D tax credits (see, for example, Stoneman, 1987), although it sits a little uneasily with the findings of several recent studies that the US tax credit had relatively large effects on the amount of reported company R&D (see Griffith *et al.* (1995) for a recent survey). Nevertheless, even if R&D subsidies do raise total R&D, it is not clear how much of an effect this will have on the production of patents and innovations.

References

ARELLANO, M. and BOND, S. (1991) 'Some Tests of Specification for Panel Data: Monte Carlo Evidence and an Application to Employment Equations', *Review of Economic Studies*, vol. 58, pp. 277–98.

BLUNDELL, R., GRIFFITH, R. and VAN REENEN, J. (1995a) 'Dynamic Count Data Models of Technological Innovation', *Economic Journal*, vol. 105, pp. 429, 333–44.

BLUNDELL, R., GRIFFITH, R. and VAN REENEN, J. (1995b) 'Market Dominance, Market Value and Innovation in a Panel of British Manufacturing Firms', Discussion Paper 95/19, University College London.

BLUNDELL, R., GRIFFITH, R. and WINDMEIJER, F. (1995c) 'Individual Effects and Dynamics in Count Data Models', Discussion Paper 95/03, Discussion Paper 95/03, University College London.

BOND, S. and MEGHIR, C. (1994) 'Dynamic Investment Models and the Firm's Financial Policy', *Review of Economic Studies*, vol. 61, pp. 197–222.

CHAMBERLAIN, G. (1993) 'Feedback in Panel Data Models', Mimeo, Harvard University, Cambridge, Mass.

CHIRINKO, R. (1997) 'Finance Constraints, Liquidity and Investment Spending: Theoretical Restrictions and International Evidence', *Journal of the Japanese and International Economies*, vol. 11, pp. 185–207.

COHEN, W. and KLEPPER, S. (1992) 'The Anatomy of Industry R&D Intensity Distributions', *American Economic Review*, vol. 82, pp. 773–99.

COHEN, W. and LEVIN, R. (1989) 'Empirical Studies of Innovation and Market Structure', in R. Schmalensee and R. Willig (eds), *Handbook of Industrial Economics*. Amsterdam: North-Holland.

COHEN, W. and LEVINTHAL, D. (1989) 'Innovation and Learning: The Two Faces of R&D', *Economic Journal*, vol. 99, pp. 569–96.

FAZZARI, S., HUBBARD, G. and PETERSEN, B. (1988) 'Financing Constraints and Corporate Investment', *Brookings Papers on Economic Activity*, vol. 1, pp. 141–95.

GEROSKI, P. (1991) 'Entry and the Rate of Innovation', *Economics of Innovation and New Technology*, vol. 1, pp. 203–14.

GEROSKI, P. (1994) 'Do Spillovers Undermine the Incentive to Innovate?', in S. Dowrick (ed.), *Economic Approaches to Innovation*. Aldershot: Edward Elgar.

GEROSKI, P. (1995) *Market Structure, Corporate Performance and Innovative Activity*, Oxford University Press.

GEROSKI, P. and WALTERS, C. (1995) 'Innovative Activity Over the Business Cycle', *Economic Journal*, vol. 105, pp. 916–28.

GEROSKI, P., MACHIN, S. and VAN REENEN, J. (1993) 'The Profitability of Innovating Firms', *Rand Journal of Economics*, vol. 24, pp. 198–211.

GEROSKI, P., VAN REENEN, J. and WALTERS, C. (1997) 'How Persistently Do Firms Innovate?', *Research Policy*, vol. 26, pp. 33–48.

GOODACRE, A. and TONKS, I. (1994) 'Finance and Technological Change', in P. Stoneman (ed.), *Handbook of the Economics of Innovation and Technical Change*, Oxford: Basil Blackwell.

GOURIEROUX, C., MONFORT, A. and TROGNON, A. (1984) 'Pseudo Maximum Likelihood Methods: Applications to Poisson Models', *Econometrica*, vol. 52, pp. 701–20.

GRIFFITH, R., SANDLER, F. and VAN REENEN, J. (1995) 'Tax Incentives for R&D', *Fiscal Studies*, vol. 16, pp. 21–44.

GRILICHES, Z. (1979) 'Issues in Assessing the Contribution of R&D to Productivity Growth', *Bell Journal of Economics*, vol. 10, pp. 92–115.

GRILICHES, Z. (1990) 'Patents Statistics as Economic Indicators: A Survey', *Journal of Economic Literature*, vol. 28, pp. 1661–707.

GRILICHES, Z., HALL, B. and PAKES, A. (1991) 'R&D, Patents and Market Value Revisited: Is There a Second (Technological Opportunity) Factor?', *Economics of Innovation and New Technology*, vol. 1, pp. 183–202.

HAUSMAN, J., HALL, B. and GRILICHES, Z. (1984) 'Econometric Models for Count Data with an Application to the Patents R&D Relationship', *Econometrica*, vol. 52, pp. 909–38.

HIMMELBERG, C. and PETERSON, B. (1994) 'R&D and Internal Finance: A Panel Study of Small Firms in High-tech Industries', *Review of Economics and Statistics*, vol. 76, pp. 38–51.

JAFFEE, A. (1986) 'Technological Opportunity and Spillovers of R&D: Evidence from Firms' Patents, Profits and Market Value', *American Economic Review*, vol. 76, pp. 984–1001.

JOVANOVIC, B. and ROB, R. (1990) 'Long Waves and Short Waves: Growth through Intensive and Extensive Search', *Econometrica*, vol. 98, pp. 1391–409.

KAPLAN, S. and ZINGALES, L. (1997) 'Do Investment Cash-flow Sensitivities Provide Useful Measures of Financing Constraints?', *Quarterly Journal of Economics*, vol. 112, pp. 169–215.

LACH, S. and SHANKERMAN, M. (1989) 'The Interaction between Capital Investment and R&D in Science-based Firms', *Journal of Political Economy*, vol. 97, pp. 880–904.

PAKES, A. (1984) 'Patents, R&D and the Stockmarket Rate of Return', in Z. Griliches (ed.), *R&D, Patents and Productivity*, University of Chicago Press.

PAKES, A. (1985) 'On Patents, R&D and the Stock Market Rate of Return', *Journal of Political Economy*, vol. 93, 390–409.

ROBSON, M. and TOWNSEND, J. (1984) 'Users Handbook for the ESRC Archive File on Innovations in Britain since 1945', Mimeo, Science Policy Research Unit, University of Sussex, Brighton.

ROBSON, M., TOWNSEND, J. and PAVITT, K. (1988) 'Sectoral Patterns of Production and Use of Innovations in the UK: 1945–83', *Research Policy*, vol. 17, pp. 1–14.

SEATON, J. and WALKER, I. (1997) 'Corporate R&D in the UK: Spillovers and Credit Market Failure', in: *Economics of Innovation and New Technology*, vol. 5, pp. 75–90.

SCHANKERMAN, M. and PAKES, A. (1986) 'Estimates of the value of Patent Rights in European Countries During the Post-1950 Period', *Economic Journal*, vol. 96, pp. 1052–76.

SCHLIEFER, A. (1986) 'Implementation Cycles', *Journal of Political Economy*, vol. 94, pp. 1163–90.

SCHMOOKLER, J. (1966) *Invention and Economic Growth*. Cambridge, Mass.: Harvard University Press.

STONEMAN, P. (1987) *The Economics of Technology Policy*. Oxford University Press.

WINKELMANN, R. and ZIMMERMANN, K. (1995) 'Recent Developments in Count Data Modelling: Theory and Application', *Journal of Economic Surveys*, vol. 9, pp. 1–24.

WHITE, H. (1980) 'A Heteroscedastic-Consistent Estimator and a Direct Test for Heteroscedasticity', *Economica*, vol. 50, pp. 1–16.

3 The Mutual Relation between Patents and R&D

Hans van Ophem, Erik Brouwer,
Alfred Kleinknecht and Pierre Mohnen *

3.1 INTRODUCTION

Because of the lack of long time series on R&D and patents, few studies have examined the causal link in the Granger sense between these two innovation indicators. The existing evidence gathered by Griliches (1981), Pakes (1985), Hall *et al.* (1986) and Griliches *et al.* (1991) points to an almost instantaneous relationship, and, to the extent that any lag effects can be established, causality seems to run from R&D to patents. The Dutch innovation surveys which contain questions on patent applications allow us to re-examine this issue using information of four-year lagged amounts of R&D expenditures and numbers of patent applications for a sample of 460 firms from the 1992 survey that also responded to the 1988 survey.

Section 3.2 discusses the model which relates R&D expenditures and patent count mutually. Section 3.3 introduces the data, and the estimation results are presented in Section 3.4. Section 3.5 concludes.

3.2 MODEL

As discussed in the introduction, we want to investigate the relation between R&D expenditures and our measure of the rate of success of these expenditures, the number of patents acquired. Clearly, stating that R&D in year t ($R\&D_t$) depends on the patent count of year t (y_t) and that the patent count of year t depends on $R\&D_t$ gives rise to a model with an internal inconsistency which it is impossible to estimate. The problem is that y_t cannot cause $R\&D_t$ and at the same time be caused by $R\&D_t$. Also, from economic theory one would not expect such a relation. Economic theory suggests that y_t and $R\&D_t$ depend on past R&D expenditures and past

---

* Pierre Mohnen thanks the Social Science and Humanities Research Council of Canada for financial support.

acquired patents, respectively. In the panel data set used in this chapter, we have two waves available with a time lag of four years (1988–92). We shall denote these past R&D expenditures by $R\&D_{t-1}$, and the past patent counts by y_{t-1}. It is not very likely that using these past observations specify the determination process of $R\&D_t$ and y_t correctly. One would expect many past values to have an influence on this process (cf. Bound *et al.*, 1984). However, as we do not have better information, we have to rely on our expectation that $R\&D_{t-1}$ and y_{t-1} are good proxies. We do not expect that R&D expenditures fluctuate wildly over time. Moreover, once a firm has established a high-quality research department, it is probable that a relatively constant flow of patents will be generated.[1]

Assume that the distribution of the patent count given y_{t-1} is given by:

$$\Pr(y_{ti} = y_i | R\&D_{t-1_i}) = f(y_i, R\&D_{t-1_i}; \lambda_i) \tag{1}$$

where λ_i is a vector of parameters of the distribution. One (or more) of the elements of λ_i can be made a function of the characteristics of the firm. If we choose the Poisson distribution, λ_i only consists of the expectation of the count. If X_i represents a vector of characteristics of firm i, the usual specification for this expectation is:

$$\lambda_i = \exp(\beta' X_i + \alpha R\&D_{t-1i}) \tag{2}$$

For the R&D expenditures we specify the following relation:[2]

$$R\&D_{ti} = \gamma' Z_{ti} + \delta y_{t-1i} + \varepsilon_{ti} \tag{3}$$

where Z_{ti} is again a vector of explanatory variables of firm i and ε_{ti} an error term. Given the fact that both $R\&D_{t-1i}$ and y_{t-1i} are proxies of the past, we cannot expect that the distributions of y_{ti} and $R\&D_{ti}$ are independent. The relevant conditional loglikelihood looks something like:[3]

$$\log(L | y_{t-1i}, R\&D_{t-1i}) = \sum_{i=1}^{N} \log(L_i | y_{t-1i}, R\&D_{t-1i})$$
$$= \sum_{i=1}^{N} \log(g(y_{ti}, R\&D_{ti}; \rho | y_{t-1i}, R\&D_{t-1i})) \tag{4}$$

where N is the number of observations and $g(., .; \rho | .)$ the conditional bivariate distribution of y_{ti} and $R\&D_{ti}$ where the correlation between the variables is given by ρ. Very few distribution functions combining a discrete and a continuous variable are available. However, by following the method of van Ophem (2000) g can be specified for any combination of a discrete count and a continuous distribution.

We start by specifying the marginal distributions of the random variables under investigation. The conditional marginal distribution of the patent count is given by Equation (1) and the conditional marginal distribution of the R&D expenditures is based on the assumption that the ε_{ti} has a conditional distribution $h(\varepsilon_{ti}|y_{t-1i})$.

If we assume that the patent count takes a finite number of outcomes (say, a maximum of Y) and that λ_i takes on a particular value, we can always determine numbers $\eta_0, \eta_1, \ldots, \eta_{Y-1}$ such that:

$$\Pr(y_{ti} = y; \lambda_i \,|\mathrm{R\&D}_{t-1i}) = \int_{\eta_{y-1}}^{\eta_y} \phi(u)\,du \quad y = 1, \ldots, Y-1 \tag{5a}$$

where $\phi(.|.)$ is the density of the standard normal distribution function. For observations $y=0$ and $y=Y$ we specify:

$$\Pr(y_{ti} = 0; \lambda_i|\mathrm{R\&D}_{t-1i}) = \int_{-\infty}^{\eta_0} \phi(u)\,du$$

$$\Pr(y_{ti} = Y; \lambda_i|\mathrm{R\&D}_{t-1i}) = \int_{\eta_{K-1}}^{+\infty} \phi(u)\,du \tag{5b}$$

Equations (5a) and (5b), given some λ_i, define $\eta_0, \eta_1, \ldots, \eta_{Y-1}$ uniquely. The relation between the probabilities $P(y_{ti} = y; \lambda_i|\mathrm{R\&D}_{t-1i})$ and the η_ys can also be written as:

$$\Pr(y_{ti} \le \kappa; \lambda_i|\mathrm{R\&D}_{t-1i}) = \sum_{y=0}^{\kappa} P(y_{ti} = y; \lambda_i|\mathrm{R\&D}_{t-1i})$$

$$= \Phi(\eta_\kappa) = \int_{-\infty}^{\eta_\kappa} \phi(u)\,du \tag{6}$$

where we define $\eta_y = +\infty$; Consequently:

$$\eta_\kappa = \Phi^{-1}\left(\sum_{y=0}^{\kappa} P(y_{ti} = y; \lambda_i|\mathrm{R\&D}_{t-1i}) \right) \tag{7}$$

This relation defines η_y ($y = 0, \ldots, Y-1$) uniquely for any value of θ, and clearly η_y is a function of λ_i: $\eta_y(\lambda_i)$. As a result, we have related an arbitrary discrete distribution to the normal distribution. For count data the random variable y_{ti} is unbounded. However, this does not cause any problems in the estimation of the model. The log-likelihood function only contains the probability of actual, and therefore bounded, observations.

The density of R&D$_{ti}$ can also be written in terms of the normal distribution whatever the distribution $h(.)$ (Lee, 1983):

$$R\&D_{ti}^* = \Phi^{-1}\left(H(R\&D_{ti}|y_{t-1i})\right) \tag{8}$$

where $\Phi^{-1}(.)$ is the inverse of the standard cumulative normal distribution function and $H(R\&D_{ti}) = \int_{-\infty}^{R\&D_{ti}} h(v)\,dv$. R&D$_{ti}^*$ has a standard normal distribution. Following Lee (1983), if ε_j follows the distribution $F_j(\varepsilon_j)$, $u_j = \Phi^{-1}(F_j(\varepsilon_j))$ has a standard normal distribution.

A cumulative bivariate distribution having marginal distributions $F_1(\varepsilon_1)$ and $F_2(\varepsilon_2)$ and a correlation ρ_ε between ε_1 and ε_2 is given by:

$$H(\varepsilon_1, \varepsilon_2; \rho_\varepsilon) = B(u_1, u_2; \rho_u) = B(\Phi^{-1}(F_1(\varepsilon_1)), \Phi^{-1}(F_2(\varepsilon_2)); \rho_u) \tag{9}$$

where $B(., .; \rho_u)$ is the cumulative bivariate normal distribution with zero means, unit variances and correlation ρ_u.[4] In our case, we have a combination of a discrete and an actually observed continuous random variable, and therefore we need the first derivative of Equation (9) with respect to the continuous variables (say, ε_2):

$$\frac{\partial}{\partial \varepsilon_2} H(\varepsilon_1, \varepsilon_2; \rho_\varepsilon) = \frac{f_2(\varepsilon_2)}{\phi(F_2(\varepsilon_2))} \frac{\partial B(u_1, u_2; \rho_u)}{\partial u_2} \tag{10}$$

The likelihood function of the observed pair $(y_{ti}, R\&D_{ti})$ equals:

$$\begin{aligned} L_i &= g(y_{ti} = y, R\&D_{ti} = r | R\&D_{t-1i}, y_{t-1i}) \\ &= g(y_{ti} \le y, R\&D_{ti} = r | R\&D_{t-1i}, y_{t-1i}) \\ &\quad - g(y_{ti} \le y-1, R\&D_{ti} = r | R\&D_{t-1i}, y_{t-1i}) \end{aligned} \tag{11}$$

Using Equation (10) we have:

$$g(y_{ti} \le y, R\&D_i = r | R\&D_{t-1i}, y_{t-1i})$$

$$= \frac{h(r)}{\phi(H(r))} \frac{\partial B\left(\Phi^{-1}\left(\sum_{k=0}^{y} P(y_{ti} = k)\right), \Phi^{-1}(H(r)); \rho_u\right)}{\partial \Phi^{-1}(H(r))} \tag{12}$$

This simplifies to (Maddala, 1983, p. 273):

$$g(y_{ti} \leq y, R\&D_i = r | R\&D_{t-1i}, y_{t-1i})$$

$$= h(r) \, \Phi\left(\frac{\Phi^{-1}\left(\sum_{k=0}^{y} P(y_{ti} = k)\right) - \rho_u \Phi^{-1}(H(r))}{\sqrt{1 - \rho_u^2}} \right) \qquad (13)$$

which can be substituted into Equation (11) and then Equation (4).

3.3   DATA

We use data from the Dutch part of the *Community Innovation Survey* (CIS), which is available for the years 1988 and 1992. The population of interest in this survey are the firms with ten or more employees in all manufacturing and service sectors of the Dutch economy. The original sample size consists of about 4000 firms for both years. We restrict this sample to the firms conducting permanent R&D activities and of course, for which we have information for both years. The resulting sample contains 460 observations. Additional information about the CIS can be found in Brouwer (1997). The endogenous variables of the analysis are the patent count and the natural logarithm of R&D expenditures. The patent count relates to the patents submitted to the European Patent Office in Munich. We must be content with using R&D expenditures, since we have no information of past R&D to construct an R&D stock. Summary statistics are listed in Table 3.1. A salient detail is the large difference between the mean and variance of the patent counts. At first sight it is therefore questionable to assume a Poisson distribution for the count, where the mean and the variance are the same. The patent count ranges from 0 to a maximum of 22, but the mean is below 1 patent per firm. There is thus a high frequency of zero counts.

The explanatory variables used in the estimations all relate to 1988. They are:

- *Firm size: the logarithm of the number of employees in the firm.*
  Firm size is expected to have a positive effect on R&D. What is less clear-cut is whether R&D increases more or less proportionately with firm size. There might be scale advantages, but there might also be a threshold effect (see Bound *et al.* (1984) for empirical evidence). Since the size effect is not our primary concern, we only introduce a linear term. The impact of size on patent count is also debatable. On the one

hand, large firms might exploit their first-mover advantage rather than patenting to secure the appropriation of R&D benefits, but, on the other hand, large firms are better equipped to apply for patents and face future litigation battles.

- *R&D collaboration: a dummy variable equal to 1 if the firm is engaged in an R&D collaboration with other firms.*
R&D collaboration will probably have a positive impact on both the patent count and R&D. Collaborating firms will have a higher propensity to seek patent protection since they have to reveal information to their partners. We expect the effect of R&D collaboration on R&D to be positive. R&D collaboration allows firms to internalize their mutual R&D spillover and thereby to increase the returns to their R&D efforts (see d'Aspremont and Jacquemin (1988) for a theoretical discussion of this result).

- *Sectoral dummy variables equal to 1 if the firm's principal activity is in that sector, and zero otherwise.*
The sectors are service, food and beverages, wood processing, chemicals, plastics and rubber, metals, machinery, electrical equipment, and transportation equipment. The reference group is all other sectors.

- *Average product life cycle in a sector in years.*
The average product life cycle should show up with a negative coefficient in both the patent count and R&D, since a shorter life-cycle of

Table 3.1   Sample characteristics of the variables

Variables	Mean	St. dev.	Minimum	Maximum
Patent count 1992	0.457	1.662	0	22
Log (R&D) 1992	1.270	1.603	−2.794	8.939
Firm size (log of employees)	4.998	1.214	1.386	11.082
R&D collaboration	0.452	0.498	0	1
Service	0.211	0.408	0	1
Food & beverages	0.091	0.288	0	1
Wood processing	0.072	0.258	0	1
Chemicals	0.080	0.272	0	1
Plastics & rubber	0.035	0.183	0	1
Metals	0.126	0.332	0	1
Machinery	0.174	0.379	0	1
Electric equipment	0.050	0.218	0	1
Transportation equipment	0.065	0.247	0	1
Average product life-cycle	10.638	1.945	4.526	14.821
Patent count 1988	0.663	2.200	0	33
Log (R&D) 1988	1.315	1.530	−3.219	9.616

products will increase the efforts of firms to renew their products more frequently.

3.4   EMPIRICAL RESULTS

Tables 3.2 and 3.3 give the estimation results of the model described in Section 3.2 under the assumptions of a Poisson distributed patent count – Equation (1) – and a normal distribution for the error term of the $\log(R\&D_t)$ Equation (3). Table 3.2 contains the estimates for the case that patent count and $\log(R\&D_t)$ are not correlated. This case can be estimated by a Poisson regression and ordinary least squares. R&D increases with size, patents not, whereas cooperative R&D increases the number of patents but not the amount of R&D. R&D and patents are not related to the average product life cycle but are cross-correlated over time. Table 3.3 contains the full maximum likelihood estimation for the specification that allows a non zero correlation between the error terms of the R&D and patent equations.

Table 3.2   ML estimation of a Poisson distributed patent equation and OLS estimation of log (R&D), 1992

Variables	Patent count	Log (R&D)
Constant	−3.087 (0.886)**	−2.248 (0.452)**
Firm size (log of employees)	0.164 (0.089)	0.679 (0.049)**
R&D collaboration	0.369 (0.160)*	0.194 (0.117)
Service	0.320 (0.513)	0.289 (0.221)
Food & beverages	−0.124 (0.652)	0.251 (0.267)
Wood processing	0.942 (0.579)	0.066 (0.284)
Chemicals	2.084 (0.520)**	1.648 (0.282)**
Plastics & rubber	2.078 (0.550)**	0.221 (0.361)
Metals	1.336 (0.528)**	0.234 (0.251)
Machinery	1.901 (0.483)**	0.663 (0.232)**
Electric equipment	0.049 (0.586)	1.421 (0.317)**
Transportation equipment	0.543 (0.577)	0.773 (0.294)**
Average product life-cycle	−0.054 (0.073)	−0.049 (0.035)
$\log(R\&D_{1988})$	0.301 (0.067)**	
Patent count 1988		0.101 (0.027)**

Notes: Mean log-likelihood (count part) $= -0.877$; number of observations $= 460$; R^2 (R&D part) $= 0.445$; variance R&D error $= 1.468$; asymptotic standard errors in parentheses.
* = significant at 5%; ** = significant at 1% (two-sided test).

Table 3.3   ML estimation patents/R&D model, 1992: Poisson specification
of the count

Variables	Patent count	Log (R&D)
Constant	−3.001 (0.936)**	−2.883 (0.561)**
Firm size (log of employees)	0.157 (0.095)*	0.822 (0.062)**
R&D collaboration	0.317 (0.164)*	0.207 (0.143)
Service	0.304 (0.519)	0.354 (0.275)
Food & beverages	−0.250 (0.649)	0.423 (0.330)
Wood processing	0.918 (0.580)*	0.101 (0.355)
Chemicals	1.721 (0.523)**	2.068 (0.344)**
Plastics & rubber	1.942 (0.543)**	0.493 (0.440)
Metals	1.189 (0.525)*	0.422 (0.312)
Machinery	1.679 (0.486)**	0.959 (0.287)**
Electric equipment	0.386 (0.587)	1.620 (0.383)**
Transportation equipment	0.609 (0.574)	0.977 (0.360)**
Average product life cycle	−0.017 (0.072)	−0.092 (0.043)*
Log (R&D$_{1988}$)	0.189 (0.075)*	
Patent count 1988		0.094 (0.032)**
	Model parameters	
Correlation	0.082 (0.062)	
Variance error term log (R&D)	2.042 (0.159)**	

Notes: Mean log-likelihood = −2.385; number of observations = 460; standard errors in parentheses.
* = asymptotically significant at 10%; ** = significant at 1% (two-sided test).

Size now exerts a positive effect on both patent applications and R&D expenditures. The estimated marginal effect of size on the number of patent applications increases. The average product life cycle shows a negative coefficient on the amount of R&D. The correlation coefficient between the two error terms is, however, insignificantly different from zero. Causality between patents and R&D still seems to run both ways. The causality running from R&D to patents weakens when a contemporaneous correlation between both is introduced through the error term.

   If we look at the distribution of the count (cf. Table 3.7, second column on page 67), we observe a very large proportion of zero counts. The question is whether this is not a little out of line with the Poisson distribution estimated. To check this we have estimated a Without Zero Poisson model, as proposed by Mullahy (1986). Broadly speaking, only the positive counts follow a Poisson distribution in this model and the probability of

Table 3.4   ML estimation patents/R&D model for 1992: without zero specification for the count

Variables	Patent count	Log (R&D)
Constant	−2.689 (1.352)*	−2.841 (0.559)**
Firm size (log of employees)	0.422 (0.121)**	0.824 (0.061)**
R&D collaboration	0.462 (0.186)*	0.240 (0.141)*
Service	0.603 (0.628)	0.394 (0.275)
Food & beverages	−0.146 (0.788)	0.440 (0.330)
Wood processing	1.196 (0.792)	0.106 (0.354)
Chemicals	1.727 (0.693)*	2.023 (0.341)**
Plastics & rubber	1.320 (0.695)*	0.394 (0.435)
Metals	1.224 (0.670)*	0.434 (0.311)
Machinery	1.833 (0.603)**	0.939 (0.285)**
Electric equipment	0.694 (0.644)	1.562 (0.379)**
Transportation equipment	0.971 (0.732)	0.984 (0.358)**
Average product life cycle	−0.071 (0.126)	−0.098 (0.043)*
Log (R&D$_{1988}$)	0.053 (0.095)	
Patent count 1988		0.078 (0.032)*
	Model parameters	
Correlation	0.322 (0.095)**	
Variance error term log(R&D)	2.047 (0.159)**	
ψ	0.692 (0.039)**	

Notes: Mean log-likelihood = −2.213; number of observations = 460; standard errors in parentheses.
* = asymptotically significant at 10%; ** = significant at 1% (two-sided test).

the zero count is estimated by a constant. The following distribution is estimated:

$$\begin{aligned} \Pr(y_{ti} = 0) &= \psi + (1 - \psi)\, \phi(0), \\ \Pr(y_{ti} = y) &= (1 - \psi)\, \phi(y) \text{ for } y > 0 \end{aligned} \tag{14}$$

where $\phi(y)$ is the chosen basic distribution function of the count. As we can see from Table 3.4, treating the frequent occurence of zero patents differently from the other patent counts increases the contemporaneous correlation between R&D and patents but reduces their cross-intertemporal effects. The coefficient of R&D on patents becomes insignificant. The estimates of the R&D equations are robust to this change of specification. The additional parameter ψ is significant.

To investigate whether the assumption of a Poisson distributed count is too restrictive, we now turn to the Katz family of distributions (Katz, 1995 or Winkelmann, 1997, p. 35). This type of distribution nests several other distributions for non-negative integers, while maintaining a parsimonious parameterization. It is defined by the recursive probabilities:

$$\frac{\Pr(y_{ti} = y | \text{R\&D}_i)}{\Pr(y_{ti} = y - 1 | \text{R\&D}_i)} = \frac{\omega + \theta(y - 1)}{y}$$

$$y = 1, 2, \ldots; \ \omega > 0 \quad \text{and} \quad y \leq \omega/\theta \ \text{for} \ \theta < 0 \qquad (15)$$

The Poisson ($\omega = \lambda$, $\theta = 0$), Negative Binomial, Geometric and Binomial distributions are special cases (Winkelmann, 1997, p. 36). To make the Poisson specification of Section 3.3 a special case we assume that ω is individual specific ($\omega = \exp(X_i'\beta)$) and that θ is not. Because the implicit probabilities have to sum up to 1, the probability of a zero count can be simply derived:

$$\Pr(y_{ti} = 0 | \text{R\&D}_i) = 1 - \sum_{k=1}^{\infty} \Pr(y_{ti} = k | \text{R\&D}_i)$$

$$= 1 - \sum_{k=1}^{\infty} \prod_{j=1}^{k} \frac{\omega + \theta(j - 1)}{j} \Pr(y_{ti} = 0 | \text{R\&D}_i)$$

$$= \left(1 + \sum_{k=1}^{\infty} \prod_{j=1}^{k} \frac{\omega + \theta(j - 1)}{j}\right)^{-1} \qquad (16)$$

From this probability all other probabilities can be derived, and the application of the method proposed in Section 3.3 is straightforward. The estimation results can be found in Tables 3.5 and 3.6 (respectively, the with and without zero patent count specifications). The new parameter θ is significantly different from zero, proving formally our suspicion that the Poisson distribution is too restrictive. If we compare Tables 3.3 and 3.5, we notice that the estimated correlation between the error terms increases. In the patent equation, size and lagged R&D become insignificant. The estimates of the R&D equation remain pretty much the same. Combining the Katz distribution and the without zero patent specification increases the contemporaneous correlation coefficient of the error terms, reinforces the size elasticity in the patent equation, but does not resurrect any causality running from R&D to patents. The absence of Granger causality from R&D to patents is broadly consistent with the predominantly contemporaneous R&D effect and the non-significance of lagged R&D effects on patents found in most other studies (see Cincera, 1997). Again, the R&D estimates remain largely unaffected.

Table 3.5   ML estimation patents/R&D model, 1992: Katz-system specification of the count

Variables	Patent count	Log (R&D)
Constant	−4.430 (1.329)**	−2.891 (0.562)**
Firm size (log of employees)	0.193 (0.151)	0.817 (0.061)**
R&D collaboration	0.085 (0.240)	0.203 (0.143)
Service	−0.213 (0.721)	0.350 (0.275)
Food & beverages	−0.189 (0.816)	0.429 (0.330)
Wood processing	1.036 (0.718)	0.119 (0.356)
Chemicals	1.602 (0.678)*	2.067 (0.344)**
Plastics & rubber	1.643 (0.731)**	0.497 (0.440)
Metals	0.924 (0.674)**	0.422 (0.313)
Machinery	1.465 (0.620)*	0.958 (0.287)**
Electric equipment	1.062 (0.751)	1.639 (0.383)**
Transportation equipment	0.759 (0.725)	0.987 (0.361)**
Average product life cycle	0.027 (0.099)	−0.089 (0.043)*
Log (R&D$_{1988}$)	0.055 (0.126)	
Patent count 1988		0.082 (0.032)*

	Model parameters
Correlation	0.319 (0.118)**
Variance error term log (R&D)	2.050 (0.159)**
θ	0.712 (0.052)**

Notes: Mean log-likelihood = −2.229; number of observations = 460; standard error in parentheses.
* = asymptotically significant at 10%; ** = significant at 1% (two-sided test).

To investigate the fit we employ the method discussed in Winkelmann (1997, p. 162). We predict the patent count distribution of the firms, and after aggregating across all firms, we obtain a sampling distribution under the specified model. A Pearson χ^2-test is performed to check whether the sampling distribution fits the data. In doing this we need to limit the count, and we opted for a maximum count of eight (only two firms where granted more than eight patents). The results of these calculations are listed in Table 3.7.

From Table 3.7 we can conclude that the best-performing model is the one based on the Katz system of distributions and a without zero patent count specification. Based on these estimates, we can assert that one additional patent applied for (assuming that on average an application gets granted) four years down the road yields, a 7.5 per cent increase in R&D

Table 3.6 ML estimation patents/R&D model for 1992: without zero
Katz-system specification of the count

Variables	Patent count	Log (R&D)
Constant	−4.314 (1.409)**	−2.961 (0.563)**
Firm size (log of employees)	0.500 (0.151)**	0.838 (0.061)**
R&D collaboration	0.452 (0.233)*	0.255 (0.142)**
Service	−0.129 (0.738)	0.345 (0.276)
Food & beverages	−0.328 (0.854)	0.414 (0.332)
Wood processing	1.207 (0.811)	0.117 (0.358)
Chemicals	1.838 (0.703)**	2.046 (0.342)**
Plastics & rubber	1.204 (0.748)	0.374 (0.437)
Metals	1.231 (0.697)*	0.444 (0.313)
Machinery	1.982 (0.641)**	0.980 (0.287)**
Electric equipment	1.071 (0.736)	1.602 (0.380)**
Transportation equipment	1.111 (0.764)	1.009 (0.360)**
Average product life cycle	−0.030 (0.108)	−0.094 (0.043)*
Log ($R\&D_{1988}$)	0.057 (0.115)	
Patent count 1988		0.075 (0.032)*
	Model parameters	
Correlation	0.390 (0.102)**	
Variance error term log (R&D)	2.059 (0.161)**	
θ	0.402 (0.103)**	
ψ	0.589 (0.061)**	

Notes: Mean log-likelihood $= -2.202$; number of observations $= 460$;
standard errors in parentheses.
* = asymptotically significant at 10%; ** = significant at 1% (two-sided test).

Table 3.7 Predicted patent count

Count (Y)	Sample	Poisson $\rho = 0$	Poisson	Poisson	Katz	Katz WZ
0	381	360	317	375	374	379
1	36	75	101	41	42	37
2	21	16	28	21	19	18
3	6	4	8	10	10	10
4	3	2	3	5	6	5
5	5	1	1	3	3	3
6	5	1	1	1	2	2
7	0	0	0	1	1	1
8	1	0	0	1	1	1
≥9	2	0	0	3	2	4
Pearson-χ^2	–	66.5*	114.0*	15.9	10.0	10.6

* = H_o: predicted count fits sample count, rejected at 1%.

expenditures. The interpretation could be that patents pave the way to a stream of development expenditures in order to bring the patented product to the market, or to additional R&D aiming to develop complements to the patented product. The elasticity of patents with respect to R&D (from the contemporaneous correlation of the error terms) is in the order of 0.4, which is closer to the time series estimates reported in the literature (see Griliches, 1990) than to the cross-section estimates to which they are supposed to be comparable.

3.5   CONCLUSION

From cross-sectional data on contemporaneous and four-year lagged patent applications and R&D expenditures, we have re-examined the causality direction between R&D and patents. The two equations have been estimated jointly with a contemporaneous correlation working through the error terms. We have experimented with different specifications of the count data for patent applications: the Poisson distribution, the negative binomial distribution, and the Poisson and negative binomial without zero patent specifications. The negative binomial without zero patent specification model performs best (as was also found by Licht and Zoz (2000) and Crépon and Duguet (1997)).

We find that patents Granger-cause R&D in all specifications. One additional patent increases R&D four years later by 7.5 per cent. The reverse causality from R&D to patents vanishes as soon as we depart in one way or another from the simple Poisson specification of patent counts. Although our result should be confirmed by analyzing other datasets and by checking how sensitive our estimates are to other specifications (such as including non-linear size effects, modelling more explicitly the contemporaneous linkage between R&D and patents, and introducing innovative sales into the picture) we might have uncovered a different causality from the conventional one estimated by other authors.

Notes

1.   This argument would allow us to use $R\&D_t$ and y_t as proxies for the past R&D expenditures and the patent count. A statistical inconsistency would still be present in the model (cf. Maddala, 1983, p. 118).
2.   In fact, we use the log of $R\&D_{ti}$ and the log of $R\&D_{t-1i}$ in the empirical analysis. For notational conciseness we shall delete log in the section.

3. Here we have abstracted from conditioning on the explanatory variables.
4. Although ρ_ε and ρ_u are closely related, they are not the same. Numerical analysis shows that the signs and the order of magnitude are always the same (cf. van Ophem, 1999).

References

ACS, Z. and AUDRETSCH, D. B. (1989) 'Patents as a Measure of Innovative Activity', *Kyklos*, vol. 42, pp. 171–80.

D'ASPREMONT, C. and JACQUEMIN, A. (1988) 'Cooperative and Noncooperative R&D in Duopoly with Spillovers', *American Economic Review*, vol. 78, no. 5, pp. 1133–7.

BOUND, J., CUMMINS, C., GRILICHES, Z., HALL, B. H. and JAFFE, A. (1984) 'Who Does R&D and Who Patents?', in Z. Griliches (ed.), *R&D, Patents, and Productivity*. Chicago: National Bureau of Economic Research, University of Chicago Press.

BROUWER, E. (1997) *Into Innovation: Determinants and Indicators*, Ph.D. thesis, University of Amsterdam.

CINCERA, M. (1997) 'Patents, R&D and Technological Spillovers at the Firm Level: Some Evidence from Econometric Count Models for Panel Data', *Journal of Applied Econometrics*, vol., 12, no. 3, pp. 265–80.

CRÉPON, B. and DUGUET, E. (1997) 'Estimating the Innovation Function from Patent Numbers: GMM on Count Panel Data', *Journal of Applied Econometrics*, vol. 12, no. 3, pp. 243–64.

DOSI, G. (1988) 'Sources, Procedures, and Microeconomic Effects of Innovation', *Journal of Economic Literature,* vol. 26, pp. 1120–71.

GRILICHES, Z. (1981) 'Market Value, R&D and Patents', *Economics Letters*, vol. 7, pp. 183–7.

GRILICHES, Z. (ed.) (1984) *R&D, Patents, and Productivity.* Chicago: National Bureau of Economic Research, University of Chicago Press.

GRILICHES, Z. (1990) 'Patent Statistics as Economic Indicators: A Survey', *Journal of Economic Literature*, vol. 28, pp. 1661–707.

GRILICHES, Z. (1995) 'R&D and Productivity: Econometric Results and Measurement Issues', in P. Stoneman (ed.), *Handbook of the Economics of Innovation and Technological Change*. Oxford: Basil Blackwell.

GRILICHES, Z., HALL, B. and PAKES, A. (1991) 'R&D, Patents and Market Value Revisited: Is There a Second (Technological Opportunity) Factor?', *Economics of Innovation and New Technology*, vol. 1, no. 3, pp. 183–201.

HALL, B. H., HAUSMAN, J. and GRILICHES, Z. (1986) 'Patents and R and D: Is There a Lag?', *International Economic Review*, vol. 27, pp. 265–83.

HAUSMAN, J., HALL, B. H. and GRILICHES, Z. (1984) 'Econometric Models for Count Data with an Application to the Patents–R&D Relationship', *Econometrica*, vol. 52, pp. 909–38.

KATZ, L. (1995) 'Unified Treatment of a Broad Class of Discrete Probability Distributions', in G. P. Patil (ed.), *Classical and Contagious Discrete Distributions*. New York: Statistical Publishing Society, Pergamon Press.

LEE, L. F. (1983) 'Generalized Econometric Models with Selectivity', *Econometrica*, vol. 51, pp. 507–12.

LICHT, G. and ZOZ, K. (2000) 'Patents and R&D, An Econometric Investigation Using Applications for German, European and US Patents by German Firms', in D. Encaoua, B. Hall, F. Laisney and J. Mairesse (eds), *The Economics and Econometrics of Innovation*. Boston, Mass.: Kluwer.

MADDALA, G. S. (1983) *Limited-Dependent and Qualitative Variables in Econometrics*, Cambridge University Press, Cambridge, Mass.

MONTALVO, J. G. (1997) 'GMM Estimation of Count-Panel-Data Models with Fixed Effects and Predetermined Instruments', *Journal of Business and Economic Statistics*, vol. 15, pp. 82–9.

MULLAHY, J. (1986) 'Specification and Testing of Some Modified Count Data Models', *Journal of Econometrics*, vol. 33, pp. 341–65.

PAKES, A. (1985) 'On Patents, R&D, and the Stock Market Rates of Return', *Journal of Political Economy*, vol. 93, 390–409.

PATEL, P. and PAVITT, K (1995) 'Patterns of Technologival Activity: Their Measurement and Interpretation', in P. Stoneman (ed.), *Handbook of the Economics of Innovation and Technological Change*. Oxford: Basil Blackwell.

STONEMAN, P. (ed.) (1995) *Handbook of the Economics of Innovation and Technological Change*. Oxford: Basil Blackwell.

VAN OPHEM, H. (1999) 'A General Method to Estimate Correlated, Discrete Random Variables', *Econometric Theory*, vol. 15, pp. 228–37.

VAN OPHEM, H. (2000) 'Modeling Selectivity in Count-Data Models', *Journal of Business and Economic Statistics*, vol. 18, pp. 503–11.

WANG, P., COCKBURN, I. M. and PUTERMAN, M. L. (1998) 'Analysis of Patent Data – A Mixed-Poisson-Regression-Model Approach', *Journal of Business and Economic Statistics*, vol. 16, pp. 27–41.

WINKELMANN, R. (1997) *Econometric Analysis of Count Data*, 2nd edn. Berlin: Springer-Verlag.

Part II
Determinants of Innovative Behaviour

4 Innovation and Farm Performance: The Case of Dutch Agriculture

*Paul Diederen, Hans van Meijl
and Arjan Wolters*

4.1 INTRODUCTION

The agricultural sector in The Netherlands, as elsewhere in Europe, is confronted with three related types of change in its environment. First, markets are changing. Over the years, shortage markets have changed into surplus markets. Prices for basic bulk products fluctuate around, or just above, average production costs. Prices substantially higher than costs can only be obtained on niche markets by offering products with specific extra qualities (in terms of taste, health or production mode). Second, policies are changing. Whereas in the past, the government assumed a role in taking care of the economic fate of farmers, it is now putting more emphasis on the private sector's own responsibilities. Policies under the Common Agricultural Policy (CAP) are gradually reformed and the market is left to do its work. The farmer is expected to change from an artisan into an entrepreneur. Third, the institutional environment is changing. Until recently, a system of political representation and product and industry boards was in place, to take care of the collective interests of the agricultural community. In the Netherlands, this system has largely broken down as a consequence of the growing differentiation between farmers, and under increasing pressure from within-industry competition.

These three kinds of change have an important impact on innovation in agriculture. As markets change, the required directions for innovation also change. Where formerly the focus was almost exclusively on productivity increase and efficiency on the farm, major themes are now quality increase in all its guises and co-ordinated innovation at the level of the production chain. As government is reducing its steering role in the running of agricultural businesses, it is also withdrawing from the responsibility of producing and diffusing technical change in the industry. It leaves innovation to the initiative of the farmers, at most stimulating them indirectly to invest in technological change (see, for example, Possas *et al.*, 1996). If, in addition, organizations for the representation of shared interests disintegrate, as they have in the Netherlands, innovation tends no longer to be organized collectively. Again, it is left to the individual farmer. Thus, on the one hand, innovation in farming has become a more varied and complex issue than in the past, and on the other, it has become increasingly the task of the individual entrepreneur.

Innovation in agricultural firms is plagued by a number of market failures (over and above the ones usually cited in relation to technical change). Because of their small scale of operations, they have limited opportunities to develop and implement innovations profitably, they have limited financial resources and in-house specialized expertise, and limited management resources. Also, the institutional structure for the sale of output, characterized by co-operative trading organizations and auctions, makes it difficult to market a differentiated product, and may thereby hamper product innovation. Because of these difficulties, agriculture is often characterized as a 'supplier dominated' industry with respect to technical change (Pavitt, 1984). Innovation is traditionally infused from outside the sector, be it through government-sponsored research stations[1] or by suppliers of capital goods and production inputs.

Changing circumstances are now forcing the farmers themselves to take responsibility for innovation. This raises the question whether individual farmers are able to take up this role, to organize and carry out the innovation process themselves to a satisfactory degree. This research looks the extent to which farmers are able to do this.

To tackle this topic, we collected data at the farm level through an innovation survey among about 1500 farms. Questions concerned innovative activities, innovations recently implemented, and determinants and effects of innovativeness. The Section 4.2 will introduce our research questions and hypotheses, and in the following sections we present evidence and results from these tests; Section 4.7 concludes.

4.2   RESEARCH QUESTIONS

In this chapter, we address three types of questions about innovation in agriculture. With each question we give a number of hypotheses, which we test in the sections below.

1. *How do farmers go about innovating; how do they organize innovation?*
   - Innovative firms take advantage of a wide range of available sources of knowledge;
   - Vertical and horizontal co-operation is important for innovation; innovative firms are active in networks; and
   - Innovative firms protect their innovations.
2. *Who is innovative in agriculture: what structural characteristics and incentives determine whether a farmer innovates?*
   - Large firms are more innovative than smaller ones (this hypothesis on the relationship between absolute size and innovation is known as the first Schumpeterian hypothesis). Larger firms have more resources to invest in innovation and more opportunity to apply an innovation profitably (Schumpeter, 1943; Kamien and Schwartz, 1982; Scherer and Ross, 1990);
   - Firms with a larger market share are more innovative than those with a smaller market share (this hypothesis, looking at relative size and thereby market power, is called the second Schumpeterian hypothesis);
   - Farmers who engage in all sorts of entrepreneurial behaviour aimed at change and renewal are more successful in technical innovation than those that do not. Innovative farmers are not only looking for improvements in their business processes by introducing new technologies, but also by engaging in new marketing and management activities, and new forms of organization and co-operation; and
   - Innovativeness is related inversely to the age of the farmer: older farmers may have a lower level of education and a shorter planning horizon.
3. *What is the economic impact of innovation?*
   - Innovative firms are more profitable; and
   - Innovative firms grow faster.

4.3   THE DATABASE

Data were collected among 1250 farms participating in the Dutch Farm Accountancy Data Network (FADN), maintained at the Agricultural Economics Research Institute (LEI). This is a stratified sample, representative of the Dutch agricultural and horticultural industry. Additional data were collected among about 250 farmers and growers that were identified a priori as being in the technological lead (these data were added to the

Table 4.1 Innovativeness per sector

	Number of firms in each sector	Of which innovative (%)
Greenhouse vegetables	70	23
Intensive livestock farming	120	22
Greenhouse flowers	111	17
Other horticulture	126	17
Mushrooms	26	15
Arable farming	236	12
Dairy farming	432	8
Fruit	87	7
Total	1208	13

sample to compute Tables 4.2 and 4.3 (see pages 77 and 78), but were not used for the regressions in this chapter).

An innovation is commonly defined as the first commercial application of new practical knowledge. We are not so much interested in the very first farmer in this industry of thousands to adopt a new technology, but in the group of farmers that move faster than the average. In our survey, we therefore defined an innovation as a *relatively* new commercial application of, mostly technical, knowledge. By relatively new we mean: used by less than 25 per cent of potential users. Thus, in our database, an innovative firm is one of the front runners, but not necessarily the very first firm to adopt an innovation.

Farmers were classified as innovative if they answered positively to both of the following questions: (1) Did you adopt an important innovation in the period 1995–7? and (2) Were you among the early adopters of this innovation (the first quarter of potential adopters)? If they answered positively, they were asked about the nature of their innovation, their activities aimed at innovation in general, personal and firm characteristics, and results from innovation.

Table 4.1 shows the distribution of firms in the FADN sample over sectors and the share of firms in each sector that were classified as innovative. The data suggest that there are significant differences between sectors. On average, firms in horticulture seem more innovative than those in arable and dairy farming.

4.4 INNOVATIVE FIRMS IN AGRICULTURE

In the Netherlands, the collective structures taking care of technological innovation and diffusion in agriculture are grinding to a halt. Individual

Table 4.2 Sources of information (percentages)

	Important or very important	Only moderately important	Not important
Inside company	68	14	18
Trade journals	65	24	11
Trade fairs	54	30	16
Competitors	54	19	27
Cutomers	49	17	34
Suppliers	44	19	37
Research organizations	25	15	60
Governmental organizations	13	12	75
Patent information	10	5	85

farmers are taking over. In this section we look at some evidence on how they go about it.

For the farmer, the main sources of information and inspiration relevant to the innovation process are his own business, contacts with colleagues, trade journals, and agricultural trade fairs (see Table 4.2). Of the innovative farmers, more than 70 per cent are members of a 'study group' (that is, an organization of farmers aimed at information exchange), whereas, of the non-innovators, just over half are members. Suppliers and buyers are of secondary importance as sources of information, though they do play an important role indirectly through their presence at fairs and in trade journals. Sector organizations and public technical services play a minor role.

Where, in larger manufacturing firms, innovations are mostly developed in-house by the R&D department, smaller agricultural firms tend to organize the innovation process together with external partners. Asked about the origin of the idea for their main innovation in 1995–7, more than half of the respondents answered that it was their own, 18 per cent said it came from a supplier, and 10 per cent mentioned a colleague. Technical consultants and services offered by the public knowledge infrastructure were hardly mentioned as sources of ideas at all. In developing and implementing innovations, co-operation is frequent (see Table 4.3). In three-quarters of the cases, innovations came about with the help of others, mostly suppliers. Colleagues were partners in a quarter of the cases.

In the past, diffusion of innovations in the agricultural sector used to be fast, because technological development was organized collectively. Also, because in regulated markets competition between farmers was limited, nobody had an incentive to prevent the spreading of knowledge and

Table 4.3　Co-operation in innovation (percentages)

Number of innovative firms	292
The innovation was developed by the firm itself with the help of others	45
The innovation was developed by the firm itself	23
The innovation was developed by others, introduced on the market and	18
adapted to the specific needs of the firm	14
The innovation was developed by others, and without changes introduced in the firm	

technology to other firms. Now that competition is increasing and innovation becoming more of an individual process, fears are that innovators will protect their inventions, and that diffusion of new technology will be hampered. Up to the time of writing, we have found little evidence that this process has proceeded very far. Only 14 per cent of respondents answered that they have taken action to protect their innovation (through a patent or through secrecy), whereas 66 per cent answered that they saw no problem in their innovation being adopted by colleagues, or even that they thought they would benefit from diffusion.

4.5　DETERMINANTS OF INNOVATION

There is an extensive empirical literature on the relationship between firm size (absolute or relative to the market) and innovation (Cohen and Levin, 1989; Brouwer and Kleinknecht, 1996). A look at the raw data in Figure 4.1, showing the distribution of innovative and non-innovative firms across a number of size categories, suggests that in our sample there is also a relationship between size and innovativeness: non-innovative firms are smaller, on average.

To test whether this impression is realistic, we estimated a logit function. The dependent variable is the probability of being classified as innovative. Apart from the size variables we included the age of the farmer, membership of a study group, introduction of non-technical changes, familiarity with innovation policy, and a sector dummy as independent variables.

Table 4.4 shows the estimation results. The reference case is a farm with a size of 100 nge, a relative size of 0.3 per cent, the age of the farmer being 35 years, and in the fruit sector. Furthermore, the value of all the dummy variables are set equal to zero. For such a firm, the probability of being innovative is 8 per cent. In accordance with the first Schumpeterian

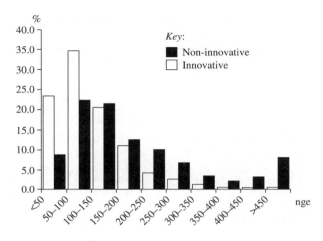

Figure 4.1   Size and innovativeness

Note: Size is measured in nge (Nederlandse grootte-eenheid), which stands for 'Dutch standard unit of size'.[2]

hypothesis, larger firms have a higher probability of being innovative than smaller firms. The estimate of the coefficient is statistically significant at the 1 per cent level. An estimated value of 0.55 implies that the estimated probability of being innovative increases from 8 to 13 per cent if firm size doubles from 100 to 200 nge. This indicates that the probability of being innovative increases quickly as firms sizes increase. Not only the absolute but also the relative size or market share of a firm has a positive impact on the probability of being innovative (absolute size and relative size show a correlation of 0.3). This result is in accordance with the second Schumpeterian hypothesis, which states that firms with a larger market share are likely to be more innovative. The value of the estimated coefficient is equal to 1.39 and statistically significant at the 5 level. This implies that the probability of being innovative increases from 8 to 11 per cent if the relative size of a firm increases from 0.3 to 0.6 per cent. In agriculture, relative sizes are relatively small in any subsector; there are hardly any oligopolies. Nevertheless, firms in sectors such as greenhouse flowers, for example, produce for much more differentiated markets than firms in dairy farming, which produce a fairly homogeneous good. The second Schumpeterian hypothesis would suggest that flower producers would be much more able to capitalize on their innovations by exploiting their market position in a niche market than are dairy farmers. We think we picked up this influence with our indicator of relative size.

The age of a farmer has a significantly negative influence on the probability of being innovative. The estimated probability of being innovative

Table 4.4   Factors influencing the probability of being
innovative (1995–7)

Exogenous variables	Coefficient	Wald statistic
Intercept	−2.71	18.32**
Size[1]	0.55	27.53**
Relative size[2]	1.50	4.89**
Age of farmer	−0.02	5.22**
Member of a study group	−0.04	0.04
Non-technical change in:[3]		
Farm organization	0.44	4.42**
Management structure	0.20	0.47
Marking	0.73	8.56**
Quality control	−0.23	0.91
Chain integration/ vertical co-ordination	0.50	3.16*
Horizontal co-operation	0.47	3.09*
Finance	0.47	1.64
Sector[4]		
Arable farming	0.73	2.18
Dairy farming	0.38	0.63
Intensive livestock farming	1.26	6.19**
Greenhouse vegetables	0.79	1.92
Greenhouse flowers	0.29	0.28
Mushrooms	0.62	0.72
Other horticulture	0.63	1.50

Notes: Size and relative size were measured in 1994; age of
the farmer and member of a study group measured in 1997.
Non-technical changes recorded over the period 1995–7.
1.   Size is measured in nge/100;
2.   The relative size of a firm is calculated at the size of a
firm (measured in nge; see note to Figure 4.1) divided by
the summation of all firm sizes in a sub-market (measured
in nge). We have defined 40 sub-markets in the total agricultural market.
3.   Non-technical changes in the period 1995–7.
4.   Categorical variable of which the fruit sector is the
reference case. The Wald statistic for the variable categorical variable 'sector' (as a whole) is 12.10, significant at
10% level.
* = coefficient is significant at 10% level; ** = coefficient is
significant at 5% level;
−2 Log likelihood model   785.2;
−2 Log likelihood baseline   904.0;
Cox and Snell R^2 0.10;
Number of observations   1171.

decreases from 8 to 5 per cent for a farmer of 55 years relative to a farmer of 35 years. Possible explanations for this finding could be that older farmers have, on average, a lower level of education or a shorter planning horizon (which is often the case if there is no successor in the family).

An often-voiced opinion is that membership of a 'study club', an informal association of producers aiming at the exchange of experiences in production and management, is conducive to innovativeness. We do not find evidence to support this. We do find support, however, for the hypothesis that farmers who are engaged in entrepreneurial activities regarding management and organization are also more innovative in a technical sense. In particular, we find that innovativeness is related positively to renewal of marketing and distribution, and in organization of the firm. There is also a positive relationship between innovativeness on the one hand, and finding new ways of vertical co-ordination and horizontal co-operation, but this is less pronounced.

Structural differences between sectors have been accounted for by including sector dummies in the regression equation. We have taken the fruit sector as the reference sector; the coefficients of the dummies in Table 4.4 indicate the differences relative to this sector. To our surprise, most of the coefficients are insignificant: the probability of being innovative hardly varies systematically by sector. The only sector in which firms show a significantly higher probability of being innovative than in the fruit sector is the intensive livestock sector.

4.6   THE IMPACT OF INNOVATION

We turn now from the determinants of innovativeness to its effects on performance. We study whether being innovative has a positive impact on the profit level and/or the growth rate of a firm. Table 4.5 shows the results of an OLS regression of profit rate in 1997 on the dummy variable for being innovative. Given that we found above that innovativeness varies with size, sector and age of the farmer, we include these variables in the regression equation to control for their influence on performance.

The regression results indicate a statistically significant positive influence of being innovative in the 1995–7 period on the profit rate of 1997. The expected profit rate for an innovative firm is 331 Dutch guilders (150 euro) per nge higher than that of a firm not classified as innovative. For the average farm in our sample of around 140 nge, this would be somewhere near 46 000 guilders (21 000 euro). These results indicate that innovative efforts indeed enhance the performance of firms. Furthermore, as expected, we find a positive influence of firm size (though not of

Table 4.5   Factors influencing profit rates (1997)

Exogenous variables	Coefficient	t-statistic
Intercept	−736	−3.26**
Innovative	331	2.83**
Size	584	11.92**
Relative Size	−126.52	−1.03
Age of farmer	−12.07	−3.61**
Non-technical changes in:		
Farm organization	205	2.26**
Management structure	−67.80	−0.50
Marketing	−43.04	−0.36
Quality control	−162	−1.71
Chain integration/	353	2.75**
vertical co-ordination		
Horizontal co-operation	10.24	0.08
Finance	−127	−0.74
Sector		
Arable farming	94.33	0.56
Dairy farming	−349	−2.18**
Intensive livestock farming	466	2.42**
Greenhouse vegetables	193	0.88
Greenhouse flowers	197	1.00
Mushrooms	32	0.11
Other horticulture	−411	−2.14

Notes: Size and relative size were measured in 1994; age of the farmer and member of a study group measured in 1997. Non-techincal changes recorded over the period 1995–7. Profit rate is measured as profit level (in 1997 in Dutch guilders) over size (in age); Innovative: classified as innovative in 1995–7; See notes under Table 4.4 for further definitions of variables.
** = coefficient is significant at 5% level; R^2 = 0.24; Number of observations: 1114.

relative firm size), change in farm organization and chain integration. We find a negative influence of age on profitability, notwithstanding the fact that young start-up farmers are likely to be more heavily indebted than older farmers. Finally, we find some sector specificity; general market conditions in agriculture vary across sectors.

Finally, we studied whether innovative firms grow faster (measured in nge's) than firms that are not innovative. It is likely that there is a lag between the introduction of innovations and their effect on performance. Innovations introduced in the period 1995–7 may not have their full impact on performance until the years beyond 1997 and 1998. The regression results in Table 4.6 show that the growth rate of innovative firms is significantly higher than the growth rate of firms that are not innovative. The remaining variables, except for those measuring new developments in farm organization and chain integration, do not explain growth in a statistically significant way. Furthermore, the causal relationship between performance and innovativeness most probably goes two ways: not only do innovators perform better, high performers are also more likely to get involved in innovation.

Table 4.6 Factors influencing the average rate of growth of production (1997–8)

Exogenous variables	Coefficient	t-statistic
Intercept	0.13	0.98
Innovative	0.17	2.58**
Size	−0.32	−1.16
Relative size	−5.00	−0.74
Age of farmer	−0.00	−0.98
Non-technical changes in:		
Farm organization	0.10	1.94*
Management structure	0.01	0.16
Marketing	−0.08	−1.15
Quality control	−0.03	−0.57
Chain integration/ vertical co-ordination	0.27	3.66**
Horizontal co-operation	−0.07	−0.95
Finance	0.07	0.74
Sector		
Arable farming	0.09	0.96
Dairy farming	−0.00	−0.04
Intensive livestock farming	−0.08	−0.77
Greenhouse vegetables	−0.06	−0.50
Greenhouse flowers	0.03	0.25
Mushrooms	0.11	0.63
Other horticulture	−0.01	−0.11

Notes: Size and relative size were measured in 1994, age of the farmer and member of a study group measured in 1997. Non-technical changes recorded over the period 1995–7. Average growth rate of production 1997–8 measured in nge's; Innovative: classified as innovative in 1995–7; See notes under Table 4.4 for further definitions of variables.
** = coefficient is significant at 5% level; R^2 = 0.03; Number of observations: 1158.

4.7   CONCLUSIONS

Most of the literature on technological change in agriculture looks at the adoption behaviour of farmers, on the assumption that innovations are developed mainly outside the sector. Changing circumstances are forcing farmers increasingly to pick up the process of innovation themselves, and not to rely on new technologies coming from outside. Taking this context into account, we have not limited our analysis to innovation adoption as such in this chapter; we have made an attempt to take a broader perspective by looking at the innovative activities and entrepreneurial behaviour at the farm level. The main questions dealt with concern the activities and characteristics of farmers that are involved more than the average in innovative activities. Table 4.7 sums up our hypotheses and the evidence we uncovered.

We found some indication that there are innovative firms in agriculture that manage to organize the innovation process and exploit opportunities profitably. However, in most cases they draw on sources of information that are close at hand. In the development stage there often develops a dependence on competitors or suppliers, and when the innovation process

Table 4.7   Summary of outcomes

Hypothesis	Evidence
1. How do farmers go about innovating?	
Innovators take advantage of a wide range of available sources of knowledge	Innovators develop ideas themselves on the basis of 'near' information
Innovators exploit networks	They often collaborate to implement innovations
Innovative firms protect their innovations	We found no substantive evidence to support this claim
2. What determines innovativeness?	
Size determines innovativeness	Confirmed
Relative size determines innovativeness	Confirmed
Entrepreneurs are more innovative	Confirmed
Age is inversely related to innovativeness	Confirmed
Study groups membership enhances innovation	Not confirmed
3. What are the effects of innovation?	
Innovative firms are more profitable	Confirmed
Innovative firms grow faster	Confirmed

has been successful, little attention is given to the protection of innovations. This suggests that the professional management of innovation in most agricultural firms is still lacking.

Our hypotheses about the size characteristics of innovative firms are confirmed strongly. Innovative firms are, on average, larger firms. This may be so because larger firms can mobilize larger resources to invest in risky projects; they can diversify the risk of their innovation using a larger portfolio; they have a sufficient degree of division of labour to have a specialist care for new technology; and they have a sufficiently large in-house pool of both technical and commercial knowledge.

Notes

1. Inside the Dutch agricultural system of innovation, the research stations perform near-market research (testing, experimenting, etc.) and give advice to farmers.
2. The number of nge's is measured as follows: for each product a standard gross value added (SVGA) per unit (an animal or a hectare) is calculated. The number of nge's at one company equals SVGA times the number of units at that specific company, divided by a specific factor (equal to 1310 in 1994) that compensates for inflation. So a company that has two hectares of tomatoes (SVGA for tomatoes = 202 000 ECU per hectare) has [(202 000*2)/1310] = 308.40 nge's. This method allows the aggregation of different products.

References

BROUWER, E. and KLEINKNECHT, A. (1996) 'Determinants of Innovation. A Microeconometric Analysis of Three Alternative Innovation Output Indicators', in A. Kleinknecht (ed.), *Determinants of Innovation*, London: Macmillan, pp. 99–124.
COHEN, W. M. and LEVIN, R. C. (1989) 'Empirical Studies of Innovation and Market Structure', in R. Schmalensee and R. D. Willig (eds), *Handbook of Industrial Organization*, Amsterdam: North-Holland.
KAMIEN, M. I. and SCHWARTZ, N. L. (1982) *Market Structure and Innovation*, Cambridge University Press.
PAVITT, K. (1984) 'Sectoral Patterns of Technological Change. Towards a Taxonomy and a Theory', *Research Policy*, vol. 13, pp. 343–73.
POSSAS, M. L., SALLES-FILHO, S. S. and DA SILVEIRA, J. M. (1996) 'An Evolutionary Approach to Technological Innovation in Agriculture: Some Preliminary Remarks', *Research Policy*, vol. 25, pp. 933–45.
SCHERER, F. M. and ROSS, D. (1990) *Industrial Market Structure and Economic Performance*, Boston, Mass.: Houghton Mifflin.
SCHUMPETER, J. A. (1943) *Capitalism, Socialism, and Democracy*, revised 2nd edn, London: Allen & Unwin.

5 Determinants of Innovative Activity in Canadian Manufacturing Firms

John Baldwin, Petr Hanel and David Sabourin*

5.1 INTRODUCTION

The topic of innovation has garnered the interest of a select group of economists from Schumpeter (1939) to Nelson and Winter (1982), who have stressed that it is the key to economic growth. However, until the advent of panel data sets, there was little empirical evidence to link the innovative stance of firms and their performance. Recent work that links dynamic panel datasets on the performance of firms, and special surveys on the strategies that are being pursued by firms, has demonstrated the importance of innovation to the growth of firms. Baldwin *et al.* (1994) demonstrate that in small and medium-sized Canadian firms, a measure of success that is based on growth, profitability and productivity is related strongly to the emphasis that firms place on innovation. Baldwin and Johnson (1999) use a sample of entrants to show that growth in new firms depends upon whether the firm innovates. Crépon *et al.* (1998) find that innovation in French firms increases productivity.

While we have evidence, therefore, on the connection between success and innovation, there is less evidence on the factors that condition whether a firm adopts an innovation policy. Not all firms innovate despite the benefits of doing so. Research has therefore been aimed at understanding the conditions that are associated with being innovative.[1] A number of questions have been posed in this literature – the extent to which the intellectual property regime stimulates innovation; whether the exclusive emphasis that is given to R&D ignores the importance of other inputs; the effect of firm size and market structure on the intensity of innovation; and the extent to which multinational firms are more innovative. In this chapter, we use data from the 1993 Canadian Survey of Innovation and Advanced Technology to study the differences between firms that innovate and those that do not, and to address the following issues.

The first is the extent to which the intellectual property regime stimulates innovation. Patents are seen as a key form of protection for innovation, but Mansfield (1986) and Levin *et al.* (1987), using data from firm-based surveys, have presented empirical work that suggests that patents may not be very important in many sectors. More recently, Cohen *et al.* (1996) and Baldwin (1997a) present additional survey evidence for the USA and Canada, respectively, that other ways of protecting intellectual property, such as being first in the market, using trade secrets, and developing complex designs, are more effective than patents.

The second issue is whether the existence of an R&D unit is essential to innovation. While it is traditional to emphasize the importance of R&D facilities to the innovation process, Mowery and Rosenberg (1989) have stressed that a good deal of innovation comes out of engineering departments and production facilities.

The third issue is the extent to which a larger average firm size and less competition stimulate innovation. Often described as the Schumpeterian hypothesis, it is sometimes claimed that innovation is fostered by a climate where firms are large, or in industries where there is less competition. While there is mixed evidence that of these either matter (Scherer, 1992), the issue continues to receive attention (Cohen and Klepper, 1996a, 1996b).

The fourth question deals with the effect of the nationality of a firm on its innovative tendencies. Both Dunning (1993) and Caves (1982) have stressed the special role of the multinational firm in transferring special innovation skills from one nation state to another. The role of multinationals in Canada is particularly important since they control over half of the manufacturing sector. McFetridge (1993) stresses the importance of linkages from Canada into the world innovation system that are carried out through multinationals.

Finally, we examine the importance of the scientific infrastructure that is stressed by Tassey (1991). The environment facing each industry is seen to condition a firm's ability to innovate. On the one hand, the availability and quality of education, private and public technical services such as test laboratories, and standardization institutes, as well as research institutes, favours innovation. On the other hand, firms also need educational infrastructure to take account of new knowledge. The state of a country's higher educational facilities will affect a firm's ability to digest new information.

The chapter is organized as follows. The survey data used for this study are described in Section 5.2; a description of the empirical model used for the analysis is provided in Section 5.3; and Section 5.4 contains the results for the model that estimates the determinants of innovation for the Canadian manufacturing sector.

5.2 THE INNOVATION SURVEY

The data for this study come from the 1993 Survey of Innovation and Advanced Technology (SIAT). This survey was conducted by Statistics Canada in 1993 and is based on a frame of all firms possessing a Canadian manufacturing establishment. The frame is taken from Statistics Canada's Business Register.[2] Firms were sampled randomly using strata based on firm size, region, and two-digit industry. The sample consisted of 1595 head offices (which answered questions on firm strategies, R&D facilities, innovation, and the use of intellectual property protection) and 1954 plants that belonged to these firms (which answered questions on technology use). The overall response rate to the survey was 86 per cent. For more details, see Baldwin and Da Pont (1996).

In this chapter, we focus only on those firms for whom Statistics Canada maintains a profile in its Business Register. Firms in this group range from 20 employees upwards and tend not to include the very small enterprises. They account for over 80 per cent of the output in manufacturing.

The material collected in the survey covers a number of issues relating to the innovative and technological capabilities of Canadian manufacturing firms. The questionnaire for the survey consisted of five sections: a general section covering some basic characteristics of the firm; a section on research and development; a third section on innovation; a fourth section on intellectual property rights; and a final section dealing with advanced technology.

Because of the breadth of the survey, a firm's activity in the way of innovation, research and development, and intellectual property protection can be linked together. This allows us to ask how research and development activity affects innovation, and the extent to which firms that have learned to protect their intellectual property also tend to be more innovative.

5.3 EMPIRICAL MODEL

5.3.1 The Model

Firms innovate in the expectation of receiving an increase in profits because of innovation. The expected post-innovation return to innovation activity r_i^* for firm i is taken to be a function of a set of firm-specific variables that determine how the firm responds to profitability incentives and industry-specific exogenous variables that condition the profitability of innovative activities. This may be expressed formally as:

$$r_i^* = bx_i + u_i \tag{1}$$

Even though r_i^* is not observable directly, we can observe whether firm i innovated or not. We assume that when the expected return from innovation is positive, firms innovate. The observable binary variable I_i takes a value of one when the firm is an innovator, and zero otherwise. Thus we can write:

$$I_i = 1 \quad \text{if } r_i^* > 0$$
$$I_i = 0 \quad \text{otherwise}$$

The expected return from innovation, given the characteristics of the firm and the industry to which it belongs, is:

$$E(r_i^* | x_i)$$

Thus the probability of observing that a firm is innovative is given by:

$$\text{Prob}(I_i = 1) = \text{Prob}(u_i > -bx_i) = 1 - F(-bx_i)$$

where F is the cumulative density function for the residuals u_i.

The choice of the statistical model depends on assumptions about the form of the residuals u_i. If the cumulative distribution of residuals is normal, the probit model is the appropriate choice; if it conforms to a logistic function, the logit model is appropriate. For practical purposes, the difference between the results of the two models is usually small. The probit model will be used for our analysis.

Differences in expected profits from innovation, and therefore differences in profitability, are hypothesized to be related to differences in firm size, market structure, appropriability conditions, technological opportunities, technological competency, and R&D activity.[3]

5.3.2 Dependent Variable

Innovation surveys allow us to examine the determinants of the output of the innovative process. In this respect, they differ from previous studies using R&D expenditures (Levin and Reiss, 1984) or patents (Pakes and Griliches, 1984). Innovation surveys ask whether a firm has produced an innovation, and then proceed to explore the various firm and industry characteristics associated with innovation.

Innovation in the 1993 Canadian innovation survey refers to the successful commercialization of an invention for either the production of a new product or process, or the improvement of an existing product or process. Changes that are purely aesthetic or involve minor design alterations are not considered to be innovations. The concept of an innovation that was emphasized in the definitions given to the survey respondents focused on 'major' changes in products and processes that had an important impact on the profitability of the company. According to the survey results, some 32 per cent of Canadian manufacturing firms in the sample used in this study are innovative (Baldwin and Da Pont, 1996).

In this study, we divide innovations into those associated with a new product or a new process. A product innovation is the commercial adoption of a brand new product or an existing product of higher quality. A process innovation is the use of new or improved production methods that lead to a reduction in unit production costs. Often, product and process innovations occur simultaneously, since the production of a new product may require a new or improved production method.

Some 35 per cent of innovators used in the sample drawn for this study introduced a product-only innovation, while 46 per cent introduced a process-only innovation, and 45 per cent introduced a combined product–process innovation.

We examine the determinants of product as opposed to process innovation using two dichotomous variables. The first variable contrasts product innovators with non-innovators. It takes a value of one if the firm is a product innovator and zero if it is not. Product innovators include those firms that have produced at least one product innovation over the three-year period prior to the survey, with or without an associated process innovation. The second binary variable contrasts process-only innovators against non-innovators. This binary variable takes a value of one for process-only innovators, and zero for non-process innovators.

5.3.3 Explanatory Variables

Innovation is highly idiosyncratic. Firms are heterogeneous. Some of the differences in innovative capabilities will be related to differences in industry environment, while others are attributable to differences in innovative tendencies of individual firms. Therefore, innovation is postulated here to be a function of both firm-specific and industry-specific variables. Firm-specific variables include characteristics variables – such as firm size, ownership, and the competition each firm faces, and activity variables – such as R&D and patenting. The only industry-specific variable included here is technological opportunity.

5.3.3.1 Firm Characteristics

Size

A measure of firm size is used to test whether there are inherent advantages associated with size. Large firms, it is often argued, tend to be more innovative than their smaller counterparts. Reasons for this include scale advantages of large firms; a greater likelihood of engaging in risky projects; and economies of scope (Cohen, 1996). Larger firms have easier access to finance, can spread the fixed costs of innovation over a larger volume of sales, and may benefit from economies of scope and complementarities between R&D and other manufacturing activities. Counterarguments, however, exist to suggest that, as firms grow large, their R&D becomes less efficient. Levin and Reiss (1988) review the empirical evidence and observe that it is inconclusive. Economies of scale and scope may exist, but they may be exhausted long before the largest size classes.

Size is measured here by the total number of employees in a firm, including both production and non-production workers. Firms are classified as belonging to one of three size categories – fewer than 100 employees, 100 to 499 employees, and 500 employees or more. Some 66 per cent of our surveyed firms fall into the first category, 25 per cent into the second, and 9 per cent into the third. The summary statistics for these and other variables over the population of large firms used in this chapter are provided in Table 5.1. In order to capture size effects, three binary variables corresponding to each of our three size categories have been constructed.

Nationality of Ownership

Canada, because of its size and proximity to the USA, has a mixture of both Canadian-owned and foreign-owned firms. Some 17 per cent of firms in the survey were foreign-owned.

Existing studies, relying on R&D intensity, are inconclusive as to whether or not the nationality of ownership of a firm has an impact on its innovative activity. Caves *et al.* (1980, p. 193) suggest that foreign activity reduces the rate of R&D activity in Canada. However, lower R&D intensity may not signify less innovation if multinational subsidiaries import innovations from their parents. Using a survey for a limited number of firms in five industries, De Melto *et al.* (1980) reported that foreign firms operating in Canada were less R&D-intensive than their domestic counterparts, but that they accounted for a disproportionately large percentage of process innovations.

Table 5.1   Summary of variables (company weighted)

Variable	Description	Mean[4]	Standard deviation
Dependent variables			
Innovation			
PRODINV	Product innovator	0.23	0.42
PROCINV	Process innovator	0.15	0.36
Intellectual property rights			
PATENTS	Use of patents	0.17	0.37
SECRETS	Use of trade secrets	0.12	0.32
Independent variables			
Firm characteristics			
Size	Employment size		
ENTSIZE 1	Fewer than 100 employees	0.66	0.47
ENTSIZE 2	100 to 499 employees	0.25	0.43
ENTSIZE 3	500 or more employees	0.09	0.29
Ownership	Nationality of ownership		
FOREIGN	Canadian or foreign-owned	0.17	0.37
Competition	Number of competitors		
COMP 1	Five or fewer competitors	0.27	0.44
COMP 2	Six to 20 competitors	0.36	0.48
COMP 3	More than 20 competitors	0.35	0.48
Intellectual property strategy	Intellectual property strategy		
IPSTRATEGY	Emphasis attached to IP	2.59	1.20
Firm activities			
R&D activity		0.80	0.40
R&D	R&D performer or not		
Industry characteristics			
Technological opportunity			
TECH_OPP	Technological opportunity	6.38	4.81

In order to investigate whether foreign-controlled firms are more likely to be innovative, a binary variable – taking a value of one if the firm is foreign-owned, and zero otherwise – is included.

Competitive Conditions

Firms active in highly concentrated markets have been hypothesized to be more likely to innovate. Monopoly power, it is claimed, makes it easier for firms to appropriate the returns from innovation and provides the incentive to invest in innovation. However, this view is far from universal. Others

Arrow, 1962) have argued that the gains from innovation at the margin are larger in an industry that is competitive than under monopoly conditions. Moreover, insulation from competitive pressure can breed bureaucratic inefficiency (Scherer, 1980). Finally, if market structure is determined largely by the life-cycle of an industry, and innovation is more intensive in the early stages of the industry,[5] we should expect innovation to be higher when markets are less concentrated.[6] The empirical evidence on the relationship between concentration and innovation is mixed (Cohen and Levin, 1989).

Since the intrinsic concept that we want to measure is the degree of competition faced, and concentration is a poor proxy for this (Baldwin and Gorecki, 1994), we choose to measure the potential competition that a firm faces by the number of competitors that the firm tells us it faces. Firms are grouped according to whether they face five or fewer competitors, six to twenty competitors, or more than twenty competitors. Some 27 per cent of firms in the survey fall into the first category, 36 per cent in the second category, and 35 per cent in the third category. Three binary variables are used to capture these groups.

5.3.3.2 Firm Activities

Research and Development

Although R&D is neither a necessary nor a sufficient condition for innovation (Äkerblom *et al.*, 1996; Baldwin, 1997b), it is an important input into the innovation process.[7] Some 80 per cent of firms in the survey reported that they conducted R&D.

Firms that have established an effective R&D program are more likely to innovate, for several reasons. First, R&D directly creates new products and processes. Second, firms that perform R&D are also more receptive to the technological advances made by others (Mowery and Rosenberg, 1989; Cohen and Levin, 1989). A binary variable was constructed to capture the effect of having an R&D program; it takes a value of one if the firm engages in R&D, and zero otherwise.

Appropriability and Intellectual Property Rights

Firms commercialize new products and processes expecting, in return, certain rewards – usually an increase in profits. If inventions are copied easily by competitors, there is little incentive to innovate. To protect themselves from being copied, they use various forms of intellectual property protection, such as patents or trade secrets. Some 17 per cent of manufacturing

firms in this study possessed at least one patent. Some 12 per cen
employed trade secrets.

Despite the widespread belief that the existence of intellectual property
protection is critical to the innovation process, empirical evidence as to the
beneficial effects on innovative activity is sparse (Cohen, 1996). Indeed
there is evidence to suggest the opposite. In a study examining the effec
tiveness of patents in protecting intellectual property rights, Mansfiel
(1986) found that only in the pharmaceutical and chemical industries di
patents play an important role. Levin *et al.* (1987) also found that produc
patents were more important for pharmaceuticals and chemicals
Moreover, Levin *et al.* (1987) found that other forms of intellectual prop
erty rights protection were perceived by firms to be more effective thai
patents. Complementary marketing activities and lead-time were found to
be the most effective in protecting product innovations. For process inno
vations, patents were found to be much less effective, while secrecy wa
found to be the most effective. Cohen (1996) concludes that, althougl
there is growing evidence of inter-industry differences in appropriability
conditions, there is little empirical evidence as to the beneficial effect o
these conditions on innovative activity across a wide range of industries.

Other studies have tended to define appropriability at the industry level
We choose to move to the level of the firm, because there is evidence tha
shows firms, even within well-defined industries, are idiosyncratic when i
comes to their tendency to develop a capacity to protect their ideas
Baldwin (1997a) investigates the determinants of patent and trade secre
use by manufacturing firms, and finds that the industry in which a plant i
located only partly accounts for inter-firm differences. Thus, appropriabil
ity is only partially conditioned by the nature of the industry – whether the
product is sufficiently definable that it can be patented. Even within indus
tries where patents and trade secrets are generally not used, there will be
some firms that develop a strategy of protection. These firms make appro
priability work. Appropriability may be partially exogenous in that it stems
from some inherent product characteristic that varies considerably across
industries; but a substantial part of the appropriability environment stems
from individual decisions taken at the firm level to develop product
characteristics that are patentable, or that can be protected by trade secrets,
or to develop the legal expertise that protects what otherwise might not be
protected.

In this study, we construct two variables to capture the intellectual prop
erty environment that might help to stimulate innovation. Two binary vari
ables are used to capture a firm-based appropriability effect on innovation.
The first is based on whether or not a firm uses patents to protect its

innovations. This binary variable takes a value of one if patents are used, and a value of zero if they are not. This is a direct measure of the extent to which the firm finds patents to be important, or the degree to which it is able to devise a strategy to protect its intellectual property. Learning how to do this is not straightforward and requires the development of specific competencies – legal skills, and design skills, and marketing and service skills. The second variable captures whether trade secrets are used to protect innovations. The binary variable takes a value of one if trade secrets are employed, and a value of zero if they are not.

It should be noted that these variables capture another factor. They also proxy whether a firm has innovated successfully in the past, since it is past innovation that leads a firm to possess a patent or a trade secret at the time of the survey. There is a considerable lag between the act of innovation and the receipt of a patent for an innovation. If both past innovation success and an appropriability strategy foster innovation, the appropriability variable that we employ here will have a positive coefficient. If, however, past success is correlated negatively with success (see Geroski *et al.*, 1997), the coefficient on the variable may take on a negative value.

We also experimented with an alternative variable to capture the intellectual property regime of a firm. We used the score (on a scale of 1 – not very effective – to 5 – extremely effective) that a firm gave to the efficacy of patents, trade secrets and other intellectual property rights as a means of protecting their innovation. This effectiveness variable provides a measure that does not depend upon past activity. Whereas the patent-use variable at the firm level reflects both past innovative activity and attitude towards intellectual property right protection, in addition to skill in protecting intellectual property, the patent-effectiveness variable measures more directly existing attitudes towards the value of patent protection. However, existing attitudes are, of course, conditioned by past innovative activity and experience with intellectual property rights.

We chose not to focus our results on this alternative appropriability variable, for two reasons. First, fewer firms answered this question in the survey, and those that did so were not representative. Firms that answered this question were much more likely to have taken out a patent (Baldwin, 1997a). Therefore, average scores at the industry level using this variable really reflected differences in the propensity to patent – the variable that is used here at the plant level. Second, the average score on the efficacy of patents has a strong relationship to the propensity to patent (Baldwin, 1997a). Since the patent-efficacy score was related so closely to the propensity to patent, and there were many more observations on the latter variable, the propensity to patent is used here.

5.3.3.3   Industry Effects

Technological Opportunities

Technological opportunities differ across industries, since the scientific environment provides more fertile ground for advances in some industries than others. As a result, the technical advance generated per unit of R&D is greater in some industries than others (Cohen, 1996).

Two proxies that were suggested by Levin *et al.* (1987) have been used in various studies.[8] The first is a measure of the extent to which an industry relies on science-based research, while the second measures the extent to which an industry relies on external sources of knowledge, such as customers and suppliers, for technological advance. In this study, we use the first approach, since we believe that it comes closer to the concept of the advanced scientific knowledge base that is available to a firm. The second is more a function of the ease with which knowledge flows from firm to firm, and represents the extent to which knowledge is easily transferable rather than representing differences in the underlying scientific environment.

To capture the first concept, technological opportunity is measured here by the percentage of R&D performers within an industry that have collaborative R&D agreements with universities, colleges or external R&D institutions.

5.3.4   Estimation Procedures

We employ two systems of equations – one system for product innovations, and one for process innovations. Each system contains an equation for the incidence of innovation, and one for the determinants of the use of intellectual property. We test whether product innovation is related to the intellectual property regime connected to patents, and whether process innovations are a function of the intellectual property regime related to the use of trade secrets. This division results from earlier work that suggests patents are used for product innovation while trade secrets are used predominantly for process innovation (Baldwin, 1997a). Thus, we have product innovation and patent use in the first set of equations, and process innovations and trade secret use in the second set. The equations are:

PRODUCT INNOVATION:

$$\text{PRODINV} = \alpha_0 + \alpha_1^*\text{PATENTS} + \alpha_2^*\text{SIZE} + \alpha_3^*\text{R\&D}$$
$$+ \alpha_4^*\text{COMPET} + \alpha_5^*\text{TECH\_OPP} \qquad (1)$$

$$\text{PATENTS} = \alpha_0 + \alpha_1^*\text{PRODINV} + \alpha_2^*\text{SIZE}$$
$$+ \alpha_3^*\text{FOREIGN} + \alpha_4^*\text{IPSTRATEGY} \qquad (2)$$

PROCESS INNOVATION:

$$\text{PROCINV} = \beta_0 + \beta_1^*\text{SECRETS} + \beta_2^*\text{SIZE} + \beta_3^*\text{R\&D}$$
$$+ \beta_4^*\text{COMPET} + \beta_5^* \text{FOREIGN} \qquad (3)$$

$$\text{SECRETS} = \beta_0 + \beta_1^*\text{PROCINV} + \beta_2^*\text{SIZE}$$
$$+ \beta_3^*\text{FOREIGN} + \beta_4^*\text{IPSTRATEGY} \qquad (4)$$

Each of these two-equation models contains two endogenous variables – innovation and the use of either patents or trade secrets. Innovation is assumed to be a function of the intellectual property regime, firm size, R&D, and competitive conditions. In addition, product innovation is assumed to be a function of technological opportunity, and process innovation a function of nationality of ownership.

While the main focus of this chapter is on the determinants of innovation, we treat patent and trade secret use as endogenous because of previous work (Baldwin, 1997a) that finds such a strong relationship between the use of intellectual property rights and innovation activity. We recognize that other variables, such as market structure, may be endogenous, but do not consider these relationships here.

Patent use is assumed to be related primarily to product innovation, and trade secrets are assumed to be primarily a function of process innovation, since Baldwin (1997a) finds that patents are generally used for product innovations and trade secrets are used more intensively for process innovations. Both patent and trade secret use are taken to be a function of size, and foreign ownership. In addition, we recognize that the likelihood of using either form of protection depends on the culture of an organization. Some firms pursue actively strategies that protect their intellectual property. These strategies are purposive and require the expenditure of resources to protect intellectual property. Intellectual property strategy is measured by the importance plant managers attach to intellectual property management competency. Measured on a scale of 1 to 5 (1 – not important, 3 – important, and 5 – crucial) it indicates the importance firms place on 'intellectual property management' as part of their general development strategy. We include this variable in both the patent and trade secrets equation. It can be regarded alternately as a proxy for the resources expended (and the equation as a type of production function), or as a proxy for the importance attributed to an intellectual property strategy. *Ceteris paribus*, a firm that stresses intellectual property protection should be more likely to make use of patents and trade secrets if they are innovative.

PRODINV and PROCINV are binary dependent variables indicating whether or not a firm is a product innovator, and process innovator, respectively. Intellectual property rights are captured by two variables PATENTS and SECRETS, which measure whether or not a firm uses patents and trade secrets, respectively. SIZE is the employment size of a firm, while FOREIGN is a binary variable indicating that a firm is controlled from abroad. R&D represents a firm that engages in R&D activity, while COMP measures the number of competitors a firm faces. Finally, one industry variable has been included in the analysis – technological opportunity (TECH_OPP), a measure of the prevalence of basic science within an industry. This variable is presumed only to have an effect on product innovation because of the strong connection between R&D and product innovation. IPSTRATEGY is a variable taking a value of 1 to 5, and measuring the importance given to the strategy of intellectual property protection within the firm.

5.3.5 Estimation Issues

Three issues arise in choosing the estimation procedure – because of problems associated with the use of a dichotomous dependent variable, the use of survey data, and simultaneity.

First, since the dependent variable used for the innovation equations is a binary variable, we tried both probit and logit regression. We also experimented with ordinary least squares in this situation, using a generalized routine to handle the heteroscedastic error term that emerges from simple OLS. The latter produced results that are qualitatively quite similar to those reported here.

Second, since the data used for the analysis come from a survey that randomly samples a population stratified by region, industry and size, a decision had to be made to use weighted or unweighted regression analysis. Survey data must be weighted by sampling weights if they are to give an accurate picture of the population. Multivariate analysis of this data, if it is to represent the behaviour of the population, also needs to take into account the sampling weights attached to each observation – unless the variables to be included in the analysis and the functional form are perfectly specified. If this is the case, unweighted results will be the same as weighted results. Since it is unlikely that we can meet the rigid conditions for relying completely on the unweighted results, we experimented with both routes. The formulation reported here produces quite similar results for both. We therefore report only the unweighted results.

Third, a method for dealing with endogeneity must be chosen. Innovation is taken to be a function of the extent to which a firm can appropriate the benefits of innovating, as measured by its use of patents or trade secrets, as well as by a set of firm-specific and industry-specific characteristics. Firms that can protect their innovations effectively – through the use of patents, trade secrets or other forms of intellectual property rights – are expected to have a greater likelihood of being innovative. They are more likely to have established capable legal departments for handling patent applications, or perhaps their organization is better suited to the prevention of the disclosure of trade secrets.

Patent use and trade secret use, on the other hand, are likely to be a function of innovation and a set of firm-specific and industry-specific characteristics. Once an innovation is discovered, a firm may turn to patents or trade secrets to protect its innovation from being imitated.

Innovation and appropriability are, therefore, not independent of each other. Because of this, using a single-equation model can lead to biased and inconsistent estimates. We employ a simultaneous equation model to overcome this difficulty, recognizing that a poorly specified simultaneous model can worsen rather than improve bias in the estimates. It is primarily for this reason that we do not extend our simultaneous model to other variables.

Two different methods were used to estimate the simultaneous equations. The first, referred to as the simultaneous bivariate probit model, uses a three-step procedure for simultaneous estimation of the probit function. This is implemented by the statistical computer software package MECOSA (Arminger *et al.*, 1996), which builds on Amemiya's (1978) suggestions for the estimation of a simultaneous-equation generalized probit model.

The second method employs a two-stage logit model. In the first step, single-equation logit models are estimated for each of the endogenous variables. Then, in the second step, the single-equation models are re-estimated using the predicted values from the first stage, instead of the observed values, for the endogenous variables in the estimation. Each of the equations is identified.

Similar results were obtained using both of these methods as well as the simultaneous generalized least squares model. We report the values of the coefficients derived from the simultaneous probit in Table 5.2. The t-statistics are provided in brackets after the parameter estimates. All regressions are estimated against an excluded firm that is small, does not perform R&D, is domestic owned, and faces few competitors.

Table 5.2 Simultaneous-equation estimates (*t*-statistics in brackets)

	Product innovation model		Process innovation model	
	Product innovation	Patents	Process innovation	Trade secrets
Intercept	−2.72 (−7.08)	−0.98 (−6.50)	−2.25 (−6.17)	−1.06 (−4.62)
Endogenous variables				
Innovation				
Product	−	0.56 (4.32)	−	−
Process	−	−	−	0.46 (2.98)
Appropriability				
Patents	−0.25 (−1.39)	−	−	−
Trade secrets	−	−	−0.17 (−0.87)	−
Exogenous variables				
Firm characteristics				
Firm Size				
100 to 499 employees	0.26 (1.95)	0.34 (3.04)	0.24 (2.05)	−0.02 (−0.14)
500 or more employees	0.95 (4.82)	0.41 (2.58)	0.91 (5.90)	0.11 (0.58)
Ownership				
Foreign	−	0.20 (1.82)	0.21 (1.83)	0.02 (0.17)
Strategies				
Intellectual Property	−	0.10 (2.34)	−	0.11 (2.37)
Competition				
6–20 competitors	0.30 (2.75)	−	0.42 (3.40)	−
Over 20 competitors	−0.06 (−0.55)	−	0.12 (0.99)	−
Firm activities				
R&D Activity				
R&D performer	1.70 (7.24)	−	0.91 (5.17)	−
Industry characteristics				
Technological opportunity				
Collaborative agreements	0.01 (1.59)	−	−	−
Summary statistics:[9]				
N		1196		1078
$Q_T(\theta)$: χ^2		11.3		5.6
R^2	0.32	0.24	0.23	0.11

Since the coefficients of the probit model by themselves do not reveal fully the magnitude of the effects of the variables, we also report the probability values associated with each explanatory variable (Table 5.3). Probability values provide a quantitative estimate of the partial effects of an activity or firm characteristic on the likelihood of introducing an innovation. The probabilities are calculated by estimating the probit function at the sample means using the parameter estimates. For binary explanatory variables, two probabilities are calculated. The first estimates the probability of innovating, given that the explanatory variable takes a value of one, while the second provides the probability of innovating given that the explanatory variable takes a value of zero. The difference in the two probabilities provides the quantitative effect of this variable on the decision to innovate.

For the continuous variable (technological opportunity), we adopt a different approach. The probability of introducing an innovation is first estimated for a given explanatory variable at its mean value. It is then estimated at its mean value minus one standard deviation, and finally at its mean value plus one standard deviation.[10]

5.4. REGRESSION RESULTS

5.4.1 Incidence of Innovation

Firms that perform R&D are more likely to innovate. R&D activity has a positive and significant impact on both forms of innovation. This accords with other studies (Cohen and Klepper 1996a; Baldwin, 1997b).[11] If a firm does not perform R&D, it has only a 1 per cent chance of introducing a product innovation, whereas a firm performing R&D has a 25 per cent chance of innovating. The same probabilities for process innovation are 3 and 18 per cent. While being neither a necessary nor a sufficient condition for innovation, R&D increases the probability of success by 24 percentage points for product innovation and about 15 percentage points for process innovation. This confirms the greater importance of R&D for product than for process innovation.

Firm size is also highly statistically significant, for both product and process innovation. Small firms have a 12 per cent probability of introducing a product innovation; large firms have a 40 per cent probability, a difference of 28 per cent. Small firms have a 9 per cent probability of introducing a process innovation; large firms have a 34 per cent probability, a difference of 25 per cent. The largest firms are three times as likely

Table 5.3 Estimated probability of introducing product and process innovations, and using patents and trade secrets

	Product innovation model		Process innovation model	
	Product innovation	Patents	Process innovation	Trade secrets
Endogenous variables				
Innovation				
Product innovator	–	52	–	–
Process innovator	–	–	–	38
Non-innovator	–	31	–	22
Appropriability				
Patent user	17	–	–	–
Non-patent user	17	–	–	–
Trade secret user	–	–	14	–
Non-trade secret user	–	–	14	–
Exogenous variables				
Firm characteristics				
Firm size				
1 to 99 employees	12	31	9	25
100 to 499 employees	17	43	14	25
500 or more employees	40	46	34	25
Nationality of ownership				
Foreign	–	43	18	25
Canadian	–	35	13	25
Intellectual property strategy				
Intellectual property strategy	–	37	–	25
+ standard deviation	–	41	–	29
– standard deviation	–	32	–	21
Number of competitors				
0 to 5	14	–	11	–
6 to 19	22	–	21	–
20 or more	14	–	11	–
Firm activities				
R&D activity				
R&D performer	25	–	18	–
Non-R&D performer	1	–	3	–
Industry characteristics				
Technological opportunity				
Technological opportunity	17	–	–	–
+ standard deviation	17	–	–	–
– standard deviation	17	–	–	–

as the smallest ones to introduce both a product innovation, and a process innovation, which is not consistent with the findings of Cohen and Klepper (1996b) who argue that size matters more for process innovation.

Nationality of ownership was included in the first round of estimates, but it was found to have no significant effect on the probability that a firm is more likely to introduce a product innovation. It should be noted that nationality does become significant if size or R&D is omitted. Foreign-owned firms are larger, and more likely to perform R&D, but once these factors are taken into account, there is no additional effect of nationality on product innovation.

Foreign ownership is more likely to be associated with process innovations, but even here the effect is marginal.

Technological opportunity has a positive effect on product innovation that is not significant. In associated experiments this variable becomes significant when both forms of innovation are combined. Firms in industries relying on science-based research are more likely to be innovative. This finding gives weak corroboration to other studies which find there are greater opportunities for innovation in industries for which basic science is important (Arvanitis and Hollenstein, 1994; Crépon *et al.* 1996).

One of the most striking results is the negative effect of patent use on product innovation, and trade secret use on process innovation.[12] However, in neither case is the variable significant.

It should be recalled that this variable captures two effects – previous success, on the one hand, and the appropriability environment, on the other. The negative relationship between taking out patents and innovating, found in the simultaneous probit model, indicates that previous experience does not guarantee future success. The fact that the effect is negative tends to indicate that reliance on past success has a stronger negative effect than the positive impact hypothesized to arise from the appropriability environment. This accords with the findings of Geroski *et al.* (1997), who report that very few innovative firms are persistently innovative.

Innovation is also related significantly to the number of competitors that a firm faces, but the relationship is not monotonic. Firms facing moderate competition – six to twenty competitors – are significantly more likely to innovate. Moderate competition increases the probability of innovating by 8 percentage points over both high and low competitive conditions for product innovation, and 10 percentage points for process innovation.

Various alternatives were tried in order to test whether our results are affected by other specifications of the innovation equation. First, we moved to the industry level to define appropriability conditions. That is, we defined the environment in which the firm operated as being determined by the average two-digit industry patent use. This has two effects. First, it means that the environment is more likely to be exogenous, and therefore the need for a simultaneous equations framework is less persuasive. Second, it overcomes the criticism that the use of patents at the firm level may reflect not so much how a firm engineers its intellectual property environment as its past innovation success. However, when patent use, defined at the industry level, is included, it is found to be insignificant.

We also experimented with an alternative measure of the importance of the intellectual property environment – the score (from 1, not very effective – to 5, extremely effective) that the firm gave to the effectiveness of various instruments in 'preventing competitors from bringing to market copies of its new product or process technology'. The instruments considered included seven formal options – copyrights, patents, industrial design, trade secrets, trade marks, integrated circuit designs and plant breeders' rights. In addition, the scores given to other strategies – complexity of product design, being first in the market – were included. When the average scores at the two-digit industry level for patents, trade secrets and other strategies are included, the patent score is insignificant, but the score on trade secrets is positive and significant. In industries where trade secrets are seen to be effective, the probability that innovation occurs is higher. When patent and trade secret use, as well as the efficacy variables, are included, the use variables are insignificant, but the efficacy scores given to trade secrets and other strategies (product complexity and trade secrets) remain positive and significant.

Industry effects were also included. For this purpose, we broke our sample down into three broad groups that differ in terms of the innovation intensity of the industry. Industries were classified to one of three groups based on the classification system used by Robson *et al.* (1988), who investigated differences in innovative tendencies of two-digit industries. The first industry group produces the most innovations and tends to disseminate more innovations than they use to the other two groups of industries. The first group includes electrical and electronic products, chemicals and chemical products, machinery, and refined petroleum and coal. The second group produces fewer innovations and does less dissemination to other industries. It consists of transportation equipment, rubber products, non-metallic mineral products, plastics, fabricated metals and primary metals. The last group of industries produces the least number of innovations and tends to use innovations produced in the first two sectors. This group consist of textiles, paper, wood, clothing, leather, beverages, food, furniture and fixtures, and printing and publishing. When we include binary variables for these three classifications, very little changes. Thus, the inclusion of broad industry effects, which we know are associated with innovation tendencies, does not affect our results.

The innovation equations were also estimated using efficacy scores for patents, trade secrets and lead-time at the firm level. The sample for which these scores are available is considerably smaller than that for which patent and trade secret use is available. In this formulation, strategies relating to complexity of product and lead-time are significant – much as they are in the equation that summarizes these at the industry level, but patent efficacy has an insignificant coefficient.

We also included the score given to whether a firm gets its innovative ideas from its competitors or from its customers. Arvanitis and Hollenstein (1996) have included a variant of this variable to capture the technological opportunities; however, it also could approximate conditions under which information flows are transmitted easily and difficult to protect. This hypothesis is confirmed by its negative coefficient in the formulation in which it is included.

In summary, the results of these various experiments suggest that appropriability stimulates innovation. But it is not patents that matter as much as trade secrets and other strategies that allow a firm to appropriate the fruits of its investments in intellectual capital.[13] Moreover, in industries where ideas are taken easily from competitors, or transferred from others, innovation is less likely.

5.4.2 Patent and Trade Secret Use[14]

Patent use is related strongly to whether a firm is an innovator.[15] Some 52 per cent of firms introducing product innovations use patents, compared to only 31 per cent of non-innovative firms (Table 5.3). Similarly, process innovators are significantly more likely to use trade secrets. But here the effect is somewhat lower. Introducing a process innovation raises the probability of making use of trade secrets from 22 to 38 per cent.

Both innovation and patent use are related to size.[16] While there was a monotonic increase in the probability of innovating and using patents with increasing firm size, the effect of size is greater for innovation: Being large adds only 15 percentage points to the probability of patenting. On the other hand, size is not significant for trade secret use.

Whereas moderate competition leads to more innovation, it has no effect on either the patenting or the trade secret decision, and it was omitted from these regressions. Technological opportunity leads to more innovation but has no effect on the likelihood that patents will be pursued.

The emphasis given to intellectual property is significant for both patents and trade secrets. The difference in the probability of employing each form of intellectual property protection varies by about 8 percentage points over the range of the mean, plus or minus one standard deviation.

5.5   CONCLUSION

Because Canada is a small, developed country with an open economy and a substantial amount of foreign investment, it might be expected to have a different innovation system. An innovation system is made up, on the one hand, of institutions that govern the way in which knowledge is created and disseminated and, on the other, of the firms that make up the economy.

In order to examine the characteristics of Canada's innovation system, this chapter has focused on the characteristics of firms that are innovators. The characteristics – appropriability conditions, nationality, R&D, and size – that were chosen for the analysis are all relevant to the debate over the uniqueness of the Canadian innovation system. First, foreign-controlled firms are important in the Canadian economy. We are interested in knowing whether they have a particular innovation advantage. Second, Canada has a lower intensity of R&D spending than most other developed countries. At issue here is the extent to which R&D is relatively unproductive in Canada. Third, the Canadian industrial structure has more small firms than elsewhere. Is there evidence, then, that small firms tend to be less able to innovate? Fourth, patents tend to be used less in Canada than elsewhere – especially when calculated in number of patents granted to residents in per capita terms?[17] Is this because patents are seen as a particularly ineffective device for protecting the intellectual capital that is invested in innovations?

Several findings are of note. First, while there is a close connection between innovation and the appropriability climate or patent use, the causal relationship is much stronger going from innovation to the decision to use patents than from the use of patents to innovation. This extends the findings, based on survey evidence (Mansfield, 1986; Levin *et al.*, 1987; Cohen *et al.*, 1996), that patents are not seen by firms as being a very effective means of protecting innovations, even though they tend to be used once an innovation occurs. More important, the lack of impact of patent use on innovation may explain the relatively low rates of patenting in the Canadian innovation system.

Second, as has been found elsewhere, R&D is an important factor contributing to innovation. Firms that have an R&D capability have a higher probability of introducing an innovation compared to those that do not. Nevertheless, while developing an R&D capability is important, having this capability still leads to a relatively low probability of successful innovation – only about 25 per cent for product innovators, and only about 18 per cent for process innovation. If both are considered together, the probability of success is still less than 50 per cent. These low probabilities may explain partly why R&D activity is not as intense as elsewhere.

Third, the two variables that are often used in testing the Schumpeterian hypothesis give mixed results. Size is related positively to innovation. The probability of innovating increases monotonically with size.[18] Moreover, this effect is quite dramatic. The largest firms are three times more likely to introduce an innovation. Elsewhere (Baldwin *et al.*, 2000), we find that size matters most for those innovations that are the most complex – those that combine products and processes, or those that are world-firsts.

While larger firms are more likely to be innovators, a lack of competition is not related positively to innovation. Indeed, intermediate levels of competition are more conducive to innovation than the lowest levels of competition – though the relationship is non-linear. That is, as we increase the number of competitors, the probability of innovating first increases, and then decreases. This effect is particularly evident for the least novel innovations (Baldwin *et al.*, 2000). Competition matters more in the diffusion process than for the introduction of the most novel world-first innovations.

Fourth, it is noteworthy that foreign-controlled firms are not significantly more likely to introduce a product innovation once consideration is given to size and R&D performance. Thus differences in product innovation rates that exist between foreign and domestic firms are accounted for by differences in size and R&D competencies.

Finally, the scientific regime affects the rate of innovation, but only marginally. This points to the importance of the scientific infrastructure provided by university research in Canada. But it also indicates that the Canadian industry structure is unique in that innovation in Canada originates more in sectors that are not highly R&D intensive.

Notes

* We would like to thank Bronwyn Hall, Alfred Kleinknecht, Pierre Mohnen and other members of the European Innovation Network for their comments. The opinions expressed herein are those of the authors and do not necessarily reflect the views of Statistics Canada.

1. For related studies covering France, Germany, Italy, The Netherlands and Switzerland, see Crépon *et al.* (1996), Felder *et al.* (1996), Sterlacchini (1994), Brouwer and Kleinknecht (1996), and Arvanitis and Hollenstein (1994, 1996).
2. The Business Register maintains a listing of all establishments and firms in the Canadian manufacturing sector.
3. See Cohen (1996) for a review of previous studies that examine the determinants of innovation.
4. For all but intellectual property strategy and technological opportunity, the mean value refers to the proportion of the large-firm population that exhibit a particular characteristic, for example, being foreign-owned. For intellectual property strategy it refers to the mean score – on a scale of one (not important) to five (crucial) – given to the importance of 'intellectual property management' in firms' overall development strategy. For technological opportunity, it refers to the percentage of R&D performers within an industry that have collaborative R&D agreements with universities, colleges or external R&D institutions.
5. For a discussion of the relationship between innovation and structure, see Abernathy and Utterbach (1978), Rothwell and Zegveld (1982), Gort and Klepper (1982), Klepper and Millar (1995), and Klepper (1996).
6. See also Acs and Audretsch (1991).
7. Baldwin (1997b) reports that only 56% of firms conducting ongoing R&D reported a product or process innovation, while only 49% of firms with a product or process innovation reported that they had an ongoing R&D programme.
8. Sterlacchini (1994) uses the percentage of those firms investing in R&D that have collaborative projects with universities. Arvinitis and Hollenstein (1994) use the extent to which outsiders such as competitors and customers contributed to the innovation.
9. Using the same simultaneous probit approach that we have adopted in this Chapter, Lenz (1997), in his investigation of innovative and co-operative behaviour in Swiss manufacturing firms, reports similar values for his simultaneous model summary statistics.
10. Assuming the variable to be normally distributed, this range – from the mean minus one standard deviation to the mean plus one standard deviation – covers 68% of the distribution of the variable.
11. When R&D is broken down into those doing R&D occasionally and those doing it continuously, the coefficient on the latter was found to be 50 per cent higher than the former. Brouwer and Kleinknecht (1996) also report that in The Netherlands, firms with continuous R&D facilities have a higher probability of innovating.
12. If simultaneity is not considered, patent use always has a positive and significant effect.
13. Schankerman (1991) provides evidence that at least 75 percent of the private returns to inventive activity are obtained from sources other than patents.
14. For a more detailed examination of the determinants of the intensity of use of a wide range of intellectual property rights, see Baldwin (1997a).
15. In complementary research (Baldwin, Hanel and Sabourin 2000), we show that patent use is related more closely to product innovations and to world-first innovations.
16. See Brouwer and Kleinknecht (1999) for similar results.

17.   This is not the case if we measure patents granted per research scientist. See Baldwin (1997a).
18.   We also experimented with continuous variables using a quadratic term to capture non-linearities. Essentially the same results were obtained.

References

ABERNATHY, W. J. and UTTERBACH, J. M. (1978) 'Patterns of Industrial Innovation', *Technology Review*, vol. 80, pp. 41–7.
ACS, Z. J. and AUDRETSCH, D. (eds) (1991), *Innovation and Technological Change*. Hemel Hempstead: Harvester Wheatsheaf.
ÄKERBLOM, M., VIRTAHARJU, M. and LEPPÄAHTI, A. (1996) 'A Comparison of R&D Surveys, Innovation Surveys and Patent Statistics Based on Finnish Data', *Innovation, Patents and Technological Strategies*, Paris: OECD.
AMEMIYA, T. (1978) 'The Estimation of a Simultaneous Equation Generalized Probit Model', *Econometrica*, vol. 46, pp. 1193–205.
ARMINGER, G., WITTENBERG, J. and SCHEPERS, A. (1996) *MECOSA, A Program of the Analysis of General Mean- and Covariance Structures with Non-Metric Variables, User Guide*, Friedrichsdorf, Germany: Additive Gmbh.
ARROW, K. (1962) 'Economic Welfare and the Allocation of Resources for Invention', in R. R. Nelson (ed.), *The Rate and Direction of Inventive Activity*. Princeton, NJ: Princeton University Press.
ARVANITIS, S. and HOLLENSTEIN, H. (1994) 'Demand and Supply Factors in Explaining the Innovative Activity of Swiss Manufacturing Firms', *Economics of Innovation and New Technology*, vol. 3, pp. 15–30.
ARVANITIS, S. and HOLLENSTEIN, H. (1996) 'Industrial Innovation in Switzerland: A Model-based Analysis with Survey Data', in Alfred Kleinknecht (ed.), *Determinants of Innovation: The Message from New Indicators*, London: Macmillan, pp. 13–62.
BALDWIN, J. R. (1997a) *Innovation and Intellectual Property*, Catalogue 88-515-XPE, Ottawa: Statistics Canada.
BALDWIN, J. R. (1997b) *The Importance of Research and Development for Innovation in Small and Large Canadian Manufacturing Firms*, Research Paper Series No. 107, Ottawa: Statistics Canada.
BALDWIN, J. R. and DA PONT, M. (1996) *Innovation in Canadian Manufacturing Enterprises*, Catalogue 88–513, Ottawa: Statistics Canada.
BALDWIN, J. R. and GORECKI, P. (1994) 'Concentration and Mobility Statistics', *Journal of Industrial Economics*, vol. 42, pp. 93–104.
BALDWIN, J. R. and JOHNSON, J. (1999) 'Innovation and Entry', in Z. Acs (ed.), *Are Small Firms Important?* Dordrecht: Kluwer.
BALDWIN, J. R., HANEL, P. and SABOURIN, D. (2000) *Determinants of Innovative Activity in Canadian Manufacturing Firms*, Research Paper Series No. 122, Ottawa: Statistics Canada.
BALDWIN, J. R., CHANDLER, W., LE, C. and PAPAILIADIS, T. (1994) *Strategies for Success: A Profile of Growing Small and Medium-Sized Enterprises in Canada*, Catalogue 61–523R, Ottawa: Statistics Canada.
BROUWER, E. and KLEINKNECHT, A. (1996) 'Determinants of Innovation. A Microeconometric Analysis of Three Alternative Innovation Output Indicators',

in A. Kleinknecht (ed.), *Determinants of Innovation: The Message from New Indicators*, London: Macmillan, pp. 99–124.

BROUWER, E. and KLEINKNECHT, A. (1999) 'Innovative Output and a Firm's Propensity to Patent. An Exploration of CIS Micro Data', *Research Policy*, vol. 28, pp. 615–24.

CAVES, R. E. (1982) *Multinational Enterprise and Economic Analysis*, Cambridge: University Press.

CAVES, R. E., PORTER, M. E. and SPENCE, A. M. with SCOTT, J. T. (1980) *Competition in the Open Economy: A Model Applied to Canada*, Cambridge, Mass.: Harvard University Press.

COHEN, W. (1996) 'Empirical Studies of Innovative Activity', in P. Stoneman (ed.), *The Handbook of the Economics of Technological Change*, Oxford: Basil Blackwell, pp. 182–264.

COHEN, W. and KLEPPER, S. (1996a) 'A Reprise of Size and R&D', *Economic Journal*, vol. 106, pp. 925–52.

COHEN, W. and KLEPPER, S. (1996b) 'Firm Size and the Nature of Innovation within Industries: The Case of Process and Product R&D', *Review of Economics and Statistics*, vol. 78, pp. 232–43.

COHEN, W. and LEVIN, R. C. (1989) 'Empirical Studies of Innovation and Market Structure', in R. Schmalensee and R. D. Willig (eds), *Handbook of Industrial Organization: Vol 2*, Amsterdam: Elsevier Science Publishers.

COHEN, W. M., NELSON, R. R. and WALSH, J. (1996) 'Appropriability Conditions and Why Firms Patent and Why They Do Not', NBER Working Paper, Cambridge, Mass.

CRÉPON, B., DUGUET, E. and KABLA, I. (1996) 'Schumpeterian Conjectures: A Moderate Support from Various Innovation Measures', in A. Kleinknecht (ed.), *Determinants of Innovation: The Message from New Indicators*, London: Macmillan, pp. 63–98.

CRÉPON, B., DUGUET, E. and MAIRESSE, J. (1998) 'Research Investment, Innovation, and Productivity: An Econometric Analysis at the Firm Level', Cahiers Economiques and Mathematiques, No. 98.15, University of Paris 1-Pantheon-Sorbonne.

DE MELTO, D., McMULLEN, K. and WILLS, R. (1980) *Innovation and Technological Change in Five Canadian Industries*, Discussion Paper No. 176, Ottawa: Economic Council of Canada.

DUNNING, J. H. (1993) *Multinational Enterprises and the Global Economy*, Toronto: Addison-Wesley.

FELDER, J., LICHT, G., NERLINGER, E. and STAHL, H. (1996) 'Factors Determining R&D and Innovation Expenditure in German Manufacturing Industries', in A. Kleinknecht (ed.), *Determinants of Innovation: The Message from New Indicators*, London: Macmillan, pp. 125–54.

GEROSKI, P. A., VAN REENEN, J. and WALTERS, C. F. (1997) 'How Persistently Do Firms Innovate?', *Research Policy*, vol. 26, pp. 33–48.

GORT, M. and KLEPPER, S. (1982) 'Time Paths in the Diffusion of Product Innovations', *Economic Journal*, vol. 92, pp. 630–53.

KLEPPER, S. (1996) 'Entry, Exit, Growth and Innovation over the Product Life Cycle', *American Economic Review*, vol. 86, pp. 562–83.

KLEPPER, S. and MILLAR, J. H. (1995) 'Entry, Exit and Shakeouts in the Unites States in New Manufactured Products', *International Journal of Industrial Organization*, vol. 13, pp. 567–91.

LENZ, S. (1997) 'R&D Cooperation and Innovation: Some Evidence from Swiss Manufacturing Industries', Mimeo, Swiss Federal Institute of Technology, Zurich.

LEVIN, R. and REISS, P. (1984) 'Tests of a Schumpeterian Model of R&D and Market Structure', in Z. Griliches (ed.), *R&D, Patents and Productivity*. Princeton, NJ: National Bureau of Economic Research Princeton University Press, pp. 175–208.

LEVIN, R. C. and REISS, P. C. (1988) 'Cost-reducing and Demand-creating R&D with Spillovers', *Rand Journal of Economics*, vol. 19, pp. 538–56.

LEVIN, R. C., KLEVORICK, A. K., NELSON, R. R. and WINTER, S. G. (1987) 'Appropriating the Returns from Industrial Research and Development', *Brookings Papers on Economic Activity*, vol. 3, pp. 783–820.

MANSFIELD, E. (1986) 'Patents and Innovation: An Empirical Study', *Management Science*, vol. 32, pp. 173–181.

McFETRIDGE, D. (1993) 'The Canadian System of Innovation', in R. R. Nelson (ed.), *National Innovation Systems*, Oxford University Press, pp. 299–323.

MOWERY, D. C. and ROSENBERG, N. (1989) *Technology and the Pursuit of Economic Growth*. Cambridge University Press.

NELSON, R. R. and WINTER, S. G. (1982) *An Evolutionary Theory of Economic Change*. Cambridge, Mass.: Harvard University Press.

PAKES, A. and GRILICHES, Z. (1984) 'Patents and R&D at the Firm Level: A First Look', in Z. Griliches (ed.), *R&D, Patents, and Productivity*, Chicago: National Bureau of Economic Research, University of Chicago Press.

ROBSON, M., TOWNSEND, J. and PAVIT, K. (1988) 'Sectoral Patterns of Production and Use of Innovations in the UK: 1945–83', *Research Policy*, vol. 17, pp. 1–14.

ROTHWELL, R. and ZEGVELD, W. (1982) *Innovation and the Small and Medium-Sized Firm*. London: Frances Pinter.

SCHANKERMAN, M. (1991) 'How Valuable is Patent Protection? Estimates by Technology Field Using Patent Renewal Data', National Bureau of Economic Research Paper No. 3780, Cambridge (Mass.).

SCHERER, F. M. (1980) *Industrial Market Structure and Economic Performance*, 2nd edn. Chicago: Rand McNally.

SCHERER, F. M. (1992) 'Schumpeter and Plausible Capitalism', *Journal of Economic Literature*, vol. 30, pp. 1416–34.

SCHUMPETER, J. A. (1939) *Capitalism, Socialism, and Democracy*, New York: Harper.

STERLACCHINI, A. (1994) 'Technological Opportunities, Intraindustry Spillovers and Firm R&D Intensity', *Economic Innovation and New Technology*, vol. 3, pp. 123–37.

TASSEY, G. (1991) 'The Functions of Technology Infrastructure in a Competitive Economy', *Research Policy*, vol. 20, pp. 345–61.

6 Differences in the Determinants of Product and Process Innovations: The French Case

Alexandre Cabagnols and Christian Le Bas*

6.1 PURPOSE OF THE STUDY

Empirical studies have noticed the differing impact of product and process innovation on international competitiveness, the level of employment and the types of skills used, and on the profit rate of firms (Vernon, 1966; Rottmann and Ruschinski, 1997; Duguet and Greenan, 1997; Capon *et al.*, 1992). These studies show that the *type* of innovative behaviour of firms is important. However, little is known from either a theoretical or an empirical point of view, about the determinants of these different types of innovation. Therefore, the purpose of this study is to identify the microeconomic determinants of the innovative behaviour of French manufacturing firms. Studying a sample of innovative firms, we try to understand why they develop product innovations rather than process innovations, or product *and* process innovations simultaneously.

We do not try to predict whether a firm will innovate or not. We know that a particular firms innovate, and we want to discover what type of innovation is undertaken: (i) product innovation; or (ii) process innovation, or product *and* process innovation at the same time? The distinction between concurrent product and process (product & process) and the other types of innovation should help to highlight some particularities of this kind of innovation. In particular, product & process innovations may be the result of specific strategies of appropriation.

In Section 6.2, we describe our database. In Section 6.3 we survey briefly the existing literature dealing with determinants of product and process innovations, and present our expected results. In Section 6.4, we present the empirical methodology and econometric tools that will be used. In Section 6.5, we discuss our results and try to evaluate their robustness.

6.2 DATA SOURCES

We use here the results of three French innovation surveys and using only responses from innovating firms (see Table 6.1 for details).

The first survey was conducted by SESSI (Service des Statistiques Industrielles) in 1991. It covered a five-year period (1985–90) and involved 25 000 firms with more than twenty employees, with a sampling rate of 100 per cent for firms with more than 500 employees, and 83 per cent for firms with fewer than 500 employees. For this first survey our analysis uses 10 137 innovating firms, distributed as follows: 2038 product innovators, 1855 process innovators and 6244 product & process innovators.

The second survey was carried out in 1993 by SESSI according to the Oslo manual. In the following it will be referred to as CIS (Community Innovation Survey). It covers a three-year period (1990–2) and involved 4500 firms, each with more than twenty employees. The sampling rate was 100 per cent for firms with more than 1000 employees, 50 per cent for those with 500 to 1000 employees, and 33 per cent for those with fewer than 500 employees. These firms were sampled from the 1991 innovation survey. For this survey, our analysis uses 1645 innovating firms distributed as follows: 482 product innovators, 355 process innovators, and 808 product & process innovators.

Table 6.1   Summary statistics for each survey

Survey	Number of innovating firms implementing			Total number of innovating firms
	Product innovation	*Process innovation*	*Product & process innovation*	
1990 (1985–90) >20 employees	2038	1855	6244	10137
Distribution for the 1990 survey (%)	20	18	62	100
CIS (1990–2) >20 employees	482	355	808	1645
Distribution for the CIS survey(%)	29	22	49	100
Appropriability (1990–2) >50 employees	317	147	533	997
Distribution for the appropriability survey (%)	32	15	53	100

The third survey deals with conditions for appropriation of innovation benefits, and was also conducted by SESSI in 1993. It covers a three-year period (1990–2) and involved firms with more than fifty employees. The sampling rate is 100 per cent for firms with more than 1000 employees, 50 per cent for those with 500 to 1000 employees, and 33 per cent for those with fewer than 500 employees. Firms in this survey are not necessarily in the CIS survey, but are all present in the 1991 survey. This third survey is interesting in that it often makes a distinction between responses about product innovation and about process innovation in the same question. For this survey, our analysis uses 997 innovating firms, distributed as follows: 317 product innovators, 147 process innovators, and 533 product & process innovators.

In addition to these surveys on innovation we use three annual French EAE (Enquête Annuelle Entreprise) surveys of firms for 1987, 1990 and 1992. They provide us with information about the number of employees, cash flow and so on. We completed this information with data about the firms' lines of activity for the same periods (1987, 1990 and 1992). In lines of business surveys, the unit of analysis is the firm in each of the particular lines of business in which it evolves. This allows for the calculation of a diversification index according to the distribution of cash flow across different lines of business. It is also possible to compute a specific index of concentration faced by each firm according to its particular diversification profile.

In all surveys, our data cover only the manufacturing industry, excluding the building and food industries.

6.3   DETERMINANTS OF THE TYPE OF INNOVATION: A MANSFIELD–PAVITT–SCHERER APPROACH

Few analyses deal explicitly with the balance between product and process innovations. The distinction between product innovations and process innovations on the one hand, and product & process innovations on the other is even more unusual. Nevertheless, interest has grown recently in distinguishing between these different types of innovation. The intuition for this is as follows: if different types of innovation do not have the same economic consequences in terms of market share and/or profit rate, a better understanding of their determinants would help to better understand the economic dynamics induced by technological change.

Currently we do not have convincing models that explain why firms innovate in products and not in processes, or vice versa. However, the years of empirical and theoretical research since the mid-1970s have highlighted the impact of specific types of variable on the occurrence of innovation in firms. Driven by the work of Mansfield (1995) (about the impact of size, technological opportunities, strategies and so on); Pavitt (1984) (technological learning, sources of the technological change, strategies and so on); and Scherer (1986) (appropriability conditions and market structures), progress has been made in defining a suitable framework for grasping the complexity and multidimensionality of the determinants of innovative behaviour. At the time of writing, scholars of technological change are trying to check whether these explanatory variables have different impacts on product and process innovations. Six lines of inquiry can be distinguished, according to their reference to:

• characteristics of a firm's demand (price elasticity, level, evolution, homogeneity and so on);
• conditions for appropriation of innovation benefits;
• sources of technological knowledge (customers, users and so on);
• market structures (concentration level, intensity of technological competition);
• characteristics of the firm (size, market share, diversification level); and
• firm strategy (towards quality, marketing and so on).

Until recently these variables were studied mainly at the sectoral level. Our data allow us to evaluate their impact at the firm level. We now present our hypotheses.

6.3.1   Demand Conditions

Both product and process innovators face technological uncertainty during the development process. However, product innovators also face market (or demand) uncertainty that is less easily managed than is technological uncertainty (Freeman, 1982). In such a situation, factors resulting in lower uncertainty about demand should favour product innovation. In this view, the volume of demand and its growth rate should have a stronger effect on product innovation than on process innovation. This should be particularly the case in sectors with high technological opportunities (Muller, 1967; Hambrick and MacMillan, 1985; Lunn, 1986). In contrast, according to life-cycle theories (Utterback and Abernathy, 1975; Klepper, 1996), product innovation should be the solution developed by firms to overcome market uncertainty. Indeed, while firms develop new products, they can also discover the real characteristics of demand (level, quality). The progressive reduction in uncertainty concerning the exact nature of demand resulting from product innovations leads to the optimization of the production process and the development of process innovations. In turn, this optimization process tends to reduce flexibility and to make product innovations more costly. In this view, product innovation should be related positively to market uncertainty, and process innovation should be related negatively to it.

Akin to the life-cycle view about uncertainty, the heterogeneity of demand directed towards small series should enhance product innovations and inhibit process innovations (Pavitt, 1984). A high price elasticity of demand should stimulate process innovations because the opportunity for cost-reducing strategies is greater when the increase in demand resulting from lower prices is high (Kamien and Schwartz, 1970; Spence, 1975). In contrast, a high product innovation elasticity of demand would stimulate product innovations more than process innovations (Gomulka, 1990).

In our estimates we only include one variable related to micro-level demand conditions: the development of the market share of the firm over the 1987–90 period (DMS). This variable captures the evolution of demand directed towards a specific firm in comparison to other firms in the same sector. According to life-cycle theories, we expect that increasing demand should induce more *process* innovation, because the firm gains knowledge about demand and knows that it has developed a solution that can now be optimized. And a negative evolution of past market share should induce more *product* innovation, because it means that the firm has not yet discovered its market.

6.3.2   Appropriability Conditions

Despite a higher efficiency of patents for product innovations than for process innovations, empirical studies have shown that the appropriability conditions of product innovations are on average worse than those of process innovations: secrecy is not as efficient for product innovations as it is for process innovations; patents are not a perfect substitute for secrecy (Von Hippel, 1982a; Levin *et al.*, 1987; Harabi, 1995; Brouwer and Kleinknecht, 1999). As a result, product innovations should be sensitive to the capacity of the firm to take advantage of the response time of its competitors. This ability is related positively to the extent of learning that results from innovation (Von Hippel, 1982a; Grubber, 1994). In addition to response time, complementary assets should stimulate product innovations positively, because they can reinforce their appropriability (Teece, 1986). In this perspective, process innovations should be considered as a complementary asset to product innovations: in the case of low appropriability of product innovations, process innovation linked narrowly to product innovations, and whose degree of secrecy is higher, should enable the firm more easily to reap the benefits of its innovative activity.

It is impossible in this study to measure firm-level appropriability conditions. However, it *is* possible to measure sector-specific appropriability conditions by using the indicators that measure:

- the efficiency of patents and models for protecting product innovation in comparison to process innovation (PAT);
- the efficiency of secrecy for protection of product innovation in comparison to process innovation (SEC);
- the efficiency of complexity of design for protection of product innovation in comparison to process innovation (CPX); and
- the efficiency of 'lead time' for the protection of product innovation in comparison to process innovation (TIM).

For all these appropriability variables we expect a positive relationship with product innovation according to the logic that the better the protection of a type of innovation, the greater the incentive is to choose it. But this logic has some limitations: greater protection also means a lower speed of diffusion (particularly in the case of product innovation) and in turn, lower opportunity if external intraindustry sources of knowledge are important for innovation (Mohnen, 1991). Therefore, the net effect, in particular for product innovation at the sectoral level, is hard to predict.

6.3.3 Sources of Technological Knowledge

Most of the studies dealing with opportunity conditions are based on sectoral analyses or use micro-data but conclude with a sectoral analysis (for example Pavitt, 1984). We shall try to check whether such sectoral patterns (linking the sources of technological knowledge and the type of innovation) can also be observed at the firm level, after control for sectoral fixed effects. At this firm-level context there is a shift in terminology because the question is not about the existence or level of the opportunity itself, but about the ability of the firm to develop successful interactions with its environment, so as to take advantage of them (that is, its 'absorptive capacity') (Cohen and Levinthal, 1990). From an empirical point of view we distinguish the following variables.

Extra-Industry Sources

- Upstream links as a source of technological knowledge (UP). Previous empirical studies have shown that this source of technological knowledge mainly enhances process innovation rather than product innovation (Pavitt, 1984; Levin *et al.*, 1987; Kleinknecht and Reijnen, 1992).
- Downstream links as a source of technological knowledge (DOWN). This variable is supposed to boost product innovation according to the user–producer interaction model developed by Von Hippel (1982a) and later by Lundvall (1988). Links to users would reduce market uncertainty associated with product innovations (both for users and producers) and result in more product innovations (Pavitt, 1984; Von Hippel 1982b; Lundvall, 1988).
- Providers of technological services (STT): as a source of technological knowledge, these can be used more easily to develop product innovations based on the hypothesis that they have a more disembodied form than process innovations because patents can be sold for products but not for processes. Processes would include too many idosyncratic elements (Cohen and Klepper, 1996; Klepper, 1996).
- General information (IGAL) as a source of technological change the influence of which is hard to predict.
- Technological information (ITECH): no a priori hypothesis.
- French sources of technological knowledge (NSI).[1] In a National System of Innovation perspective this variable represents the degree of national integration of the firm. This integration should reduce both technological and market uncertainty associated with the development of innovations. We expect a stronger impact on product innovation because this type of innovation is the most sensitive to uncertainty on the sides of both user and producer (Lundvall, 1988; Leo, 1996).

Progress in Scientific Knowledge

Science as a source of technological knowledge (SCI): both product and process innovations should be influenced positively by scientific progress (Levin *et al.*, 1987). This would be the reason why product & process innovations appear more frequently in 'science based' sectors (Pavitt, 1984).

Intra-Industry Sources

Competitors as a source of technological knowledge (HORI for horizontal links): the main problem of product innovation is its low level of appropriability (Mansfield, 1985; Levin *et al.*, 1987). Hence, we can put forward the hypothesis that HORI is an important source of technological knowledge for product innovators, whereas it is not a significant variable for process innovation; in the latter case, secrecy is a more efficient means of protection. This variable can also be considered as a measure of the ability of firms to take advantage of 'Marshallian externalities'.

6.3.4 Market Structure

Concentration Index and the Intensity of Economic Competition

Our concentration index is a proxy for the intensity of economic competition. Since the first empirical study by Scherer (1983) finding a stronger relationship between concentration and product R&D than with process R&D, no clear empirical conclusions have emerged. In line with Scherer, some authors refer to a stronger positive impact of concentration on product innovations than on process innovations (Kraft, 1990) while others tend to conclude that there is a reverse relationship (Lunn, 1986, 1987; Zimmermann, 1987) or to no clear difference at all (Pohlmeier, 1992; Flaig and Stadler, 1998). Recent theoretical research using the distinction between Bertrand and Cournot competition tends to obtain mixed conclusions concerning the link between product and process innovations, and the intensity of economic competition. Bertrand (price) competition is a more intensely competitive regime when compared to Cournot competition. Concerning this issue, Bonanno and Haworth (1998) obtain the following results: 'for the high quality firm, whenever there is a difference between the choice made by a Cournot competitor and the choice made by a Bertrand competitor, the former opts for product innovation, while the latter prefers process innovation. For the low quality firm the result is reversed' (p. 495).

As a measure of competition we use the Herfindahl index. According to Kraft (1990) we expect a positive impact on product innovation because concentration should make the appropriation of product innovations easier.

Intensity of Technological Competition

According to Lunn (1986, 1987), the intensity of technological competition should be higher in high technological opportunity sectors. As a measure of the intensity of technological competition (LPCI) we shall compute the percentage of innovating firms in the sector for the period of investigation. This variable can also be considered as a proxy for technological opportunity. According to life-cycle theory, we should observe the highest rates of product & process innovations in sectors with high LPCI

(Klepper, 1996). In contrast, process innovation should be correlated negatively with this variable. It should be noted, however, that life-cycle theory tends to be applied to product-line data, while we deal with firm-level data.

6.3.5   Characteristics of the Firm

Firm Size

Empirical studies by Pavitt (1984) Pavitt *et al.* (1987) and Scherer (1991) have shown a negative link between firm size and product innovation. The conclusion is that firm size should influence the trade-off between product and process innovations, because product innovations can be sold in a disembodied form. So, increased size should decrease the profitability of product innovations in comparison to process innovations (Cohen and Klepper, 1996). In a game theoretic framework (duopoly), and using a firm's market share as a measure of its size, Xiangkang and Zuscovitch (1998) obtain similar results: the smallest firm (initially producing low-quality good) has a greater inducement to invest in product innovation than the largest firm (initially producing the high-quality good), and conversely for process innovation. The largest firm has a comparative advantage in producing the existing high-quality good. This will engender investment in process R&D to increase its margin rather than investment in a new product that could also depress demand for its existing production. In contrast, the smallest firm has more benefits in product innovation because it gains a new market.

In our model we use the market share of the firm as a measure of its size. According to the model developed by Cohen and Klepper (1996) and Xiangkang and Zuscovitch (1998), firms with higher market shares should innovate more in processes than firms with lower market shares.[2] But we could also follow Von Hippel (1982a), Levin *et al.* (1987), and Kraft (1990), for whom product innovations are difficult to appropriate with traditional tools. Hence, market power could be used as a means of appropriation, and enhance product innovation in comparison to process innovation.

Degree of Diversification

While the impact of this is not clear, Lunn (1987) shows a positive and significant impact of the degree of diversification on product and process innovations. This impact should be higher for product than for process innovations because diversification may be a tool to spread risks over different projects. In other words, diversified firms could more easily develop risky product innovation projects (Lunn, 1987). Nevertheless, causality is not clear and we have to be careful: product innovation could be the engine of diversification rather than its consequence. We shall measure the diversification level of the firm inversely by a concentration measure: the Herfindahl index calculated over the different branches in which a firm operates (LCON). We expect a negative link with product innovation.

Nature of Skills

External interfaces should be more heavily used for product innovations because firms have to look for opportunities and to manage uncertainty emerging from outside the firm (that is, in the market) (Cohen and Levinthal, 1990). The internal interface between sub-units should be more heavily used for process innovations in that both the implementation and the search process take place in the firm (Cohen and Levinthal, 1990; Clark and Fujitomo, 1987). In this context, the nature of the human capital involved in each kind of innovation would be different: diversified skills to ensure external interfaces for product innovations; specialized skills to optimize internal interfaces for process innovations (Leiponen, 1997). An increase in the internal flexibility of the firm would reduce this trade-off between product and process innovations, leading to the development of product and process innovations at the same time (Athey and Schmutzler, 1995). Unfortunately we do not have data about skills.

Another point of interest relates to the ability of the firm to learn from its past innovative activity (whatever its past type of innovative behaviour). To measure the impact of this process of technological accumulation we use a binary variable, taking the value 1 if a firm has innovated previously over the period 1985–90, and 0 otherwise.

6.3.6 Firm Strategy

The strategy of the firm can be considered in two ways. First, in a long-term perspective, what are the structures developed to sustain technological development? Two major questions arise. The first deals with the choice by a firm to rely on its own capability (inside the firm), or to rely on a larger set of capabilities provided by a consortium. The second question concerns its choice of laboratory research versus non-laboratory development of its technological ability. Second, in a shorter-term perspective, what are the goals of its technological activity? What are the main orientations of its problem-solving activity? Previous studies at a sectoral level have highlighted the link between the types of innovation and the main questions raised by the problem solving activities of firms. For example, Klevorick *et al.* (1995) have shown that sectoral trajectories characterized by problem-solving activities orientated towards the improvement of technical characteristics of products and processes induce process innovations. In contrast, trajectories characterized by the filling of demand needs mainly result in product innovations. The current microeconomic literature dealing with product and process innovations distinguishes the concepts of 'sales-enhancing' product innovation and 'cost-reducing' process innovation.

In this chapter, we take into account six different strategies:

A Long-Term Perspective

- Laboratory versus non-laboratory strategies for the production of technological knowledge (L_F): theory does not provide clear predictions. However, we can make the hypothesis that laboratory inputs increase the probability of process innovation more than product innovation, because product innovation would rely on less specific skills (Cohen and Levinthal, 1990; Leiponen, 1997).
- Firm versus consortium strategy for the production of technological knowledge (F_C): as with the strategy of L_F, we can assume that, given that human interactions inside the firm are easier than inside the whole consortium, the strategy of firms should stimulate product rather than process innovations.

A Medium-term Perspective

- Marketing strategy (MKT): this variable indicates the importance of marketing in relation to technological change. We expect that marketing strategies tend to induce product innovations rather than process innovations.
- Strategy of flexibility (FLEX): this variable indicates the importance of flexibility in relation to technological change. According to Athey and Schmutzler (1995) we expect a positive link with product & process innovation. Flexibility should be a means of increasing both product and process profitability.
- Quality strategy (QUAL): this variable indicates the importance of quality in relation to technological change. Quality improvements involve both the production process and the product itself. We have no prediction of its impact.

- Cost-reducing strategy (COST): this variable indicates the importance of cost reduction in relation to technological change. We expect a positive link with process innovation.

6.4 ESTIMATION PROCEDURE, SCOPE AND LIMITS OF OUR ANALYSIS

6.4.1 Estimation Procedure

In order to model the link between, on the one hand, the discrete choice of certain types of innovation k (k being product innovation, process innovation, or product *and* process innovation, the three categories being mutually exclusive) and, on the other hand, a set of firm-specific explanatory variables (X_i), we use a multinomial logit model with three levels: product innovation, process innovation, and product & process innovation. The category 'product & process innovation' serves as an initial baseline. Alternatively, we use the 'process' category as a baseline to highlight the difference between product and process innovations. In all cases, we take account of sampling weights.

We develop our analysis in two steps. First, we study the specific determinants of (i) product, (ii) process and (iii) product & process innovation for the period 1990–2. We run a multinomial logit model with a three-level endogenous variable (product, process, product & process). In other words, we estimate the relative odds in time t of the jth and the kth kinds of innovation. Firm-level explanatory variables (Xi) are mainly extracted from the CIS survey (that is, we explain current innovative behaviour using current explanatory variables). Variables relating to appropriability conditions are estimated at sectoral level using the appropriability survey for the same period. We add another sectoral variable representing the degree of technological competition in the sector (called LPCI) (for details about the construction of the variables, see Appendix 6.2 of page 134).

Second, we try to reproduce a 'similar' model with data from the 1985–90 period as a means of checking the robustness of our findings. Not all the variables in the CIS survey for 1990–2 are available in the 1990 survey. In particular, for the 1990 survey, we do not have information about the past evolution of a firm's market share, nor about past technological experience, and, at the sectoral level, we do not have information about appropriability conditions. Most of the time, when the same concept is found in both surveys, it is not measured with identical questions. This is why we do not expect the results to be exactly the same.

We only want to check whether the signs are the same for the two periods (for details about the construction of the variables see Appendix 6.3 on page 138).

6.3.7   Scope and Limits of our Analysis

The surveys were conducted according to specific sampling procedures. SESSI developed appropriate sampling weights for each observation, and these have been included in all our computations. Despite an overlap for the year 1990, the first innovation survey partly covers a different period of time than the other two surveys.

We face two important limitations. The first is that the questions and concepts are not always the same in the three surveys. The 1991 survey does not use exactly the same definitions for product and process innovations as those used in the CIS and in the survey on appropriation of innovation benefits. Questions about product and process innovations are not exactly the same but can easily be matched, as is indicated in Appendix 6.1 (see page 133). It is thus, strictly speaking, not possible to compare the different proportions of product, process, and product & process innovations calculated for each period. Concepts such as the 'intensity of the relationship with customers' or with 'suppliers' are not measured in the same way in the three surveys. Nevertheless, we have tried to construct proxies that are as close as possible to each other. The second problem is the different length of time covered by the first survey (five years) and the second (three years). It is obvious that the probability of achieving an innovation over a five-year period is higher than over a three-year period. This again limits comparisons between the two surveys.

6.5   RESULTS ON DETERMINANTS OF PRODUCT, PROCESS AND PRODUCT & PROCESS INNOVATIONS FOR 1985–90 AND 1990–2

6.5.1   Main Results

Demand Conditions

The estimated coefficient of LDPM (past evolution of the market share) is not significant. In contrast to the Cohen and Klepper (1996) hypothesis, we do not observe a significant decrease in the probability of product innovation in contrast to process innovation when the market share grows.

Appropriability Conditions at the Sectoral Level

Appropriability conditions (measured at the sector level), have no impact on the balance between product, process and product & process innovations. We have also made a similar model (not documented here) using firm-level appropriability variables from the appropriability survey. In this latter model, higher appropriability conditions for products result in more product innovations and fewer process innovations. However, these results are not very reliable because of high item non-response.

External Sources of Technological Knowledge

The main characteristic of product innovators in contrast to process innovators is their heavy use of technological information coming from their competitors (HORI) and their lower use of upstream information (UP). In contrast to our expectations, the estimated coefficient of downward links (DOWN) is not highly significant (at 10 per cent) for the second period. What distinguishes product innovators from product & process innovators in external knowledge sourcing is not only HORI (use of information coming from competitors) but also SCI (use of scientific sources of technological knowledge). Scientific inputs increase the probability of making product & process innovation compared to mere product innovation. This is in line with the views of Pavitt (1984). For process innovators, the distinction between simultaneous product and process innovators is mainly caused by the impact of UP (upstream activities have positive impact on process inovation) but also to NSI (National System of Innovation). Process innovators use significantly fewer technological inputs from their national environment than product & process innovators. This is consistent with Leo's (1996) results, even though in our case we do not observe any significant difference for product versus process innovators for this variable. The variables ITECH (technological information) and IGAL (general information) have no significant impact on the probability of innovation in product versus process and product versus product & process innovation.

Market Structure

In terms of the Herfindahl index (LH) or the firm's market share (LMS), firms operating in more concentrated markets tend to innovate more in products than in products & processes, or in processes only.[3] This is consistent with the findings of Scherer (1983) and Kraft (1990), but not with other empirical studies. Concerning the intensity of technological competition (LPCI), we notice a systematic difference between product & process innovation and process innovation alone. An increase in the overall number of innovating firms enhances product & process innovation rela tive to process innovation. At least for the 1985–90 innovation survey, i also tends to result in a higher probability of product innovation compared to process innovation. This result confirms the life-cycle theory view, in which greater technological competition results in more product innova tions than process innovations.

Characteristics of the Firm

Higher market shares (LMS90) induce higher probabilities of product inno vations in comparison to product innovation, at least for the 1990–2 period This result is not consistent with the literature. The explanation may be that in our study, in contrast to the theoretical work, we deal with outputs and no inputs of the innovative process. For the concentration (versus diversity variable (LCON), we obtain homogeneous results for both periods. Produc and product & process innovators are not very different according to this cri terion. In contrast, process innovators are much less diversified than produc and product & process innovators. This suggests that product innovation i stimulated by the heterogeneity of the economic activity of the firm, and tha diversification leads to spillovers from one activity to another. The impact o the technological past of the firm (IA4) is positive on the probability o innovation in products & processes, but negative on the probability of inno vation in products only (weakly significant) and on the probability o process innovation (highly significant). The probabilities of product versu process innovations are not affected by this variable. This means that it is no because a firm has innovated in the past that it will be more likely to inno vate in products rather in the processes in the future. On the contrary, a firm with past experience, if it keeps on innovating, is more likely to innovate products & processes: continuous innovators tend to develop a widening rather than a specializing profile of innovation.

Strategy of the Firm

Regarding laboratory versus non-laboratory organization of technological development (L_F), results are clear: the stronger the strategy of labora tory research, the higher the probability of product innovation in compari son to process and product & process innovation. Process innovators are the least intensive users of laboratory research.

Concerning the strategies of problem-solving pursued by firms, we obtain interesting results showing that the occurrence of product versus process innovations cannot only be understood using the distinction between cost-reducing process innovations and sales enhancing product innovations. As expected, a firm's goal of increased sales (MKT) strongly and significantly (at 0.1 per cent level with and without dummies for sectors) increases the probability of product innovation as opposed to process innovation. In contrast, the reverse relationship from a cost reducing strategy (COST) to process innovation is not so strong (significant at 10 per cent with dummies for sectors, not significant at all without these dummies). Interestingly, cost-reducing problem-solving activities do not lead to a significant trade-off between product and process innovations, but they do lead to a significant trade-off (at 5 per cent) between product and product & process innovations. This result contrasts sharply with current theoretical developments that use the 'cost-reducing, sale-enhancing trade-off' as a starting point to model the innovative behaviour of firms.

Turning now to the impact of flexibility strategy (FLEX), we notice its surprising importance (greater than the strategy of cost reduction). Athey and Schmutzler (1995) would have predicted a positive link between increased flexibility and the probability of product & process innovation in comparison to product innovation, as well as with respect to process innovations. We observe only one opposition: a stronger strategy of flexibility leads to a higher probability of product & process innovation in contrast to product innovation, but it does not reduce the probability of process innovation.

The discussion about cost, quality, marketing and flexibility strategies depends strongly on the typology that is used. For example, flexibility strategies can be considered as a special mean of cost reduction. Quality strategies may be seen either as a tool to reduce scrapping (and hence costs), or to increase the utility of consumers and, as a result, sales. Depending on the typology results may change.

6.5.2 Robustness of the Results

The coefficients reported in Table 6.2 tend to be more significant for the 1985–90 survey than for that of 1990–2. This is probably due to the size of the sample (10 137 innovating firms for the first period versus 1645 for the second), and to the fact that in the first period we use eleven explanatory variables, whereas in the second period we use twenty-six.

The two models produce, most of the time, coefficients with the same sign. Nevertheless, three differences are observed. First, the coefficient for STT (providers of research) is not significant for the 1992 survey, but it is significant in that of 1985–90 for the distinction between product innovators, and process innovators, and between process innovators and joint product & process innovators. This means that during the 1985–90 period,

Table 6.2 The determinants of product, process, and product & process innovations. Results from a multinomial logit model with survey weights. Exogenous variables from 1990 to 1992 and from 1985 to 1990. Maximum likelihood estimates

	1990–2				1985–90		
	Name	P(iprod/ prod& proc)	P(iproc/ prod&proc)	P(iprod/ iproc proc)	Name	P(iprod/ prod& proc)	P(iprod/ proc& proc)	P(iprod/ proc)
Demand conditions								
Past market share evolution (1987–90)	Intercept	.089	.142	−.052	Intercept	−.368**	−1.485****	1.117****
	LDMS	.011	.071	−.060				
Sectoral appropriability conditions								
Efficiency of patent for product in comparison to process	PAT	−.081	−.378*	.296				
Efficiency of secret for product in comparison to process	SEC	−.021	−.223	.201				
Efficiency of complexity for product in comparison to process	CPX	.478	.388	.089				
Efficiency of time advance for product in comparison to process	TIM	.242	.164	.077				

Variable	Code				Code			
Upstream activities	UP	−.082	.206***	−.288****	UP	−.677****	.169****	−.846****
Downstream activities	DOWN	.070	−.067	.138*	DOWN	.033	−.302****	.335****
Competitors	HORI	.197***	−.050	.248***				
Science	SCI	−.177**	−.172	−.004	SCI	−.234****	−.149****	−.084**
Providers of research	STT	.067	−.003	.071	STT	−.034	−.120****	.085**
General information	IGAL	−.129	.021	−.151				
Technical information	ITEC	.049	−.001	.051				
French sources (NSI)	NSI	−.561	−1.189***	.627				
Market structures								
Concentration level (Herfindahl index)	LH90				LH87			
Percentage of innovative firms in the sector	LPCI90-92	−.376	−.827***	.450	LPCI185-90	.149	−.707****	.856****
Microeconomic characteristics of the firm								
Market share	LMS90	−.115***	−.279****	.163***	LMS87	−.093****	−.199****	.026
Concentration index	LCON90	−.132	.872***	−1.00****	LCON87	−.077	.400****	−.478****
Technological past	IA4	−.329*	−.496***	.167				
Strategy of the firm								
Relative importance of laboratory and non-laboratory research	L_F	.066	−.204***	.271****	L_F	.039*	−.121****	.161****
Relative importance of research inside the firm and research in the consortium	F_C	.103**	−.146**	.250****	F_C	−.067****	−.230****	.163****

Table 6.2 Continued

	1990–2			1985–90			
	Name	P(iprod/ prod& proc)	P(iproc/ prod&proc)	P(iprod/ iproc)	Name	P(iprod/ prod& proc)	P(iproc/ prod& proc)	P(iprod/ proc)
Marketing	MKT	.117	−.904****	1.021****				
Flexibility	FLEX	−412****	.078	−.490****				
Cost	COST	−.191**	−.024	−.167				
Quality	QUAL	−.138*	.073	−.211**				
Number of observations		1645	10137					
L0 (Log likelihood with intercept only)		−1762	−9556					
L1 (Log likelihood with all coefficients)		−1418	−8665					
Chi² (degrees of freedom)		chi²(46)=686	chi²(18)=1780.80					
Prob. > X2		0.0000	0.0000					
Pseudo R² (1-L1/L0)		0.1949	0.0932					

Notes: For more detailed results (tests of slopes for each of the equations and tables of prediction) see Appendixes 6.4 and 6.5. See Appendix 6.6 for results with dummies for sectors in 1990–2 (23 industrial sectors). Variables calculated at sectoral level such as appropriability conditions, concentration level and percentage of innovative firms in the sector are dropped in this last model. The estimated coefficients are consistent with those obtained without dummies for sectors, the pseudo R² slightly rises from 0.19 (without dummies) to 0.21 (with dummies for sectors).

Significance: *: 10%; **: 5%; ***:1%; ****: 0.1%.

product & process innovators were the heaviest users of specialized suppliers of technological services. Product innovators use STT more intensively than process innovators. This tends to be in line with the idea that product innovation can be exchanged on a market much like a specific good, whereas process innovations (or at least their technological inputs) are less easily sold and exchanged. However, this relationship vanishes in the second period. Second, in Table 6.2, the estimated coefficient of F_C (firm versus consortium) in the equation opposing product innovators and product & process innovators i.e. in columns entitled P (iproc/prod & proc) is not stable over the two periods. In the first period, higher internally generated technological change leads to a smaller probability of product innovation in comparison to product & process innovation, whereas in the second period the link is slightly positive and significant. Third, mainly for the 1985–90 period, we may have a problem of multicolinearity between LH (Herfindahl concentration index) and LMS (market share). Because of this, the total effect of a variable in one survey could be spread over two or more variables in the other, resulting in a change in estimated parameters. Apart from these points, the two estimates give some similar results, and can thus be considered as robust.

6.6 CONCLUSIONS

What are the distinguishing determinants of product, process and combined product & process innovations in France? We have investigated this question using three French surveys covering the 1985–90 and 1990–2 periods.

Surprisingly, we do not find a significant impact of sectoral appropriability conditions on the relative probabilities of product, process or concurrent product & process innovations. The sources of technological knowledge are important. Upstream sources tend to promote process innovation, whereas horizontal and downward links enhance product innovation. These results are entirely consistent with the economic literature. The intensity of competition can also modify the balance between product and process innovations. Stronger competition (that is, a lower Herfindahl index) induces more process innovations, whereas technological competition stimulates more product innovations.

Firms' characteristics are important. Large firms (large market shares) mainly develop product & process innovations. In contrast to theoretical predictions, we did not observe a negative link between market share and the probability of product in contrast to process innovation. Perhaps this is because of the use indicators of output rather than input. On the other hand, consistent with theoretical expectations, we observe that more diversified firms tend to innovate more in products than in processes. Finally, a firm's learning process and its accumulation of technological capabilities increases the probability of product & process innovation. We can interpret this finding as saying that continuous innovators tend to follow widening technological trajectories rather than specialized ones.

Firms' strategies also have a significant impact on the balance between product, process and product & process innovations. When the production of new technology is based on laboratory activities and on the firms' own abilities (rather than on those of a consortium), the probability of product innovation tends to increase in contrast to process innovation. The contrast between sales-enhancing product innovations and cost-reducing process innovations is not as strong as expected. The marketing strategy goes in the direction of product innovations, but process innovations are not driven strongly by the cost-reducing strategy.

Appendix 6.1: Definition of the Type of Innovation in Different Survey

- For the 1991 survey, product and process innovations are identified by the answers to the following questions.

During the past five years the firm has:

Product innovations

Products substantially improved from a technological point of view:	0/1 (U1)
Introduced on the market a new product that is technologically innovating:	
(i) products new to the market:	0/1 (U2)
(ii) products new to the firm but already known in the market:	0/1 (U3)

Process innovations

Been the first to develop:	0/1 (U4)
Substantially improved the production process from a technological point of view:	0/1 (U5)

The definition for product, process and product & process innovators is the following:

If (u1 = 0 and u2 = 0 and u3 = 0) and (u4 = 0 and u5 = 0) then Non-innovator;
If (u1 = 1 or u2 = 1 or u3 = 1) and (u4 = 0 and u5 = 0) then Product innovator;
If (u1 = 0 and u2 = 0 and u3 = 0) and (u4 = 1 or u5 = 1) then Process innovator;
If (u1 = 1 or u2 = 1 or u3 = 1) and (u4 = 1 or u5 = 1) then Product & process innovator.

- In the Community Innovation Survey (CIS) and in the survey on appropriation of innovation benefits, the type of innovation is identified using the following questions.

During the past three years (1990–2), has your firm developed or introduced:
 (i) product innovations?   0/1 (Q110)
(ii) process innovations?   0/1 (Q120)

Definitions of product, process and product & process innovations are the following:

If q110 = 0 and q120 = 0 then Non-innovator;
If q110 = 1 and q120 = 0 then Product innovator;
If q110 = 0 and q120 = 1 then Process innovator;
If q110 = 1 and q120 = 1 then Product & process innovator.

Appendix 6.2

Table A6.1 Definitions of the Variables Used to Identify the Determinants of Product, Process and Product & Process Innovations in 1990–2

Name	Notation	Definition of the variable	Statistical source	Mean	Variance
Demand conditions					
Market share evolution	LDpm	log(PM90/PM87)	EAE 1990 and 1987	−0.057	1.183
Efficiency of protection against imitators at sector level					
Efficiency of patent for product in comparison for product in to process comparison	PAT	Sectoral mean score obtained by (AQ21a, AQ22a) minus (AQ21b, AQ22b) using only answers from innovating firms (product and/or process).	SESSI's appropriability survey	0.954	2.016
Efficiency of secrecy for product in comparison to process	SEC	Sectoral mean score obtained by (AQ23a) minus (AQ23b) using only answers from innovating firms (product and/or process).	SESSI's appropriability survey	−0.283	1.345
Efficiency of complexity for product in comparison to process	CPX	Sectoral mean score obtained by (AQ31a) minus (AQ31b) using only answers from innovating firms (product and/or process).	SESSI's appropriability survey	0.148	1.347
Efficiency of time lead for product in comparison to process	TIM	Sectoral mean score obtained by (AQ32a, AQ33a) minus (AQ32b, AQ33b) using only answers from innovating firms (product and/or process).	SESSI's appropriability survey	0.940	1.954

135

Sources of technological knowledge

		Description	Source		
Relative importance of research in laboratory and non-laboratory research	L_F	The difference between the mean score of LAB=(Q311+Q321)/2 and FLOR= (Q312+Q322)/2 (L_F=(LAB-FLOR)) as sources of technological knowledge	SESSI's CIS survey	2.930	7.246
Relative importance of research inside the firm and research in a consortium	E_C	The difference between the mean score of ETS=(Q311+Q312)/2 and CON = (Q321+Q322)/2 (E_C=(ETS-CON)) as sources of technological knowledge	SESSI's CIS survey	0.814	7.067
Upstream activities	Up	Mean score obtained by Q344, Q345 about suppliers of material and components and suppliers of equipment as sources of technological knowledge.	SESSI's CIS survey	2.238	7.056
Downstream activities	Down	Mean score obtained by Q346 about customers as sources of technological knowledge	SESSI's CIS survey	2.314	9.784
Competitors	HORI	Mean score obtained by Q347 (competitors as sources of technological knowledge)	SESSI's CIS survey	1.823	6.542
Science	Science	Mean score obtained by Q331, Q332 (public laboratories, universities as sources of technological knowledge)	SESSI's CIS survey	1.412	3.226
Providers of technological services	SSTT	Mean score obtained by Q341, Q342, Q343 (centres techniques de profession, prestataires de service de R&D, sociétés de consultants)	SESSI's CIS survey	1.474	2.385
General information	IGAL	Mean score obtained by Q352, Q353 (meetings, publications, fair, exhibitions as sources of technological knowledge)	SESSI's CIS survey	2.171	5.877

Table A6.1 Continued

Name	Notation	Definition of the variable	Statistical source	Mean	Variance
Technical information	ITECH	Score obtained by Q351 (data bases, patents, patterns as sources of technological knowledge)	SESSI's CIS survey	1.639	5.377
National system of innovation (French sources)	NSI	Mean score obtained by French sources of knowledge for the questions (Q41a, Q42a, Q43a, Q44a, Q45a, Q46a, Q47a, Q48a, Q49a, Q410a, Q411a, Q412a)	SESSI's CIS survey	0.250	0.204
Market structure					
Concentration in 1990	LH90	log(weighted mean concentration level (measured by the Herfindahl index) a firm meets according its diversification pattern by branch).	EAE 1990	−3.463	6.919
Intensity of technological competition	LPCI 90–2	log(percentage of innovative firms in the sector over 1990–2 (NAF in 24 sectors)	SESSI's CIS survey	−0.875	0.737
Firms' characteristics					
Market share in 1990	LPM90	log(market share in 1990 using branch data. Weighted means of each firm's market share on the whole set of branches in which it operates)	EAE 1990	−5.687	13.877
Diversification in 1990	LCON	log(Herfindahl index calculated over the different branches in which a firm operates)	EAE 1990	−0.184	0.465

Technological past	IA4	1 if the firm declares an innovation (product or process or product & process) in 1985–90, 0 otherwise	SESSI's 1990 survey	0.83	
Strategy					
Marketing	Mrkt	Mean score obtained by Q211, Q213, Q214 about obsolescence, range of products, exploration of new products.	SESSI's CIS survey	2.867	5.597
Flexibility	Flex	Mean score obtained by Q221, Q226 about the flexibility of the production and the reduction of the product conception cycle.	SESSI's CIS survey	2.590	7.926
Quality	Qual	Mean score obtained by Q212, Q225 about improvement in product quality and rejects reduction.	SESSI's CIS survey	2.930	7.246
Cost	Cost	Mean score obtained by Q222, Q223, Q224 about the reduction in labour costs, energy costs, consumption of materials	SESSI's CIS survey	2.098	5.273

Appendix 6.3

Table A 6.2   Description of the Variables Used to Identify the Determinants of the Innovative Behaviour in 1985–90

Name	Notation	Definition of the variable	Statistical source	Mean	Variance
Sources of technological knowledge					
Upstream activities	Up	W7	SESSI's 1990 survey	1.539	13.105
Downstream activities	Down	V1	SESSI's 1990 survey	2.362	10.500
Science	SCI	V2	SESSI's 1990 survey	1.719	11.983
Providers of technological services	SSTT	(W4+W6)/2	SESSI's 1990 survey	0.756	11.213
Market structure					
Concentration index in 1987	LH87	log of weighted mean concentration level (measured by the Herfindahl index) a firm meets given its diversification pattern by branch.	EAE 1987	−3.596	13.138
Intensity of the technological competition in 1985–90	LPCI 85–90	log of percentage of innovative firms in the sector over 1985–90 (NAP90)	SESSI's 1990 survey	−0.525	3.002
Firms' characteristics					
Market share in 1987	LMS 87	log of market share in 1990 using branch data. Weighted means of each firm's market share in all branches in which it operates.	EAE 1990	−6.282	20.786

Concentration in 1987	LCON 87	log (Herfindahl index calculated over the different branches in which a firm operates)	EAE 1987	−0.149	3.314
Strategy of the firm					
Relative importance of research in laboratory and non-laboratory research	L_F	The difference between LAB=W1 and FLOR=W2 (L_F=(LAB-FLOR)) as sources of technological knowledge	SESSI's 1990 survey	−0.255	17.998
Relative importance of research inside the firm and research in a consortium	E_C	The difference between the mean score of ETS=max(W1, W2) and CON=W3 (E_C=(ETS-CON)) as sources of technological knowledge	SESSI's 1990 survey	0.591	17.313

Appendix 6.4:   Detailed Results of Estimates for 1990–2

Table A6.3(a)   Determinants of product, process and product & process innovations in 1990–2 in a multinomial logit model with survey weights; test of equality of all slopes for each equation

Whole model	F(446, 1599)	= 8.74
	Prob > F	= 0.0000
Product/product & process	F(23, 1622)	= 5.72
	Prob > F	= 0.0000
Process/product & process	F(23, 1622)	= 9.91
	Prob > F	= 0.0000
Product/process	F(23, 1622)	= 11.14
	Prob > F	= 0.0000

Table A6.3(b)   Determinants of product, process and product & process innovations in 1990–2 using a multinomial logit model with survey weights; table of observed and predicted types of innovation

		Predicted			Total
		Product	Process	Product & process	
	Product	234	43	206	483
		48.45	8.90	42.65	100.00
		55.58	13.44	22.66	29.27
		14.18	2.61	12.48	29.27
	Process	49	189	117	355
		13.80	53.24	32.96	100.00
Observed		11.64	59.06	12.87	21.52
		2.97	11.45	7.09	21.52
	Product & process	138	88	586	812
		17.00	10.84	72.17	100.00
		32.78	27.50	64.47	49.21
		8.36	5.33	35.52	49.21
	Total	421	320	909	1650
		25.52	19.39	55.09	100.00
		100.00	100.00	100.00	100.00
		25.52	19.39	55.09	100.00

Appendix 6.5: Detailed Results of Estimates for 1985–90

Table A6.4(a) Determinants of product, process and product & process innovations in 1985–90 using a multinomial logit model with survey weights; exogenous variables from 1985–90; test of equality of all slopes for each equation

Whole model	F(18, 10118)	= 79.06
	Prob > F	= 0.0000
Product/product & process	F(9 10127)	= 94,16
	Prob > F	= 0.0000
Process/product & process	F(9 10127)	= 70,79
	Prob > F	= 0.0000
Product/process	F(9 10127)	= 98,43
	Prob > F	= 0.0000

Table A 6.4(b) Determinants of product, process and product & process innovations in 1985–90 using a multinomial logit model with survey weights; exogenous variables from 1985–90; table of observed and predicted types of innovation

		Predicted			Total
		Product	Process	Product & process	
	Product	373	33	1632	2038
		18.30	1.62	80.08	100
		49.67	13.64	17.85	20.10
		3.68	0.33	16.10	20.10
	Process	99	109	1647	1855
		5.34	5.88	88.79	100
		13.18	45.04	18.01	18.30
		0.98	1.08	16.25	18.30
Observed	Product & process	279	100	5865	6244
		4.47	1.60	93.93	100
		37.15	41.32	64.14	61.60
		2.75	0.99	57.86	61.60
	Total	751	242	9144	10 137
		7.41	2.39	90.20	100
		100.00	100.00	100.00	100
		7.41	2.39	90.20	100

Appendix 6.6

Table A6.5 Estimation for 1990–2 with dummies for sectors. The determinants of product, process, product & process innovations in 1990–2; multinomial logit with survey weights and dummies for sectors

	Variable	P(iprod/ prod& proc)	P(iproc/ prod& proc)	P(iprod/ iproc)
	INTERCPT	−.599	2.06**	−2.66**
Demand conditions				
Past market share evolution (1987–90)	DPM1	.018	.058	−.039
Sectoral appropriability conditions				
Efficiency of patent for product by comparison to process	BRV			
Efficiency of secret for product by comparison to process	SEC			
Efficiency of complexity for product by comparison to process	CPX			
Efficiency of time advance for product by comparison to process	TIM			
External origins of the technological knowledge				
Upstream activities	UP	−.076	.233***	−.309****
Downstream activities	DOWN	.084	−.064	.148*
Competitors	HORI	.185***	−.071	.257***
Science	SCI	−.170*	−.200	.030
Subcontractors	STT	.052	−.018	.071
General informations	IGAL	−.133	−.0153	−.117
Technical informations	ITEC	.051	.023	.027
French sources	FR	−.525	−1.23***	.707
Market structures				
Concentration level (Herfindhal index)	LH			
Percentage of innovative firms in the sector	LPCI			
Microeconomic characteristics of the firm				
Market share in 1990	LPM	−.118***	−.3150323****	.196***
Concentration index 0 in 199	LDIV	−.160	.7928741***	−.952***
Technological past	IA4	−.336*	−.515***	.179

Table A6.5   Continued

Variable		P(iprod/ prod &proc)	P(iproc/ prod &proc)	P(irod/ iproc)
Strategy of the firm				
Relative importance of research in laboratory and non-laboratory research	L_F	.073	−.193***	.266****
Relative importance of research inside the firm and research in the consortium	E_G	.096*	−.153**	.249****
Marketing	MKT	.124	−.925****	1.04****
Flexibility	FLEX	−.430****	.098	−.529****
Cost	COST	−.212**	.019	−.232*
Quality	QUAL	−.138*	.088	−.226**
		Dummies for sectors (22 dummies)		
Number of observations	1650			
L0 (Initial log likelihood)	−1767			
L1 (Final log likelihood)	−1389			
Chi^2(degrees of freedom)	chi^2(80) = 755.65			
Prob. > X^2	0.0000			
Pseudo R^2 (1-L1/L0)	0.21			

Explanation: * = Significant at 90% level; ** = Significant at 95% level;
*** = Significant at 99% level.

Appendix 6.7

Table A6.6 The determinants of product, process, product & process innovations (including Herfindahl index) in 1990–92 and 1985–90; results from a multinomial logit model with survey weights; exogenous variables from 1990–92 and from 1985–90; maximum likelihood estimates

		1990–2				1985–90		
	Name	*P(prod/ prod & proc)*	*P(iproc/ prod & proc)*	*P(iprod/ iproc)*	*Name*	*P(iprod/ prod & proc)*	*P(iproc/ prod & proc)*	*P(iprod/ iproc)*
	Intercept	.996*	1.45**	−.461	Intercept			
Demand conditions								
Past market share evolution (1987–90)	LDMS	−.006	.041	−.047				
Sectoral appropriability conditions								
Efficiency of patent for product in comparison to process	PAT	−.046	−.413*	.367				
Efficiency of secret for product in comparison to process	SEC	.004	−.305	.309				
Efficiency of complexity for product in comparison to process	CPX	.418	.380	.038				
Efficiency of time advance for product in comparison to process	TIM	.205	.251	−.045				

External sources of technological knowledge

Upstream activities	UP	-.080	.196***	-.276****	UP	-.685****	.156****	-.841****
Downstream activities	DOWN	.085	-.038	.124*	DOWN	.024	-.308****	.332****
Competitors	HORI	.191***	-.0602	.251***				
Science	SCI	-.185**	-.206*	.021	SCI	-.230****	-.149****	-.081**
Providers of research	STT	.055	-.034	.089	STT	-.037	-.119****	.081**
General information	IGAL	-.113	.053	-.166				
Technical information	ITEC	.036	-.037	.074				
French sources (NSI)	NSI	-.544	-1.1468**	.602				

Market structures

Concentration level (Herfindahl index)	LH90	.031	-.154**	.185**	LH87	.034	-.222****	.257****
Percentage of innovative firms in the sector	LPCI90-92	-.349	-.648**	.298	LPCI85-90	.055	-.475****	.531****

Microeconomic characteristics of the firm

Market share	LMS90	Dropped due to multicolinearity with LH			LMS87	Dropped due to multicolinearity with LH		
Concentration index	LCON90	-.046	.904***	-.950***	LCON87	.094	.319***	-.22*
Technological past	IA4	-.361**	-.541***	.180				

Table A6.6   Continued

		1990–2				1985–90		
	Name	P(iprod/ prod & proc)	P(iproc/ prod & proc)	P(iprod/ iproc)	Name	P(iprod/ prod & proc)	P(iproc/ prod & proc)	P(iprod/ iproc)
Strategy of the firm								
Relative importance of research in laboratory and non-laboratory research	L_F	.051	−.227****	.278****	L_F	.027	−.124****	.151****
Relative importance of research inside the firm and research in the consortium	F_C	.106**	−.143**	.250****	F_C	−.063****	−.230****	.166****
Marketing	MKT	.123	−.880****	1.00****				
Flexibility	FLEX	−.402****	.107	−.510****				
Cost	COST	−.220**	−.083	−.136				
Quality	Qual	−.152**	.058	−.211				
Number of observations		1645				10137		
L0 (Initial log likelihood)		−1762				−9556		
L1 (Final log likelihood)		−1432				−8660		
Chi²(degrees of freedom)		chi²(46) =660				chi²(18) =1780		
Prob. > X²		0.0000				0.0000		
Pseudo R² (1-L1/L0)		**0.1874**				**0.0932**		

Explanation: * = significant at 90% level; ** = significant at 95% level; *** = significant at 99% level.

Notes

*   We thank Jean-Paul François who has provided us with the data used in this study. We also thank participants of the TSER workshop 'Innovation and Economic Change: Exploring CIS Micro Data' at Delft University of Technology, the Netherlands, in February 1999 for their comments, in particular Emmanuel Duguet, Petr Hanel, Alfred Kleinknecht, José Labeaga, Pierre Mohnen, and Louis-André and Elisabet Lefebvre.

1.   In the 1990–2 survey, firms were asked about the geographical origin of their different sources of technological knowledge (users, suppliers, competitors etc.). We computed the mean score obtained by French sources for the whole set of questions.
2.   This is an indirect interpretation of the model of Cohen and Klepper (1996). The original model deals with size and not market share. It deals with R&D expenses and not output (even though its empirical model uses patent data).
3.   Because of high multicollinearity between the Herfindhal index (LH) and the market share of firms (LMS) we performed two estimates: one with LMS and without LH, another with LH but without LMS. Results were very similar.

Bibliography

ATHEY, S. and SCHMUTZLER, A. (1995) 'Product and Process Flexibility in an Innovative Environment', *Rand Journal of Economics*, vol. 26, no. 4, pp. 557–74.

BONANNO, G. and HAWORTH, B. (1998) 'Intensity of Competition and the Choice Between Product and Process Innovation', *International Journal of Industrial Organization*, vol. 16, pp. 495–510.

BROUWER, E. and KLEINKNECHT, A. (1999) 'Innovative Output, and a Firm's Propensity to Patent. An Exploration of CIS Micro Data', *Research Policy*, vol. 28, pp. 615–24.

CAPON, N., FARLEY, J. U., LEHMANN, D. R. and HULBERT, J. M. (1992) 'Profiles of Product Innovators Among Large U.S. Manufacturers', *Management Science*, vol. 38, no. 2, pp. 157–69.

COHEN, W. M. and KLEPPER, S. (1996) 'Firm Size and the Nature of Innovation within Industries: The Case of Process and Product R&D', *Review of Economics and Statistics*, vol. LXXVII, no. 2, pp. 232–43.

COHEN, W. M. and LEVINTHAL, D. A. (1990) 'Absorptive Capacity: A New Perspective on Learning and Innovation', *Administrative Science Quarterly*, vol. 35, pp. 128–52.

DUGUET, E. and GREENAN, N. (1997) 'Le Biais Technologique: Une Analyse Économétrique sur Données Individuelles', *Revue Economique*, vol. 48, no. 5, pp. 1061–89.

FLAIG, G. and STADLER, M. (1998) 'On the Dynamics of Product and Process Innovations: A Bivariate Random Effects Probit Model', *Jahrbücher fur Nationalükonomie und Statistik*, pp. 401–17.

FREEMAN, C. (1982) *The economics of industrial innovation*, London: F. Pinter.

CLARK, K. B. and FUJIMOTO, T. (1987) 'Overlapping problem solving in product development', Technical Report, Harvard University Press.

GOMULKA, S. (1990) *The Theory of Technological Change and Economic Growth.* London: Routledge.

GRUBBER, H. (1994) *Learning and Strategic Product Innovation: Theory and Evidence for the Semi-Conductor Industry.* Amsterdam: Elsevier Science.

HAMBRICK, D. C. and MACMILLAN, I. C. (1985) 'Efficiency of Product R&D in Business Units: The Role of Strategic Context', *Academic Management Journal*, vol. 28, pp. 527–47.

HARABI, N. (1995) 'Appropriability of Technological Innovations: An Empirical Analysis', *Research Policy*, vol. 24, pp. 981–92.

KAMIEN, M. and SCHWARTZ, N. (1970) 'Market Structure, Elasticity of Demand, and Incentive to Invent', *Journal of Law and Economics*, vol. 13, pp. 241–52.

KLEINKNECHT, A. and REIJNEN, J. O. N. (1992) 'Les Nouvelles Données sur l'Innovation: l'Expérience des Pays-Bas', *STI Revue*, OCDE, no.11.

KLEPPER, S. (1996) 'Entry, Exit, Growth, and Innovation over the Product Life Cycle', *American Economic Review*, vol. 86, pp. 562–83.

KLEVORICK, A. K., LEVIN, R. C., NELSON, R. R. and WINTER, S. G. (1995) 'On the Sources and Significance of Interindustry Differences in Technological Opportunities', *Research Policy*, vol. 24, pp. 185–205.

KRAFT, K. (1990) 'Are Product and Process Innovations Independent of Each Other?', *Applied Economics*, vol. 22, pp. 1029–38.

LEIPONEN, A. (1997) *Dynamic Competencies and Firm Performance*, Working Paper, IIASA.

LEO, H. (1996) 'Determinants of Product and Process Innovation', *Economies et Sociétés*, series Dynamique Technologique et Organisation, no. 7, pp. 61–78.

LEVIN, R. C., KLEVORICK, A. K., NELSON, R. R. and WINTER, S. (1987) 'Appropriating the Returns from Industrial Research and Development', *Brooking Papers on Economic Activity*, vol. 3 (special issue), pp. 783–831.

LUNDVALL, B.-A. (1988) 'Innovation as an Interactive Process: From User–Producer Interaction to the National System of Innovation', in: G. Dosi, C. Freeman, R. R. Nelson and G. Silverberg (eds), *Technical Change and Economic Theory*, London: Pinter, pp. 349–69.

LUNDVALL, B.-A. (1992) *National System of Innovation: Towards a Theory of Innovation and Interactive Learning*, London: Pinter.

LUNN, J. (1986) 'An Empirical Analysis of Process and Product Patenting: A Simultaneous Equation Model', *Journal of Industrial Economics*, vol. xxxiv, no. 3, pp. 319–30.

LUNN, J. (1987) 'An Empirical Analysis of Firm Process and Product Patenting', *Applied Economics*, vol. 19, pp. 743–51.

MANSFIELD, E. (1985) 'How Rapidly Does New Industrial Technology Leak Out?', *Journal of Industrial Economics*, vol. xxxiv, no. 2, pp. 217–23.

MANSFIELD, E. (1995) *Innovation, Technology and the Economy*, vol. 2, Aldershot: Edward Elgar.

MOHNEN, P. (1991) 'Survol de la Littérature sur les Externalités Technologiques', in F. De Bandt and D. Foray (eds), *L'évaluation Economique de la Recherche et du Changement Technologique*, Paris: Editions du CNRS.

MUELLER, D. C. (1967) 'The Firm Decision Process: An Econometric Investigation', *Quarterly Journal of Economics*, vol. 81, pp. 58–87.

PAVITT, K. (1984) 'Sectoral Patterns of Technological Change: Toward a Taxonomy and a Theory', *Research Policy*, vol. 13, no. 6, pp. 343–73.

PAVITT, K., ROBSON, M. and TOWNSEND, J. (1987) 'The Size Distribution of Innovative Firms in U.K.: 1945–1983', *Journal of Industrial Economics*, vol. xxxv, no. 3, pp. 297–316.

POHLMEIER, W. (1992) 'On the Simultaneity of Innovations and Market Structure', *Empirical Economics*, vol. 17, pp. 253–72.

ROTTMANN, H. and RUSCHINSKI, M. (1997) 'Beschäftigungswirkungen des Technischen Fortschritts. Eine Paneldaten-Analyse für Unternehmen des Verarbeitenden Gewerbes in Deutschland', *IFO-Studien*, vol. 43, no. 1, pp. 55–70.

SCHERER, F. M. (1983) *Innovation and Growth. Schumpeterian Perspectives.* Cambridge, Mass.: MIT Press.

SCHERER, F. M. (1986) 'Concentration, R&D, and Productivity Change', *Southern Economic Journal*, vol. 50, pp. 221–5.

SCHERER, F. M. (1991) 'Changing Perspectives on the Firm Size Problem', in: Z. J. Acs and D. B. Audretsch (eds), *Innovation and Technological Change.* London: Harvester Wheatsheaf, pp. 24–38.

SPENCE, M. (1975) 'Monopoly, Quality and Regulation', *Bell Journal of Economics*, vol. 6, pp. 417–29.

TEECE, D. J. (1986) 'Profiting from Technological Innovation: Implications for Integration, Collaboration, Licensing and Public Policy', *Research Policy*, vol. 15, no. 6, pp. 285–305.

UTTERBACK, J. M. and ABERNATHY, W. J. (1975) 'A Dynamic Model of Product and Process Innovation', *Omega*, vol. 3, no. 6, pp. 639–56.

VERNON, R. (1966) 'International Investment and International Trade in the Product Life cycle', *Quarterly Journal of Economics*, vol. Lxxx, May, pp. 190–207.

VON HIPPEL, E. (1982a) 'Appropriability of innovation benefits as a predictor of the source of innovation', in: *Research Policy*, vol. 11, no. 2, pp. 95–115.

VON HIPPEL, E. (1982b) 'Get New Product from Customers', *Harvard Business Review*, March–April, pp. 117–22.

XIANGKANG, Y. and ZUSCOVITCH, E. (1998) 'Is Firm Size Conducive to R&D Choice? A Strategic Analysis of Product and Process Innovations', *Journal of Economic Behaviour and Organization*, vol. 35, pp. 243–62.

ZIMMERMANN, K. F. (1987) 'Trade and Dynamic Efficiency', *Kyklos*, vol. 40, pp. 73–87.

7 Modelling Innovation Activities Using Discrete Choice Panel Data Models

Ester Martínez-Ros and José M. Labeaga*

7.1 INTRODUCTION

The main purpose of this chapter is to analyze the determinants of innovation activity using Spanish data at firm level corresponding to the manufacturing sector. We focus on the relationship between the R&D effort undertaken by firms, and the innovation decision claimed by them. We are really estimating a research production function (see, for example, Crépon and Duguet, 1997), where we include other controls as firm characteristics and market conditions in addition to the typical inputs.

Previous studies (Bound *et al.*, 1984; Hall *et al.*, 1986; or García-Montalvo, 1993) have examined the research function using lagged R&D expenditures as a measure of inputs, and patents as the output. This chapter departs from those studies in several ways. First, we explain the innovation decision rather than the number of patents. Moreover, we exploit the information available in the survey about the possibility of distinguishing product innovation from process innovation. An advantage of this indicator, as Griliches (1990) argues, is that it retrieves more closely the innovation activity because not all-technical research transforms into patents. Another advantage is the possibility of assessing the kinds of innovation carried out, which is not possible when using patents.

Second, we use the knowledge capital stock instead of lagged R&D expenditures as input within the research production function. It assumes that the firm's effort takes R&D as a specific input, in order to explain value-added differences among firms. The use of these variables has precedents in Hall and Mairesse (1993), and Crépon and Duguet (1997), using French data. Following this idea, we also introduce the industrial knowledge capital removing the own-firm R&D expenditures, in order to capture opportunity externalities in the product market.

Third, we consider additional determinants of innovation activity in the research production function and we separate them into two categories: firm characteristics and market conditions. In the former, we include firm size, capital intensity or the degree of vertical integration. In the latter, we assume that market concentration, growth of demand or the product elasticity could modify the firm innovation strategy.

The econometric treatment takes into account both that the dependent variables are binary, and that we have panel data at hand. We use several alternatives for estimating static and dynamic versions of the models. First, we estimate a pooled logit in levels under the assumption of absence of unobserved heterogeneity (see Amemiya, 1986). Second, we assume a specific distribution for the unobserved heterogeneity and estimate random effects logit models. Third, we use a two-step method following Chamberlain (1984), where in the first step we specify linearly the conditional mean of the effects, and in the second we devise the parameters of interest using a within-groups procedure.

There are important differences among the alternatives. When moving from one method to one another, we try to emphasize the importance of controlling for unobserved heterogeneity, but also the need to allow for specific feedback effects among some of the determinants of the innovation decision and the innovation itself (as in Blundell *et al.*, 1995, for example). Moreover, we relax the absence of correlation among firm heterogeneous effects and regressors, which is a crucial matter in the models, including the lagged dependent variable, as has been revealed in previous empirical applications (see, for example Hausman *et al.*, 1984). Finally, we take account of the possible simultaneity between the decisions to innovate in process and product.

The empirical evidence indicates that in the decisions to carry out innovations, there are different determinants (or effects) in the two equations. Moreover, we find that the lagged own dependent variable is important, while, after controlling for this dynamic effect, the significance of the alternative innovation indicator vanishes. Large firms in a highly concentrated market only find it profitable to carry out product innovations. On the other hand, we observe that the effect of technological opportunity disappears when we control for both experience and firm effects. Spanish manufacturing firms fulfil the Schumpeterian hypothesis in terms of the degree of market competition, but it is not possible to make conclusive comments as regards firm size. Size seems to be important for carrying out product innovation, but this is not the case for process innovation decisions.

The chapter contains four sections. Section 7.2 describes briefly the data supporting the specification used in the empirical section. We set up the theoretical framework, specify the model and explain the econometric techniques in Section 7.3. The empirical results are reported in Section 7.4, and Section 7.5 concludes.

7.2   AN INFORMAL LOOK TO THE DATA

It is very difficult to find satisfactory measures of new knowledge and the value of an invention to be used in empirical analyses (Griliches, 1990). In fact, the measure of technical change or innovations is approximated by a variety of variables, distinguishing between inputs and outputs of an innovation. One feature of this chapter is the use of an alternative output of innovation: the product and process innovation indicators. Our data set allows us the use of this kind of information. It corresponds to the Encuesta Sobre Estrategias Empresariales (ESEE) which was conducted over the period 1990–3 and surveyed over 2000 firms. This is an unbalanced panel, since some firms did not continue to provide information, for several reasons (mergers, changes to non-industrial activity, or ceasing production). New companies were included in the survey each year in an attempt to maintain representativeness. It therefore constitutes a mixed data set, where small companies (with fewer than 200 employees) are selected randomly using strata corresponding to four size intervals and twenty-one groups of two-digit industry codes of the CNAE,[1] while for large firms (more than 200 employees) the sample is exhaustive. After selecting the sample for inconsistencies in the variables, we have a balanced panel with 923 firms for each year.[2]

In order to offer a brief description of this survey, we group the sample using production activity and firm size. Production activity refers to the industries whose firms belong to, and the classification corresponds to, the NACE-CLIO. In this classification, we have available eighteen manufacturing sectors, but these have been aggregated into five for our analysis. Table A7.1 in the Appendix (see page 168) presents the definition of the industry variables and their correspondence with the original classification of sectors. The size aggregation is constructed using the number of employees at 31 December. It implies that we have to weight temporary workers using the period during which they have been hired by the firm. The ESEE uses specific size intervals: fewer than 20 workers, between 21 and 50, between 51 and 100, between 101 and 200, between 201 and 500, and more than 500. This aggregation is suitable for the typical Spanish structure (Segura, 1993). The industry classifications as well as the size intervals are constructed to maintain the representativeness of the sample.

Table A7.2 in the Appendix (see page 168) presents some descriptive statistics for three sample classifications as well as definitions of the variables.

The first column corresponds to all firms in the sample, while the remaining two columns correspond to samples for product and process innovating firms, respectively. Although there are differences among the three sub-samples, the main ones appear between the whole sample and the two sub-samples of innovating firms. The share of exporters with foreign capital ownership is larger in the subsamples of innovators than in the whole sample. On the other hand, firms with high levels of physical capital or more vertical integrated are not necessarily the most innovative. Comparing the frequencies by sector, there are more firms innovating in the electrical materials and machinery, motors and vehicles than in the whole sample, and fewer firms in the food and beverages, and leather, wooden and paper than in the whole sample. Finally, these simple measures do not show that large firms are significantly more innovative than small ones.

Two of the main issues addressed when analyzing innovation equations (either the number of patents or the innovation counts) are the dynamic structure of the input variables which enter the equation of interest and the experience effects; that is, the dynamics of the lagged dependent variables. In this chapter, we are only interested in estimating the decision to innovate,[3] but it should also be crucial to account for the experience effect, in the sense that the probability of innovating today could be affected not only by past realizations but also by the probability of innovating in the past. On the other hand, there could be some lag between the effort that the firm makes and the possible success (see Hall *et al.*, 1986). Our sample only contains four periods, and this small time series dimension could cause problems of lag truncation or lack of identification of the dynamic structure of the model. In the rest of this section, we try to justify the empirical specification used below concerning a way of solving these problems.

Table 7.1 shows the unconditional probabilities of innovating in product and process as well as several conditional frequencies; 25.5 per cent of the sample made product innovations over the whole period, and 31.1 per cent conducted process innovations. Looking at the frequencies over the four years, we observe the expected path. Frequencies for product innovations are 19.5, 27.52, 28.49 and 26.54 in 1990, 1991, 1992 and 1993, respectively, while for process innovations the respective frequencies are 19.07, 37.38, 33.91 and 34.13. The innovation frequencies are affected by the economic crisis of 1992. However, this crisis affected process innovations before product innovations. We can observe a big jump in the frequency when moving from unconditional probabilities to conditional on the most recent past. Firms innovating in product in the previous year, increase the probability of innovating in product today to more than 150 per cent. Firms innovating in process in the previous year increase the probability of

Table 7.1   Frequencies of innovation

	Product innovation in t	Process innovation in t
Unconditional probability	**0.255**	**0.311**
Conditional probabilities		
Product innovation in t	–	0.628
Process innovation in t	0.515	–
Product innovation in t − 1	0.637	0.529
Process innovation in t − 1	0.436	0.655
Product innovation in t − 1 and in t−2	0.734	0.575
Process innovation in t − 1 and in t−2	0.476	0.736
Product innovation in t − 1, in t−2 and in t − 3	0.790	0.629
Process innovation in t − 1, in t − 2 and in t − 3	0.566	0.829
Product and Process innovations in t − 1	0.679	0.695
Product and Process innovations in t − 1 and t − 2	0.744	0.763
Product and Process innovations in t − 1, t − 2 and t − 3	0.784	0.811

innovating in process today by 110 per cent. This *experience effect* is smaller after two or more periods engaging innovations. When conditioning on two previous years, the probabilities increase by 15 and 12 per cent respectively, while the respective increments are 7.6 and 12.5 per cent when conditioning on innovating in three previous periods.

Finally, we also report in Table 7.1 the conditional frequencies when the condition subset includes not only experience of own innovation but also of the alternative. Once we condition on the own past decision, the frequencies do not change a lot when augmenting the conditioning set by the alternative innovation event. For instance, the probability of innovating in product (process) is 6.6 (6.1) per cent larger for a firm innovating simultaneously in product and process in t − 1 than for a firm only innovating in product (process). These changes in the frequencies reduce as we extend the conditioning set. While all these empirical findings must be confirmed in the regression analysis, they seem to allow us the use of a parsimonious specification in the innovation decision equations. Some models, as proposed by Heckman (1981), it seems, do not need estimating. We do not estimate a model in which the experience effect is multiplicative (that is, a product of the innovation indicator for all lags of the dependent variable), for instance. Moreover, once controlling for own effect, the alternative measure of innovation does not seem to produce an improvement in the innovation frequencies.

7.3 THEORETICAL FRAMEWORK, EMPIRICAL SPECIFICATION AND ECONOMETRIC METHODS

7.3.1 A Model for Innovation Decisions

We measure the different determinants of technological innovation assuming the existence of a dynamic process in both decisions. This chapter considers the technological research as a heterogeneous activity, being important to distinguish between research addressed towards process innovation, and research addressed towards product innovation. Since process innovation is more related to firm costs, and product innovation focuses on product differentiation, we expect that the determinants of innovation types and the effects of other variables will be different (Lunn, 1986; Martínez-Ros, 1998).

We estimate the research production as a function of past research (S) and other control variables (X) which reinforce the achievement of new inventions:

$$E(I_{it}) = f_i(S_{it-1}, X_{it-1}) \tag{1}$$

Past research is measured as a knowledge stock variable rather than by using the traditional proxy R&D expenditures. So, we substitute expenditure on R&D by knowledge research, G_{it}, constructed as actual R&D expenditures produced within the firm plus the past-period knowledge which depreciates at a rate (δ) as a result of imitation:

$$G_{it} = S_{it} + (1-\delta)G_{it-1} \tag{2}$$

With this formulation, we assume that research contributes towards the innovation stock by generating a constant stream of incremental innovations.[4] In this equation, the relative productivity of research is a function of the technological opportunity in the industry, τ, so the marginal productivity will be $\partial f_{it}/\partial S_{it} = \tau_{it}$. Technological opportunity or product market externalities reflect the influences of technological push in the industry which occurs when exogenous changes in scientific and engineering knowledge reduce the costs of new processes and so increase the benefit of the firm (Lunn, 1986).

Related to other conditionings, X contains variables as firm characteristics or market environment that could affect the firm innovation decision. Specifically, we focus on testing the effect of *firm size* and *market competition*. On the one hand, following the Schumpeter tradition, we expect a positive sign in the innovation probabilities for larger firms, since they have more complementary financial, physical and commercial resources that provide for the development of more innovation activity. However, large firms may also be subject to controls that are more bureaucratic and this may have a negative effect on their capacity to translate capital stock into innovations. Moreover, if size is associated positively with market power, the incremental benefits of innovation may be lower for larger firms than for smaller ones. On the other hand, we could also think that the relationship between innovation activity and firm size is not monotonic. In the case of observing a size threshold, we must allow for quadratic profiles, for example (see Pavitt *et al.*, 1987, or Kleinknecht, 1989).

Market concentration would also increase innovation probabilities, both in product and process, according to the Schumpeter hypothesis, because firms that act as a monopoly have more incentives to maintain innovations as a barrier to entry. However, we can find a reverse effect, where firms in a more competitive market obtain larger profits when they develop innovation activity (Arrow, 1962). So the empirical evidence on this issue is not conclusive (see Levin and Reiss, 1989).

7.3.2   The Empirical Specification

Since we have available in our database the kinds of innovation in which firms engage (product or process), we can separate the innovation output in these two types and estimate the research production function for the two innovation decisions. Consequently, we are going to estimate the following two specifications for Equation (1):

$$IPROD_{it}^* = g(G_{it-1}, XFIRM_{it-1}, \tau_{it-1}, XMARKET_{it-1}, \varepsilon_{2it}) \qquad (3)$$

$$IPROC_{it}^* = g(G_{it-1}, XFIRM_{it-1}, \tau_{it-1}, XMARKET_{it-1}, \varepsilon_{1it}) \qquad (4)$$

where *IPROD* is the indicator of product innovation of firm i in period t, so that $IPROD_{it} = 1$ if $IPROD_{it}^* > 0$, and $IPROD_{it} = 0$ otherwise, and *IPROC* is the indicator of process innovation with $IPROC_{it} = 1$ if

$IPROD_{it}^* > 0$, and $IPROC_{it} = 0$ otherwise. We denote by ε_{1it} and ε_{2it} the error terms, which are decomposed into mixed errors and heterogeneous effects in some of the models estimated below.[5]

Equations (3) and (4) explain the innovation activities through their main determinants. We use as dependent variables the two dummies (*IPROD* and *IPROC*) because the ESEE provides this information directly from the firm's questionnaire. The effect of experience is introduced using the lagged latent dependent variables $IPROD_{it-1}^*$ and $IPROC_{it-1}^*$ or the lagged observed dependent ones, depending on the specification. These two cases differ in assuming whether only past innovation is important, or if the probability to innovate in the past could affect the current probability.

Notice that innovation activity is conditioned on the technological capital stock of the firm (G_{t-1}) which captures the previous R&D effort carried out by a firm affected by a depreciation rate. We assume a depreciation rate of 30 per cent as do numerous studies. It is constructed as in Equation (2) and normalized by firm sales. It represents the depreciated sum of past innovation search relative to sales. This implies that Equations (3) and (4) can be interpreted as pseudo-production functions of innovations, where *XFIRM* and *XMARKET* are explanatory variables of the innovation activity of the firm, for a given capital stock. Some variables included in *XFIRM* and *XMARKET* may also affect the capital stock G_{t-1}; that is, the stock should be considered endogenous. To account for this, G_{t-1} will be instrumented by its prediction $GINST_{t-1}$, which has been obtained by regressing G_t on industry and time dummies, firm characteristics, market characteristics and the past knowledge stock, under the assumption that the error term in this auxiliary regression is not autocorrelated.

Among *XFIRM* we include size, production technology, vertical integration, export activity and foreign ownership. Firm size is measured by the logarithm of the number of employees (ln *EMP*). As explained above, a positive sign would be in line with the Schumpeter propositions. But as there may also be negative effects of size on innovation activity after a threshold has been passed, we account for this possibility by using a quadratic relationship (ln *EMP2*).

The production technology is proxied by the ratio of fixed assets to sales of the firm (*KSA*). It represents the replacement value of the firm's machinery capital stock and is constructed following the traditional literature about the measure of capital stock (Blundell *et al.*, 1992). The tangible capital captures the positive effect of internal financing on research activity via reduction in costs. We also consider a dummy variable that captures the foreign ownership (*CAPEXT*). We like to test whether there is a discipline effect of firms with foreign capital on national ownership firms (see Baldwin *et al.*, 1999).

We also include a variable which proxies the firm export activity: *DEXP* is a dummy variable equal to one if a firm exports in any moment of the sample period. We assume that the development of export activities will produce incentives to innovate in order to compete in foreign markets. As a control of the vertical integration, we introduce the share that the intermediate products represent over the total firm production (*CISP*). The maintained hypothesis is that the higher the degree of vertical integration in their production activities, the lower the innovation.

On the other hand, in *XMARKET* we include industry shifters that try to characterize the market structure. We refer first to the degree of competition in the product market, proxied inversely by market concentration (*AVGMBE*). *AVGMBE* represents the average gross profit margin and is constructed taking means of the margin each year for the firms belonging to the same sector. It tries to capture whether market competition encourages innovation activity. A positive sign would give support to Schumpeter's hypothesis, while a negative sign would be in accordance with Arrow's predictions.

In order to take into account the demand structure, we consider the demand growth (*RECES*). Specifically, it is a dummy variable equal to one when the firm considers a recession in its product markets. Then we can determine how the business cycle affects innovation strategies. When firms are in a declining period we expect that, whatever the innovation, the decision to innovate will be lower. But we also expect that recessions affect process much more than product innovation decisions. Related to the demand function, we introduce an approximation of the product homogeneity. We use a dummy variable taken directly from the questionnaire, which measures whether the product is standard (*EP*). We expect a different effect of this indicator in product innovation decisions than in process innovation ones. While product innovation needs an elastic demand to create innovation gains, process innovation drives in the reverse direction. The more inelastic the demand, the more incentives to innovate in process.

Technological opportunity is approximated using the industry knowledge stock (*SPILL*), constructed again as in Equation (2). We try to retrieve the experience of an industry in the production of innovation effort, but removing the own-firm R&D expenditure and normalizing by industry sales. As Crépon and Duguet (1997) pointed out, it is also capturing an externality of R&D capital. The sign of the coefficient of this variable in the empirical model is ambiguous. We expect a positive sign because in an industry with a high level of R&D activity there will also be more spillovers that may facilitate innovation. However, it may also happen that in high-tech intensive industries, firms have more opportunities to imitate innovations, so the competitive advantage obtained by innovating firms vanishes because of imitation. Finally, in order to capture common time shocks and time invariant industry effects, we also include time and industry dummies in the specifications.

7.3.3 Econometric Methods

We are interested in this chapter in analyzing the determinants of innovation activity using data at firm level. Moreover, we would like to test whether these determinants are different in conducting process and/or product innovation. For these purposes, we are going to estimate discrete choice models for panel data. Let us assume, as it is the case in this chapter, that we have observations about the characteristics of N firms (N large) over T periods (T small). Our model of interest as presented in Equations (3) and (4) can be written in a more compact notation as:

$$y_{it} = 1(\beta' x_{it} + u_{it}) \quad i = 1,\ldots,N; \quad t = 1,\ldots,T \quad (5)$$

where $1(\beta' x_{it} + u_{it})$ is the indicator function of event $(\beta' x_{it} + u_{it} > 0)$. The probability that $y_{it} = 1$ (that is, firm i takes the decision of innovating in period t) is given by $P(u_{it} \geq -\beta' x_{it}) = 1 - F(-\beta' x_{it})$ where β are unknown parameters for our model of interest $P(y_{it} = 1/x_{it})$.

There are several alternatives for estimating these kind of models. Under the specification in Equation (5), since u_{it} does not contain individual heterogeneity, the best and simplest alternative is to apply the standard probit or logit models to the pooled data. We refer to this model as the *pooled levels* and its likelihood function can be written as:

$$\log LP = \sum_{i=1}^{N}\sum_{t=1}^{T}[y_{it}\log F_{it} + (1 - y_{it})\log(1 - F_{it})] \quad (6)$$

where $F_{it} = F(\beta' x_{it})$. When F is the cumulative distribution function of the standard normal, the specification is that of the probit model, whereas if F corresponds to the logistic function we have the logit model.

However, these models are not very useful, because unobserved heterogeneity is normally very important, and their absence leads to misleading inferences (spurious state versus true state dependence; see Heckman, 1981). In the presence of relevant effects (η_i), the decision is whether to consider them fixed or random. If we assume the firm-specific effects are fixed, we have to include them as additional variables for each firm in the equation of interest (Equation (5)). However, in a typical situation using panel data on firms where T is finite, there are only a limited number of observations of y_{it} that contain information about η_i. Any estimation of η_i is meaningless in this case because of the problem of *incidental parameters*.[6]

Since the number of firms N tends to infinity, we are interested in inferences for the manufacturing sector, and the fixed effects interpretation loses some sense. Moreover, the impossibility of including non-strictly exogenous variables (predetermined, for instance) makes this model very restrictive. If the effects are treated as random, $\varepsilon_{it} = \eta_i + u_{it}$, this is known as an error components model. We do not consider a time component in the error because the time-span of the sample is very small, and time dummies will control for these effects. We can consider two possibilities: (i) η_i and x are not correlated; and (ii) η_i are not independent of x (or of some of the regressors). Assuming that the explanatory variables and the effects are orthogonal, one can write the joint likelihood of $(y_{it},...,y_{Nt})$ without taking into account heteroscedasticity. Notice that even if u_{it} are independently distributed over i and t, $E(\varepsilon_{it}, \varepsilon_{is}) = \sigma_\eta^2 \neq 0$; η_i is a random sample from a univariate distribution G, indexed by a finite number of parameters δ. Then, the log-likelihood function becomes:

$$\log LRE = \sum_{i=1}^{N}\log \int \prod_{t=1}^{T} F(\beta'x_{it} + \eta_i)^{y_{it}}[1 - F(\beta'x_{it} + \eta_i)]^{1-y_{it}}\, dG(\eta|\delta) \quad (7)$$

But the absence of correlation among η_i and x has limited interest in our exercise. Managerial ability or corporate culture could induce more innovation activity that subsequently needs more resources, for example. In that case, the unobserved effect managerial ability would be correlated with some of the regressors. Moreover, the panel nature of the data does not provide advantages over a pure cross-section, except on efficiency grounds. If the effects are not orthogonal to the explanatory variables, *ML* will yield biased estimators for β. To allow for dependence between η_i and x, we can specify a distribution for η conditional on x. A possibility suggested by Chamberlain (1984) is to assume that $\eta_i = \Sigma_{t=1}^{T}\alpha_t x_{it} + \nu_i$. Now we are assuming that the regression function $E(\eta_i/x_{it})$ is in fact linear, and that ν_i has a specific distribution. Given these assumptions, the log-likelihood function under our random-effects specification is:

$$\log LLE = \sum_{i=1}^{N}\sum_{t=1}^{T} [y_{it} \log F_{it} + (1 - y_{it}) \log(1 - F_{it})] \quad (8)$$

where now $F_{it} = F(\beta'x_{it} + \Sigma_{s=1}^{T}\alpha_s x_{is})$ and F could again be the cumulative distribution function of the standard normal (probit model) or the logistic distribution (logit model). Chamberlain (1984) shows that we can estimate each of the T (reduced form) models by maximum likelihood (that is, T probits or logits) and then we can find the parameters of interest β by minimum distance in a second step. We derive the parameters of interest using a within-groups procedure at the second stage instead of minimum distance for simplicity (see Bover and Arellano, 1997), although at the cost of obtaining parameter estimates that are inefficient relative to those obtained by minimum-distance.[7] Our two-step procedure runs as follows. First, we estimate T discrete choice models (one for each cross-section) and form predictions for each i and t using the reduced-form parameters. At the second stage we use the predicted latent indicators, which are now observed variables, to estimate the structural form parameters. Since the model incorporates firm heterogeneity, we transform the variables to deviations from individual means (within-groups) in order to rule out these effects at the level of the structural form of the model.

7.4   EMPIRICAL RESULTS AND DISCUSSION

Tables 7.2 and 7.3 present the estimates of the models reported in the previous section. We assume that the distribution of the mixed errors is logistic. Results using probit models are very similar because the logistic is very close to the normal distribution (see Cox, 1970). In econometric terms, there are two issues in which we are interested. The first concerns individual heterogeneity while the second considers the experience effect.

In order to see the impact on the estimators of controlling for firm effects, we focus first on the static specifications (Table 7.2). The importance of unobserved effects can be checked by comparing the results in columns one and three (product innovation), or columns two and four (process innovation). The impact of all factors affecting innovation probabilities is reduced when moving from homogeneous to heterogeneous models. If, as expected, time invariant unobserved variables (managerial ability, corporate culture or specific know-how) affect innovation frequencies positively, the magnitude of the effects of the observables are biased upwards when we do not consider them. The homogeneity tests (LR) compare the likelihood values of specifications with and without heterogeneity, and clearly reject the null at standard significance levels. So, firm effects are important determinants of the innovation frequencies, and their absence could lead to wrong inferences.

Table 7.2   Static models

	Pooled levels		Random effects		Linear effects	
	IPROD	*IPROC*	*IPROD*	*IPROC*	*IPROD*	*IPROC*
Intercept	−2.713*	−3.767*	−2.705*	−4.167*	–	–
	(1.27)	(1.18)	(1.05)	(1.02)		
GINST/10	0.810*	0.638*	0.413*	0.604*	−0.089	0.026
	(0.15)	(0.15)	(0.15)	(0.16)	(0.08)	(0.06)
SPILL	0.022	0.101	−0.027	0.030	−0.013	0.006
	(0.51)	(0.09)	(0.05)	(0.05)	(0.01)	(0.01)
DEXP	0.841*	0.410*	0.585*	0.292*	−0.173*	−0.068
	(0.12)	(0.10)	(0.13)	(0.12)	(0.06)	(0.05)
KSA	−0.012*	−0.007*	−0.009*	−0.005**	−0.022*	0.001
	(0.004)	(0.003)	(0.005)	(0.003)	(0.003)	(0.002)
CAPEXT	0.024	0.101	−0.032	0.102	−0.338*	0.145*
	(0.12)	(0.09)	(0.14)	(0.14)	(0.10)	(0.07)
AVGMBE/	0.094	0.157**	0.083	0.157*	0.093*	0.083*
100	(0.09)	(0.08)	(0.06)	(0.06)	(0.02)	(0.01)
ln EMP	−0.211	0.286***	−0.015	0.334***	−0.472*	−0.554*
	(0.18)	(0.17)	(0.22)	(0.21)	(0.21)	(0.16)
ln EMP2	0.036*	0.000	0.023	−0.003	0.088*	0.069*
	(0.017)	(0.02)	(0.02)	(0.02)	(0.02)	(0.02)
RECES	−0.248*	−0.184**	−0.089	−0.158**	0.017	−0.169*
	(0.10)	(0.10)	(0.09)	(0.09)	(0.03)	(0.03)
EP	0.552*	−0.265*	0.558*	−0.256*	–	–
	(0.11)	(0.10)	(0.14)	(0.13)		
CISP	−0.326	−0.216	−0.199	−0.242	−0.359*	−0.479*
	(0.21)	(0.21)	(0.20)	(0.22)	(0.09)	(0.07)
χ^2	333.0	322.1	136.7	163.0	898.2	264.8
	(17)	(17)	(17)	(17)	(13)	(13)
LR	136.7	159.9	238.7	209.1	375.38	368.24
	(1)	(1)	(142)	(142)	(143)	(143)

Notes: Sample size: 2769 observations; Time and industry dummies included; Standard errors are in parenthesis; * Significant at 1 per cent; ** at 5 per cent; *** at 10 per cent. Pooled levels present estimates of Equation (6). Random effects correspond to estimates of Equation (7). Linear effects present estimates of Equation (8). χ^2: Chi-squared test of joint significance of the estimates (degrees of freedom): LR: Likelihood ratio test of random effects versus pooled levels (cols one and two), linear effects versus random effects (cols three and four) and linear effects versus pooled levels (cols five and six) (degrees of freedom).

However, since firm effects are potentially correlated with the regressors, as explained above, the random effects specification could provide inconsistent parameter estimates. The columns under the heading 'linear effects' report parameter estimates of Equation (8), allowing for correlation among effects and variables. These results show that managerial ability or other unobserved time-invariant characteristics of the firm are important determinants of the innovation frequencies. For example, firms with foreign

Table 7.3 Dynamic models

	Pooled levels		Random effects		Linear effects	
	IPROD	IPROC	IPROD	IPROC	IPROD	IPROC
Intercept	−3.529*	−3.514*	−1.177**	−4.034*		
	(1.39)	(1.27)	(0.66)	(1.10)		
$IPROD_{t-1}$	2.020*		1.292*	–	0.845*	–
	(0.11)		(0.10)		(0.04)	
$IPROC_{t-1}$		1.774*	–	0.824*	–	0.259*
		(0.10)		(0.09)		(0.03)
GINST/10	0.444*	0.488*	0.468*	0.565*	−0.127**	−0.001
	(0.15)	(0.15)	(0.15)	(0.16)	(0.07)	(0.05)
SPILL	−0.018	0.094	−0.028	0.047	−0.048*	0.008
	(0.05)	(0.11)	(0.05)	(0.06)	(0.01)	(0.01)
DEXP	0.599*	0.314*	0.614*	0.298*	−0.068	−0.030
	(0.12)	(0.11)	(0.13)	(0.12)	(0.05)	(0.04)
KSA	−0.009**	−0.006*	−0.009**	−0.006***	0.018*	−0.001
	(0.005)	(0.003)	(0.005)	(0.004)	(0.002)	(0.002)
CAPEXT	0.029	0.091	−0.001	0.101	−0.347*	0.155*
	(0.13)	(0.12)	(0.14)	(0.13)	(0.08)	(0.07)
AVGMBE/100	0.109	0.148***	0.096	0.151*	0.078*	0.083*
	(0.10)	(0.09)	(0.08)	(0.07)	(0.02)	(0.01)
ln EMP	−0.019	0.166	−0.001	0.269	0.240	−0.561*
	(0.19)	(0.18)	(0.21)	(0.21)	(0.17)	(0.14)
ln EMP2	0.013	0.003	0.015	−0.001	−0.006	0.068*
	(0.02)	(0.02)	(0.02)	(0.02)	(0.02)	(0.02)
RECES	−0.252*	−0.238*	−0.181***	−0.198*	−0.009	−0.170*
	(0.12)	(0.10)	(0.11)	(0.10)	(0.03)	(0.02)
EP	0.487*	−0.207*	0.515*	−0.234*	–	–
	(0.12)	(0.10)	(0.13)	(0.12)		
CISP	−0.250	−0.182	−0.248	−0.213	−0.398*	−0.330*
	(0.25)	(0.24)	(0.24)	(0.24)	(0.07)	(0.06)
χ_1^2	337.2	314.7	166.9	83.82	446.3	74.53
	(1)	(1)	(1)	(1)	(1)	(1)
χ_2^2	718.3	658.3	328.6	257.1	538.7	177.9
	(18)	(18)	(18)	(18)	(14)	(14)
χ_3^2	–	–	–	–	0.42	0.12
					(1)	(1)
LR	164.6	290.6	210.1	369.6	204.06	239.34
	(1)	(1)	(143)	(143)	(144)	(144)

Notes: Sample size: 2769 observations; Time and industry dummies included. Standard errors are in parenthesis. * Significant at 1 per cent; ** at 5 per cent; *** at 10 per cent. Pooled levels present estimates of Equation (6). Random effects correspond to estimates of Equation (7). Linear effects present estimates of Equation (8). χ_1^2: Chi-squared test of dynamic versus static models (degrees of freedom). χ_2^2: Chi-squared test of joint significance of the estimates (degrees of freedom). χ_3^2: Chi-squared test on the significance of the alternative innovation indicator (degrees of freedom). LR: Likelihood ratio test of random effects versus pooled levels (cols one and two), linear effects versus random effects (cols three and four) and linear effects versus pooled levels (cols five and six) (degrees of freedom).

capital innovate significantly less in product than firms with national ownership, once we control for correlated unobserved heterogeneity. The reverse
is true in the case of process innovation. The LR tests indicate the rejection
of the null of absence of correlation, conditional on their presence, among
effects and variables at usual levels of significance.

Our second concern is to test experience. We try to capture experience
using the lagged latent or lagged observed indicators. Although all
columns present results with the lagged observed indicator as the explanatory variable, the coefficients in the linear effects specification do not differ from those including the predicted lagged latent variable. The effect of
experience is very important, as many authors have shown in other con-
texts (see Hausman *et al.*, 1984 in an application with patents). The results
are affected independently of the specification considered. There are at
least two reasons. The first one concerns misspecification of the static
models as confirmed by the χ^2 tests (see Table 7.3). The second has to do
with the correlation among effects and variables. If we include a lagged
dependent variable in a model with unobserved heterogeneity, at least this
variable is correlated with the effects, and in their absence with the mixed
error. Again, as both experience and managerial ability affect the innovation probabilities positively, the parameters of the static models are generally upwards-biased. This can be observed by comparing columns 1 to 3 in
Table 7.2 with their counterparts in Table 7.3. There is no common pattern
in the results reported in columns under the heading 'linear effects',
because the scheme of correlation is more complex, given the assumption
that the effects depend on all the exogenous variables. Therefore, static
models representing innovation decisions are too restrictive to impose on
the data. Moreover, the sign of the coefficients indicates that Spanish
manufacturing firms innovating in the past have a higher probability of
continuing to innovate, as expected.

The effect of experience once we control for the correlation among
effects and variables can be tested by comparing the corresponding
columns in Tables 7.2 and 7.3. Misspecification of the dynamic relationship has important consequences for the results. The indicator of export
activities has no influence on the decision to innovate in product once we
have controlled for the variable 'experience'. This contrasts with its
contra-intuitive sign obtained in the static specification. Moreover, the size
profile on innovation probabilities is the same in the process decision and
the reverse in the product innovation decision, a result already detected by
Martínez-Ros and Labeaga (1996) in a product innovation count equation
using this same survey. Finally, the spillover effects and the effects of the
vertical integration variable are also affected. The negative sign of the

spillover effect in the product innovation decision indicates the absence of competitive advantage because of the easy imitation.

When comparing coefficients in columns 1 to 6 on Tables 7.2 and 7.3, we observe that the results depend on both the method used to estimate the equation and the static or dynamic nature of the specification. However, the testing procedure allows us to focus in the dynamic linear effects specification in Table 7.3. This model has been estimated using the within-groups procedure, as previously stated. In the reduced form equation for each year, we include all lags and leads of the exogenous conditionings plus the lagged indicators, under the assumption of uncorrelated mixed errors. On the other hand, we consider that the knowledge stock is endogenous, and consequently we adjust an auxiliary regression using again all exogenous factors.

Concerning results, we must first emphasize that the determinants of both innovation activities are very different except for the degree of market competition and the level of firm vertical integration. High concentration in the product market encourages firms to carry out product and process innovations of the same magnitude. It confers validity to the Schumpeter hypothesis in the sense that an important degree of monopoly power *ex ante* constitutes a good source to generate innovations. On the other hand, we observe that the higher the degree of vertical integration, the lower the probability of innovation both in product and in process, as expected.

The other conditioning variables have different effects on product and process innovations. Experience affects the probability of product innovation much more than process innovation. It could be related to the process in developing the new products. The experience in carrying out product innovation jointly with the ability of the manager, the culture of the firm or the know-how lead firms to have more competitive advantage in producing such types of innovation. Justification for absence of effects in the knowledge stock could be found in the importance of both heterogeneity and experience. We must note that firm effects (managerial ability, corporate culture, know-how, or other unobserved time-invariant variable), experience and the knowledge stock act in the same way concerning innovation probabilities. Consequently, when we take into account the dynamic structure of the model and the presence of these unobserved effects, the importance of the knowledge stock vanishes in both equations. Part of the technological effort is captured by the probability of developing new products in the past and the other part of it is captured by the firm effect. Although this seems to be an important and surprising result when comparing all the estimated specifications, we can find some reasons for it. When comparing the positive and significant effect that we find in both the pooled and the random effects models, the only difference from the linear effects specification is that in the latter we allow for correlation among effects and variables. The knowledge stock is a good candidate to be correlated with any of the time-invariant characteristic captured by unobserved heterogeneity. Moreover, the effect of experience is very important independently of the maintained hypothesis about the effects. However, when including them in the specification, the magnitude of the coefficients of $IPROD_{t-1}$ and $IPROC_{t-1}$ reduces. Finally, when assuming correlated effects, these coefficients reduce their magnitude again.

Another interesting result is the different influence of technological opportunity on both decisions. For product innovation, the spillover effect is negative, while for process innovation the effect is not significant. This is reasonable, since product innovation is easier to imitate than process innovation and, as a consequence, the threat of rivals is very much more active in this kind of activity.

High-capital-intensive firms tend to innovate more in product than in process. They reduce the costs of making new products using internal financing. The coefficient of this variable in the process innovation decision is not significantly different from zero. Although we expect a discipline effect of the foreign capital variable, it only happens in the process innovation decision. Managerial ability and experience seem to be more important in the development of new products, and once we take account of these variables, foreign ownership firms have a smaller probability of innovating than national ownership ones. Concerning the export variable, we do not find a discipline effect of competing in foreign markets, either in the decision of making product innovations or in the decision to conduct process innovations. It seems that integrated markets (as the Spanish one) require the same products and processes for competing.

Neither product nor process innovation require large firms with high complementary resources. In fact, only the very largest firms (5 per cent of the sample by size) innovate more in process than the rest. So, we find a threshold at the level of 2000 employees, in such a way that the probability of conducting process innovation reduces with size, except for those firms with more than 2000 workers.

We find that process innovation probabilities are affected by the state of demand, while product innovation decisions are not. A priori, we expected both innovation decisions to be affected negatively. However, only the influence on the process innovation frequencies can be justified, since firms developing new processes need a good environment in order to extract results. Moreover, process innovation needs more financing (either internal or external) than product innovation. The state of demand, which could be considered as a subjective proxy for the state of the economy, makes firms cut sources of financing and so reduce the innovation probability.

A final comment concerns complementarity between the two innovation decisions. We have tested this assumption by including the alternative innovation indicator in each of the equations. There are important effects of the lagged product innovation variable in the process innovation frequencies, and of the lagged process innovation indicator on the product innovation decisions when we do not control by own experience (either controlling or not for unobserved heterogeneity). However, once the lagged own variable is included, the effect of the alternative decision vanishes. The χ^2 tests corresponding to both equations are reported in Table 7.3. These figures do not reject the null of absence of complementary relationships at usual significance levels. This confirms the descriptive figures already shown in Table 7.1.

7.5 CONCLUDING REMARKS

We have estimated in this chapter several alternatives of discrete choice models for panel data, with the main purpose of analyzing the determinants of innovation activity, using a Spanish survey, the Encuesta Sobre Estrategias Empresariales, for the period 1990–3. Empirical evidence indicates that in the decisions to carry out innovations, there are different determinants (or effects) in the two equations. We find that the lagged own dependent variable is important, while, after controlling for this dynamic effect, the significance of the alternative indicator vanishes. In this sense, complementarity is not a requirement for innovating in both product and process once the model is specified correctly. We can affirm that once the experience effect and the unobserved heterogeneity are controlled for, the other determinants of innovation are affected sensibly. The Schumpeter hypothesis in terms of market environment is confirmed, but it is not possible to make conclusive comments in terms of firm size, since neither for product innovation nor for process innovation is size an important factor. Only those firms with more than 2000 employees decide to develop more process innovation than the rest. Finally, unobserved heterogeneity, which captures managerial ability, corporate culture, know-how or other time invariant variables, constitute an important determinant of innovation frequencies of Spanish manufacturing firms.

Appendix: Data

Table A7.1 Industry classification

Industries	NACE–CLIO	CNAE-74[1]
1. Chemical and metal products (CHEM)	1, 2, 3, 4	22, 24, 25, 31
2. Electric materials (ELEC)	6, 7	33, 39, 34, 35
3. Machinery, motors and vehicles (MACHIN)	5, 8, 9	32, 36, 37, 38
4. Food and beverages (FOOD)	10, 11, 12	41, 42
5. Leather, wooden and paper (LEATHER)	13, 14, 15, 16, 17, 18	43, 44, 45, 46, 47, 48, 49

Explanation: [1] "CNAE" is the Spanish National Classification of Economic Activities (1974).

Table A7.2 Descriptive statistics

	All Firms		Product Innovation		Process Innovation	
	Mean	Std. dev.	Mean	Std. dev.	Mean	Std. dev.
G	0.016	0.037	0.027	0.051	0.023	0.043
SPILL	0.019	0.693	0.044	0.871	0.047	0.829
DEXP	0.543	0.498	0.769	0.422	0.721	0.448
KSA	6.355	28.01	2.131	7.971	2.534	10.53
CAPEXT	0.218	0.413	0.324	0.468	0.318	0.466
AVGMBE	0.106	0.027	0.102	0.023	0.102	0.027
ln EMP	4.320	1.595	4.986	1.668	5.031	1.605
RECES	0.350	0.477	0.357	0.479	0.354	0.478
CISP	0.595	0.212	0.586	0.263	0.587	0.251
EP	0.661	0.473	0.714	0.452	0.632	0.482
CHEM	0.268	0.443	0.247	0.432	0.278	0.448
FOOD	0.169	0.375	0.154	0.361	0.157	0.364
ELEC	0.095	0.294	0.149	0.356	0.111	0.315
MACHIN	0.121	0.326	0.157	0.364	0.162	0.368
LEATHER	0.347	0.476	0.293	0.455	0.292	0.455
No. of observations	3692 (100%)		942 (25.5%)		1149 (31,1%)	

Notes: Sample in each innovation type corresponds to the observations in the period 1990–4. The percentage over the total number of observations is in brackets.

Definition of variables: G: Knowledge stock obtained using Equation (2). SPILL: Industry knowledge stock using Equation (2) removing own-firm R&D expenditure. DEXP: Dummy variable equals one if firm exports in any period. KSA: Ratio of fixed assets to sales. CAPEXT: Dummy variable equals one if firm has foreign capital as ownership. AVGMBE: Average gross profit margin of the industry. Ln EMP: Log of total firm employment. CISP: Share of intermediate products over total firm production. RECES: Dummy variable equals one when firm considers a recession in its production market. EP: Dummy variable takes one when firm produces a standard product. CHEM, FOOD, ELEC, MACHIN and LEATHER: Industry dummies.

Notes

* This chapter is based on the paper presented at the workshop of the TSER Network on Innovation and Economic Change held in Delft in February 1999. We are grateful to participants and a referee for many useful comments. We are also grateful to the Ministry of Industry and Energy for providing the data used in the study. The authors acknowledge financial support from DGES projects PB97-0185 and PB95-0980, respectively. The usual disclaimer applies.
1. CNAE is the National Classification of Economic Activities.
2. We use the balanced panel instead of the unbalanced one both for simplicity and for the need to use the maximum number of periods, given the dynamic nature of our model. However, all the features of the models presented below are applicable to both types of data.
3. Although we have available the number of product innovations, we have not used it in this chapter, since we are interested in analyzing the determinants of the decisions to develop innovation activities. However, Martínez and Labeaga (1996) present some evidence using the count of product innovations.
4. See Griliches and Mairesse (1984), or Hall (1990).
5. Note that we could express these equations in terms of an unobserved variable, profits produced by innovation, and then link the decision with profits, assuming that we observe a firm innovating when the profits of doing this activity are larger than those corresponding to the alternative regime.
6. In order to estimate the parameters of interest consistently, several solutions have been proposed as the conditional logit, or logit with fixed effects (Andersen, 1973; and Chamberlain, 1980). Although this procedure does not place restrictions on the conditional distribution of the effects given the regressors, it requires strict exogeneity of all the regressors, thus ruling out possible dynamic specifications.
7. There are different alternatives for estimating random effects models, as Keane's (1994) method of simulated moments, which allows the estimation of models with complex patterns of serial correlation without the need to evaluate multivariate integrals. Honorè and Kyriazidou (1996) propose the estimation of models in the presence of lagged endogenous regressors, and unobserved effects in the spirit of the conditional logit (that is, without modelling the effects explicitly). However, this method rules out non-stationary variables, time-series heteroscedasticity or serially-correlated mixed errors. Finally, Arellano and Carrasco (1997) present a model which takes account of heterogeneity without restricting the form of the effects, and allows for the inclusion of predetermined variables. They propose to estimate the model either by minimum distance, maximum likelihood, or by using a generalized method of moments.

References

AMEMIYA, T. (1986) *Advanced Econometrics*. Oxford: Basil Blackwell.
ANDERSEN, E. B. (1973) *Conditional Inference and Model Measuring*. Copenhagen: Mentalhygiejnisk Forlag.

ARELLANO, M. and CARRASCO, R. (1997) 'Discrete Choice Panel Data Models with Predetermined Variables', DT 9716. Madrid: *CEMFI*.

ARROW, K. (1962) 'Economic Welfare and the Allocation of Resources for Inventions', in R. R. Nelson (ed.), *The Rate and Direction of Inventive Activity*. Princeton, NJ: Princeton University Press.

BALDWIN, J., HANEL, P. and SABOURIN, D. (1999) 'Determinants of Innovation Activity in Canadian Manufacturing Firms: The Role of Intellectual Property Rights', Paper presented at the TSER Network on Innovation and Economic Change, Delft.

BLUNDELL, R. W., BOND, S., DEVEREUX, M. and SCHIANTARELLI, F. (1992) 'Investment and Tobin's Q', *Journal of Econometrics*, vol. 51, pp. 233–57.

BLUNDELL, R. W., GRIFFITH, R. and VAN REENEN, J. (1995) 'Dynamic Count Data Models of Technological Innovation', *The Economic Journal*, vol. 105, pp. 333–44.

BOUND, J., CUMMINS, C., GRILICHES, Z., HALL, B. H. and JAFFE, A. (1984) 'Who Does R&D and Who Patents?', in Z. Griliches (ed.), *R&D, Patents and Productivity*. Chicago: University of Chicago Press and NBER.

BOVER, O. and ARELLANO, M. (1997) 'Estimating Dynamic Limited Dependent Variable Models from Panel Data', *Investigaciones Económicas*, vol. 21, pp. 141–65.

CHAMBERLAIN, G. (1980) 'Analysis of Covariance with Qualitative Data', *Review of Economic Studies*, vol. 47, pp. 225–38.

CHAMBERLAIN, G. (1984) 'Panel Data', in Z. Griliches and M. Intriligator (eds), *Handbook of Econometrics*, vol. II, Amsterdam: North-Holland, pp. 1247–318.

COX, D. R. (1970) *Analysis of Binary Data*, London: Methuen.

CRÉPON, B. and DUGUET, E. (1997) 'Research and Development, Competition and Innovation. Pseudo-maximum Likelihood and Simulated Maximum Likelihood Methods Applied to Count Data Models with Heterogeneity', *Journal of Econometrics*, vol. 79, pp. 355–78.

GARCÍA-MONTALVO, J. (1993) 'Patents and R&D at the Firm Level: A New Look', *Revista Española de Economía, Monográfico: Investigación y Desarrollo*, pp. 67–82.

GRILICHES, Z. (1990) 'R&D, Patent Statistics as Economic Indicators: A Survey', *Journal of Economic Literature*, vol. 28, pp. 1661–707.

GRILICHES, Z. and MAIRESSE, J. (1984) 'Productivity and R&D at the Firm Level', in Z. Griliches (ed.), *R&D, Patents and Productivity*, University of Chicago Press, pp. 339–74.

HALL, B. H. (1990) 'The Impact of Corporate Restructuring on Industrial Research and Development', *Brooking Papers on Economic Activity: Microeconomics*, pp. 85–124.

HALL, B. H. and MAIRESSE, J. (1993) *Exploring the Productivity of Research and Development in French Manufacturing Firms*. National Bureau of Economic Research and Centre de Reserche en Economie et Statistique, WP 9326.

HALL, B. H., GRILICHES, Z. and HAUSMAN, J. (1986) 'Patents and R&D: Is There a Lag?', *International Economic Review*, vol. 27, pp. 265–83.

HAUSMAN, J., HALL, B. and GRILICHES, Z. (1984) 'Econometric Models for Count Data and an Application to the Patents–R&D Relationship', *Econometrica*, vol. 52, pp. 909–38.

HECKMAN, J. J. (1981) 'Statistical Models for Discrete Panel Data', in C. F. Manski and D. McFadden (eds), *Structural Analysis of Discrete Data with Econometric Applications*, Cambridge, Mass.: MIT Press.

HONORÈ, B. and KYRIAZIDOU, E. (1996) 'Panel Data Discrete Choice Models with Lagged Dependent Variables', Mimeo (Princeton University).

KEANE, M. (1994) 'A Computationally Practical Simulation Estimator for Panel Data', *Econometrica*, vol. 62, pp. 95–116.

KLEINKNECHT, A. (1989) 'Firm Size and Innovation. Observations in Dutch Manufacturing Industries', *Small Business Economics*, vol. 1, pp. 215–22.

LEVIN, R. C. and REISS, P. C. (1989) 'Cost-reducing and Demand-creating R&D with Spillovers', *Rand Journal of Economics*, vol. 19, pp. 538–56.

LUNN, J. (1986) 'An Empirical Analysis of Process and Product Patenting: A Simultaneous Equation Framework', *Journal of Industrial Economics*, vol. 34, pp. 319–30.

MARTÍNEZ-ROS, E. and LABEAGA, J. M. (1996) 'The Relationship between Firm Size and Innovation Activity: A Double Decision Approach', WP 96/04, Universitat Autònoma de Barcelona.

MARTÍNEZ-ROS, E. (1998) 'Explaining the Decisions to Carry Out Product and Process Innovations: The Spanish Case', WP 98/98, Universidad Carlos III de Madrid.

PAVITT, K., ROBSON, M. and TOWNSEND, J. (1987) 'The Size Distribution of Innovating Firms in the UK: 1945–1983', *Journal of Industrial Economics*, vol. 35, pp. 297–316.

SEGURA, J. (ed.) (1993) *Las Empresas Industriales en 1991*, Madrid: MINER.

SCHUMPETER, J. A. (1942) *Capitalism, Socialism and Democracy*, New York: Harper.

Part III
Spillovers and R&D
Collaboration

8 Do Non-R&D Intensive Industries Benefit from Public Research Spillovers? The Case of the Agro-Food Industry

Vincent Mangematin and Nadine Mandran*

8.1 INTRODUCTION

The aim of this study was to enhance our knowledge about innovation mechanisms in sectors in which firms innovate without doing internal research. Greater insight into the motives behind innovation in sectors where R&D is weak enables us to define appropriate tools for supporting innovation and to identify the most relevant levels of intervention (region, state, European Union (EU)).

Agro-food has a few very large corporations (for example, Nestlé and Danone), which co-exist with a large number of small businesses. Firms in the sector seldom participate in major research programmes, and hardly benefit from tax credits for research. Case studies (Mangematin, 1997) show that agro-food SMEs form local partnerships when they innovate. This observation raises two questions: first, can innovation policies suited to agro-food firms be defined? And, if so, what is the relevant level of intervention: region, country or EU, and what are the relevant tools? Second, how can firms that do not perform formal internal research benefit from spillovers from research done elsewhere, when they have no research or absorptive capacities?

Based on a statistical analysis of the sources of innovation in agro-food firms, this chapter identifies innovation mechanisms in a sector in which R&D spending is low. By studying the link between public research in a region, the density of firms that do research in that region, and the propensity of agro-food firms to innovate, we are able to grasp the relative importance of regional infrastructure in the innovation dynamics of non-R&D-intensive firms.

The first section analyses the different ways of capturing spillovers employed by those firms that do not perform internal research. The data and methods of analysis are presented in the second section, which provides us with a typology of the intrinsic characteristics of innovative and non-innovative firms, in terms of the sources of innovation. The third section shows that not only large firms benefit from the externalities of public research on a regional basis, but also small firms without any internal research capacity. The fourth section considers the results obtained and their theoretical implications.

8.2   FROM SUPPORT FOR R&D TO INNOVATION DYNAMICS

Most of the models developed in the economics of technological change consider R&D as the main source of innovation (Cohen, 1995). However, the distribution of R&D expenditures is highly asymmetric. In the French innovation survey in 1993, almost 70 per cent of agro-food firms (with more than twenty employees) claim to have produced at least one innovation, while research expenditures account for less than 1.7 per cent of value added.

8.2.1   Innovation without Internal Research

Intersectoral comparisons show that large firms have a competitive advantage to innovate in specific sectors such as instrumentation, the automotive industry and the aircraft industry, while SMEs have a higher rate of innovation in other sectors, especially low-tech sectors (agro-food, clothing industry and so on) (Acs and Audretsch, 1988). According to the Frascati manual's definition, fewer than 3000 firms carry out R&D activities in France. These are mainly large or high-tech firms (computer, software, biotechnology, for example). As established by Kleinknecht (1987), there is an obvious lack of formal R&D in SMEs, especially in low-tech sectors. Lhuillery and Templé (1995) emphasize the role of informal R&D in French SMEs, which causes us to wonder about alternative or complementary sources of innovation in these companies. In other words, the actual sources of innovation remain peculiarly mysterious if R&D expenditures are considered as the main input of innovation.

Based on multisector analysis of US data, Jaffe (1989) suggests that the weak linkages between innovation and R&D expenditures in SMEs result from the collective nature of innovation. Small firms gain more advantages from spillovers of R&D than large firms, regardless of whether the research activities are undertaken by public or private institutions. Link and Rees (1990) point out one interesting aspect regarding large- and small-firm research behaviour: 'Although large firms are more active in university-based research per se, small firms appear to be able to utilize their university based associations to leverage their internal R&D to a greater degree than large firms' (Link and Rees, 1990, p. 30).

Acs *et al.* (1994) show that the propensity of small firms to innovate is correlated positively with research expenditures of neighbouring universities. Interestingly, this correlation is weaker for large firms. Their propensity to innovate is correlated with private research centres' expenditures, wherever the research centres are located. These empirical results are quite stimulating. They shed light on the complementarity between private and public R&D expenditures, on the one hand, and an SME's propensity to innovate, on the other. They may represent a first explanation of the distortion between R&D expenditures and the propensity to innovate in SMEs.

However, the way in which SMEs in the agro-food sector benefit from spillovers from public or private institutions remains uncertain. Are inside research capacities needed to be able to absorb research done outside the firm (Cohen and Levinthal, 1990)? Do low-tech firms require specific modes of collaboration to be able to absorb knowledge and technology from public or private institutions?

Cohen and Levinthal (1989) show that R&D investments 'develop the firm's ability to identify, assimilate, and exploit knowledge from the environment' (p. 569). Examining what they call the absorptive capacity of the firm, they elucidate the two faces of R&D investments. On the one hand, firms invest in R&D to generate innovations. On the other, research activities contribute to the constitution and broadening of the firm's absorptive capacity. Defined as a set of knowledge and competencies, the firm's knowledge base remains a preliminary condition in the assimilation of spillovers from public research institutes and private R&D efforts. For Rosenberg (1990), fundamental research inside the firm has strong complementarities with external R&D from either the public or the private sector. Cohen and Levinthal, and Rosenberg, insist on potential synergies between the firm's own knowledge base and external flows of scientific and technical knowledge. However, absorptive capacity is considered as a by-product of R&D investments (Cohen and Levinthal, 1990, p. 129) which implies that it cannot be built for its own sake.

Other contributions have paid further attention to absorptive capacity. Arora and Gambardella (1994) distinguish between the scientific and the technological capabilities of a company. The former is required in the evaluation of relevant interorganizational alliances. It is both a means of knowledge diversification and a phase of scientific specialization. The latter (that is, technological capability) implements such knowledge, leading to innovations. Convincingly, Arora and Gambardella identify the role of R&D in the building of a firm's ability to exploit external knowledge flows. Therefore, absorption mechanisms cannot be limited to passive attitudes, but must include active processes of assimilation as well. In a similar vein, Mangematin and Nesta (1999) show that a firm's absorptive capacity is linked to the characteristics of the assimilated (or absorbed) knowledge. They analyze the relationship between three basic, empirically-defined concepts: the fundamental or applied nature of knowledge, the tacit or codified form of knowledge, and the absorptive capacity of the firm. They show that a low absorptive capacity inhibits co-operation in R&D. This collaboration concerns mostly applied fields, and needs informal interaction to support transfers (such as telephone calls, informal interviews and meetings). A high absorptive capacity extends the assimilation to all kinds of knowledge (applied, fundamental) through all types of channel (PhD students, scientific papers, technical devices). In all, absorptive mechanisms seem to diversify as the firm's absorptive capacity increases. They have also shown that channels of absorption in firms with research activities differ from those in firms without them. This difference of channels of absorption of knowledge leads us to assume differences in organization. Mangematin and Nesta show that channels of knowledge transfer are more informal (personal contacts, unpublished written notes, instruments) in low-tech sectors than in high-tech sectors. Even if goals are similar in low-tech and high-tech sectors, the forms of knowledge produced are different: technical devices for low-tech; articles, patents, as well as technical devices and new materials for high-tech.

In short, innovation does exist without formal internal research activities. What we do not know is whether the propensity of firms to innovate is different in sectors in which R&D expenditures are high, and in sectors in which they are low. It is generally assumed that the propensity to innovate is correlated strongly with the level of R&D expenditure.

8.2.2 Absorptive Capacity and Intensity of Innovation

If one accepts that innovation is based on research (whether internal or contracted-out), innovation in firms that do not carry out internal R&D is based on spillovers from outside research. Economic theory remains unclear on the types of spillover from which low-tech industries benefit. Empirical evidence shows a correlation between intensity of university research in a geographic area and propensity to innovate, irrespective of the economic sector. But research undertaken to evaluate the influence of local research infrastructure in innovation dynamics does not take into account problems encountered specifically in low-tech sectors. A number of conclusions can be drawn from research undertaken in this field:

- Innovation in a given region is related closely to public and private research spending in the region (Feldman, 1994).
- Innovation in a given region is related not only to public and private R&D spending, but also to all the region's technology transfer infrastructure (presence of technical centres, of a technology transfer organization and so on) (Feldman, 1994; Llerena and Schaeffer, 1995). Thus, the presence of complementary activities generates greater spillovers, and reduces the costs and risks related to firms' innovation.
- There are no eviction effects between public and private R&D spending; they are self-reinforcing, and thus create areas of expertise (Jaffe *et al.*, 1993).
- Only Audretsch and Stephan (1995) have focused their analysis exclusively on high-tech sectors. In sectors where innovation is based on science, geographic links disappear. These authors show that 70 per cent of all relations between biotechnology firms and universities are not based on geographical proximity. Several explanations can be suggested. Ties based on geographical proximity are strong when businesses are created, since entrepreneurs maintain steady relations with their network of local contacts. Having a 'star of science', like a Nobel prize-winner, for example, creates impulsion effects in the region, since firms have less need to turn to the outside. By contrast, in other cases, ties based on geographical proximity are very quickly replaced.

If we combine the different elements, the following two assumptions can be made for low-tech sectors:

Hypothesis H1: The greater the public research in a specific area, the higher the intensity of innovation.
Hypothesis H2: Only firms that have absorptive capacity can benefit from public research externalities.

In low-tech industries, the absorptive capacity is low and the channels of technology transfer between research organizations and agro-food firms are likely to be based on the trading of tacit knowledge and expertise, rather than on trading of codified knowledge.

We intend to identify the impact on innovation in agro-food firms of spillovers from public research and from R&D-performing firms in the sector. This approach will enable us to examine empirically the notion of absorptive capacity, by linking it to both the intensity of firms' innovation (radical innovation, incremental innovation, or no innovation) and to the characteristics of those firms that innovate (size, capacity to generate added value and to invest).

8.3   METHODS AND DATA

Do innovative firms have intrinsic characteristics different from those that do not innovate?

8.3.1   Sources

The matching of three separate surveys, namely (i) 1986–90 French part of the Community Innovation Survey (CIS); (ii) the R&D survey by the Ministry of Research; and (iii) the annual survey of firms, enables us to characterize the type of enterprise, the sources of innovation, the propensity of firms to innovate, and the types of innovation performed by the firm. Although the concept of geographical proximity is more relevant in terms of the coherence of the local industrial district, we chose to base our assessment of geographical proximity on the firms' postal addresses, since that was the only available information. Despite the limits of this approach, it enabled us to make comparisons with other empirical studies carried out in the United States, in particular (Jaffe *et al.*, 1993; Audretsch and Stephan, 1995). At the time of the study, only the 1990 CIS (innovation survey) was available for agro-food firms, since the 1993 survey had excluded this category. In 1990 the number of agro-food firms in France was 4218 firms, each with over ten employees; 1902 firms participated in the innovation survey, and 1320 claimed to be innovative; 80 per cent of the firms had only one plant. We assumed that all plants belonged to the same region as the firms.

8.3.2   Innovation in the Agro-food Industry

The 1990 survey distinguishes five types of innovation: (i) product innovation (with three subcategories: (a) improvement of existing products, (b) products that are new for the firm but already exist in the market, and (c) products that are new in the market); (ii) process innovation, which distinguishes (a) technological breakthroughs, and (b) substantial improvements to an existing process; (iii) innovations in packaging; (iv) organizational innovation; and (v) commercial innovation. In order to study the types of innovation in relation to their sources and the structures of research in the vicinity of the firm, we have grouped together innovations according to their degree of innovativeness:

1. No innovation.
2. Improvement to products or processes, including innovation in packaging, that is, incremental innovation.
3. Achievement of technological breakthroughs (product or process), that is, radical innovation.

Irrespective of category, innovations are primarily market driven (58.6 per cent). A minority are technology driven (39.5 per cent). Of all firms, 43 per cent claim to be innovative in general, and 54 per cent claim to be relatively more innovative than the average in their sector.

As shown in Table 8.1, the majority of innovations concerns improvements to products or processes.

Firms rely essentially on the acquisition of capital goods (38 per cent) to innovate. Next on the list are engineering studies (32 per cent), then

Table 8.1   Types of innovation

	Number of firms innovated (%)
Incremental innovation	53
Improvement of product	69
Product new to the firm	62
Process improvement	63
Innovation in packaging	52
Radical innovation	40
Absolutely new product	39
Absolutely new process	21
Incremental and radical innovation	7
Organizational innovation	25
Commercial innovation	21

Note: Innovations are primarily improvements to products or processes. They are rarely isolated. The same firm often improves a product and a process at the same time. Very few firms introduce only commercial or organizational innovations (8 out of 1305 cases).

internal R&D (26 per cent) and, finally, external R&D acquired from other organizations (18 per cent), or from within the group (17 per cent).

Judging from data on the sources of innovation, the number of citations of 'internal R&D' as a source of innovation highlights the limits of statistical surveys. When two different sources are matched (those of the statistical service of the Ministry of Research and those of the CIS survey), the number of firms that state the use of internal R&D as a source of innovation and the number of firms that claim to have internal R&D (Frascati definition) are different. In the Ministry of Research's database only ninety firms claim to do R&D, whereas 222 firms claim to have based their innovation on their own R&D. These two sources of information give a different picture of the same reality: the presence of internal R&D capacities.

8.3.3   Five Clusters of Firms

To understand innovation dynamics within firms, we characterized our sample in terms of the sources of innovation used by a firm when it wished to market new products or processes. Most of the variables are qualitative ones. Thus, we used a multiple correspondence analysis (Lebart *et al.*, 1995) on the sources of innovation (internal R&D, R&D in the group, external R&D, and engineering studies). It revealed three structuring dimensions: first, there is a contrast between firms that use engineering studies and those that do not; second, there is a contrast between firms that use R&D within the group, with those that do not; and, lastly, there is a contrast between those that do their own R&D with those that do not. We excluded from the analysis the innovative use of capital goods, new materials and patents, since these dimensions are not significant. In the multiple correspondence analysis, the different types of innovation were used as illustrative variables, which makes it possible to situate them on factorial axes structured by the implemented means of innovation. Thus, radical innovations seem related to internal R&D and engineering studies. Incremental innovations are equidistant from internal and external R&D, since innovations of this type tend to use these two types of resource. The firm creates new products in the context of research which mobilizes external R&D.

The multiple correspondence analysis was followed by a hierarchical classification (Celeux and Nekache, 1994) of the means of innovation, which reveals five clusters of firms as described in Table 8.2. This table warrants some explanation. We based the constitution of clusters solely on the sources of innovations (R&D and engineering studies). The classification obtained was consolidated. This method enabled us to improve the

Table 8.2   Five clusters of firms

Clusters	Number of firms	Sources of innovation	Nature of innovation	Characteristics of firms (average)*
1	706	No sources of innovation	No innovation	Number of employees: 66 Turnover: 104 MF Added value of turnover: 0.20 Added value per employee: 263 KF
2	199	Engineering studies No R&D	Product new to the firm Improvement of product Packaging innovation	Number of employees: 71 Turnover: 94 MF Added value on turnover: 0.13 Added value per employee: 234 KF
3	237	Engineering studies Purchase of external R&D No internal or group R&D	Improvement of product Improvement of process Packaging innovation New product for the firm	Number of employees: 70 Turnover: 97 MF Added value on turnover: 0.15 Added value per employee: 243 KF
4	349	Internal R&D No R&D from the group Engineering studies Purchase of external R&D	All kinds of innovation	Number of employees: 160 Turnover: 222 MF Added value on turnover: 0.13 Added value per employee: 269 KF
5	381	All sources of innovation	All kinds of innovation	Number of employees: 298 Turnover: 478 MF Added value on turnover: 0.12 Added value per employee: 343 KF

Note: * See text, page 184, for explanation of figures.

first classification based on the factorial analysis of multiple components. After three iterations, inter-cluster inertia is stable (ratio of inter-cluster inertia on total inertia: 0.7300 before consolidation, and 0.7344 after). From one iteration to the next, classes 2, 3 and 4 are very stable, and classes 1 and 5 slightly distorted.

We then characterized the nature of the innovation in the five clusters, and the firms in these clusters, by estimating the average value for four indicators:

(i)   *Number of employees*: average number of employees in the firm.
(ii)   *Turnover*: average turnover expressed in millions of francs.
(iii) *Ratio of added value on turnover* (AVTO): the AVTO ratio gives an indication of the firm's capacity to generate added value. It also constitutes an estimate of the degree of integration of the firm. The higher the ratio, the less the firm contracts out work.
(iv)   *Value added per person*: average VAPE expressed in kilo francs.

A Fisher test enables us to show that a substantial difference exists between the averages of each of the indicators, for each of the classes. The clusters obtained from R&D resources are different from the point of view of firms' structural variables.

Economic Significance of Clusters

Cluster 1 describes the firms that do not innovate and have no innovation resources. These firms are generally small in terms of both staff and turnover, are highly integrated, contract out very little, and have an average of two factories.

Cluster 2 describes firms which, through engineering studies, achieve product improvement innovations. These firms are small (in terms of staff and turnover), do not make use of formal R&D, and base their innovations on engineering studies. They contract out work on a large scale and have a weak capacity to generate added value per franc of turnover or per employee.

Cluster 3 describes small firms which rely on engineering studies and on R&D bought from other organizations to improve products or processes, and to create products that are new for the firm. These firms contract out work on a large scale.

Cluster 4 describes firms that have internal R&D capacities. They do not use R&D from within the group to innovate; they buy R&D from outside and carry out their own engineering studies. These are firms that are substantially larger than those in the preceding clusters. They contract out on a large scale and are integrated to a very small degree, although they have a good capacity to generate added value per employee. They produce innovations of the first type: products or processes.

Firms in *Cluster 5* are larger than those in the other clusters and carry out all types of innovation. They are integrated to a very small degree and have a very high level of productivity.

8.3.4 Structure of Public Research in the Life Science Sector

One of the characteristics of the environment of innovative firms is the presence of a public research organization in the vicinity. We therefore tried to estimate the weight of public research in each of the regions. No existing database combines the three key dimensions: scientific discipline, location, and resources.

The relative weight of public research in a region is a value that corresponds to a relative index. Indexes of the presence of public research are calculated both for spending (spending by research organizations, colleges in the agricultural field, grants from the ministry) and for employees. The data used do not take into account the research expenditures of the regions.

The resources devoted by public research to scientific and technological production in the four fields studied (agriculture, sea, life sciences, and environment) are spread as shown in Table 8.3. Public research is spread unequally across the territory in the four fields related to the agro-food sector (all four taken together). Thus, the regions have highly polarized research capacities. Links between the research capacities of the region and the innovative intensity of firms are not at all clear. An overall link appears to exist, but the specialization of each region is not correlated with the intensity of firms' innovation.

8.3.5 Density of the Industrial Fabric in the Agro-food Industry and Innovation

To explain regional differences in the propensity of firms to innovate, it can be assumed that innovations appear in localized clusters. First, a leading firm innovates and others follow suit, especially if they are located close to

Table 8.3 Relative weight of public research in each of the regions

Presence of public research	Weak	Average	Strong
Regions	Champagne, Franche Comté Limousin, Picardie, Basse Normandie, Haute Normandie	Alsace, Bourgogne, Lorraine, Midi Pyrénées, Nord, Auvergne, Centre, Aquitaine	Rhône Alpes, Pays de Loire, Languedoc, Bretagne, Ile de France, PACA.

Table 8.4   Presence of comparatively large firms (>150 employees)

	Fewer than 15% of firms with >150 employees (LD)	More than 15% of firms with >150 employees (HD)
Regions	Limousin, Franche Comtés, Languedoc, Basse Normandie, Auvergne, Lorraine, Haute Normandie, Bourgogne, Picardie, PACA, Poitou, Centre, Champagne, Alsace	Midi-Pyrenees, Aquitaine, Rhône-Alpes, Pays de Loire, Nord, Bretagne, Ile de France

the first one. We have chosen to describe the industrial district in the agro-food sector in relation to the sizes of firms: regions in which the density of large firms (>150 employees) is greater than 15 per cent, and regions in which the density is lower. We have chosen the threshold of 150 employees to distinguish large agro-food firms because 99 per cent of all firms with over 150 employees innovate. The small firms (20–50 employees) account for 55 per cent of the sample, while medium-sized firms (50–150 employees) account for 30 per cent of the sample. Relatively large firms account for only 15 per cent of the sample.

Table 8.4 reveals two groups of regions: (i) Low density of large firms (LD); and (ii) High density of large firms (HD). The propensity of firms to innovate (by type of innovation) is related to their size. However, the industrial structure of the region, as described in these two classes, is not linked to their propensity to innovate.

The construction of the three databases gives an idea of the national innovation system in the agro-food industry. These three bases describe all the institutions (public and private) on which the innovation dynamics in the agro-food industry are based. They are used to measure the extent to which a regional or national system exists.

8.4   RESULTS

8.4.1   Firms without any Formal Internal Research Capacity Do Not Have a Weaker Propensity to Innovate than Others

The innovation survey in the agro-food sector, matched with other surveys (on firms, on research in firms, on public research), enables us to map the linkages between the propensity to innovate (all types of innovation versus no innovation) and R&D expenditures in the industrial sector. Seventy per cent of firms in the agro-food industry innovate, although research spending is very low. The propensity of agro-food firms to innovate is similar to that of firms in high-tech sectors (information technology, electronics and so on), where R&D spending is greater than 5 per cent of the turnover. Figure 8.1 exhibits no significant correlation between the propensity to innovate and the percentage of added value dedicated to R&D.

If one analyses the links between R&D and innovation at the sectoral level, no significant correlation appears. But when one examines the relations between the intensity of firms' innovation (radical, incremental or no innovation) and sources of innovation (defined according to the above clusters), the Chi-square test shows that a link does exist. The more intense are firms' R&D activity, the more they achieve technological breakthroughs. The example of the agro-food sector shows that firms without any formal internal research capacity do not have a weaker propensity to

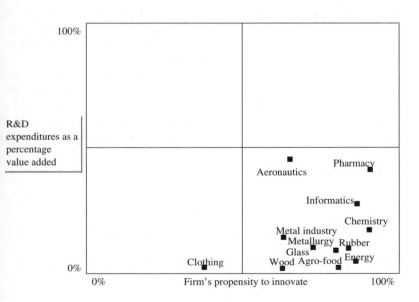

Figure 8.1 Propensity to innovate and R&D expenditures in some sectors in France

innovate than do others. By contrast, the nature of their innovations depends on the firms' research and absorptive capacities.

8.4.2   Intensity of Innovations, Spillovers and Characteristics of Firms

Hypotheses H1 (the greater the amount of public research in a specific area, the higher the intensity of innovation) and H2 (only firms that have an absorptive capacity can benefit from public research externalities) can be tested simultaneously. There are two complementary analyses: first, the study of determinants of innovation intensity (radical innovation, incremental innovation, and no innovation), and second, the analysis of the effects of geographical proximity with public research, or of large innovative firms, on the propensity to innovate. The typology of firms (see Section 8.3.3) reveals the influence of intrinsic characteristics on the propensity to innovate.

The study of the influence of each of the variables that describe the characteristics of firms, and the externalities of public research and of other firms in the sector, generates a better understanding of the relative role of factors influencing innovation in the agro-food industry. The method used to analyze the influence of various variables on the dependent variable is a multinomial logout model.

The endogenous variable is the intensity of innovation (radical, incremental, and no innovation). The models presented in Appendix 8.2 compare the marginal influence of exogenous variables on the intensity of innovation. The exogenous variables are grouped into two categories (individual characteristics of firms, and spillovers from public or private research).

Several models are estimated:

Model 1: $\text{Prob}(\text{Inno} = \text{intensity of innov}) = \text{cste} + \alpha\text{AVTO} + \beta\text{INVA} + \gamma\text{NBE} + \varepsilon$.

Model 2: $\text{Prob}(\text{Inno} = \text{intensity of innov}) = \text{cste} + \alpha\text{AVTO} + \beta\text{INVA} + \gamma\text{NBE} + \delta\text{DENSITY} + \varepsilon$.

Model 3: $\text{Prob}(\text{Inno} = \text{intensity of innov}) = \text{cste} + \alpha\text{AVTO} + \beta\text{INVA} + \gamma\text{NBE} + \varphi\text{PUBLIC R\&D} + \varepsilon$.

All the coefficients α, β, γ, δ and φ describe the marginal influence of a variable compared to the reference group 'incremental innovation' of the endogenous variable.

AVTO is value added as a percentage of turnover; INVA is investment as a percentage of value added; NBE is the number of employees; DENSITY describes the percentage of large firms in the region; and PUBLIC R&D is the intensity of public research in the region.

Individual Characteristics of Firms

Estimates in Table 8.2 can be summarized as follows:

(i)   Compared to firms that have a low AVTO (Added Value over Turnover) ratio, firms that have a high ratio have a significantly higher marginal probability of realizing radical innovation than realizing incremental innovation. Those that have a high AVTO ratio have no significant difference of marginal probability of realizing incremental innovation, and of realizing no innovation.

(ii) The higher the INVA (Investment over Value Added) ratio, the higher is the intensity of innovation. Firms that have a high INVA ratio have significantly lower marginal probability of realizing no innovation than of incremental innovation.

(iii) The higher the number of employees, the higher the intensity of innovation. There seems to be an obvious relation between the size of the firm and the propensity to innovate. But, in that case, what are called 'large firms' describe relatively small companies (over 50 employees). The intensity of innovation is higher (radical innovation) in firms with over 50 employees.

Spillovers from Public or Private Research

(i)   The proportion of large firms in a region has no relation to the intensity of innovation.

(ii) The degree of presence of public research in life science increases the probability of having some innovations. The intensity of innovation is not linked with the degree of presence of public research in life science in the geographic area. The presence of academic labs influences the marginal probability of firms to innovate, but does not determine the intensity of innovation.

Empirical analysis in Table A8.1 in Appendix 8.2 confirms the relationship between the size of the firm and the intensity of its innovations (radical, incremental, and no innovation). There are relations between the firm's propensity to invest (INVA) and its number of employees, on the one hand, and the intensity of innovation, on the other. For the firm's capacity to generate added value (AVTO), the logit model does not enable the highlighting of a marginal difference between firms that produce incremental innovations and those that do not innovate. The intensity of innovation does not influence the capacity of the firm to generate added value.

8.4.3   Sources of Innovation, Spillovers and Characteristics of Firms

The methodology outlined in Section 8.3 is based on the sources of innovation used by firms. To what extent are the characteristics of firms and the spillovers they can benefit from linked to the sources of innovation ? Table A8.2 presented in Appendix 8.3 explains a firm's belonging to one of the following classes 1. No sources of innovation; 2. No R&D, but engineering studies; 3. Purchase of external R&D; 4. All sources except R&D in the group; or 5. All sources of innovation. Does the propensity to invest influence membership of a class? Does the number of employees influence the class to which the firm belongs?

Individual Characteristics of Firms

The results obtained in Table A8.2 confirm the typology presented in Table 8.2 in Section 8.3.3 (see page 183). As pointed out in Table 8.2, compared to firms that do not innovate, firms that do innovate do not have a greater capacity to generate added value per franc of turnover, except for Class 2, which characterizes firms that produce incremental innovations without R&D.

Investments in tangible and intangible capital goods by firms that innovate are significantly greater than those of firms that do not innovate, except for firms in Cluster 3, which produce incremental innovations by buying R&D from outside.

The number of employees of firms that innovate is significantly greater than that of firms that do not innovate, for Clusters 4 and 5, that is, for firms that have in-house research capacities.

Confirmation has been found of the results obtained in the typology of firms, with significant differences of structure between firms, depending on the sources of innovation they mobilize.

Spillovers from Public or Private Research

By contrast, the presence in the region of a high density of large firms does not affect the overall innovation dynamics. In general, the greater the presence of academic labs in a region, the higher the proportion of firms that have done some innovation. But the role of public research depends on the source that firms are using for innovation: the most significant effects are for Type 2 firms (no R&D as a source of innovation and incremental innovations) and Type 5 firms (all sources of innovation) when the presence of public research is strong, and only for Type 2 firms when the presence is average. It seems that firms can benefit from public research of the same region even if the firm has no formal internal R&D but they realize mainly 'small' innovations. The geographic proximity allows firms to benefit from the spillovers on an informal basis (advice, use of public research equipment and so on).

8.5   CONCLUSIONS

The above sheds light on the specific dynamics of local spillovers of R&D, and provides empirical material to define public policy to support innovation in low-tech. The propensity to innovate of firms in a particular a region is not linked with the density of large firms in the same geographic area. Spillovers from agro-food firms that have research capacity seem to be very low, and firms that have their own R&D capacities are more likely to realize radical than incremental innovation.

The presence of academic labs in a geographic area influences the propensity of firms to innovate, but not the intensity of innovation. However, the presence of academic labs in a specific geographic area seems to stimulate mainly incremental innovation in firms. Academic labs seem to play a role as a catalyst in innovation. They increase the linkages between actors potentially involved in agro-food innovation, and allow small firms without any research capacities to innovate. But they provide no specific help to firms that want to realize radical innovation. Spillovers are more technical than scientific in that way. Expertise from public research and access to specific equipment as well as skilled human capital (public research and universities are closely linked) contribute to the production and diffusion of knowledge and expertise. It increases the propensity to innovate of SMEs that do not have any internal research facilities.

As public policy supports formal R&D rather than innovation, low-tech SMEs are excluded from public authority support because they do not have a formal R&D structure. Our analysis shows that academic research plays a part in each cluster of agro-food firms. Such an observation questions the tools that can be used to stimulate innovation that is not based on internal research. To what extent do subsidies given to academics stimulate innovation? And what is the relevant level of intervention by public authorities?

Appendix 8.1:   Methodology to Estimate Public Expenditures by Region in Life Sciences and Agro-food Sciences

The procedure used to estimate public expenditures per region and per scientific field is based on the matching of three databases:

- Resources devoted to research (spending and staff) by research organizations and universities;
- Distribution by socioeconomic fields and by research organization and university; and
- Regional distribution of research organizations and universities.

The translation of a scientific discipline into a business sector is a tricky exercise. We chose to adhere to two principles:

(i)   Firms are capable of using knowledge, equipment and generic research equipment produced by public research in several sectors. In this way we are not, strictly speaking, limited to disciplines related to agriculture.
(ii)   The breakdown into sectors of activity (NAF at INSEE) introduces a problem. It is not possible to distinguish between equipment manufacturers that are related to the agro-food industry, and to what degree, and those that are not. The technology transfer by equipment manufacturers to the agro-food industry remains impossible to capture in firm-level statistics. It is also difficult to map the links between public research in the equipment and agro-food sectors.

The Ministry's databases reveal four fields related to the agro-food sector: agriculture, life sciences, sea, and environment. Resources devoted to research are broken down in the following way in terms of region and in terms of fields:

(i)   Distribution of resources in terms of fields, institutes and scientific departments, for the institutes and scientific departments which state that one of the preceding fields is a primary objective.
(ii)   Sum of spending per objective, per institute.

(iii) Location of firms, per region.
(iv) Breakdown of the resources devoted to research, per region and per objective.
(v) Calculation of the relative weight of the region.

Appendix 8.2: Intensity of Innovations, Spillovers and Characteristics of Firms

The characteristics of the model are detailed below.

The endogenous variable covers three categories: radical innovation, incremental innovation and no innovation. The models compare the marginal influence of exogenous variables on the intensity of innovation.

The exogenous variables are grouped into four categories:

- Individual characteristics of firms;
- Ratio of Value Added/Turnover (AVTO) (strong, weak); the break is set at 0.2;
- Ratio of Investment over Value Added (INVA) (strong, weak); the break is set at 0.2; and
- Number of employees (fewer than 49; more than 50).

In this model, we analyze the structural characteristics of firms rather than the source of innovation. Structural characteristics describe firms in the agro-food industry with no a priori relation to sources of innovation.

- Intensity of the presence of public research;
- Public research in the four fields (PUBLIC R&D), divided up into 3 classes: strong, average, weak);
- Density of large firms in the industrial district;
- Density of large firms in the region (DENSITY), divided up into 2 classes, >15% of the total number of firms and <15%.

We tested several models. All coefficients of intensities of innovation are compared to the reference group 'incremental innovation'.

Appendix 8.3: Sources of Innovation, Spillovers and Characteristics of Firms

The endogenous variable is the firm's belonging to a cluster. Exogenous variables are the characteristics of the firm, the density of large firms in the industrial fabric and the degree of presence of public research. The data are interpreted as a marginal probability in relation to class 1 (no source of innovation). The endogenous variables are the same as in Table A8.1.

Table A8.1 Analysis of the variables that influence the intensity of innovation, by multinomial logistic regression

	Intensity of innovation	Model 1		Model 2		Model 3	
		Coefficient (st. deviation)	Probability	Coefficient (st. deviation)	Probability	Coefficient (st. deviation)	Probability
Intercept	Radical/incremental	−0.200 (0.067)	0.003 (***)	−0.193 (0.067)	0.000 (***)	−0.200 (0.07)	0.006 (***)
	No innovation/ incremental	−0.357 (0.074)	0.000 (***)	−0.366 (0.074)	0.000 (***)	−0.283 (0.07)	0.002 (***)
AVTO High	Radical/incremental	0.101 (0.06)	0.09 (**)	0.105 (0.062)	0.08 (**)	0.098 (0.062)	0.002 (***)
High	No innovation/ incremental	−0.083 (0.06)	0.17	−0.088 (0.06)	0.151	−0.106 (0.06)	0.614
INVA High	Radical/incremental	0.16 (0.06)	0.001 (***)	0.161 (0.06)	0.01 (**)	0.157 (0.06)	0.08 (**)
High	No innovation/ incremental	−0.131 (0.071)	0.06 (**)	−0.134 (0.07)	0.05 (**)	−0.141 (0.07)	0.04 (**)
Number employees High	Radical/incremental	0.243 (0.059)	0.000 (***)	0.247 (0.05)	0.000 (***)	0.242 (0.05)	0.000 (***)
High	No innovation/ incremental	−0.227 (0.059)	0.000 (***)	−0.228 (0.05)	0.001 (***)	−0.221 (0.05)	0.002 (***)

Variable		Category	Model 1		Model 2		Model 3	
DENSITY	<15	Radical/incremental			0.0375 (0.05)	0.531		
	<15	No innovation/ incremental			−0.0423 (0.058)	0.467		
PUBLIC R&D	High	Radical/incremental					0.035 (0.08)	0.669
	High	No innovation/ incremental					−0.191 (0.08)	0.017 (***)
	Medium	Radical/incremental					−0.053 (0.086)	0.535
	Medium	No innovation/ incremental					−0.166 (0.081)	0.043 (***)
Likelihood ratio			DF = 8	0.346	DF = 22	0.220	DF = 36	0.184
Number of observations	1785							

Notes: *How to read Table A8.1*

1. The likelihood ratio gives the general quality of the model. Thus, Model 3 appears to have a better quality than the others.

2. For example, in Model 1, variable AVTO: compared to firms that have a low Value added over Turnover ratio, firms with a high ratio have a significantly higher marginal probability to realize radical innovation than to realize incremental innovation. Those that have a high AVTO ratio have no significant difference of marginal probability of realizing incremental innovation and realizing no innovation.

*** significance 1%; **significance 5%; *significance 10%.

196

Table A8.2 Analysis of the variables that influence the presence in a cluster, by multinomial logistic regression

Presence in cluster number		Model 1		Model 2		Model 3	
		Coefficient (st. deviation)	Probability	Coefficient (st. deviation)	Probability	Coefficient (st. deviation)	Probability
Intercept	Cluster 2/Cluster 1	-1.22 (0.099)	0.00 (***)	-1.22 (0.10)	0.00 (***)	-1.39 (0.11)	0.00 (**)
	Cluster 3/Cluster 1	-1.12 (0.099)	0.00 (***)	-1.11 (0.09)	0.00 (***)	-1.21 (0.10)	0.00 (***)
	Cluster 4/Cluster 1	-0.63 (0.08)	0.00 (***)	-0.62 (0.08)	0.00 (***)	-0.68 (0.08)	0.00 (***)
	Cluster 5/Cluster 1	-0.60 (0.08)	0.00 (***)	-0.60 (0.08)	0.00 (***)	-0.68 (0.08)	0.00 (***)
AVTO High	Cluster 2/Cluster 1	0.14 (0.08)	0.10 (*)	0.14 (0.08)	0.10 (*)	0.15 (0.08)	0.09 (**)
High	Cluster 3/Cluster 1	0.04 (0.08)	0.61	0.04 (0.08)	0.61	0.04 (0.08)	0.57
High	Cluster 4/Cluster 1	0.09 (0.07)	0.18	0.09 (0.07)	0.19	0.09 (0.07)	0.18
High	Cluster 5/Cluster 1	-0.05 (0.07)	0.42	-0.05 (0.07)	0.42	-0.05 (0.07)	0.44
INVA High	Cluster 2/Cluster	0.18 (0.09)	0.06 (**)	0.18 (0.09)	0.05 (**)	0.19 (0.09)	0.04 (***)
High	Cluster 3/Cluster 1	-0.03 (0.09)	0.78	-0.02 (0.09)	0.78	-0.02 (0.09)	0.87

Variable	Level	Comparison	Est. (SE)	p	Est. (SE)	p	Est. (SE)	p
	High	Cluster 5/Cluster 1	0.29 (0.08)	0.00 (***)	0.29 (0.07)	0.00 (***)	0.30 (0.08)	0.00 (***)
Number employees	High	Cluster 2/Cluster 1	0.05 (0.08)	0.58	−0.60 (0.08)	0.00 (***)	0.04 (0.08)	0.61
	High	Cluster 3/Cluster 1	0.13 (0.08)	0.09 (**)	0.04 (0.08)	0.61	0.12 (0.08)	0.10 (*)
	High	Cluster 4/Cluster 1	0.34 (0.069)	0.000 (***)	0.13 (0.07)	0.08 (**)	0.34 (0.06)	0.00 (***)
	High	Cluster 5/Cluster 1	0.72 (0.07)	0.000 (***)	0.35 (0.06)	0.00 (***)	0.71 (0.07)	0.00 (***)
DENSITY	<15	Cluster 2/Cluster 1			−0.03 (0.08)	0.72		
	<15	Cluster 3/Cluster 1			0.03 (0.07)	0.61		
	<15	Cluster 4/Cluster 1			0.05 (0.06)	0.43		
	<15	Cluster 5/Cluster 1			−0.01 (0.07)	0.82		
PUBLIC R&D	High	Cluster 2/Cluster 1					0.38 (0.12)	0.00 (***)
	High	Cluster 3/Cluster 1					0.21 (0.11)	0.05 (**)
	High	Cluster 4/Cluster 1					0.18 (0.09)	0.09 (**)
	High	Cluster 5/Cluster 1					0.26 (0.09)	0.00 (***)
	Medium	Cluster 2/Cluster 1					0.24 (0.12)	0.05 (**)

Table A8.2 Continued

Presence in cluster number		Model 1		Model 2		Model 3	
		Coefficient (st. deviation)	Probability	Coefficient (st. deviation)	Probability	Coefficient (st. deviation)	Probability
Medium	Cluster 3/Cluster 1					0.17 (0.11)	0.12
Medium	Cluster 4/Cluster 1					0.06 (0.09)	0.48
Medium	Cluster 5/Cluster 1					0.08 (0.10)	0.42
Likelihood ratio	DF = 8	DF = 16	0.322	DF = 44	0.222	DF = 72	0.632
Number of observations	1785						

Notes: ***significance 1%; **significance 5%; *significance 10%.

Note

* The authors wish to thank the Rhône Alpes Region and the INRA/DADP for their financial support for this research. Aupelf/Urelf enabled us to initiate collaboration with UQAM, and we are indebted to them for that assistance. We also benefited from comments by the steering committee and the scientific committee of the INRA/DADP – Rhône-Alpes project, and wish to thank them for their stimulating remarks. We similarly benefited from comments made at the TSER workshop *Innovation and Economic Change: Exploring CIS Micro Data*, Delft, 12–13 February 1999. Of course, the usual restrictions about the responsibility of mistakes apply.

References

ACS, Z., AUDRETSCH, D. and FELDMAN, M. (1994) 'R&D Spillovers and the Recipient Firm Size', *Review of Economics and Statistics*, vol. 76, no. 2, pp. 336–40.

ACS, Z. J. and AUDRETSCH, D. B. (1988) 'Innovation in Large and Small Firms: An Empirical Analysis', *American Economic Review*, vol. 78, no. 4, pp. 678–90.

ARORA, A. and GAMBARDELLA, A. (1994) 'Evaluating Technological Information and Utilizing It', *Journal of Economic Behavior and Organization*, vol. 24, pp. 91–114.

AUDRETSCH, D. and STEPHAN, P. (1995) 'Company Scientist Locational Links: The Case of Biotechnology', CEPR Working Paper.

CELEUX, G. N. and NAKACHE, J. P. (1994) *Analyze Discriminante sur Variables Qualitatives*, Paris: Polytechica.

COHEN, W. (1995) 'Empirical Studies of Innovative Activity', in P. Stoneman (ed.), *Handbook of the Economics of Innovation and Technological Change.* London: Basil Blackwell, pp. 182–263.

COHEN, W. M. and LEVINTHAL, D. A. (1989) 'Innovation and Learning: The Two Faces of R&D', *Economic Journal*, vol. 99, pp. 569–96.

COHEN, W. M. and LEVINTHAL, D. A. (1990) 'Absorptive Capacity, a New Perspective of Learning and Innovation', *Administrative Science Quarterly*, vol. 35, pp. 128–52.

FELDMAN, M. (1994) *The Geography of Innovation.* Boston, Mass.: Kluwer.

JAFFE, A. (1989) 'Real Effects of Academic Research', *American Economic Review*, vol. 79, no. 5, pp. 958–70.

JAFFE, A., TRAJTENBERG, M. and HENDERSON, R. (1993) 'Geographic Localization of Knowledge Spillovers as Evidenced by Patent Citations', *Quarterly Journal of Economics*, vol. 108, no. 3, pp. 577–98.

KÉRIHUEL, A. (1995) 'L'Innovation dans les Industries Agro-alimentaires', in SESSI (French Ministry of Industry, ed.), *L'Innovation Technologique.* Paris, Dunod, pp. 307–10.

KLEINKNECHT, A. (1987) 'Measuring R&D in Small Firms: How Much Are We Missing?', *Journal of Industrial Economics*, vol. 36, pp. 253–6.

LEBART, P., MORINEAU, L. and PIRON, R. (1995) *Statistiques Exploratoires Multi-dimensionnelles.* Paris: Dunod.

LHUILLERY, S. and TEMPLÉ, P. (1995) 'Organization de la R&D et Innovation', in SESSI (French Ministry of Industry, ed.), *L'Innovation Technologique*. Paris, Dunod, pp. 239–47.

LINK, A. and REES, J. (1990) 'Firm Size, University Based Research and the Return to R&D', *Small Business Economics*, vol. 2, no. 1, pp. 25–32.

LLERENA, P. and SCHAEFFER, V. (1995) 'Politiques Technologiques Locales de Diffusion: Recherche Interne et Mode de Coordination', in A. T. Rallet and A. Torre (eds), *Economie Industrielle et économie Spatiale*. Paris, Economica, pp. 403–20.

MANGEMATIN, V. (1997) 'De la Capacité d'Absorption à la Capacité de Gestion: l'exemple des P.M.I. de l'Agro-alimentaire en Rhône Alpes', *Cahiers d'Economie et Sociologie Rurales*, vol. 44, pp. 85–105.

MANGEMATIN, V. and NESTA, L. (1999) 'What Kind of Knowledge Can a Firm Absorb?', *International Journal of Technology Management*, vol. 37, no. 3, pp. 149–72.

ROSENBERG, N. (1990) 'Why Companies Do Basic Research (with Their Own Money)?', *Research Policy*, vol. 19, pp. 165–74.

9 The Effect of Spillovers and Government Subsidies on R&D, International R&D Cooperation and Profits: Evidence from France

*Florent Favre, Syoum Negassi and Etienne Pfister**

9.1 INTRODUCTION

Firms in industrial countries invest vast sums in research and development (R&D) to create new products and new production processes. On a broader level, the ability of firms and of national innovation systems in general, to create, diffuse and use new knowledge has become a key to their success. Accordingly, economic research has devoted much effort towards understanding the links between R&D, innovation and productivity (Hall and Mairesse, 1995). Another path of research has focused on what drives R&D efforts from demand evolution to intellectual property rights, from technological opportunities to increased competition. Yet another series of works have stressed that R&D is not the sole determinant of innovation. While many empirical studies have highlighted the link between R&D and innovation (see Griliches, 1990) or between R&D and total factor productivity (see Mairesse and Sassenou, 1991), the use of panel and survey data has helped to underline that innovation also depends on the relations of the firm with its competitors, suppliers and customers, science institutes and so on (OECD, 1997).

Thanks to a wide set of data, this Chapter brings new evidence on these different aspects of R&D and innovation. More precisely, we focus on the links between internal R&D intensity and externally acquired knowledge, and on the impact of R&D subsidies. We show that the relation between internal R&D investment and externally acquired technological capital is complementary rather than substitutive, and this holds for a wide array of forms of access to external technologies.

This work is original in its data use. Various strategies have been employed to assess the empirical relevance of spillovers.[1] Bernstein and Nadiri (1989) use the total R&D capital of the industry. Wolff and Nadiri (1987) use capital and intermediate purchases matrix weights, thus assuming that borrowed R&D is embodied in the purchase of inputs. Studies of international spillovers combine domestic R&D investment and import-weighted sums of trade partner's cumulative R&D spending (Coe and Helpman, 1993). In these studies, trade is often used as a proximity index: the more a firm trades with another, the more the spillovers between them will be important. But other indexes of proximity have also been used, such as the flow of patents (Mohnen and Lepine, 1991) or the position of firms within a patent space (Jaffe, 1986). Here we undertake a simultaneous assessment of various forms of spillover, some national, some international. More precisely, we introduce foreign direct investment, international trade in patents and licences, international and domestic trade in machine tools, and other intermediate inputs. We find evidence that although the impact of spillovers on firm-level performance is smaller than that of internal factors (R&D intensity, market share, capital intensity), it cannot be neglected. Moreover, we observe a greater impact for international spillovers than for national spillovers.

The second aspect addressed by this chapter is the effectiveness of R&D subsidies in promoting R&D and innovation. Innovation and its inputs are subjected to many market imperfections (uncertainties, imperfect property rights, high fixed costs) that justify government intervention. Indeed, this kind of intervention is one of the lucky few that have not been dismissed as undesirable by neoclassical economists. Research and development (R&D) subsidies are among the most widely used devices to reduce the under-investment in R&D stemming from these market imperfections. We distinguish subsidies from the French government from those of the European Union (EU). State funding of R&D for France has always been quite substantial. Between 1959 and 1995, the share of government financed R&D varied between 50 and 71 per cent of total national R&D (Boyer and Didier, 1998). A large part of these expenses are linked to the military industry and to fundamental research, but projects conducted by other private firms are also subsidized. At the EU level, R&D subsidies remain relatively low, less than 5 per cent of total public expenditures on science and technology (S&T) in Europe. Another difference lies in the declared objective of the subsidies: because the Rome Treaty forbids the promotion of particular firms, European subsidies aim at fostering pre-competitive and collaborative networks so that many firms benefit from the European Framework Programme (EUFP).[2]

Whatever their origin, subsidies have been criticized for various reasons. First, publicly-funded research demonstrates a consistently lower return rate than does private research. There is also evidence that the system is targeted more at large firms than at small ones (Guillaume, 1998).

The EUFP is very hard to rate: many studies (DeMontgolfier and Husson, 1995) stress the weaknesses of data collection (low response rates; no control group). Moreover, as Luukkonen (1998) points out, the effects of the EUFP on competitiveness would be hard to assess, since studies are mostly conducted at micro-level. Given the small amounts of money involved, their effects can hardly be drastic. Last, it is hard to separate the effect of the EUFP from other subsidies (Georghiou, 1994). It has sometimes been emphasized that the EU Framework Program may demonstrate specific efficiency effects. Indeed, the benefits from collaboration between European firms, which could be highly beneficial thanks to scale economies, synergies and so on (see Teece, 1992, or Hagedoorn and Schakenraad, 1990), may remain too low because of many obstacles (language and cultural barriers, fear of insider competition, low appropriability of knowledge). By providing subsidies for co-operation projects, the EUFP may then help firms to overcome part of these problems. But, according to many studies (for example, Lagrange *et al.*, 1996), the EUFP did not help to prompt projects that would not have been decided without EU support, although it has sometimes increased their scope, scale and speed.[3] Other limits include the administrative burden and the very open way in which these programs are conducted (Lagrange *et al.*, 1996; Luukkonen and Niskanen, 1998).[4] For Lagrange *et al.* (1996), more convincing positive effects stem from how the support of an EUFP may convince financial and strategic departments of the desirability of a project. For Georghiou (1994), EU networks help firms to find new partners; the desire to remain an attractive partner, to build upon a competitor's knowledge or gain competitiveness drives the R&D investment upwards.

Our empirical findings cast doubt on the effectiveness of these European subsidies. Although they display a positive relationship with the international R&D co-operation budget, their influence is a lot smaller than those of the French government, or of privately financed R&D investment. Moreover, they have a negative influence on R&D intensity (while subsidies from the French government have a positive impact).

9.2   SAMPLE, VARIABLES AND EQUATIONS

9.2.1   The Sample

The results presented in this chapter are based on 2879 French firms distributed over fourteen industries, thus accounting for the bulk of production in the French manufacturing sector. To separate innovators from non-innovators, we used the CIS/Eurostat survey carried out in 1993, covering the years 1990–2, and the SESSI survey carried out in 1998, covering the years 1994–6. We assume that a firm has innovated if it reported an innovation in both surveys. The resulting sample of 2879 firms contains 1736 innovating and 1143 non-innovating firms. Lastly, we assume that firms that report an increase in total sales of more than 70 per cent in one year are likely to have been involved in a merger. These firms form a special case because they can be expected to have experienced productivity changes resulting from the merger alone.

Our dataset is the combination of three data sources:

(i) The SESSI database provided by the French Ministry of Industry. Among the many available sources of information, we focused especially on the:
- 'Annual firm database' (EAE–Enquête Annuelle d'Entreprise), which contains most financial and economic firm-level data (sales, market share, number of employees and so on) for the years 1985 to 1996;
- 'Innovation survey', providing qualitative information on innovating activities at the firm level; and
- 'Appropriation and diffusion survey', a survey that replicates the so-called 'Yale study' for French firms.
(ii) The 'Research' database provided by the Ministry of Education. It presents precise data on firms' research expenditures.
(iii) The 'INPI' (Institut de la Propriété Intellectuelle).

9.2.2 Variables and Equations

Table 9.1 presents our independent and dependent variables. Two variables deserve a short comment. Our measure of national rent spillover is described in detail in Appendix 9.1. Basically, we relate a firm's trade with its partners from all industries to the importance of external knowledge for this particular firm, and to its internal absorption capacity (measured by R&D and human capital intensity). Adding an internal absorption capacity variable to a rent spillover variable may seem somewhat paradoxical, since by definition rent spillovers can be captured simply by adopting a new process or product. However, we expect that the importance of the spillover variable will depend on the quality of the adopted good or

Table 9.1 Dependent and independent variables

Variable	Definition	Source
Dependent variables		
Y_{1git}	International R&D co-operation, calculated as the sums a firm devotes to international R&D co-operation	'Research'
Y_{2git}	R&D intensity; the level of R&D stock is calculated following the permanent inventory method with a constant depreciation rate of 25% and a three-year lag	'Research'
Y_{3git}	Firm level profit rates	EAE
Independent variables		
X_{1git}	Physical capital intensity; stock of physical capital is calculated from the flow of investments with a depreciation rate of 5%	EAE
X_{2git}	Research subsidies received by each firm from the French government	'Research'
X_{3git}	Inward foreign direct investment is the amount of inward foreign direct investment in the industry of firm i by European, US and Japanese plants. In this study, we include 1174 plants for Europe, 91 for USA and 54 for Japan	INPI
X_{4git}	Foreign technology payments	INPI
X_{5git}	International rent spillovers in machine tools; see Appendix 9.1 for construction	EAE
X_{6git}	National rent spillovers; see Appendix 9.1 for construction and 'Appropriation'	EAE and Appropriation
X_{7git}	Research subsidies received from the EU	'Research'
X_{8git}	Part of the turnover attributable to exports – exporters are likely to co-operate with foreign firms	CIS
X_{9git}	Market share in the sector of principal activity	EAE
X_{10git}	Concentration index of the sector of principal activity	EAE
X_{11git}	Demand elasticity in industry g, the industry of principal activity of firm i	EAE
$X_{12git-1}$	Innovation performance, i.e., the part of turnover realized attributable to innovation with one-year lag.	CIS
$X_{13git-1}$	Short-term (year) growth rates of sales	EAE

Notes: i, g, t denote, respectively, the firm, the industry and the year under study.

process. We approximate this quality by adding an internal absorption capacity, assuming that firms that have a high absorption capacity will be better able to extract productivity gains from a given process or good.

A similar procedure is used for our measure of international rent spillovers. Here, we measure a firm's imports in machine tools. As with national rent spillovers, we cannot compute the R&D content of these imports. Hence, we approximate the quality of the imported machine tool with the R&D stock of the importing firm. Once again, we assume that firms with a high R&D stock will be better able to make productivity gains from a given machine tool. Note also that foreign technology payments are another measure of international rent spillovers; however, since the technological dimension of these spillovers is obvious, we did not include a proxy for the quality of these imports, or for the quality of the importing firm. The construction of our national and international rent spillovers is given in Appendixes 9.1 and 9.2.

9.2.3   The Equations

The model contains three structural equations:

(i)   An equation for the budget devoted to international R&D *co-operation*:

$$Y_{1git} = f(Y_{2git}, X_{2git}, X_{3git}, X_{4git}, X_{5git}, X_{7git}, X_{8git-1}, v_{git}) \tag{1}$$

(ii)   An equation for *R&D capital intensity*:

$$Y_{2git} = g(Y_{1git}, Y_{3git}, X_{3git}, Y_{4git}, X_{6git}, X_{7git}, X_{9git}$$
$$X_{10git}, X_{11git}, X_{12git-1}, u_{git}) \tag{2}$$

(iii)   An equation for *firm-level profit rates*:

$$Y_{3git} = g(Y_{1git}, Y_{2git}, X_{1git}, X_{2git}, X_{4git}, X_{5git}, X_{6git}, X_{8git}$$
$$X_{9git}, X_{10git}, X_{11git}, X_{13git-1}, W_{git}) \tag{3}$$

Before we present our empirical method and results, let us first briefly discuss the rationale behind these three econometric specifications.

In Equation (1), the budget a firm devotes to international R&D co-operation is explained by the firm's:

- *R&D intensity*: firms that are already R&D intensive can attract new partners, detect new opportunities for collaboration and so on. Alternatively, one might imagine that firms with high R&D intensities may not indulge in co-operation projects because they already have the necessary R&D capital; so we shall test whether R&D co-operation is a complement or a substitute for internal R&D programmes;
- *Foreign direct investment*, which may have two different influences. First, it is an increased competitive pressure and firms will seek opportunities to face this new competition; R&D co-operation may be a strategic decision in a context of increased competition. Second, an increase in FDI may generate higher opportunities for collaboration. Overall, we thus expect a positive influence of FDI on international R&D co-operation;
- *Foreign technology payments*: as in the case of R&D intensity, the effects of foreign technology payments are theoretically ambiguous. Indeed, if firms can buy technology from foreign firms, there is no need to co-operate with them. Alternatively, this may increase the firm's technological capital as well as help to develop new opportunities for co-operation;
- *International rent spillovers* (defined here as imports of machine tools from foreign countries): while the complementary/substitute relation holds here, as with foreign technology payments, we expect it to work in the same direction but also to be less significant, since machine tools are less technology-based and thus leave less room for R&D co-operation than licensing contracts and patent acquisitions;
- *EU research subsidies*: these are directed towards firms that are developing an R&D international co-operation project. Critics may argue, however, that firms would engage in co-operation even without EU subsidies. On the other hand, supporters of EU subsidies claim that these funds help firms to overcome internal bureaucratic barriers; and
- *Export intensity of innovating products*: firms that are competing on a global scale are more likely than others to resent the need of R&D international co-operation; this helps them to remain informed about new technological developments and to organise competition.

In Equation (2), we explain the R&D intensity with:

- *International R&D co-operation*: as before, a complementarity/substitution relationship may exist between R&D co-operation and R&D.

However, while the previous relation was dynamic, since R&D was computed with a three-year lag, here it is simultaneous, so high international R&D co-operation may induce a decrease in R&D investment. Alternatively, a firm that co-operates may sustain its R&D efforts in order to remain able to absorb its partner's knowledge;

- *Profit rates*: the most profitable firms are also those financially most able to invest in R&D; because of financial market imperfections, we expect a positive relationship between profit and R&D intensity;

- *Subsidies from the French government* may crowd out private R&D investment; alternatively, they may also encourage it, by alleviating financial and appropriation imperfections;

- *Inward foreign direct investment* is an increased competitive pressure that encourages firms to increase their R&D investment so as to develop new products and processes, and be more competitive;

- *Foreign technology payments (FTP)*: as R&D collaboration, FTP may be complementary to, or a substitute for, internal R&D investments;

- *National rent spillovers*: the external acquisition of inputs (machines and machine tools) should spur internal R&D investment by increasing its productivity; alternatively, if many goods are available through market contracts, developing them inside the firm should be less rewarding, and R&D investment should decrease;

- *EU research subsidies*: the substitute/complement effects are obvious; they may displace private R&D resources; alternatively, by increasing the incentive to co-operate, they may encourage higher R&D investment;

- *Market share*: is a traditional determinant of R&D investment. We expect a positive relationship because high market share entails the financial capacity to finance R&D. It also facilitates the appropriation of the R&D results;

- *Concentration index*: higher concentration can be associated with higher R&D investment, since concentrated industries are composed mainly of large firms able to finance and appropriate their innovations; however, greater concentration may also induce lower competition, and thus lower innovation;

- *Demand elasticity*: there is higher price elasticity of demand in the sector of activity of the firm, competition becomes intensive because competing firms have an incentive to reduce their prices to increase quantities sold. Innovations may then be viewed as a way to overcome the competition constraint. The need to innovate entails higher R&D investment; and

- *Innovation performance*: Innovation performance is the part of turnover produced by innovation. Success in R&D encourages higher

R&D investment. Conversely, one might imagine that a successful firm will stabilize its R&D investment.

Finally, in Equation (3), we explain the profit rates with: *international R&D co-operation, R&D intensity, physical capital intensity, foreign technology payments, international rent spillovers, and national rent spillovers.* These variables reflect different forms of investment that should have a positive effect on performance and on profits. Profit rates are also related to various firm characteristics such as *export intensity of innovative products, market share,* and the *growth of sales,* whatever the level of its investment. Regarding industry characteristics, profit intensity should be related positively to concentration, and negatively to demand elasticity (since this makes price competition more probable). Finally, we also include research subsidies from the French government in the profit intensity equation (EU subsidies did not prove to be significant).

9.3   THE ECONOMETRIC PROCEDURE

9.3.1   Specification of the Random Coefficients Model

We obtain inconsistent and biased estimates of our functions when running ordinary least squares (OLS). This is so for many reasons. Assuming homoscedasticity and independent error, the direct estimation of a model by OLS provides optimal estimators of the coefficients. But in our case, the hypothesis of perfect homogeneity among the different industries is too restrictive.

We have also run two fixed-effect estimators: the 'between' and 'Within' methods[5]. We find that whereas the OLS are over-restrictive because they disregard the variability between industries, the covariance method (within estimator) and the indirect method (between estimator), i.e. the use of dummy variables, goes too far the other way, by taking out an excessive proportion of the variability that exists between the different industries.

In our case, the main reason for using a random model is not only empirical (high test statistic)[6]: we believe strongly that the observed variability is of a more fundamental nature in that it is related directly to differences in behaviour. The random model we use is not the well-known error component method developed by Balestra and Nerlove (1966), but an original random coefficient model[7]. The formulation of the problem in terms of a random coefficient model in which allowance is made for an individual (industry) effect seems to be the best choice. We therefore assume that the coefficients of the three-equation system have two components: a fixed component (equal for all firms and industries) and a random component (constant within an industry, but varying across industries).

More precisely, our simultaneous equation system stems from a model of individual behaviour. We extend the econometric research initiated by Hildreth and Houck, 1968, and Swamy, 1970. In particular, we propose a pooling method based on the segmentation of groups rather than individuals. Here, individuals are grouped following their distribution over industries: each firm is related to the industry of its main activity, and each industry has a specific coefficient of reaction. More concretely, a coefficient Γ_g will represent permanent differences in industry performance, while an error term (stochastic variable) ε_g will represent temporary fluctuations in performance around the industry specific means caused by the effects of individual production projects. Finally, the estimator is a weighted matrix average of the pooled industry estimators, as the loads are inversely proportional to their variance–covariance matrix.

The system entails N ($N = 3$ in our case) structural equations (and therefore N endogenous variables) and M ($M = 13$ in our case) exogenous variables. The sample is made up of G industries ($G = 14$ in our case) observed over T_g periods. We assume that all observations of the same industry are taken from the same population (regardless of the number of firms comprising the industry). Naturally, if an industry was composed of a single firm, and if all the firms were observed over the same T_g periods, we would resort to the standard panel model.

The normal matrix notation for a simultaneous equation system for each industry g lends it self to the following expression:

$$Y_g\beta_g + X_g\Gamma_g = \varepsilon_g \quad g = 1,...,G$$

$$Y_{g1} = Y_{g1*}\beta_{1*} + X_{g1*}\Gamma_{g1*} - \varepsilon_{g1} \qquad (4)$$

$$\beta_g = \beta \ \forall g$$

$$\Gamma_g = \Gamma + U_g$$

where Y_g is the matrix $T_g \times N$ of the endogenous variables of industry g; β_g is the matrix $N \times N$ of the coefficients of the endogenous variables; X_g is the matrix $T_g \times M$ of the exogenous variables of industry g; Γ_g is the matrix $M \times N$ of the coefficients of the exogenous variables; ε_g is the matrix $T_g \times N$ of the terms of error:

$$
Y_g = \begin{bmatrix} Y_{1git} \\ Y_{2git} \\ Y_{3git} \end{bmatrix}, \quad \text{all the other variables are in } X_g = \begin{bmatrix} X_{1git} \\ X_{2git} \\ \dots \\ X_{13git} \end{bmatrix}
$$

It can obviously be assumed that the usual identification conditions of the structural parameters have been met. In addition, our simultaneous equation system must be provided with a set of the following assumptions:

Assumption 1: Concerning the Variability of the Structural Coefficients

The elements of the coefficient matrix of the exogenous variables are assumed to be random (with industry effect), while the element of the coefficient matrix of the endogenous variables are assumed to be fixed; that is, non-stochastic. This asymmetric treatment of exogenous variables and endogenous variables is surprising at first sight, but can be justified in three ways. First, concerning the endogenous variables, a large part of their residual variance (not explained by the model) is already incorporated in the error terms. Adding to it a new random element via the reaction coefficient might appear to be superfluous. Second, introducing randomness only in the coefficients of the exogenous variables amounts to assuming randomness in the coefficients of the reduced form.[8] Third, and this is a compelling practical reason, the assumption of a random matrix β_g raises intractable difficulties at the level of identification and estimation. It is perhaps instructive to mention that, in the study of dynamic random models, one is led to make a similar set of assumptions: random coefficients for exogenous variables and fixed coefficients for the lagged endogenous variables.

Assumption 1 can be stated formally as follows:

$\beta_g = \beta \; \forall_g$, β being non-singular of fixed (but unknown) elements.
$\Gamma_g = \Gamma + U_g$, where Γ is a matrix of fixed elements and U_g is a matrix of random elements.

Assumption 2: Concerning the residual errors

As in the traditional simultaneous-equation framework, we assume a full (non-diagonal) constant contemporaneous variance–covariance matrix and time independence. For the sake of clarity, and in order to establish operational analysis instruments, only individual heterogeneity will be considered in the estimations. The hypothesis of time homogeneity is not inconvenient when, as is usually the case with panel data, the number of firms is large and the number of periods rather small. However, the analysis can be extended easily to the case where individual and time effects are present simultaneously (see Hsiao, 1994).

Assumption 3: The elements of ε_g and U_g are mutually independent

9.3.2 Estimation Methods in the Case of Random Coefficients Model: Structural Parameter Estimation Based on Instrumental Variable Method

We consider the estimation of a single equation in the structural model. To estimate the gth structural equation, we take account only of a priori restrictions affecting that equation and ignore the restrictions affecting all other equations. Therefore, suppose we are interested in estimating the first equation. Our prior requirement is to specify this first structural equation. In compliance with the usual exclusion restrictions and the normalization of the explained (the first) endogenous variable, the first equation for industry g is written in the following manner:

$$Y_{g1} = Y_{g1*}\beta_{1*} + X_{g1*}\Gamma_{g1*} - \varepsilon_{g1} \qquad (5)$$

where Y_{g1} is the $T_g \times 1$ vector of the observations concerning the endogenous variable explained in the first equation (the first column of Y_g); Y_{g1*} is the $T_g \times N_*$ (with $N_* \leq N - 1$) matrix of the observations concerning the explanatory endogenous variables (a selection of the columns of Y_g, except for the first); β_{1*} is the $N_* \times 1$ vector of the coefficients of the explanatory endogenous variables, static and non-stochastic by assumption; X_{g1*} is the matrix of order $T_g \times M_*$, where $M_* < M$ is the number of the observations concerning the exogenous variables which appear in the first equation (a selection of the columns of X_g); Γ_{g1*} is the $M_* \times 1$ vector of the coefficients of the exogenous variables. In agreement with the chosen assumption, this vector comprises a static part Γ_{g1*} and a random part U_{g1*}, or:

$$\Gamma_{g1*} = \Gamma_{1*} + U_{g1*}$$

By pooling the random components of (5), one can write:

$$Y_{g1} = Y_{g1*}\beta_{1*} + X_{g1*}\Gamma_{1*} + (X_{g1*}U_{g1*} - \varepsilon_{g1}) = Z_{g1}\alpha_1 + W_{g1} \qquad (6)$$

where

$$Z_{g1} = [Y_{g1*}X_{g1*}]$$

$$\alpha_1' = [\beta_{1*}' \; \Gamma_{1*}']$$

$$W_{g1} = X_{g1*}U_{g1*} - \varepsilon_{g1}$$

$$E(W_{g1}) = 0 \quad \text{and} \quad E(W_{g1}W_{g1}') = X_{g1*}\Delta_{11*}X_{g1*}' + \sigma_{11g} + I_N^d = A_{g11}$$

The matrix X_g of the observations relating to all the exogenous variables of the industry g is *the matrix of appropriate instruments* in this context (there is no other available information). The instrumental variable method (IV) presents the following steps:

(i)   The Equation (6) is multiplied by a suitable instrument matrix;
(ii) The matrix of the variance–covariance derived from the previous processing is computed; and
(iii) The model thus processed by the GLS method is finally estimated.

By calling F_{g1} the following quantity:

$$F_{g1} = A_{g11}^{-1}X_g(X_g'A_{g1}^{-1}X_g)^{-1}X_g'A_{g11}^{-1}$$

$$= X_g(X_g'A_{g11}^{-1}X_g)^{-1}X_g'$$

which is therefore equal in both perspectives, the following estimator is derived:

$$\hat{\alpha}_1 = \left[\sum_g [Z_{g1}'F_{g1}Z_{g1}]^{-1} \right]^{-1} \sum_g Z_{g1}'F_{g1}Y_{g1}$$

$$= \left[\sum_g (Z'_{g1} F_{g1} Z_{g1})^{-1} \right]^{-1} \sum_g (Z'_{g1} F_{g1} Z_{g1})(Z'_{g1} F_{g1} Z_{g1})^{-1} Z'_{g1} F_{g1} Y_{g1}$$

$$= \left[\sum_g [Z'_{g1} F_{g1} Z_{g1}]^{-1} \right]^{-1} \sum_g (Z'_{g1} F_{g1} Z_{g1}) \hat{\alpha}_{g1} \tag{7}$$

where $\hat{\alpha}_{g1}$ is the estimator by the classical IV of industry g. Yet again, we attain the well-known result that the global estimator is a weighted matrix average of the individual estimators.

9.4   RESULTS

Our econometric results are summarized in Table 9.2. The Readers can find in this table the results we obtained by using a special pooling method. Our estimates provide evidence of the extent to which the within firm estimates are biased downwards because of the unresponsiveness of the endogenous variables to the transitory component of most exogenous variables. The random coefficient method gives estimators that are twice the within firm estimates in the case of most variables, but are very close to the between firm estimates. The results indicate that the within firm method under-estimates to a greater extent the effect of the exogenous variables on the endogenous variables. Our comments are based on the random model results in which we have the most confidence.

9.4.1   Budget for International R&D Co-operation

International R&D co-operation is measured by the budget a firm devotes to international R&D co-operation. Using the random coefficient model, we get the following set of results:

● Internal R&D investment is complementary to international R&D co-operation. In fact, there are numerous explanations for such a result. First, firms that have the highest internal R&D capacity are also those most able to identify collaboration opportunities and to attract new partners. They are also more able to absorb external knowledge and thus profit from collaboration. Given their high R&D investment, they are less likely to adopt opportunistic behaviour.

- In accordance with the previous results, we note that all our measures of internal R&D capacity are linked positively to international R&D collaboration. Foreign technology payments and international rent spillovers (acquisitions of machine tools) do not replace international R&D co-operation, but are complementary because, just like R&D intensity, they increase the firm's technological capital. As expected, the effect of foreign technology payments is larger than that of machine tool acquisitions. Lastly, consistently with these results, we also note that research subsidies received from the French government have a positive effect on the international cooperation budget.
- We observe that EU research subsidies are linked positively to international R&D co-operation. Contrary to what critics have argued, they do have a significant influence on the propensity to co-operate. What is more intriguing, however, is that this effect is smaller than the effect of French subsidies that are not specifically aimed at promoting co-operation.
- Finally, increased openness to international trade and investment flows, or to international competition, exerts a positive and significant influence on the propensity to engage in international co-operation in R&D.

9.4.2 R&D Intensity

R&D intensity is mainly dependent on factors reflecting the financing capacity, previous innovation success and competitive pressure. Hence, we see that market share and firm-level profit intensity exert a strong positive influence on R&D. Similarly, the turnover realized thanks to innovative products or processes in the years preceding the year of study also exerts a strong positive influence. Again, foreign direct investment exerts a competitive pressure on R&D: faced with the threat of foreign competition, French firms spend higher amounts in R&D. Demand elasticity has a weakly significant influence. Conversely, concentration (the lack of competitive pressure) has a negative (though not significant) influence on R&D investment.

But we also find less conventional results. First, firms that co-operate spend more on R&D. Hence it is unlikely that firms co-operate in order to reduce their R&D costs. We would rather argue that co-operation increases the productivity of R&D and allows the better internalization of technology spillovers. However, foreign technology payments tend to be a substitute for in-house R&D investment (the effect is small and only weakly

Table 9.2 Summary of estimates

	Y_1 random	Y_1 between	Y_1 within	Y_2 random	Y_2 between	Y_2 within	Y_3 random	Y_3 between	Y_3 within
Intercept	0.0766 (0.899)		0.2159* (2.431)	0.134** (1.810)		1.954** (1.932)	0.1070 (1.636)		0.0985* (3.543)
Y_1: international R&D co-operation				0.1229* (3.787)	0.1390* (3.089)	0.1701* (2.297)	0.1080* (3.752)	0.1218* (3.429)	0.0908* (2.029)
Y_2: R&D intensity	0.4978* (2.974)	0.4070* (2.694)	0.3986* (2.411)				0.1549* (2.486)	0.1649* (2.160)	0.2896* (2.546)
Y_3: firm-level profit intensity				0.2811* (4.909)	0.2211* (3.906)	0.1810* (1.981)			
X_1: physical capital intensity	0.3291* (3.658)	0.3331* (2.219)	0.2031** (1.698)				0.4290* (3.642)	0.3996* (2.603)	0.2616* (4.033)
X_2: research subsidies from French government				0.0984* (2.001)	0.1084** (1.839)	0.1494* (3.392)	0.1301* (4.813)	0.1001* (3.898)	0.1074** (1.880)
X_3: foreign direct investment	0.2209* (3.002)	0.1909* (1.970)	0.1199** (1.970)	0.1210* (2.385)	0.1011* (2.085)	0.1811 (1.005)			
X_4: foreign technology payments	0.1918* (4.029)	0.1618* (3.803)	0.0910* (2.001)	-0.0874** (1.780)	-0.0980* (2.580)	-0.1200* (2.908)	0.1008* (2.434)	0.1281** (1.984)	0.0713* (2.946)
X_5: international rent spillovers	0.0995* (5.937)	0.0605* (3.901)	0.1605* (2.879)				0.1600* (4.311)	0.1509* (3.990)	0.1893** (1.692)
X_6: national rent spillovers				0.0796* (3.453)	0.0972* (2.974)	0.1249 (1.547)	0.1098* (2.270)	0.1118* (2.098)	0.1384 (0.098)
X_7: research subsidies to co-operation pg (EU)	0.1721* (2.637)	0.1521* (2.037)	0.1345 (1.499)	-0.1333* (2.972)	-0.1137* (2.034)	-0.0678 (0.034)			

X_8: Export intensity of innovating products	0.1809* (3.198)	0.1799* (1.998)	0.1604* (2.281)				0.2006* (2.968)	0.1871** (1.801)	0.1716* (2.854)
X_9: market share				0.4196* (2.783)	0.3796* (2.631)	0.2899* (3.904)	0.1448* (3.994)	0.1315* (2.897)	0.1217** (1.870)
X_{10}: concentration index				−0.0701 (0.0930)	−0.0901 (0.1309)	−0.1492 (1.912)	0.0980* (2.488)	0.1090* (2.100)	0.1902* (2.708)
X_{11}: price elasticity of demand in the sector of principle activity				0.1020** (1.741)	0.0900 (1.019)	0.1850 (1.452)	0.1069 (1.507)	0.0909** (1.794)	0.0693** (1.798)
X_{12}: innovation performance				0.4223* (2.810)	0.3727* (2.099)	0.3727* (2.099)			
X_{13}: growth rates of sales							0.1919* (6.900)	0.1696* (5.198)	0.1432* (2.890)
DW		2.487	2.467		2.746	2.786		2.618	2.698
R^2	0.5373	0.5437	0.5418	0.5799	0.5879	0.5679	0.5867	0.5174	0.5164

Notes: The variables are in logarithms; in parenthesis: t of Student; sign and significance of the coefficients are analyzed at 5%;
*significant at 5%; **significant at 10 %.

significant). Those who are dependent on buying licences have a weaker R&D and knowledge base.

Second, EU research subsidies tend to have a negative influence on R&D intensity. This is an unexpected result, since it has not been set out in the theoretical literature, but also because other results tend to stress the complementarity that exists between co-operation and R&D intensity. Since EU subsidies do facilitate co-operation, although at a lesser rate than private R&D investment, we would also expect them to have a positive effect on R&D intensity. However, our results show that this is not the case: EU subsidies facilitate R&D international co-operation, but they also induce a decrease in internal R&D investment. Reasons behind this result are unclear. It could be because of the bureaucracy, the co-ordination costs and the cultural differences (lack of communication) induced by the framework programmes, and thus to a lower productivity of these collaboration projects. It is all the more surprising that French subsidies have a positive influence on R&D intensity. A tentative interpretation would be that French subsidies tend to increase the productivity of R&D investment while EU subsidies do not, possibly because of the increased bureaucracy.

Finally, unlike the co-operation equation, the R&D intensity equation displays significant differences among the different estimation methods. In the within estimation, foreign direct investment, national rent spillovers, EU research subsidies and demand elasticity lose significance, while concentration and foreign technology payments gain some. Signs never change. In the between model, French research subsidies and demand elasticity lose some significance, while foreign technology payments gain some. Again, signs never change. Traditionally, the within and between methods tend to take out an excessive proportion of the variability that exists between industries; accordingly, some effects that appeared as sector-specific in these estimations turn out to be firm-specific.

9.4.3   Firm-level Profit Rates

Looking at profit rates, we observe that traditional internal factors (R&D intensity, capital intensity, exports of innovative products, market share, and sales) as well as industry concentration, exert a very strong and positive influence on firm performance. More specific to this chapter is the significant influence of externally acquired technological capital. International R&D co-operation, foreign technology payments, imports of machine tools and inter-firm trade have a positive and significant impact on a firm's profits.

An interesting point is that national rent spillovers seem to have a smaller impact than international rent spillovers. Coe and Helpman (1993), and more recently Engelbrecht (1997), have discussed the international dimension of spillovers. These studies used country-level data, where spillovers were simply approximated by the R&D stocks of the trade partners; international trade was used to weight the flow of spillovers from one country to another. However, Keller (1997) obtains substantial positive spillovers with specifications that do not include any particular international trade pattern, thus casting doubt on the construction scheme used by Coe and Helpman. Here, as in Branstetter (1996), we present firm-level evidence of the existence of international spillovers. Unlike Branstetter, however, we conclude that international spillovers have a *greater* impact than national spillovers.

9.5 CONCLUSION

This chapter addressed two of the many aspects developed by the literature on R&D and productivity. We show that spillovers have a mostly positive influence on R&D intensity, as well as on the budget a firm devotes to international R&D co-operation. It also has a significant and positive impact on performance, and we observe that international rent spillovers appear to be more significant than national spillovers.

Regarding public R&D subsidies, we find empirical evidence of the doubts many have cast on the effectiveness of European subsidies. While they do exert a positive effect on the budget a firm devotes to co-operation, the effect is a lot smaller than if these R&D expenses were funded privately. More fundamentally, they exert a negative influence on R&D intensity, suggesting that they substitute for internal R&D intensity. In contrast, French subsidies exert a positive influence on R&D intensity as well as on international R&D co-operation, suggesting that European subsidies have some specific inefficiency.

Appendix 9.1: Constructing the National Rent Spillover Variables

Rent spillovers reflect the fact that the input prices do not completely reflect the input's real value. Thus, these spillovers occur via a transfer of goods, and the environment of the firm (what kinds of firms are its partners, and how important are the exchanges between the company and these firms?) influences the total knowledge accumulated by the firm. Two types of rent spillover are considered: national and international.

National Rent Spillovers

We propose two domestic types of externalities: inter- and intra-sectoral externalities. Through the former, a firm can capture technological knowledge derived from firms that are outside its sector, whereas the latter enable the firm to profit from the technological knowledge produced in its sector. However, appropriation of outside technological knowledge requires an absorption capacity (Cohen and Levinthal, 1989). We measure the absorptive capacity of firms by human capital and R&D expenses.

In measuring intra- and inter-industry externalities, we use four types of indicators:

(i)   *An indicator of the importance of external technological sources* (defined as v_i in what follows). It results from scientific and technical knowledge that exists in the firm's environment. We have calculated this indicator using the 'Appropriation and diffusion survey' (SESSI). The question on external technology sources is part of a set of questions about factors impeding innovative activity, and was answered by firms on a scale of significance ranging from 0 (i.e., nil) to 4 (i.e., very strong). We then built an indicator denoted $v_{ij} = TC_{ij}/5$, where TC_{ij} is the judgement of the ith firm in sector j for technology sources concerning their innovation. If firm i values external technology sources as 'very strong', the indicator takes on the value of 1.

(ii) *An indicator for the inter- and intra-industrial exchanges of each firm* (input–output table of the INSEE). The transfer of technology achieved through intermediary consumption was joined by those picked up by the R&D. Then, we drew up a concordance matrix between the original industry and the user industry from an inter-industrial exchange table. This matrix retraces the exchange of intermediary goods between the industrial branches, and more precisely the exchange of knowledge (as R&D is taken in account). The elements θ_{si} of the main diagonal of the matrix illustrate the extent of intra-sectoral exchanges. The elements θ_{hsi} outside the diagonal describe inter-sectoral exchanges.

(iii) *An indicator of the firm's human capital intensity.* The stock of human capital is $H_{it} = (1 - \delta_H)H_{i,t-1} + I_{it}^H$ where I_{it}^H is the rate of investment in human capital, and δ_H is the human capital depreciation. We then calculated the proportion of human capital in the firm: $h_i = H_{it}/\Sigma_{i=1}^m H_{it}$ where m is the number of firms in the industry and $\Sigma_{i=1}^m H_{it}$ is the stock of human capital in the industry.

(iv) *An indicator of the R&D intensity of the firm:* $r_i = RD_i/\Sigma_i^m RD_i$, where R&D is firm i's total R&D expenditure (a discount rate of 15% stock was applied to this five-year stock measure).

(v)   *The absorption capacity of the firm* is then written as:

$$\alpha_i = (h_i + r_i)\,v_i(\theta_{si} + \theta_{hsi})$$

where: r_i is the R&D intensity, i.e., the ratio between firm i's total R&D expenditure and R&D expenditure in all industries ($0 \le r_i \le 1$). If $r_i = 1$, the firm shows a significant capacity of absorption of technology; whereas $r_i = 0$ in the opposite case; and $\nu_i\,\theta_{si}$ and $\nu_i\,\theta_{hsi}$ are respectively the intra- and inter-sectorial rate of appropriation of external knowledge for the firm i. The firm i appropriates knowledge belonging to firms inside and outside its sector. $\nu_i\theta_{si}$ and $\nu_i\theta_{hsi}$ are close to 1 when the firm i greatly benefits from the research of the firms from other industries, and 0 in the opposite case.

We are now able to draw up two externality variables.

(i) *The intra-industry externalities* that result from relationships with nearby firms. This variable describes the links that a firm maintains with its nearest environment, i.e. its sector of activity. In addition to its R&D expenditure, the firm's stock of knowledge includes intra-industry spillovers, defined as:

$$E_{1i} = (h_i + r_i)\nu_i\theta_{si} \sum_{j\neq i \text{ and } j\in s} RD_{si}$$

(ii) *The inter-industry externalities*, similarly defined as:F

$$E_{2i} = (h_i + r_i)\nu_i\theta_{hsi} \sum_{j\neq i \text{ and } j\in s} RD_{hsj}$$

where: RD_{sj}: the stock of R&D expenditure in sth industry; RD_{hsj}: the stock of R&D expenditure of other industries than s; Thus, the national rent spillover is:

$$X_6 = E_{1i} + E_{2i}$$

Appendix 9.2:   International Rent Spillovers

The analysis of productivity growth should also include the indirect benefits stemming from the technological improvement of imported goods and services produced by trade partners. We make the assumption that international rent spillovers are transmitted through goods purchased in foreign countries. For this purpose, we define the foreign R&D capital as the import-share-weighted sums of domestic R&D stocks of trade partners:

$$X_5 = \sum_{j\neq i} \frac{m_{ij}}{tm_{ij}} SRD_i$$

where m_{ij} is the flow of machines tools imported by the firm i from the world. tm_{ij} is the total import of the industry of i from foreign countries. SRD_i is the domestic R&D capital stock for machine tools by the industry i.

222   *The Effect of Spillovers and Government Subsidies*

Notes

*   We gratefully acknowledge the support of CNRS. We also thank two anony-
mous referees for their useful comments on an earlier version.
1.   See Griliches (1979, 1991) for surveys of these works.
2.   See Peterson (1991) and Larédo (1995,1998) for a more exhaustive description of the European Framework Programmes (EUFP).
3.   A study of Japanese R&D consortia sponsored by the government came to
the same conclusion (Sakakibara, 1997)
4.   Hence, EUFP are very rare in the pharmaceuticals industry because firms
fear the leakage of strategic information.
5.   In the within firm method, we use the standard method of sweeping out the
fixed effects by transforming variables to deviations from their firm-specific
means. The standard approach obtaining the between firm result is to regress
the firm-specific means of the dependent variable. The random coefficients
model is a model with coefficients varying over industry.
6.   This random coefficient model is developed by Balestra and Negassi (1992).
7.   See Balestra and Negassi (1992).

References

BALESTRA, P. and NERLOVE, M. (1966) 'Pooling Cross-Section and Time
Series Data in the Estimation of a Dynamic Model: The Demand for Natural
Gas', *Econometrica*, vol. 34, pp. 585–612.
BALESTRA, P. and NEGASSI, S. (1992) 'A Random Coefficients Simultaneous
Equation System with an Application to Direct Foreign Investment by French
Firms', *Empirical Economics*, vol. 17, no. 1, pp. 205–20.
BERNSTEIN, J. and NADIRI, M. (1989) 'Interindustry R&D Spillovers Rates of
Return and Production in High Tech Industries', *American Economic Review
Papers and Proceedings*, vol. 78, pp. 429–34.
BOYER, M. and DIDIER, R. (1998) '*Innovation et Croissance, Rapport du Conseil
d'Analyse Economique*', Paris La Documentation Française.
BRANSTETTER, L. (1996) 'Are Knowledge Spillovers International or Intranational
in Scope? Microeconometric Evidence from the US and Japan', NBER Working
Paper No. 5800.
COE, D. and HELPMAN, E. (1993) 'International R&D Spillovers', NBER Working
Paper No. 4444.
ENGELBRECHT, H. (1997) 'International Spillovers, Human Capital and
Productivity in OECD Economies: An Empirical Investigation', *European
Economic Review*, vol. 41, pp. 1479–88.
GEORGHIOU, L. (1994) *Impact of the Framework Programmes on European Industry*,
EUR 15907 EN. Luxembourg: Office for Official Publications of the EC.
GRILICHES, Z. (1979) 'Issues in Assessing the Contribution of R-D to Productivity
Growth', *Bell Journal of Economics*, vol. 10, no. 1, pp. 92–116.
GRILICHES, Z. (1990) 'Patent Statistics as Economic Indicators: A Survey',
Journal of Economic Literature, vol. 28, pp. 1661–797.

GRILICHES, Z. (1991) 'The Search for R&D Spillovers', NBER Working Paper No. 3724, June.

GUILLAUME, H. (1998) *Rapport de Mission sur la Technologie et l'Innovation*, Paris: Report to the Cabinet of the Prime Minister.

HAGEDOORN, J. and SCHAKENRAAD, J. (1990) 'Inter Firm Partnerships and Co-operative Strategies in Core Technologies', in C. Freeman and L. Soete (eds), *New Explorations in the Economics of Technical Change*. London: Pinter.

HALL, B. and MAIRESSE, J. (1995) 'Exploring the Relationship between R&D and Productivity in French Manufacturing Firms', *Journal of Econometrics*, vol. 76, no. 1, pp. 263–93.

HILDRETH, C. and HOUCK, J. P. (1968) 'Some Estimations for Linear Models with Random Coefficients', *Journal of the American Statistical Association*, vol. 63, pp. 584–95.

HSIAO, C. (1989) *Analysis of Panel Data*. Cambridge University Press.

HSIAO, C. (1992) 'Random Coefficients Models', in L. Matyas and P. Sevestre (eds), *The econometrics of Panel Data*, Dordrecht: Kluwer.

JAFFE, A. B. (1986) 'Technological Opportunity and Spillovers of R-D: Evidence from Firm's Patents, Profits and Market Value', *American Economic Review*, vol. 76, no. 5, pp. 984–1001.

KELLER, W. (1997) 'Trade Patterns, Technology Flows, and Productivity Growth', Mimeo, Madison, Wisc.: University of Wisconsin.

LAGRANGE, V., ZOLA, J. M., FORGIA, A., GARZELLO, F., HARTMAN-WALL, H., LEITL, J. and SEARLE, C. (1996) *RTD Strategies of the Top 500 European Industrial Companies and Their Participation in the Framework Programme and EUREKA*, EUR 17244 EN. Luxembourg: Office for Official Publications of the EC.

LARÉDO, P. (1995) *The Impact of EU Research Programs in France*, Paris: PEM.

LARÉDO, P. (1998) 'The Networks Promoted by the Framework Programme and the Questions They Raise about its Formulation and Implementation', *Research Policy*, vol. 27, pp. 589–98.

LUUKKONEN, T. P. and NISKANEN, S. (1998) 'Learning Through Collaboration: The Finnish Participation in EU Programmes'. Espoo; Finland: VTT Industry for Technology Studies.

LUUKKONEN, T. (1998) 'The Difficulties in Assessing the Impact of EU Framework Programmes', *Research Policy*, vol. 27, pp. 599–610.

MAIRESSE, J. and SASSENOU, M. (1991) 'Recherche-Développement et Productivité: Un Panorama des études économétriques sur Données d'Entreprises', reprinted in J. De Bandt and D. Foray (eds), *L'Evaluation Economique de la Recherche et du Changement Technique*, Paris CNRS.

MOHNEN, P. and LEPINE, N. (1991) 'Payment for Technology as a Factor of Production', *Structural Change and Economic Dynamics*, vol. 1, no. 2, pp. 156–68.

DE MONTGOLFIER, P. and HUSSON, P. (1995) 'The Impact of EC R&D Policy on the European Science and Technology Community', National Impact Studies Final Report, Mimeo, *Axion*, May.

OECD (1997) *Policy Evaluation in Innovation and Technology: Towards Best Pratices*, Paris: OECD.

PETERSON, J. (1991) 'Technology Policy in Europe: Explaining the Framework Programme and Eureka in Theory and in Practice', *Journal of Common Market Studies*, vol. 29, pp. 269–90.

SAKAKIBARA, M. (1997) 'Evaluating government sponsored R&D consortia in Japan: Who Benefits and How?', *Research Policy*, vol. 26, pp. 447–73.

SWAMY, P. A. V. B. (1970) 'Efficient Inference in a Random Coefficient Repression Model', *Econometrica*, vol. 38, pp. 311–23.

TEECE, D. (1992) 'Strategies for Capturing the Financial Benefits from Technological Innovation', in N. Rosenberg (ed.), *Technology and the Wealth of Nations*. Stanford, Calif.: Stanford University Press.

WOLFF, B. and NADIRI, M. (1987) 'Spillover Effects, Linkage Structure and Research Development', New York University, Starr Center Research Report 43, 1987.

10 The Impact of Spillovers and Knowledge Heterogeneity on Firm Performance: Evidence from Swiss Manufacturing

*Spyros Arvanitis and Heinz Hollenstein**

10.1 INTRODUCTION

This chapter explores the impact of knowledge capital (computed on the basis of firm patent counts and R&D expenditures, respectively) and patent, as well as R&D spillovers, on total factor productivity at the firm level for Swiss manufacturing in the usual setting of a Cobb–Douglas production function. We introduce spillovers from R&D or patents by constructing two types of spillover measures: one based on material flows between sectors, and the other one reflecting technological proximity at the firm level. In a further step, international R&D as well as patent spillovers from eight technologically highly developed countries are taken into consideration.

Moreover, we exploit systematically qualitative firm data on the innovation process in order to investigate some additional aspects of the knowledge–performance relationship. To this end, we first try to obtain a more differentiated picture of the spillover mechanism by taking into account appropriability, technological potential and the effects of various external knowledge sources (users, suppliers, universities and so on) at the firm level. The analysis shows that different appropriability conditions and/or different modes of external knowledge absorption may reflect different kinds of knowledge capital. Thus, heterogeneity of knowledge capital resulting from differing knowledge absorptive capacity is an important feature of the knowledge-generation process at the firm level, which presumably explains some of the performance differences among firms.

In a last step we try to identify further sources of knowledge-capital heterogeneity, which seem to exert an influence on firm performance. For this purpose we use proxies for several inputs and objectives of innovative activity, as well as measures of the 'degree of innovativeness' of new products and new processes, to qualify knowledge capital by taking into account its heterogeneity.

The firm data used in the study (apart form patent data) come from the 1990 Swiss Innovation Survey conducted in the manufacturing sector; these data were combined with firm patent data (Ifo-Institute for Economic Research, Munich), and data on research and development, international trade and so on at the industry level from various published sources.

The results point to the existence of substantial spillovers from other domestic industries for both types of spillover measures used, as well from industries of foreign trade partners. In addition, we find that the extent of protection from imitation as well as the specific use of various external knowledge sources exert a significant influence on the magnitude of the impact of knowledge capital on firm performance. In evaluating the impact of knowledge capital on productivity it is necessary to take into account its heterogeneity, represented in this study by different types of innovation inputs, innovation objectives and varying 'degree of innovativeness' of products/ processes (new for the firm, new for the industry and so on). We find that such factors have a substantial influence on a firm's productivity.

10.2 THEORETICAL BACKGROUND AND MODEL SPECIFICATION

10.2.1 Basic Model

The usual framework in which to study the impact of technological knowledge on economic performance at the firm level is the production function (see, for example, Griliches, 1979; Hall and Mairesse, 1995). It is assumed that the production process of manufacturing firms can be approximated by a Cobb–Douglas function with the three inputs: labour L, physical capital C, and knowledge capital K:

$$Q_i = A L_i^{\alpha} C_i^{\beta} K_i^{\gamma} \tag{1}$$

(where Q_i denotes value added of firm i). The parameter we are focusing on is γ, the elasticity of value added with respect to knowledge capital. Of particular interest for this study is the reformulation of Equation (1) in order to obtain an expression for total factor productivity f_i; in logarithmic form we get:

$$f_i \equiv q_i - s_i l_i - (1 - s_i) c_i = a' + \gamma k_i \qquad (2)$$

(where s_i stands for the wage share of value added; lower case letters denote the logarithms of the variables).[1]

10.2.2 Introduction of Knowledge Spillovers (Extended Model)

A crucial aspect of innovative activity is the generation of knowledge, which to some extent has the character of a public good. This gives rise to externalities ('spillovers') which are a central theme in the literature on innovation in industrial economics (see, for example, Spence, 1984; Cohen and Levinthal, 1989; and Geroski, 1995).

A general, though rather simplistic, way to address this externality problem is to assume the diffusion of new private knowledge as leading to a 'spillover pool of knowledge' from which other economic actors can draw information useful for their own innovative activities. To this end, the production function framework is extended to include an additional input for knowledge capital which the firm does not itself generate, but collects from different sources (see Griliches, 1979, 1992):

$$Q_i = A L_i^\alpha C_i^\beta K_i^\gamma KE_i^\delta \qquad (3)$$

where KE is knowledge spillover. Thus, the total impact of knowledge on firm output is measured by $\gamma + \delta$ the sum of the effects of a firm's own knowledge capital and the knowledge obtained by spillovers from enterprises and institutions of the firm's economic environment.

A general formulation for the spillover capital as a (weighted) sum of the knowledge capital of a firm's relevant economic environment (knowledge pool) is given by the following expression (see Griliches, 1979, 1992):

$$KE_i = \sum_j w_{ij} K_j; \quad i \neq j \qquad (4)$$

where w is a weighting variable to be further specified.

What should such a weighting variable be based on? Broadly speaking, two distinct concepts of knowledge spillovers have been applied in recent literature (see van Pottelsberghe de la Potterie, 1997, for a review). According to the first concept, spillover knowledge is related to flows of intermediate and/or capital goods, and is assumed to be proportional to the value of the stream of goods between firms/industries (see, for example, Terlekyj, 1980; Wolff and Nadiri, 1993). In the second concept, the weights in Equation (4) are some measure of scientific and technological 'distance' among firms and industries (see, for example, Jaffe, 1986; Englander *et al.*, 1988; Harhoff, 1994).

Accordingly, for total factor productivity f_i we obtain the following equation:

$$f_i = a' + \gamma k_i + \delta k e_i \tag{5}$$

10.2.3   Sources of Heterogeneity in the Extended Model

Of course, the concept of a knowledge spillover capital as a free good, accessible equally to all firms, has several weaknesses and needs further refinement. We want to focus here on three particular aspects which received special attention in recent literature on innovation (see, for example, Cohen, 1995). First, strategies of appropriation and their effectiveness are not equal across firms and industries. This means that the extent to which a firm's private knowledge 'spills' into the pool depends decisively on the firm's own actions. Effectiveness of patent protection, secrecy, time leads, complexity of design and so on may render more difficult the diffusion of information, and contribute to a better appropriation of the returns of a firm's innovative efforts. Second, the magnitude of spillovers may be related to the amount of external knowledge available, or anticipated to be available to a firm, thus the amount of existing or anticipated technological opportunities (for example, the potential of a certain technology or technological field). Third, the extent to which external knowledge can be utilized from a firm for its own innovative activity depends crucially on its 'absorptive capacity' (Cohen and Levinthal, 1989) which is a function of the 'productivity' of external knowledge with respect to the firm's own innovative activity (Levin and Reiss, 1988) and/or the amount of knowledge capital available in the firm (Cohen and Levinthal, 1989). Further, we may hypothesize that the channels by which new knowledge can reach a firm (for example, customers, suppliers, competitiors, universities and so on) may also be important for its absorptive capacity (Cohen and Levinthal, 1989; see also Mansfield, 1985).

In order to test empirically some of these effects, which are measured by qualitative variables (ordinal scale), we include 'switch' variables (a functional equivalent for interaction terms in case of qualitative variables) for the knowledge stock with respect to measures for appropriability, technological opportunities and so on in the basic model (indirect impact on firm productivity):

$$f_i = a' + \gamma_I (k_i/X_{ij} > d) + \gamma_{II} (k_i/X_{ij} \leq d) + \delta k e_i \qquad (6)$$

(in logarithmic form; X_{ij} is a qualitative measure, for example, for appropriability and so on; d indicates a threshold for the qualitative variable X_{ij}; and the index j refers to the various qualitative measures used in the empirical analysis). As a consequence, we get separate coefficients of the knowledge stock variable for the two categories ($X_{ij} \leq d$; $X_{ij} > d$) we take into consideration for each ordinal variable.

For the conceptualization of these qualitative measures we draw heavily on our earlier work on the determinants of innovation activity (see, for example, Arvanitis and Hollenstein, 1996). We expect that these factors generally will increase the impact of knowledge capital on firm performance.

In order to investigate further sources of knowledge capital heterogeneity, we use a group of characteristics of innovative activity which may affect the type of knowledge capital used in a firm. First, the structure of inputs required for the generation of new products and processes (research, development, engineering/design, follow-up investment in physical capital, organizational adjustment; see Table 10.5 on page 243) may reflect particular features of a firm's knowledge capital. Second, the objectives pursued by a firm while introducing product and process innovations (for example, increasing production flexibility, reducing energy consumption, and so on; see Table 10.6 on page 244) are part of a firm's innovation strategy. It is reasonable to assume that the type of strategy, and the types of technology and knowledge capital used are related to each other. Third, we expect that the 'degree of innovativeness' of new products and processes (for example, new to the firm only, or new to the industry worldwide; see Table 10.7 on page 245) should also reflect some special traits of knowledge capital. To test these effects we apply again the approach of Equation (6).

10.3 DATA AND VARIABLE SPECIFICATION

10.3.1 Data Sets

The firm data set used in this study was constructed by matching information from different sources, namely, is data on innovative activity and R&D expenditure 1988–90 from a survey of Swiss manufacturing firms conducted in November 1990 (see Arvanitis *et al.*, 1992); data on sales as well as labour, material and wage costs 1988–92 from a complementary survey conducted especially for this purpose; and patent data 1982–90 from the patent data bank of the Ifo-Institute for Economic Research, Munich. The matched data set contained 316 firms (Data set 1; see Appendix Table A10.1 on page 247). This sample was used for the estimations based on the patent variables. The computation of R&D capital and R&D spillover variables based on R&D expenditures led to a reduction of the sample size to 174 firms (Data set 2; see Appendix Table A10.1 on page 247).

10.3.2   Corrections for the Labour and Capital Variables

Throughout the econometric estimations total factor productivity computed according to Equation (2) was used as dependent variable (see Appendix Table A10.2 on page 247). The labour and physical capital measures used in the computation of total factor productivity have been corrected for double-counting of personnel and equipment used in R&D activities (Schankerman, 1981). Specifically, we computed labor input as the total number of full-time employees minus the number of employees working in research and development. The correction for R&D employees proved to be important; it caused an increase of about 30 per cent of the value of the coefficient of the patent capital variable (see Hall and Mairesse, 1995, for similar findings). Capital input was approximated by capital income (value added minus wage costs; flow measure) and by the book value of physical capital (stock measure). Capital income has mainly been used. We also corrected for R&D equipment by assuming that the share of the capital expenses for R&D equipment equals the value-added share of total R&D expenditure. This correction led to a slight increase in the patent capital coefficient of about 3 per cent in estimations not presented here.

10.3.3   Construction of Patent and R&D Capital Variables

The knowledge capital variables were computed according to the 'perpetual inventory method'. We used a depreciation rate of 0.25 for the construction of patent capital variables.[2] No time series for R&D expenditures were available. In order to be able to compare our calculations with the bulk of existing studies considering only R&D variables, we constructed a crude approximation for R&D capital based on the cumulated R&D expenses for the period 1988–90, which were distributed linearly over this period and depreciated with a (rather high) rate of 0.33. The effect of the initial stock of knowledge capital is not important for our estimations, because of the use of a relatively large depreciation rate. We also experimented with several time lags between the dependent variable and the patent stock variable. Within a range of three years (1988–90) the coefficients of the patent variables are almost constant; hence the mean lag seems to be about three years, in accordance with the findings of other studies (see, for example, Pakes and Schankerman, 1984; Hall *et al.*, 1986).[3]

10.3.4   Construction of Spillover Measures

We computed variables for *domestic* R&D and patent spillover variables (*IORDSO, IOPATSO*) based on the material flows between two-digit industries in manufacturing. The formulation of the spillovers (see Table 10.1) assumes that the amount of information gained from supplier industry k's R&D or patents is proportional to its importance in industry j's (to which the focusing firm i belongs) input structure, and its R&D or patent capital (see Terlekyj, 1980; Wolff and Nadiri, 1993). The R&D capital stock for the two-digit industries was calculated by the 'perpetual inventory method', with a depreciation rate of 0.15. Since the Swiss Federal Statistics Office's R&D survey is conducted only every third year, values of R&D expenditures for the missing intermediate years were approximated by linear interpolation. Further, we deflated R&D expenditures by the GNP deflator. The patent stock variables for the two-digit industries were constructed in the same way as the stock variables at the firm level.

We also computed a measure of technological proximity similar to that proposed by Jaffe (1986). Firm-specific information on the importance of seven knowledge sources (measured on a five-point Likert scale; see Table 10.1) was used to construct a seven-component 'knowledge vector' which we regard as characteristic for the knowledge basis of a firm. The 'technological proximity' between firms was computed as a distance measure between the corresponding 'knowledge vectors' (see formula for PRDSO and PPATSO in Table 10.1). These proximity measures, theoretically, can take the value of 1 in case of technologically 'similar' firms ('parallel vectors' as a geometrical analogy) and the value of 0 when no technological affinity exists ('orthogonal vectors'). The computed measures covered only a relatively narrow value range of 0.56–0.99.

The *foreign R&D* spillover variable (*FRDSO*) were constructed by the procedure described in Coe and Helpman (1995) on the basis of intra-industry trade flows between countries with high R&D intensity (see Table 10.1). It is assumed that the knowledge gain from supplier country k's R&D depends on the country-related import structure of the domestic

Table 10.1   Construction of spillover variables

Spillover variable		Comment
Domestic spillovers *(Weights based on a measure of material input flows)*		
$IORDSO_i = \sum_k v_{jk} KRD_k - KRD_i$	v_{jk}:	share of material input of industry j delivered by industry k;
	KRD_k:	R&D capital of industry k;
	KRD_i:	R&D capital of firm i;
	k:	$1, \ldots, 15$ (2-digit industries); firm i belongs to industry j.
$IOPATSO_i = \sum_k v_{jk} KPAT_k - KPAT_i$	$KPAT_k$:	patent capital of industry k;
	$KPAT_i$:	patent capital of firm i.
(Weights based on a measure of technological proximity)		
$PRDSO_i = \sum_k p_{ik} KRD_k - KRD_i$	$p_{ik} = \sum_s S_{is} S_{ks} \left(\sum_s S_{is} \sum_s S_{ks} \right)^{1/2}$	(measure of technological proximity);
	S:	sources of technological knowledge (users; suppliers; competitors; universities; professional associations/conferences; recruitment of experts; patent disclosures/licences); s: $1, \ldots, 7$; firm i; firm k; $k \neq i$.
$PPATSO_i = \sum_k p_{ik} KPAT_k - KPAT_i$		firm i; firm k; $k \neq i$.
Foreign spillovers		
$FRDSO_j = \mathrm{imp}_j \sum_m \mathrm{imp}_{jm} (RDE_{jm}/0.15)$	imp_j:	share of imports of industry j;
	imp_{jm}:	share of imports of industry j coming from country m;
	RDE_{jm}:	R&D expenditure of industry j in country m;
	m:	$1, \ldots, 8$ (USA, Japan, Germany, France, Italy, United Kingdom, the Netherlands, Sweden);
	j:	$1, \ldots, 11$ (2-digit industries).

Table 10.1 Continued

Spillover variable	Comment	
$FPATSO_j = \text{imp}_j \sum_m \text{imp}_m KPAT_m$	imp_m:	share of imports from country m;
	$KPAT_m$:	patent capital of country m.

Notes: Data sources: imports at the industry and country level: *Swiss Foreign Trade Statistics* (Swiss Federal Statistics Office, 1994); input–output linkages (2-digit industries): input–output table of the Swiss economy for 1990 (KOF/ETH; unpublished); patent data (Swiss 2-digit industries): sample of manufacturing firms (see Section 10.3 of this chapter); R&D expenditures (Swiss 2-digit industries): *Swiss R&D Statistics* (Swiss Federal Statistics Office, 1992); R&D expenditures (2-digit industries; several countries): *Research and Development Expenditure in Industry, 1973–92* (OECD, 1995); patent data (several years and countries): *Basic Science and Technology Statistics* (OECD, 1993). For data at the firm level, see Section 10.3.1 of this chapter.

two-digit industry j (to which the focusing firm i belongs), weighted with the import share of this industry. We calculated crude measures of R&D stocks for eleven two-digit industries of the USA, Japan and six European countries by dividing the R&D expenditure data for 1991 by 0.15 (that is, implying a small growth rate of R&D expenditure relative to the depreciation rate). This procedure can be justified on grounds of the low sensitivity of the coefficients of the R&D capital variables with respect to the depreciation rate.

A somewhat modified procedure was used to construct the *foreign patent* spillover variable (*FPATSO*). Patent stocks at the industry level were not available, therefore we computed patent capital measures at the country level by the 'perpetual inventory method' with a depreciation rate of 0.25 on the basis of the sum of yearly 'external' and 'resident patent applications' for the eight countries to be taken into consideration (see OECD, 1993). The reason for considering the sum of these two flow variables is that the ratios of external and internal patent applications vary strongly among countries.[4]

Throughout this study we used standard OLS procedures to estimate the parameters of the different equations. The occurence of heteroscedasticity was treated conventionally by applying the procedure proposed by White (1980) to calculate heteroscedasticity-robust standard errors. Dummies for thirteen two-digit industries have been used throughout in the econometric estimations to capture heterogeneity effects at the industry level.

10.4   EMPIRICAL RESULTS

10.4.1   Domestic and Foreign Spillovers

Basic Model

We estimated Equation (2) with both types of knowledge capital (patent and R&D capital). We obtained an elasticity of total factor productivity with respect to knowledge capital of 0.093 (when c_i in Equation (2) is approximated with the book value of physical capital) and 0.114 (when capital income is used as a proxy for physical capital), respectively, in the case of patent capital (columns 1 and 3 in Table 10.2); the corresponding elasticity amounts to 0.041 in the case of R&D capital (column 2 in Table 10.2). The coefficients of both knowledge variables (patent and R&D capital) are positive and statistically significant (5 per cent level and 10 per cent level, respectively) for the estimations reported in Table 10.2.[5] Thus there is a discernible contribution of knowledge capital to firm performance measured by total factor productivity.[6] Nevertheless, compared to elasticity estimates for other countries at the firm level, our figures are rather low (for recent similar studies, see Harhoff, 1998 or Hall and Mairesse, 1995).

Domestic Spillovers

We estimated Equation (5) with both knowledge capital variables and four different measures of domestic spillovers, two for each type of weighting variable (material input flows: *IORDSO*; *IOPATSO*; technological proximity: *PRDSO*; *PPATSO*); and patent as well as R&D externalities were taken into consideration for every type of weighting variable, as defined in Table 10.1.

As Table 10.2 shows, we obtained statistically significant positive coefficients of the R&D spillover variable of about the same magnitude for both types of weighting variable (for *iordso*: 0.227; see column 5 in Table 10.2; for *prdso*: 0.200; see column 9).[7] The elasticity with respect to patent spillover variable is negative but not statistically significant in the case of the weighting variable based on material input flows (for *iopatso*: −0.022; column 4 in Table 10.2). However, the estimate for the same parameter for the spillover variable based on a measure of technological proximity yielded a positive and statistical significant coefficient (for *ppatso*: 0.452; column 7). Thus we find a quite appreciable effect of domestic R&D spillovers on firm productivity; an even stronger effect is estimated for patent spillovers, at least for the technological proximity measure. The influence of weighting variables on the magnitude of the coefficients of the spillover variables is rather small in the case of R&D, but it makes quite a difference in the case of patents. The technological proximity measure is the more appropriate one from a conceptual point of view, and is measured at the firm level; however, it is based on subjective assessments of the 'knowledge profiles' of a certain number of firms considered to represent adequately the entire population of each two-digit industry. The measure based on material input flows is conceptually less satisfactory (see Section 10.2) and is measured only at the industry level; on the other hand, it is constructed on a more solid quantitative basis. On the whole, it is difficult to assess which weighting variable yielded more plausible results. However the results do not diverge very much, so we consider them a first approximation to be elaborated by further research.

The effect of the spillover variables in three out of four cases in Table 10.2 is considerably larger than the effect of a firm's own R&D or patent capital. It is difficult to assess the plausibility of this result, because there are few other studies with which we can make a direct comparison. On the whole, there is a general tendency in most studies for the spillover effect to be larger than that of a firm's own knowledge capital, but it is not clear by what magnitude (see, for example, Goto and Suzuki, 1989; Jaffe, 1986; Harhoff, 1994).

A further point to be considered is the relative strength of inter- and intra-sectoral effects (the sector being defined here as a two-digit industry). According to our results, most of the impact of spillovers can be traced back to intersectoral effects, that is, most productive knowledge comes not from the two-digit industry to which the focusing firm belongs, but from all other industries (elasticity of 0.453 versus 0.011; see columns 10 and 12 in Table 10.2).[8]

Foreign Spillovers

Patent and R&D spillovers of foreign knowledge exert a statistically significant positive effect on firm output. The coefficient of the spillover variables takes the value of 0.307 and 0.373 for R&D and patent spillovers, respectively (columns 1 and 2 in Table 10.3). Foreign R&D spillovers are somewhat stronger than foreign patent spillovers. For both kinds of spillover we find elasticities that are larger than those of the firm's own knowledge capital. Most existing studies on foreign technological spillovers are at the country level; thus, a comparison with our results is difficult. At any rate, foreign spillovers appear to have in most studies a stronger impact on firm performance than the firm's own knowledge capital (see, for example, Mohnen, 1992; Rogers, 1995). Our results do not permit a clear-cut statement as to the relative strength of domestic and foreign

236

Table 10.2 Impact of knowledge capital and domestic spillovers on total factor productivity

Explanatory variables	Basic model			Spillovers based on bmaterial input flows		Spillovers based on technological proximity				Intra-sectoral	Inter-sectoral	
	1	2	3	4	5	6	7	8	9	10	11	12
Intercept	2.980* (0.162)	2.937* (0.260)	2.954* (0.198)	4.529* (1.056)		0.844 (3.606)		0.382 (12.882)		2.963* (0.214)	0.385 (2.691)	
kpat	0.093* (0.031)		0.114* (0.030)	0.110* (0.041)		0.134* (0.036)	0.137* (0.031)			0.107* (0.047)	0.138* (0.036)	0.139* (0.030)
krd		0.041 (0.024)			0.043 (0.026)			0.036 (0.032)	0.036 (0.032)			
iordso					0.227* (0.021)							
iopatso				−0.414 (0.275)								
prdso								0.172 (0.933)	0.200* (0.022)			
ppatso						0.325 (0.542)	0.452* (0.031)					

ppatso (intra)							0.011 (0.190)					
ppatso (inter)											0.395 (0.404)	0.453* (0.032)
N	309	170	309	309	170	267	267	170	267	170	267	267
R^2adj	0.105	0.073	0.104	0.108	–	0.112	–	0.096	–	0.097	0.113	–
SER	0.669	0.651	0.716	0.715	0.652	0.693	0.692	0.682	0.679	0.697	0.693	0.691

Notes: The small letters denote the logarithms of the variables; *kpat*: patent capital; *krd*: R&D capital; see Table 10.1 for the definition of the spillover variables; OLS estimates of Equations (2) and (5); heteroscedasticity-robust coefficients (White procedure; standard errors in brackets; statistical significance at the 5 per cent level is indicated with *); 13 industry dummies (2-digit). We omitted the constant term in the Equations (5), (7) (see col. 6 for estimates with constant term), (9) (see col. 8 for estimates with constant term) and (12) (see col. 11 for estimates with constant term) in order to avoid the problem of multicollinearity of the variables *iordso, prdso, ppatso* and *ppatso* (inter) with the corresponding constant terms in these equations.

Table 10.3   Impact of foreign spillovers on
total factor productivity

Explanatory variables	1	2
kpat	0.113*	
	(0.030)	
krd		0.019
		(0.029)
frdso		0.373*
		(0.037)
fpatso	0.307*	
	(0.019)	
N	309	171
R^2adj	–	–
SER	0.718	0.739

Notes: See notes in Table 10.2; the omitted intercepts are throughout *not* statistically significant (5 per cent level); 13 industry dummies (2-digit).

spillovers; R&D spillovers point to stronger international effects, patent spillover, partly at least, to the opposite direction.

10.4.2   Impact of Appropriability and Technological Opportunities

In this section we try to obtain a more differentiated picture of the spillover mechanism by taking account of appropriability, technological potential, and the effects of various external knowledge sources (users, suppliers, universities, and so on) at the firm level. To this end we estimated Equation (6) for several Xs separately, with *kpat* as knowledge capital variable and *iopatso* as spillover variable. Thus pairs of 'switch' variables of knowledge capital were constructed to capture the effects of the following determinants of innovative activity (and, as a consequence, of firm-specific knowledge capital) on firm performance (see Table 10.4 and Appendix 10.2): an overall appropriability measure (*APPR*); a proxy for the general technological potential relevant to the firm's innovative activity (TPOT); a variable for the specific contribution of external knowledge to a firm's own generation of innovative knowledge (*EXTINT*); a measure of the extent of acquisition of external knowledge (*EXT*) and a measure of the extent of external knowledge from foreign sources (*EXTF*) (as a more specific feature of *EXT*); qualitative measures for the importance of a number of external sources of knowledge for the firm's

Table 10.4 Indirect impact of appropriability and technological opportunities on total factor productivity

X	Product		Process	
	$\gamma_I\ (k_i/X_{ij} > 3)$	$\gamma_{II}\ (k_i/X_{ij} \leq 3)$	$\gamma_I\ (k_i/X_{ij} > 3)$	$\gamma_{II}\ (k_i/X_{ij} \leq 3)$
$APPR$[1]	0.157*	0.081*	0.127*	0.109*
	(0.040)	(0.033)	(0.052)	(0.033)
$TPOT$[2]	0.157*	0.072		
	(0.029)	(0.046)		
$EXTINT$[3]	0.111*	0.115*	0.171*	0.090*
	(0.045)	(0.034)	(0.035)	(0.033)
EXT[4]	0.175*	0.085*	0.177*	0.094*
	(0.040)	(0.035)	(0.036)	(0.033)
$EXTF$[5]	0.144*	0.104*	0.146*	0.108*
	(0.048)	(0.032)	(0.063)	(0.030)
Knowledge sources				
$USER$	0.131*	0.071	0.075	0.117*
(customers/	(0.031)	(0.053)	(0.076)	(0.030)
users of				
products)				
$SUPP$	0.116	0.114*	0.103*	0.119*
(suppliers of	(0.070)	(0.032)	(0.044)	(0.035)
materials/				
equipment)				
$COMP$	0.109*	0.116*	0.209	0.111*
(competitors)	(0.035)	(0.039)	(0.117)	(0.030)
$UNIV$	0.145*	0.099*	0.124*	0.112*
(universities/	(0.036)	(0.037)	(0.058)	(0.033)
scientific				
laboratories)				
$ASSOC$	0.021	0.118*	0.016	0.115*
(professional	(0.070)	(0.030)	(0.077)	(0.030)
associations/				
conferences)				
$EXPERT$	0.103*	0.134*	0.079	0.135*
(recruitment	(0.032)	(0.051)	(0.052)	(0.033)
of experts)				
PAT	0.104*	0.118*	0.075	0.119*
(patent	(0.036)	(0.037)	(0.080)	(0.032)
disclosures/				
licences)				
$ACQUIS$	0.130*	0.108*	0.123*	0.111*
(acquisition of	(0.033)	(0.037)	(0.036)	(0.036)
other firms)				

Table 10.4   Continued

X	Product		Process	
	$\gamma_{II}\,(k_i/X_{ij} > 3)$	$\gamma_{II}\,(k_i/X_{ij} \leq 3)$	$\gamma_I\,(k_i/X_{ij} > 3)$	$\gamma_{II}\,(k_i/X_{ij} \leq 3)$
COOP	0.123*	0.080*	0.135*	0.076*
(subsidiaries/	(0.036)	(0.034)	(0.040)	(0.033)
joint ventures,				
etc.)				

Notes: 1. *APPR*: overall measure of the extent to which innovations can be protected from competition by means of patents, secrecy, lead time, etc.; 2. *TPOT*: general technological potential, i.e. scientific and technological knowledge relevant to the firm's innovative activity; 3. *EXTINT*: specific contribution of external knowledge to the firm's own innovative activity; 4. *EXT*: extent of acquisition of external knowledge; 5. *EXTF*: extent of acquisition of external knowledge from other countries. OLS estimates of Equations (6) ($N = 309$); *kpat* as knowledge capital variable and *iopatso* as spillover variable; all variables (except *COOP*, which is a dummy variable) reflect assessments of the surveyed firms measured on a 5-point Likert scale, and have been measured separately for product and process innovations (except *TPOT*). The threshold d in Equation (6) was set at the value 3. Separate regressions were run for each pair of 'switch' variables (e.g. *kpat*/*APPR* > 3 and *kpat*/*APPR* ≤ 3). We report for each regression only the coefficients of the pairs of 'switch' variables. Heteroscedasticity-robust standard errors are printed in brackets under the estimated coefficients. Statistical significance at the 5 per cent level is indicated by *. 13 industry dummies (2-digit) are included in the regression equations. A two-tailed t-test (5 per cent threshold) was performed for the difference of the parameters of every pair of switch variables used in the estimations. There is a statistically discernible *difference* of the coefficients of all pairs of variables included in this table except *EXTINT* (product) and *SUPP* (product).

innovative activity (alternatively to *EXTINT* or *EXT*).[9] Table 10.4 contains the results of the separate regressions run for each pair of 'switch' variables. In order to save space we report for each regression only the (jointly estimated) coefficients of the pairs of 'switch' variables.

We expected a positive impact of *APPR*, *EXTINT*, *EXT* and *EXTF* on a firm's total factor productivity for product as well as process innovations. The empirical results confirmed these expectations apart from in a single case (*EXTINT*/product; see Table 10.4). Both for product and process innovations, the coefficient of the patent stock variable for firms with high appropriability (*APPR*) is considerably larger than that for firms with low appropriability, and also larger than the coefficient for all firms when we do not distinguish between high and low imitation protection. This effect seems to be stronger for products than for processes. Thus a high effectiveness of appropriability strategies with respect to both products and processes leads to a larger impact of knowledge input on a firm's total factor productivity.

The results for the technological potential (*TPOT*), the acquisition of external knowledge in general (*EXT*) and of *foreign* external knowledge (*EXTF*) in particular are highly plausible as well (see Table 10.4). The positive impact of *TPOT* is quite large, and knowledge capital is more productive in firms which use much external (foreign) knowledge. A high contribution of external knowledge to a firm's own innovative activity leads only in case of new production techniques to a larger than 'average' impact on performance (*EXTINT* for process innovation). There is no statistically discernible difference between the two coefficients in case of product innovations (*EXTINT* for product innovation). We cannot find any plausible argument for this finding, which is not in accordance with the general pattern of the results we obtained for the individual knowledge sources (see below).

For new products, the intensive use of four out of a total of nine external knowledge sources is associated with a higher contribution of patent stock to total factor productivity (see Table 10.4); the largest elasticity (with respect to patent capital) is found for knowledge from universities, research institutions and scientific literature (0.145; *UNIV*). Further information sources with a positive impact on firm productivity are customers/users of products (*USER*), newly acquired firms (*ACQUIS*), and subsidiaries/joint ventures (*COOP*). For five of the knowledge sources, the coefficient of the highly intensive users is lower than (in case of suppliers, equal to) that for firms which do not use much information from these sources. This is not surprising for two of them (suppliers, professional associations/conferences), because suppliers' knowledge is of minor importance for the generation of new products, and information from professional associations refers rather to technical standards and general knowledge available to every firm. We cannot find an explanation for the missing positive effect of qualified personnel (*EXPERT*) and patent disclosures/licences (*PAT*). For process innovations we get a somewhat different pattern with respect to external knowledge used compared with that in the case of new products. A high intensity of use of knowledge coming from universities and scientific laboratories, newly acquired firms and subsidiaries/joint ventures is related also in this case to a more productive patent capital. But we find the strongest positive influence on total factor productivity having its origin in information from firms of the same industry (competitors). It seems that the comparison of production techniques with those of competitors yields important clues for the improvement of the cost structure, thus helping to raise productivity. For five out of a total of nine external knowledge sources, high intensity of use does not lead to high productivity of patent stock. This is particularly plausible in the case of knowledge from users of firm's products, which has only a distant and indirect relationship to expertise referring to production techniques. With respect to the variable ASSOC (information from professional association/ conferences) the same argument holds that we have developed easier when explaining the effect of the ASSOC variable on product innovations. It is difficult to find an explanation for the missing positive effects for *EXPERT, PAT,* and especially *SUPP.* In the case of process innovations it is quite possible that some of the improvement effects of technology are already incorporated in physical capital. On the whole, it seems that there are considerable differences among various external knowledge sources with respect to their influence on the productivity of knowledge capital for both product and process innovations.

10.4.3   Impact of Some Characteristics of Innovative Activity

In this last step we try to identify further sources of knowledge capital heterogeneity which seem to exert an influence on firm performance. In order to relax the hypothesis of homogeneous knowledge capital, we use a group of characteristics of innovative activity which may affect the type of knowledge capital used in a firm. Three sets of characteristics of the innovation process at the firm level were applied to qualify knowledge capital by taking account of possible forms of heterogeneity (see Tables 10.5–10.7). We distinguish, first, five types of input which may be used to generate new products and processes: research, development, engineering/design, follow-up investment (in plant, machinery, equipment, trial production, training and so on), and organizational inputs. Second, the output of the innovation process can be characterized by the specific objectives underlying the innovation projects pursued by a firm (in a certain time period); nine such objectives were taken into consideration in this study (decrease of energy, material, labour costs, etc.). Finally, a further characterization can be achieved on the basis of the degree of 'innovativeness' of products and processes (new only to the firm, new to the industry and so on). We applied the same approach as in subsection 10.4.2, constructing pairs of 'switch' variables and running separate regressions of Equation (6) for each pair of 'switch' variables with *kpat* as knowledge capital variable and *ioparso* as spillover variable. In Tables 10.5–10.7 we report for each regression only the (jointly estimated) coefficients of the pairs of 'switch' variables.

For product as well as for process innovations, firms with high inputs for development activities, show also a high coefficient of patent stock (0.164 and 0.152 respectively, significantly higher than the one for all

Table 10.5 Indirect impact of several inputs of innovation on total factor productivity

X	Product		Process	
	$\gamma_I (k_i/X_{ij} > 3)$	$\gamma_{II} (k_i/X_{ij} \leq 3)$	$\gamma_I (k_i/X_{ij} > 3)$	$\gamma_{II} (k_i/X_{ij} \leq 3)$
R	0.127*	0.112*	0.124*	0.113*
(research)	(0.046)	(0.033)	(0.068)	(0.032)
D	0.164*	0.056	0.152*	0.104*
(development)	(0.034)	(0.038)	(0.061)	(0.031)
ED	0.094*	0.137*	0.169*	0.098*
(engineering/ design)	(0.035)	(0.041)	(0.035)	(0.034)
FI	0.100	0.117*	0.144*	0.097*
(follow-up investment)[1]	(0.052)	(0.033)	(0.035)	(0.038)
OA	0.123*	0.112*	0.145*	0.091*
(organizational adjustment)[2]	(0.057)	(0.033)	(0.031)	(0.041)

Notes: 1. Follow-up investment linked to innovation (trial production, training, market analysis, investment in plant, machinery and equipment linked to new products and processes); 2. Organizational adjustment resulting from the introduction of new products and processes. See note in Table 10.4. There is a statistically discernible *difference* of the coefficients of all pairs of variables included in this table.

firms 'on the average'; see Table 10.5). We also find 'larger-than-average' coefficients of the patent capital variable for high inputs of research activities, but the effects are considerable smaller than those for development activities (0.127 and 0.124, respectively). Thus development is a dominant (and highly productive) feature of innovative activity of Swiss manufacturing. For product innovation, engineering/design and follow-up investment do not seem to contribute to a higher productivity of knowledge capital. Finally, a small positive effect comes from organizational adjustment (which is the fourth type of innovation input we take into account in this investigation). In the case of process-oriented innovative activity, we find that its productivity depends to a large extent on inputs in engineering, follow-up investment linked to innovation, and organizational adjustment. Such effects seem to be quite compatible with changes of work organization implied by major changes of production technology.

The objectives of innovation pursued by a firm during a certain time period should reflect important elements of its innovation strategy. Thus it seems worthwhile to investigate the impact of such objectives on performance. In particular, we examine the indirect impact on total factor productivity, that is, the effect of innovation objectives on the elasticity of total factor productivity with respect to knowledge capital. A strong orientation of goals towards the creation of new markets and the technical improvement of existing products exert a significant positive influence on the coefficient of the patent stock variable (see Table 10.6); for firms applying this strategy (among others) we obtain a productivity elasticity considerably higher than the value we get for firms that did not pursue this strategy, and higher than the elasticity value estimated for all the firms in our sample. The findings related to process-oriented objectives are more heterogenous. Two out of the three classical cost-reducing strategies included in our survey, namely reduction of material consumption and, to a lesser extent, reduction of the share of wage costs, yield a 'larger than average' coefficient of the

Table 10.6   Indirect impact of objectives of innovation on total factor productivity

X	Product		Process	
	$\gamma_I \, (k/X = 1)$	$\gamma_{II} \, (k/X = 0)$	$\gamma_I \, (k/X = 1)$	$\gamma_{II} \, (k/X = 0)$
Creation of new markets	0.158* (0.041)	0.089* (0.033)		
Technical improvement of products	0.123* (0.031)	0.054 (0.074)		
Increase of production flexibility			0.126* (0.029)	0.095 (0.055)
Reduction of the share of wage costs			0.132* (0.046)	0.100* (0.034)
Reduction of material consumption			0.187* (0.056)	0.098* (0.032)
Reduction of energy consumption			0.088 (0.080)	0.118* (0.032)
Improvement of product quality resulting from modification to the production technique			0.133* (0.039)	0.090* (0.039)
Improvement of working conditions			0.153* (0.052)	0.095* (0.031)
Reduction of environmental damage			0.075 (0.046)	0.138* (0.035)

Notes: See note in Table 10.4. X takes the value 1 for 'yes', and 0 for 'no'. There is a statistically discernible *difference* of the coefficients of all pairs of variables included in this table.

knowledge capital variable. We could not find any discernible productivity contribution of an energy-reducing innovation strategy. The introduction of new production techniques improving working conditions, the increase of product quality, and, to a lesser extent, the enhancement of production flexibility – all three strategies involving the application of advanced manufacturing technology – seemingly are associated with a substantially increased productivity of knowledge input. Finally, we could not find any positive effect of knowledge capital on total factor productivity for firms that pursued a strategy aiming at a reduction of environmental damage.

For firms that introduced products 'new to their industry worldwide' we could estimate an elasticity of total factor productivity with respect to patent capital that is about 60 per cent higher than the 'average' value for all firms (see Table 10.7). Products that are 'new only to the firm itself', as well as modifications of already existing products lead to only moderate increases of the coefficient of the patent stock variable, whereas products 'new to the industry in Switzerland' do not exert any (indirect) positive influence on total factor productivity. For process innovations, we obtained a somewhat different pattern: the largest impact on total factor productivity for process innovations was found for firms with processes 'new to the firm itself', or firms that use modifications of already applied production techniques, but

Table 10.7 Indirect impact of the degree of innovativeness of products and processes on total factor productivity

X	Product		Process	
	$\gamma_I\ (k/X = 1)$	$\gamma_{II}\ (k/X = 0)$	$\gamma_I\ (k/X = 1)$	$\gamma_{II}\ (k/X = 0)$
Modification of existing products/ processes	0.118* (0.026)	0.099 (0.088)	0.156* (0.036)	0.081 (0.039)
Product/process new to the *firm*	0.125* (0.057)	0.112* (0.031)	0.153* (0.033)	0.084* (0.038)
Product/process new to the industry in *Switzerland*	0.084 (0.078)	0.118* (0.031)	0.133* (0.030)	0.110* (0.038)
Product/process new to the industry *world-wide*	0.181* (0.046)	0.082* (0.033)	0.126* (0.050)	0.112* (0.033)

Notes: See note in Table 10.4. *X* takes the value 1 for 'yes', and 0 for 'no'. There is a statistically discernible *difference* of the coefficient of all pairs of variables included in this table.

not for firms that introduced 'world-wide new processes'. A small positive effect could be found also for processes 'new to the industry in Switzerland'.

10.5   CONCLUSIONS

We obtain positive estimates of the productivity effect of knowledge capital (measured by either R&D or patent data). The coefficients of both domestic spillover variables (R&D- and patent-based, respectively) are significantly positive when technological proximity is used as weighting variable, only the one based on R&D expenditures when material input flows are the underlying weighting variable. In all three cases, the coefficients are considerably larger than that of knowledge capital stock. Most of this effect can be traced back to intersectoral knowledge links. Thus spillovers have a substantial positive influence on firm performance in Swiss manufacturing, in accordance with the specific character of this country as a small, open economy with very intensive economic interactions with other countries. Consequently, foreign patent and R&D spillovers also exert a positive effect on total factor productivity of a firm, a finding similar to those reported in most studies dealing with international spillovers at the country level.

Furthermore, the degree of appropriability, the amount of external knowledge available to the firm, and the specific use of certain knowledge sources (universities, firm acquisitions and co-operations both for product and process innovations, information from users for new products, and competitors for new processes) exert a significant positive influence on knowledge capital's impact on a firm's total factor productivity. Development inputs dominating innovative activity of Swiss manufacturing firms enhance the productivity of a firm's knowledge stock, whereas engineering/design, follow-up investments and organizational inputs are important primarily for process innovations. There are discernible differences in the magnitude of the effects of several innovation objectives on the output elasticities of knowledge capital which have a plausible economic interpretation. We also get reasonable explanations for most of the results referring to measures of innovativeness.

On the whole, the use of the qualitative measures of several characteristics of innovative activity proved to be informative with respect to knowledge-capital heterogeneity, thus adding to our insights regarding the channels through which technical progress enhances performance.

Appendix 10.1

Table A10.1 Composition of the data sets

Industry	Data set 1		Data set 2	
	N	%	N	%
Manufacturing total	**316**	**100**	**174**	**100**
Food/beverage/tobacco	30	9.5	12	7.0
Textiles	19	6.0	10	5.7
Clothing/leather/footwear	9	2.8	4	2.3
Wood/furniture	20	6.3	6	3.4
Paper	13	4.1	6	3.4
Printing	35	11.1	15	8.6
Chemicals	20	6.3	10	5.7
Rubber/plastics	18	5.7	13	7.5
Glass/stone/clay	16	5.1	7	4.0
Metals, metalworking	46	14.6	26	14.9
Machinery/transportation	45	14.2	32	18.5
Electrical machinery/instruments	29	9.1	24	13.9
Watches	11	3.5	7	4.0
Other manufacturing	5	1.6	2	1.1
Firm size (number of employees)				
6–49		35.4		23.6
50–199		33.6		35.1
> 200		31.0		41.3

Notes: Data set 1 was used for estimations based on the patent capital variable, and data set 2 for estimations based on the R&D capital variable.

Table A10.2 Descriptive statistics of the metric variables used in the estimations (values in Swiss francs)

Variable	N	Mean	Standard deviation	Minimum	Maximum
KPAT	316	2.3	15.9	0	195.0
KRD	174	4 291 000	15 626 000	0	160 526 670
IORDSO	174	1 894 595 590	1 160 238 100	310 492 670	4 810 788 790
IOPATSO	316	191.4	142.4	16.2	530.7
PRDSO	174	915 490	46 542	661 081	989 473

Table A10.2   Continued

Variable	N	Mean	Standard deviation	Minimum	Maximum
PPATSO	316	789.0	45.3	471.5	862.7
FRDSO	316	20 331 400 000	29 112 280 000	264 111 333	82 548 080 000
FPATSO	316	38 822.5	28 570.9	5 081.7	93 038.2
Log F	316	3.223	0.663	0.901	5.340

Notes: *KPAT*: patent capital 1990 ($d = 0.25$); *KRD*: R&D capital 1990 ($d = 0.33$); *F*: total factor productivity based on capital income (value added minus wages) 1992; see Table 10.1 for the definition of the spillover variables.

Appendix 10.2

Questionnaire (for a full version, see Arvanitis *et al.*, 1992, appendix):

Question 2.1d
The introduction of product/process innovations required expenditures for:

	1	2	3	4	5
Research	☑	☑	☑	☑	☑
Development	☑	☑	☑	☑	☑
Engineering/design	☑	☑	☑	☑	☑
Follow-up investments linked to innovation	☑	☑	☑	☑	☑
Organizational adjustment	☑	☑	☑	☑	☑

(scale: 1 = none; 5 = very high)

Question 3.7
Evaluate the overall effectiveness of available methods of protecting new products/processes from imitation (e.g. patents, time lead, secrecy, etc.):

1 ☑   2 ☑   3 ☑   4 ☑   5 ☑
(Scale: 1 = ineffective; 5 = highly effective)

Question 4.1
Evaluate the technological potential available for the firm's activities:

1 ☑   2 ☑   3 ☑   4 ☑   5 ☑
(Scale: 1 = very low; 5 = very high)

Question 5.1

Indicate the importance of the following external sources of information for the innovation activities (product/process):

	1	2	3	4	5
Clients or customers	☑	☑	☑	☑	☑
Suppliers of materials, components and equipment	☑	☑	☑	☑	☑
Competitors in the firm's own line of business	☑	☑	☑	☑	☑
Firms of the same group, joint ventures, other forms of co-operation	☑	☑	☑	☑	☑
Universities / research laboratories, scientific journals	☑	☑	☑	☑	☑
Professional associations, conferences	☑	☑	☑	☑	☑
Recruitment of experts	☑	☑	☑	☑	☑
Patent disclosures, licenses	☑	☑	☑	☑	☑

(Scale: 1 = of minor importance; 5 = of major importance)

Question 5.3

Indicate the extent of use of external knowledge from other countries:

1	2	3	4	5
☑	☑	☑	☑	☑

(Scale: 1 = very small; 5 = very large)

Question 5.4

Evaluate the contribution of external knowledge to firm's own innovative activity:

1	2	3	4	5
☑	☑	☑	☑	☑

(Scale: 1 = very small; 5 = very large)

Notes

*   Our research was supported by the Swiss National Science Foundation and the Swiss Ministry of Economic Affairs.

1.   Under the assumption of constant returns to scale for the conventional inputs L and C, it is easy to show that $s_c = \alpha$ and $1 - s_c = \beta$.

2.   In accordance with the findings of most other empirical studies (see, for example, Hall and Mairesse, 1995), the particular choice of depreciation rates does not affect the estimation results by very much.

3.   For details, see Arvanitis (1999).

4.   On the other hand, we commit a measurement error by double-counting the patents applied for both at home and abroad. We assume that the first type of error (different ratios of external and internal patents) is much more important.

5.   Additional estimations with a cross-section for 1988 yielded a knowledge capital coefficient (patent) of 0.097.

6.   We obtained similar results with value-added, sales and average labour productivity as performance variables (see Arvanitis and Hollenstein, 1998; and Arvanitis, 1999).
7.   We omitted the constant term in the Equations (5), (7) (see column 6 for estimates with constant term), (9) (see column 8 for estimates with constant term) and (12) (see column 11 for estimates with constant term) in Table 10.2 in order to avoid the problem of multicollinearity of the variables *iordso*, *prdso*, *ppatso* and *ppatso* (inter), with the corresponding constant terms in these equations.
8.   This result is in accordance with the finding of the next subsection that (qualitatively measured) knowledge coming from competitors (*COMP*; see Table 10.4) does not have a positive impact on firm performance.
9.   The tightness of the relationship between *EXTINT* and the set of external knowledge sources was investigated by estimating an ordered probit model with *EXTINT* as dependent variable, and *USER*, ... , *COOP* as right-hand variables; the coefficients of all knowledge source variables were found to be positive and statistical significant at the 5 per cent level (see Arvanitis, 1999).

References

ARVANITIS, S. (1999) *Generierung von neuem technischem Wissen, Produktivität und Arbeits qualifikation in der schweizerischen Industrie: Eine Querschnitts analyse auf der Basis von Unternehmensdaten*, Unpublished dissertation, University of Zurich.

ARVANITIS, S. and HOLLENSTEIN, H. (1996) 'Industrial Innovation in Switzerland: A Model-based Analysis with Survey Data', in A. Kleinknecht (ed.), *Determinants of Innovation. The Message from New Indicators*, London: Macmillan, pp. 13–62.

ARVANITIS, S. and HOLLENSTEIN, H. (1998) 'Firm Performance, Innovation and Technological Spillovers: A Cross-section Analysis with Swiss Firm Data', in G. Eliasson, C. Green and C. R. McCann (eds), *Microfoundations of Economic Growth. A Schumpeterian Perspective*, Ann Harbor, Mich.: University of Michigan Press; pp. 271–84.

ARVANITIS, S., FRICK, A., ETTER, R. and HOLLENSTEIN, H. (1992) *Innovationsfähigkeit und Innovationsverhalten der Schweizer Industrie*, Berne: Bundesamt für Konjunkturfragen.

COE, D. T. and HELPMAN, E. (1995) 'International R&D Spillovers', *European Economic Review*, vol. 39, no. 9, pp. 859–87.

COHEN, W. M. (1995) 'Empirical Studies of Innovative Activity', in P. Stoneman (ed.), *Handbook of Innovation and Technological Change*, Oxford: Basil Blackwell, pp. 182–264.

COHEN, W. M. and LEVINTHAL, D. A. (1989) 'Innovation and Learning: The Two Faces of R&D', *Economic Journal*, vol. 99, no. 398, pp. 569–96.

ENGLANDER, A. S., EVENSON, R. and HANAZAKI, M. (1988) 'R&D, Innovation and Total Factor Productivity', *OECD Economic Studies*, no. 11, pp. 156–91.

GEROSKI, P. A. (1995) 'Do Spillovers Undermine the Incentive to Innovate?', in S. Dowrick (ed.), *Economic Approaches to Innovation*, Aldershot, UK and Brookfield, USA: Edward Elgar, pp. 76–97.

GOTO, A. and SUZUKI, K. (1989) 'R&D Capital, Rate of Return on R&D Investment and Spillover of R&D in Japanese Manufacturing Industries', *Review of Economics and Statistics*, vol. 71, no. 4, pp. 555–64.

GRILICHES, Z. (1979) 'Issues in Assessing the Contribution of Research and Development to Productivity Growth', *Bell Journal of Economics*, vol. 10, no. 1, pp. 92–116.

GRILICHES, Z. (1992) 'The Search for R&D Spillovers', *Scandinavian Journal of Economics*, vol. 94 (Suppl.), pp. 29–47.

HALL, B. H., GRILICHES, Z. and HAUSMAN, J. A. (1986) 'Patents and R and D: Is there a Lag?' *International Economic Review*, vol. 27, no. 2, pp. 265–83.

HALL, B. H. and MAIRESSE, J. (1995) 'Exploring the Relationship between R&D and Productivity in French Manufacturing Firms', *Journal of Econometrics*, vol. 65, no. 1, 263–93.

HARHOFF, D. (1994) 'Searching for R&D Spillovers among German Manufacturing Firms', Paper Prepared for the ZEW Workshop on Productivity, R&D and Innovation at the Firm Level, Mannheim, Germany, June 24–25.

HARHOFF, D. (1998) 'R&D and Productivity in German Manufacturing Firms', *Economics of Innovation and New Technology*, vol. 6, no. 1, pp. 29–49.

JAFFE, A. B. (1986) 'Technological Opportunity and Spillovers of R&D: Evidence from Firms' Patents, Profits and Market Value', *American Economic Review*, vol. 76, no. 5, pp. 984–1001.

LEVIN, R. C. and REISS, P. C. (1988) 'Cost-reducing and Demand-creating R&D with Spillovers', *Rand Journal of Economics*, vol. 19, no. 4, pp. 538–56.

MANSFIELD, E. (1985) 'How Rapidly Does New Industrial Technology Leak Out?', *Journal of Industrial Economics*, vol. 34, pp. 217–23.

MOHNEN, P. (1992) *The Relationship between R&D and Productivity Growth in Canada and Other Major Industrialized Countries*, Ottawa: Canada Communications Group Publishing.

OECD (1993) *Basic Science and Technology Statistics*, Paris: OECD.

OECD (1995) *Research and Development Expenditure in Industry, 1973–92*, Paris: OECD.

PAKES, A. and SCHANKERMAN, M. (1984) 'The Rate of Obsolescence of Patents, Research Gestation Lags, and the Private Rate of Return to Research Resources', in Z. Griliches (ed.), *R&D, Patents, and Productivity*, Chicago, Ill.: University of Chicago Press, pp. 73–88.

ROGERS, M. (1995) 'International Knowledge Spillovers: A Cross-Country Study', in S. Dowrick (ed.), *Economic Approaches to Innovation*, Aldershot, UK and Brookfield, USA: Edward Elgar, pp. 166–88.

SCHANKERMAN, M. (1981) 'The Effects of Double-Counting and Expensing on the Measured Returns to R&D', *Review of Economics and Statistics*, vol. 63, no. 3, pp. 454–8.

SPENCE, M. (1984) 'Cost Reduction, Competition and Industry Performance', *Econometrica*, vol. 25, no. 1, pp. 101–21.

Swiss Federal Statistics Office (1993) *Swiss R&D Statistics, 1992*, Berne: Federal Statistics Office.

Swiss Federal Statistics Office (1994) *Foreign Trade Statistics, 1994*, Berne: Federal Statistics Office.

TERLEKYJ, N. (1980) 'Direct and Indirect Effects of Industrial Research and Development on the Productivity Growth of Industries', in J. N. Kendrick and

B. N. Vaccaras (eds), *New Developments in Productivity Measurement and Analysis*, Chicago, Ill.: University of Chicago Press, pp. 359–86.

VAN POTTELSBERGHE DE LA POTTERIE, B. (1997) 'Issues in Assessing the Effect of Interindustry R&D Spillovers', *Economic Systems Research*, vol. 9, no. 2, pp. 331–56.

WHITE, H. (1980) 'A Heteroscedasticity-Consistent Covariance Matrix Estimator and a Direct Test for Heteroscedasticity', *Econometrica*, vol. 48, no. 4, pp. 817–38.

WOLFF, E. N. and NADIRI, M. I. (1993) 'Spillover Effects, Linkage Structure, and Research and Development', *Structural Change and Economic Dynamics*, vol. 4, no. 2, pp. 315–31.

11 Why Do Firms *Not* Collaborate? The Role of Competencies and Technological Regimes

*Aija Leiponen**

11.1 INTRODUCTION

Determinants and effects of innovation are topics of intense research interest, particularly since the fundamental relationship between economic and technological change has become acknowledged more widely. As a result, the contributions of research and development activities (R&D) to innovation and industrial evolution, especially in the manufacturing industries, are well appreciated. However, in economic models, as well as in many empirical studies, R&D is often conceptualized as an innovation production function. Such treatment may be a useful first approximation of the innovation process within a linear model of innovation. However, in qualitative empirical studies since the 1980s it has been observed that the organization of R&D is a critical determinant of both innovation (for example, Mowery, 1983) and economic performance (for example, Teece, 1986). Informal models of innovation emphasize feedbacks and complementarities among a firm's activities and knowledge bases (Kline and Rosenberg, 1986; Rothwell, 1994). Organizational choices, for instance, whether to organize knowledge-creation activities internally or outsource them, have a considerable impact on the strength of the interactions among the necessary sources of knowledge.

In this chapter, product innovation is assumed to be supported by a system of activities: internal R&D, R&D collaboration with outside partners, and outsourcing of R&D. I argue that this system is complemented by the competencies and skills of the firm. Competencies are hypothesized to be prerequisites for success in the three forms of R&D activity. Sufficient competence level may be necessary for both perceiving the benefits, locating, and making use of external knowledge.

It is well known that industries are characterized by different patterns of technological change (see, for example, Pavitt, 1984). The effects of these sectoral differences in technological change on R&D investment (Cohen and Levinthal, 1989) and industrial structure (Winter, 1984) have been studied. Here I will assess how sectoral differences affect firms' organizational choices concerning R&D and, ultimately, innovation.

I use recent innovation survey data from Finland to analyze the determinants of external R&D arrangements of firms – that is, collaboration with various partners and outsourcing. The main research question is, how is the organization of innovation activities affected by: (i) competencies; and (ii) the technological environment?

11.2   RELATED LITERATURE AND CONCEPTUAL FRAMEWORK

11.2.1   Firm Capabilities

The literature on the capabilities of firms emphasises the role of knowledge in firm performance and evolution. Original contributions include Penrose's work (1959) and the evolutionary approach to industrial dynamics (Nelson and Winter, 1982; Wernerfelt, 1984; Teece *et al.*, 1997). In this perspective, a firm's knowledge resources are critical determinants of its competitiveness. At the same time, firm specificities arising from the organizational nature of productive knowledge make firms idiosyncratic, as a result of which they may perform very differently in markets over the long run. This literature holds great promise for our understanding of firm behaviour and industrial dynamics, but it has proven quite difficult to extend the analysis from case studies of individual firms to cross-sectional empirical studies and to produce theoretical models of firm organisation.

Empirical innovation literature has emphasized the complex interactions among various internal and external sources of knowledge and capabilities (Rothwell *et al.* (1974), Rosenberg (1982), Freeman (1982), von Hippel (1988), among others). Cohen and Levinthal (1990), in line with the empirical work of many scholars in the 1980s, coined the term 'absorptive capacity', referring to the firm's capability to assimilate information from the environment. The idea is that a firm carries out R&D not only to improve its own products and technologies, but also to keep up with the technological advances made by other firms in the industry, and to be able to use that knowledge internally. In other words, external and internal knowledge sources are complementary in the firm's innovation activities.

11.2.2 R&D Collaboration

As technological change has become more rapid and complex, and dissemination and sourcing of information have become easier because of new technologies, many firms decide not to create all knowledge internally. Some of it can be acquired in the markets. However, there are no markets for certain kinds of knowledge. In particular, a significant part of firms' productive knowledge is tacit or collective, and therefore not easily transferable, and other parts are firm-specific or strategic, and thus not for sale. Nevertheless, through intensive collaboration within an R&D alliance, even some of this 'stickier' knowledge can be shared and utilized jointly. Collaborative R&D can be viewed as a transaction in organizational knowledge. Indeed, collaborative arrangements such as R&D alliances, joint ventures, and research consortia are becoming increasingly common in modern economies. However, in order to make use of another firm's knowledge, a firm needs to possess sufficient internal competencies – in other words, absorptive capacity.

As collaborative arrangements between firms have proliferated since the 1980s, various explanations for their occurrence have been offered in the academic literature (see, for example, Contractor and Lorange, 1988). The benefits of collaboration are generally emphasized in these studies, partly because of a sampling bias: usually, only collaborating firms are examined (see for example, Hagedoorn and Schakenraad, 1992; Powell *et al.*, 1996).[1] The reasons for *not* collaborating are typically not assessed. The cross-sectional approach with random sampling in this chapter reduces this bias.

One of the few more critical views on collaborative arrangements comes from the transaction cost approach, which suggests that R&D collaboration can lead to unintended leakage of strategic information to the firm's competitors (Pisano, 1989; Oxley, 1997). Other studies argue that external organization of R&D may reduce the possibility of innovating profitably, as externally sourced knowledge may be more difficult to integrate tightly with the other activities of the firm. In such a situation, the potential complementarities related to innovation may remain only partially exploited (Mowery and Rosenberg, 1989; Leiponen, 2000). External organization of R&D may be associated with a trade-off between the lower costs of developing new capabilities, on the one hand, and the transactional hazards stemming from leakage of knowledge and missed opportunities for complementarity among knowledge resources, on the other. Moreover, firms lacking complementary internal competencies will find it less profitable to engage in collaborative innovation.

According to Hagedoorn (1993), the main reasons behind strategic R&D alliances include: (i) technological complexity and complementarities (ii) reduction of the uncertainty and costs of R&D; (iii) interest in capturing partners' knowledge; and (iv) reduction of product development times. However, to my knowledge, the kinds of partner with which firms do and do not collaborate has not been examined empirically. The literature focuses generally on horizontal collaboration, perhaps as an outgrowth of economists' concern about the potential degradation of competition in the markets. Here I suggest it is likely that firms' motivations for forming alliances with customers or universities, for example, differ from those associated with partnering with competitors. The transaction cost point of view implies that the logic and cost structures supporting vertical alliances are different from those of horizontal organizational forms.

Beyond analyzing patterns of collaboration, this study seeks to examine possible interactions between collaboration and internal competence accumulation. Using Finnish survey data on innovation, we can compare the skill characteristics of firms entering collaborative arrangements with those of non-collaborating firms.

11.2.3   Technological Regimes

A stream of research on technical change argues that it is possible to identify the underlying dimensions according to which industries differ from one another (see, among others, Winter, 1984; Levin *et al.*, 1987). One approach to classification suggests characterizing the technological and innovation environment according to the presence of innovation *opportunities* and the degree of *appropriability* of the returns to innovation (Levin *et al.*, 1987; Klevorick *et al.*, 1995). It is argued that high opportunities encourage investment in R&D, but appropriability can have two opposed effects, because of the dual role of R&D: on the one hand, higher appropriability increases the returns to innovation, but on the other, lower appropriability increases the returns to imitation. Both can encourage R&D activities (Cohen and Levinthal, 1989).

Scholars in the Schumpeterian tradition (for example, Audretsch, 1995; Malerba and Orsenigo, 1993) have characterized the technological environment through reference to the degree of technological turbulence (see also Tushman and Anderson, 1986). In an entrepreneurial regime, small and flexible firms will find it easier to innovate, while in a routinized regime, big firms with large-scale R&D may be in a better position to innovate because of increasing returns to knowledge accumulation. Basically, it is a question of whether or not there are returns to scale in innovation.

Pavitt (1984) suggested another approach to technological regimes. His taxonomy of the patterns of technological change identified three principle types of industry: (i) supplier dominated; (ii) production intensive; and (iii) science-based. Pavitt argued that patterns of technological change differ markedly between these groups, and must be understood and taken into account in explaining the behaviour and evolution of industries.

Finally, Schmookler (1966), among others, has emphasized the importance of demand in creating incentives for innovation. Demand-induced innovation is economically less risky compared to 'science-' or 'technology-push' innovation, in the sense that a market already exists, provided that firms can match innovations with technological opportunities.

The effects of the technological regime on innovation outcomes have been studied less frequently, with the exception of Levin *et al.* (1985). Furthermore, the effects of the technological environment on the choice of the organization of R&D have not been examined. This is the novelty of the chapter at hand.

11.2.4   Conceptual Framework

This study examines the joint determination of R&D investment, R&D collaboration decisions, and product innovation. These activities are viewed as being highly intertwined. When the firm decides to pursue innovation, it will also choose whether to carry out formal R&D, and how to organize such a project (internally, outsource, and/or collaborate).

The main hypotheses are, first, that competence investments complement collaboration in innovation, and thus the two are associated positively. Competencies are measured through reference to educational fields and levels of employees, and firms' investments in internal R&D. Second, different types of skill complement collaboration with different types of partner. For example, research co-operation with universities and other research organizations necessitates relatively high internal research skills because of the absorptive capacity requirement. Collaboration with universities is thus expected to be associated with high research competencies. In contrast, collaboration with suppliers is expected to be associated with relatively low research competence requirements. Third, the technological regime affects the innovation behaviour of firms, as measured by their propensity to engage in R&D, collaborate in innovation, and innovate.

The proxies for technological regime include industry averages of the importance of various external sources of knowledge to the firm's innovation process. The Finnish innovation survey does not contain direct information about the appropriability of innovation returns. However, data on competitors as knowledge sources can serve as an indication of appropriability: when competitors are important sources of knowledge in an industry, it is likely that secrets will be difficult to maintain, and thus appropriability is fairly low. On this basis, low appropriability is expected to discourage collaboration and outsourcing of R&D because of the transaction hazards. Its effect on R&D investment is ambiguous, however, as R&D supports both internal innovation and absorption of spillover knowledge. The effect of low appropriability on innovation is hypothesized to be negative because of the disincentives to innovate created by spillovers.

Industry averages of importance of the other external knowledge sources – universities, customers and suppliers – are also treated as indicators of particular technological environments. Where universities are important knowledge sources, the regime is considered to be relatively science-intensive. According to Klevorick *et al.* (1995), science-intensive regimes are higher in innovation opportunities. Thus, firms in industries where universities are important knowledge sources are expected to be more likely to invest in R&D, collaborate with universities, and innovate.

The importance of customers as a knowledge source represents the demand for innovation and the need to be in touch with users, both of which bode well for profitable innovation. Therefore, firms operating in an environment in which customers frequently provide ideas and opportunities for innovation, both invest more in innovative activities and succeed in innovation more often. They are also highly likely to collaborate with customers in R&D.

Finally, industries in which suppliers represent important sources of knowledge are treated as supplier-dominated regimes (Pavitt, 1984). Supplier domination implies that a considerable part of technological development is delegated upstream – for example, to equipment suppliers. Consequently, innovations become embodied in production equipment, machinery, and service technicians. Firms in supplier-dominated regimes are often oriented towards process improvement through incremental learning in their operations, and do not necessarily introduce new products frequently. On this basis, outside their close relations with suppliers, they are not expected to collaborate in innovation.

The 'Schumpeterian' regime is hypothesized to affect the propensity of firms to externalize R&D. In a rapidly changing and unpredictable economic environment, expected returns to internally developed capabilities are lower, *ceteris paribus*. The reason is the higher risk that capabilities and associated competitive advantage will soon become obsolete because of some other firm's radical innovation. In such an unstable setting, firms can share innovation risks by collaborating instead of developing the complementary capabilities internally. Therefore, it is expected that a more turbulent, or *entrepreneurial*, environment is associated with more frequent outsourcing of, and collaboration in, R&D.

Lastly, the level of competition in the industry characterizes the firms' economic operating environment. Because of particularities of the Finnish economy, namely its small size, I use measures of international competition: the firm's export share and import intensity of its industry.[2] International competition is expected to encourage innovative activities.

11.3 ECONOMETRIC SET-UP AND THE DATA

To assess the hypotheses stated in the previous section, a system of equations needs to be estimated, because R&D investment, R&D collaboration and innovation are conceptualized as being determined simultaneously:

$$\left. \begin{aligned} RD\_inv_i &= f(COMPETENCIES_{1,i}, FIRM_{1,i}, REGIME_{1,I} \\ &\quad COMPETITION_{1,I}) \\ COLLAB_i &= g(COMPETENCIES_{2,i}, FIRM_{2,i}, REGIME_{2,I} \\ &\quad COMPETITION_{2,I}) \\ INNO_i &= h(COMPETENCIES_{3,i}, FIRM_{3,i}, REGIME_{3,I} \\ &\quad COMPETITION_{3,I}). \end{aligned} \right\} \quad (1)$$

Here, $i = 1, \ldots, N$ refers to the individual firms and $I = 1, \ldots, 14$ to industries. RD_inv is the share of R&D investment in sales; $COMPETENCIES$ is a vector of skill indicators; $FIRM$ is a vector of firm-specific control variables; $REGIME$ refers to a set of measures for the technological regime; and $COMPETITION$ consists of the measures for the competitive environment. The other dependent variables are binary, and they refer to R&D collaboration with different partners ($COLLAB$), and product innovation ($INNO$).

However, since a system with two binary dependent variables and one continuous, but censored, dependent variable cannot be subjected to a standard estimation procedure, it is modified into a system of three probit equations: $RD\_dum = 1$ if $RD\_inv > 0$, otherwise $RD\_dum = 0$:

$$\left. \begin{aligned} RD\_dum_i &= f^*(COMPETENCIES_{1,i}, FIRM_{1,i}, REGIME_{1,I} \\ &\quad COMPETITION_{1,I}) \\ COLLAB_i &= g(COMPETENCIES_{2,i}, FIRM_{2,i}, REGIME_{2,I} \\ &\quad COMPETITION_{2,I}) \\ INNO_i &= h(COMPETENCIES_{3,i}, FIRM_{3,i}, REGIME_{3,I} \\ &\quad COMPETITION_{3,I}). \end{aligned} \right\} \quad (2)$$

This approach allows us to account for the simultaneities and perform estimation with a standard procedure. Other approaches include the kind of two-stage methods suggested by Maddala (1983). However, this possibility is not pursued here because of the complexities involved in deriving the covariance matrix.

The estimation method is thus trivariate probit maximum likelihood, where the decisions to engage in R&D, to collaborate in R&D with other organizations, and to innovate, are estimated simultaneously. Collaboration data is binary, but has several 'dimensions': did the firm collaborate with rivals, customers, or suppliers and so on, or not? The choices are, of course, not mutually exclusive. Ideally, one would estimate the simultaneous determination of all types of collaboration, but because of a lack of reasonable methods, the trivariate approach will suffice.

Statistics Finland collected and compiled the data combining the innovation survey of 1997 and employment register of 1995. The sampling frame of the innovation survey was the Statistics Finland enterprise register. All firms with more than 100 employees were included, together with a random sample stratified by size of smaller firms. The response rate was 71 per cent, representing 1126 firms, 1029 of which are included in the sample used here. This attrition is a result of missing data. The Eurostat Community Innovation Survey methodology was applied. The list of variables is given in Table 11.1, and basic descriptive statistics are presented in Table 11.2. These data are weighted to represent the Finnish manufacturing sector.

The descriptive statistics for the collaboration variables show that more firms collaborate with customers (15 per cent), suppliers (15 per cent), or universities (14 per cent) than with competitors (6 per cent). Obviously, collaborating firms may have more than one type of partner. Product innovations were reported by 19 per cent of the firms between 1994 and 1996, and 30 per cent invested in R&D. Average R&D investment is 0.7 per cent of sales for the whole sample. There are 400 R&D firms ($RD\_inv > 0$) in the dataset, and their average R&D investment is 2.3 per cent of sales revenue. Employees with advanced formal educational degrees (*RESEARCH*) are few, only 0.1 per cent on average, while higher technical and natural scientific skills (*TECHNIC*) are quite common. Six per cent of the firms' employees have a higher (tertiary) degree in these fields. Among the knowledge *REGIME* variables, customers are the most important knowledge sources; and competitors and suppliers are recognized as next most important. Universities are the least commonly cited sources of knowledge among the sources considered here. Table 11.3 displays the 1029 firms broken down by industrial classification. Metal industries are slightly over-represented in the sample, but sampling weights correct for most of this bias.

Table 11.1 Variables

Dependent variables

RD_dum	Dummy for R&D_inv > 0
COL_com	Dummy for R&D collaboration with competitors
COL_cus	Dummy for R&D collaboration with suppliers
COL_sup	Dummy for R&D collaboration with universities
COL_uni	Dummy for R&D collaboration with universities
OUTRD	Dummy for outsourced R&D investment > 0
INNO	Dummy for successful product innovation (sales revenue from the commercialized new product >0)

Independent variables

			Expected effect on collaboration
COMPETENCIES	RESEARCH	Share of employees with a post-graduate degree (doctoral or licentiate)	+
	TECHNIC	Share of employees with a *higher* technical or natural scientific degree (e.g. university engineer, Master of Science in Chemistry)	+
	RD_inv	Internal Research and Development investments/sales	+
FIRM	EMPL	Number of employees	+
	GROUP	Membership in a group of firms	?
TECHNOLOGICAL REGIME	REG_com	Industry average for the importance of *competitors* as sources of knowledge	+/−
	REG_cus	Industry average for the importance of *customers* as sources of knowledge	+
	REG_sup	Industry average for the importance of *suppliers* as sources of knowledge	−
	REG_uni	Industry average for the importance of *universities* as sources of knowledge	+
	SCHUMP	Share of small firms (*EMPL* < 100) among innovating firms in the industry	+
COMPETITION	EXPORT	Firm's exports/sales	+
	IMPORT	Total imports in the product category/ domestic industry sales	

Table 11.2   Descriptive statistics (weighted)

	Mean	Standard deviation	Minimum	Maximum	N
COL_com	0.057	0.232	0	1	1029
COL_cus	0.153	0.360	0	1	1029
COL_sup	0.150	0.357	0	1	1029
COL_uni	0.136	0.343	0	1	1029
INNO	0.194	0.396	0	1	1029
RD_inv (%)	0.7	2.4	0	31.6	1029
RD_inv > 0 (%)	2.3	3.9	0.0002	31.6	400
RD_dum	0.304	0.460	0	1	1029
OUTRD	0.228	0.420	0	1	1029
RESEARCH	0.001	0.005	0	0.82	1029
TECHNIC	0.064	0.088	0	0.636	1029
EMPL	97.8	361.2	10	9602	1029
GROUP	0.30	0.46	0	1	1029
REG_com	1.500	0.136	1.27	2.67	1029
REG_cus	2.124	0.250	1.7	3	1029
REG_sup	1.514	0.264	1.04	2	1029
REG_uni	1.109	0.197	0.6	1.67	1029
SCHUMP	0.557	0.133	0	1	1029
EXPORT	0.187	0.273	0	1	1029
IMPORT	0.337	0.283	0.033	0.947	1029

Table 11.3   Industry distribution in the sample

Industry	N	Share%
Food	107	10.4
Textiles	79	7.7
Wood	76	7.4
Paper	26	2.5
Printing, publishing	98	9.5
Oil, chemicals	43	4.2
Plastics, rubber	47	4.6
Non-metallic minerals	44	4.3
Primary metals	26	2.5
Metal products	97	9.4
Machines, equipment	146	14.2
Electronics	133	12.9
Cars, vehicles	54	5.2
Furniture	53	5.2
Total	1029	100.0

11.4   ESTIMATION RESULTS

11.4.1.   R&D Collaboration

Estimation of the simultaneous equations in Equation (2) for the joint determination of R&D investment, R&D collaboration and product innovation decisions is done by trivariate probit. To provide a baseline for comparison, each of the equations is estimated with simple one-equation probit. The results are shown in Appendix 11.1 (Tables A11.1–A11.7) on pages 271–274. The multivariate model accounts for some of the endogeneities between the different innovation activities by separating the effects of being an R&D firm, and the *level* of investment in R&D. Table 11.4 contains the results when collaboration with competitors is the dependent variable of the second equation in Equation (2).

The probability of investing in internal R&D is associated with high research and technical competencies, and seems to be driven strongly by

Table 11.4   Collaboration with competitors, 3-variate probit ML system, weighted ($N = 1029$)

Dependent variable	RD_dum		COL_com		INNO	
	coeff.	t-stat.	coeff.	t-stat.	coeff.	t-stat.
Constant	−0.88	−1.33	−1.77*	−1.77	−1.48**	−2.07
RESEARCH	18.98*	1.84	9.99	1.21	22.09*	2.14
TECHNIC	2.00**	3.74	0.01	0.01	2.06**	3.61
RD_inv			2.42	1.25	2.77*	1.70
EMPL	0.16**	5.53	0.29**	4.09	0.64**	5.03
GROUP	0.94**	−2.39	0.38**	2.52		
EXPORT	0.97**	5.66	0.33	1.15	0.64**	3.40
REG_com	−0.98**	2.27	0.38	0.60	−0.75*	−1.74
REG_cus	0.60**	−2.87	−0.26	−0.57	0.55*	1.71
REG_sup	−0.63**	3.18	−0.57	−1.65	−0.45	−1.88
REG_uni	0.81*	1.82	0.31	0.74	0.53*	1.85
SCHUMP			0.61	1.09		
IMPORT					0.51**	2.68
Correlation coefficients						
R(01,02)	0.66**	8.56				
R(01,03)	0.82**	24.73				
R(02,03)	0.53**	6.55				
Log likelihood	−964.23					

Notes: ** indicates 95% level of significance; * indicates 90% level. *EMPL* is in thousands in the estimations.

industry-specific factors measured here with the technological regime variables. In accordance with the hypotheses, firms in regimes where customers and universities are important sources of knowledge are more likely to carry out R&D internally, while firms in environments that rely on spillovers from competitors or suppliers are less likely to perform R&D in-house. However, this model does not explain very well the variance in firms' engagement in collaborative arrangements with competitors. Only firm size and group membership play important roles. The third dependent variable, successful new product introduction (*INNO*), is associated closely with competence and R&D investments. In line with the demand and innovation opportunities hypotheses, firms in the customer-driven and science-based regimes are more likely to innovate. In contrast, firms in supplier- or competitor-dominated regimes are somewhat less innovative. As expected, international competition in terms of export intensity and import penetration is a positive driver of innovation.

Collaboration with customers is associated much more closely with competence investments than is collaboration with competitors (see Table 11.5). In this model, *RESEARCH* and *TECHNIC* become statistically significant coefficients, although *RESEARCH* is so only at the 90 per cent level. However, collaboration does not seem to be complementary with the *level* of R&D investment. More R&D does not increase the likelihood of engaging in collaborative innovation. Nevertheless, the high correlation between the equation for *RD_dum* and *COL_cus* (74 per cent) suggests a very close association between the activities. In the case of collaboration with customers, the technological environment is seen to come into play more significantly. Firms in regimes where 'demand pull' is strong are more likely to collaborate, while those in supplier-dominated regimes are less so.

Collaboration with suppliers requires internal competencies in the form of technical skills (see Table 11.6). The technological regime variables do not capture variation in this type of collaboration very well. Only low appropriability is associated significantly negatively with supplier collaboration. The hazard of leaking strategic information to rivals may be aggravated by collaborating with suppliers, a potential spillover channel.

Collaboration with universities is associated with very high internal research competencies, relatively high technical competencies, and a large export share (see Table 11.7). Firms in supplier-dominated regimes clearly are not likely to collaborate with universities, but, quite intuitively, firms in science-based regimes are.

Table 11.5   Collaboration with customers 3-variate probit ML, weighted (*N*=1029)

Dependent variable	RD_dum		COL_cus		INNO	
	coeff.	t-stat.	coeff.	t-stat.	coeff.	t-stat.
Constant	−0.79	−1.22	−1.93**	−2.37	−1.42**	−2.01
RESEARCH	20.00**	2.08	16.82*	1.82	24.32**	2.16
TECHNIC	2.04**	3.81	2.18**	3.69	2.05**	3.52
RD_inv			−0.46	−0.25	2.87*	1.78
EMPL	1.27**	8.34	0.64**	6.04	1.06**	5.15
GROUP	0.17*	1.93	0.43**	3.85		
EXPORT	0.99**	5.84	0.78**	4.04	0.66**	3.56
REG_com	−1.03**	−2.48	−0.54	−1.14	−0.83*	−1.87
REG_cus	0.61**	2.32	0.72**	2.03	0.60*	1.90
REG_sup	−0.62**	−2.87	−0.60**	−2.35	−0.46*	−1.88
REG_uni	0.76**	3.00	0.34	1.17	0.48*	1.69
SCHUMP			0.09	0.18		
IMPORT					0.50**	2.63

Correlation coefficients

R(01,02)	0.74**	15.79
R(01,03)	0.82**	24.17
R(02,03)	0.69**	14.42
Log likelihood	−1064.06	

Notes: ** indicates a 95% level of significance; * indicates a 90% level. *EMPL* is in thousands in the estimations.

Table 11.6   Collaboration with suppliers, 3-variate probit ML, weighted (*N*=1029)

Dependent variable	RD_dum		COL_sup		INNO	
	coeff.	t-stat.	coeff.	t-stat.	coeff.	t-stat.
Constant	−0.90	−1.38	−0.37	−0.46	−1.45**	−2.02
RESEARCH	19.09*	1.78	10.80	1.34	20.48	1.63
TECHNIC	1.89**	3.44	1.74**	2.93	2.02**	3.53
RD_inv			−2.31	−1.26	2.69	1.61
EMPL	1.46**	9.64	1.12**	4.77	1.26**	5.90
GROUP	0.15*	1.74	0.33**	2.95		
EXPORT	0.95**	5.61	0.76**	3.89	0.65**	3.44
REG_com	−0.98**	−2.35	−1.13**	−2.62	−0.80*	−1.76
REG_cus	0.63**	2.40	0.42	1.33	0.59*	1.80

Table 11.6   Continued

Dependent variable	RD_dum		COL_sup		INNO	
	coeff.	t-stat.	coeff.	t-stat.	coeff.	t-stat.
REG_sup	−0.63**	−2.99	−0.35	−1.46	−0.49**	−2.02
REG_uni	0.79**	3.08	0.28	0.92	0.51*	1.75
SCHUMP			−0.39	−0.82		
IMPORT					0.52**	2.73

Correlation coefficients

R(01,02)	0.77**	18.87
R(01,03)	0.81**	24.29
R(02,03)	0.60**	11.50
Log likelihood	−1078.73	

Notes: ** indicates 95% level of significance; * indicates 90% level. *EMPL* is in thousands in the estimations.

Table 11.7   Collaboration with universities, 3-variate probit ML, weighted (*N* = 1029)

Dependent variable	RD_dum		COL_uni		INNO	
	coeff.	t-stat.	coeff.	t-stat.	coeff.	t-stat.
Constant	−0.84	−1.29	−3.11**	−3.35	−1.30*	−1.84
RESEARCH	21.53**	2.05	30.03**	2.14	21.70	1.10
TECHNIC	1.93**	3.56	1.68**	2.82	1.91**	3.35
RD_inv			−1.61	−0.75	3.17**	1.97
EMPL	1.45**	9.10	1.29**	5.36	1.23**	5.89
GROUP	0.16*,	1.85	0.40**	3.61		
EXPORT	0.98**	5.74	0.88**	4.68	0.64**	3.38
REG_com	−1.03**	−2.47	0.01	0.01	−0.80*	−1.88
REG_cus	0.64**	2.41	0.33	0.87	0.54*	1.71
REG_sup	−0.64**	−2.96	−0.72**	−2.49	−0.49**	−2.03
REG_uni	0.78**	3.04	1.13**	3.24	0.48*	1.70
SCHUMP			0.68	1.25		
IMPORT					0.54**	2.84

Correlation coefficients

R(01,02)	0.80**	17.58
R(01,03)	0.81**	23.20
R(02,03)	0.71**	13.21
Log likelihood	−1009.10	

Notes: ** indicates 95% level of significance; * indicates 90% level. *EMPL* is in thousands in the estimations.

The last type of external R&D arrangement is contract R&D. In Table 11.8, the likelihood of outsourced R&D is associated positively with internal research competencies, high export orientation, and science-based innovation opportunities. The connection between R&D outsourcing and science intensity is interesting. Except for high innovation opportunities, science intensity may reflect the potential for codification. It may be easier both to define the research project and communicate the results in a science-based environment, as opposed to environments with highly tacit and ill-defined underlying knowledge.

The multivariate results differ slightly from the single equation probit results reported in Appendix 11.1 on page 271. The coefficients on competence measures are larger and more significant in explaining the probability of collaboration when the endogeneity of being an R&D firm is accounted for. Only the coefficient of the level of R&D investment has a different sign. Nevertheless, firms do internal R&D in order perhaps to be able to benefit from external R&D arrangements, as indicated by the high correlations between the first and second equations. However, provided that the

Table 11.8 R&D outsourcing, 3-variate probit ML, weighted ($N = 1029$)

Dependent variable	RD_dum		OUTRD_dum		INNO	
	coeff.	t-stat.	coeff.	t-stat.	coeff.	t-stat.
Constant	−0.83	−1.30	−1.68**	−2.25	−1.36*	−1.91
RESEARCH	12.77	1.40	13.82**	2.05	17.47*	1.74
TECHNIC	1.82**	3.40	0.87	1.53	2.02**	3.40
RD_inv			0.19	0.13	2.77	1.63
EMPL	1.02**	5.76	0.23**	4.98	0.86**	4.18
GROUP	0.19**	2.19	0.30**	3.16		
EXPORT	0.99**	5.86	0.96**	5.70	0.65**	3.45
REG_com	−1.01**	−2.45	−0.15	−0.33	−0.78*	−1.80
REG_cus	0.61**	2.30	0.22	0.80	0.52*	1.69
REG_sup	−0.64**	−2.94	−0.49**	−2.32	−0.47**	−1.99
REG_uni	0.83**	3.25	0.66**	2.52	0.55*	1.95
SCHUMP			0.35	1.09		
IMPORT					0.53**	2.80
Correlation coefficients						
R(01,02)	0.91**	47.83				
R(01,03)	0.81**	24.60				
R(02,03)	0.73**	18.35				
Log likelihood	−1063.27					

Notes: ** indicates 95% level of significance; * indicates 90% level. *EMPL* is in thousands in the estimations.

firm does some internal R&D, a higher level of investment does not necessarily increase further the probability of collaboration.[3]

As expected, in most cases, the coefficient of the measure of the Schumpeterian regime (*SCHUMP*) is positive, but it is never significant. Nevertheless, the variable was retained in the analysis in order to ensure identification, which was difficult to obtain in some cases. Its presence does not have an impact on the signs or significance of other coefficients.

To check the ability of the regime variables to account for the knowledge accumulation patterns within industries, the trivariate systems were estimated with a full set of industry dummies as control variables in the collaboration equation. The system for collaboration with universities is provided in Appendix 11.1 (Table A11.8) (see page 274) to demonstrate that the results on competencies do not depend on the control variables used. Research competencies and technical skills remain strong and significant determinants of university collaboration with industry dummies.

To summarize, the multivariate model seems to work quite well in explaining how the three innovation-related activities are determined jointly. The high correlations between the three equations indicate that assuming a joint distribution for the dependent variables is warranted. Thus, it makes sense to estimate their determination simultaneously. Skills play a significant and positive role in innovation. They may be complementary with R&D activities, independently of how R&D is organized. Moreover, internal competencies facilitate the internalization of the benefits of external R&D efforts. In particular, research skills are necessary to benefit from collaboration with universities and outsourcing of R&D, and technical skills are important in collaboration with customers, suppliers and universities.

11.5   DISCUSSION

This chapter took as its starting point the idea that organizational decisions related to R&D are simultaneous with the decisions to invest in innovation. The strong positive associations identified among internal competencies, R&D investment, R&D collaboration, contract R&D and product innovation are indeed in line with the notion that they are complementary, although partial correlation does not constitute a rigorous test.

Collaboration can be thought of as a vehicle to transact in tacit knowledge. The firm would probably choose to buy the necessary capabilities or information in the spot markets, if such resources were available. However, exchanging sticky or tacit knowledge may require more intensive and prolonged interaction, creating a need for a governance structure as constituted by the collaboration agreement. Collaboration involves exchanging knowledge for knowledge, while in R&D outsourcing, knowledge is exchanged for money. Evidently, outsourced research involves less sticky and less firm-specific information, and is often embodied in blueprints or artefacts.

Skills and competencies are important covariates in the firm's 'system of innovation' as defined by the various innovation activities (R&D, collaboration, outsourcing). This finding highlights the important role of absorptive capacity. Without internal capabilities, the firm is not likely to be an attractive partner in collaborative arrangements or to benefit fully from externally sourced knowledge. Estimation results here support the interpretation that high internal skills and competencies, in addition to internal R&D, help to build absorptive capacity and enhance firms' ability to engage in collaborative innovation. This is the basis for advantages accruing to incumbents, and public policies targeting small firms' capacity to compete. Of course, utilization of external sources of knowledge within innovation processes should not be over-emphasized. In-house competencies and internal R&D have very important roles in supporting innovation directly.

It is important to distinguish patterns of collaboration among different kinds of partners. First, this chapter demonstrates that competence requirements vary somewhat with the type of collaboration: research competencies are identified as being more important for university collaboration than for the other types of collaboration. Second, horizontal collaboration is not so prevalent as the extant literature on research joint ventures between rivals would seem to imply. From a market structure or competition point of view, it may be relevant to study the implications of, and reasons for, co-operation among rivals. However, to understand innovation, technological change, and the evolution of firms and industries, it is equally important that we assess the knowledge transactions firms carry out with differently positioned actors in production systems.

The analysis accounted for industry differences with a set of proxies for the technological environment. It seems that using and further developing measures for technological regimes is a worthwhile endeavour. Current measures perform quite well, and we are able to see *how* industries differ in addition to controlling for these differences. Understanding industry specificities is highly relevant from the perspective of policy analysis. For example, technological regimes may have a bearing on issues of antitrust and intellectual property rights. If patterns of co-operation in knowledge creation among firms depend on the technological environment, competition policies need to take this into account – co-operation may be beneficial in some environments, while in others it may be an indication of collusion.

Relatedly, firms' willingness to collaborate, and thus the rate and nature of innovation, may depend on intellectual property rights legislation and enforcement. Fruitful co-operation may be hindered by spillover hazards.

Limitations of this research include the structure of the data: innovation records are at the firm level, not R&D project level, potentially blurring some results. Also, the statistical association between competencies and collaboration is not sufficient evidence of complementarity – the two could be caused by more fundamental firm characteristics. This question could be addressed, at least to some extent, with longitudinal data on innovation, collaboration, and related investments, enabling us to better control for endogeneities. Such data exist for patents but, as is well known, these are a relevant measure of innovation for only a few industries.

The econometric method used in this study could be improved to make use of all available data. Instead of three-probit equations, the existing data could be used to estimate a system with a truncated regression of R&D investment, probit estimations of R&D collaboration, and an interval regression of innovation output (share of new products in current sales). As the econometric methods for limited dependent variable systems develop, this type of a system can be estimated. These shortcomings represent avenues for future work.

11.6   CONCLUSION

The principle results of this study include the fact that competencies of firms are closely associated with organizational choices for innovation activities. High levels of internal capabilities make R&D investments, collaborative R&D arrangements, contract R&D and innovation more likely. There are indications that skills contribute to absorptive capacity. In choosing partners for R&D, research competencies appear to be important determinants of collaboration with universities and customers, but not of collaboration with suppliers or competitors. Furthermore, firms with high research competencies often engage in R&D outsourcing. Research skills are likely to be useful in monitoring external R&D activities. Additionally, firm size and business group membership correlate with external collaboration. These may reflect access to resources and experience that are useful for managing collaborative innovation, but which are not available to small and independent firms. The reverse is that firms with low levels of internal or group-level competencies are less likely to benefit from external forms of R&D.

The results indicate that technological regimes affect firms' innovation behaviour. Firms in regimes of low appropriability are not likely to collaborate with suppliers, and are also less likely to undertake R&D or to innovate. Regimes of strong 'demand pull', that is, market opportunities are associated with high probabilities of R&D, collaboration with customers and product innovation. Supplier-dominated firms are significantly less likely to innovate or to collaborate with customers or universities. Lastly, science-based regimes with high innovation opportunities are associated with frequent contract R&D, collaboration with universities, internal R&D, and product innovation. Thus, the technological regime and firms' competencies have an impact not only on patterns of R&D investment and industrial structure, but also on boundaries of firms as reflected in their knowledge-procurement strategies.

Appendix 11.1

Table A11.1 Single equation probit ML estimation ($N = 1029$). Dependent variable: *RD_dum*

	Coeff.	t-stat.	Slope	t-stat.
Constant	−1.02	−1.59	−0.34	−1.59
RESEARCH	20.61**	2.04	6.84**	2.03
TECHNIC	1.98**	3.55	0.66**	3.53
EMPL	1.49**	5.29	0.49**	5.14
GROUP	0.20**	1.98	0.07**	1.99
EXPORT	1.01**	6.02	0.34**	6.01
REG_com	−0.92**	−2.18	−0.31**	−2.18
REG_cus	0.63**	2.54	0.21**	2.54
REG_sup	−0.63**	−3.24	−0.21**	−3.25
REG_uni	0.78**	3.10	0.26**	3.11
Log likelihood	−534.10			
Pseudo R^2	0.25			

Notes: ** indicates 95% level of significance; * indicates 90% level.

Table A11.2 Dependent variable: *COL_com*

	Coeff.	t-stat.	Slope	t-stat.
Constant	−1.59	−1.52	−0.15	−1.51
RESEARCH	4.08	0.42	0.38	0.42
TECHNIC	−0.69	−0.85	−0.06	−0.85
RD_inv	7.53**	3.34	0.70**	3.19
EMPL	0.29**	2.50	0.03**	2.42
GROUP	0.44**	3.05	0.04**	3.12

Table A11.2   Continued

	Coeff.	*t-stat.*	*Slope*	*t-stat.*
EXPORT	0.15	0.63	0.01	0.63
REG_com	0.56	0.91	0.05	0.91
REG_cus	−0.33	−0.79	−0.03	−0.79
REL_sup	−0.59*	−1.89	−0.05*	−1.92
REG_uni	0.16	0.42	0.01	0.42
SCHUMP	0.44	0.73	0.04	0.73
Log likelihood	−273.58			
Pseudo R^2	0.04			

Notes: ** indicates 95% level of significance; * indicates 90% level.

Table A11.3   Dependent variable: *COL_cus*

	Coeff.	*t-stat.*	*Slope*	*t-stat.*
Constant	−1.71	−2.04	−0.33	−2.06
RESEARCH	10.71	1.07	2.09	1.06
TECHNIC	1.28**	2.09	0.25**	2.08
RD_inv	8.14**	3.90	1.59**	3.81
EMPL	0.61**	3.34	0.12**	3.27
GROUP	0.51**	4.41	0.10**	4.46
EXPORT	0.62**	3.34	0.12**	3.33
REG_com	−0.41	−0.84	−0.08	−0.84
REG_cus	0.65**	2.03	0.13**	2.04
REL_sup	−0.60**	−2.53	−0.12**	−2.55
REG_uni	0.26	0.87	0.05	0.87
SCHUMP	−0.19	−0.38	−0.04	−0.38
Log likelihood	−431.91			
Pseudo R^2	0.20			

Notes: ** indicates 95% level of significance; * indicates 90% level.

Table A11.4   Dependent variable: *COL_sup*

	Coeff.	*t-stat.*	*Slope*	*t-stat.*
Constant	−0.06	−0.08	−0.01	−0.08
RESEARCH	2.31	0.27	0.48	0.27
TECHNIC	0.88	1.45	0.18	1.45
RD_inv	5.83**	2.84	1.20**	2.83
EMPL	1.08**	4.63	0.22**	4.43
GROUP	0.36**	3.18	0.08**	3.21
EXPORT	0.64**	3.47	0.13**	3.49

Table A11.4 Continued

	Coeff.	t-stat.	Slope	t-stat.
REG_com	−1.05**	−2.13	−0.22**	−2.14
REG_cus	0.37	1.22	0.08	1.22
REL_sup	−0.35	−1.53	−0.07	−1.54
REG_uni	0.16	0.51	0.03	0.51
SCHUMP	−0.67	−1.33	−0.14	−1.33
Log likelihood	−449.78			
Pseudo R^2	0.16			

Notes: ** indicates 95% level of significance; * indicates 90% level.

Table A11.5 Dependent variable: *COL_uni*

	Coeff.	t-stat.	Slope	t-stat.
Constant	−3.01**	−3.36	−0.50**	−3.36
RESEARCH	27.33**	2.65	4.52**	2.59
TECHNIC	0.82	1.26	0.13	1.26
RD_inv	7.40**	3.52	1.22**	3.42
EMPL	1.24**	4.94	0.21**	4.57
GROUP	0.49**	3.96	0.08**	4.03
EXPORT	0.74**	3.79	0.12**	3.78
REG_com	0.14	0.25	0.02	0.25
REG_cus	0.37	1.05	0.06	1.06
REL_sup	−0.63**	−2.39	−0.10**	−2.43
REG_uni	0.93**	2.87	0.15**	2.90
SCHUMP	0.15	0.27	0.02	0.27
Log likelihood	−379.53			
Pseudo R^2	0.26			

Notes: ** indicates 95% level of significance; * indicates 90% level.

Table A11.6 Dependent variable: *OUTRD*

	Coeff.	t-stat.	Slope	t-stat.
Constant	−1.57**	−2.08	−0.42**	−2.09
RESEARCH	0.46	0.05	0.12	0.05
TECHNIC	−0.47	−0.78	−0.13	−0.78
RD_inv	13.89**	6.00	3.69**	5.83
EMPL	0.22*	1.90	0.06*	1.89
GROUP	0.41**	3.89	0.11**	3.90
EXPORT	0.85**	4.96	0.23**	4.97

Table A11.6 Continued

	Coeff.	t-stat.	Slope	t-stat.
GROUP	0.41**	3.89	0.11**	3.90
REG_com	0.13	0.29	0.04	0.29
REG_cus	0.08	0.28	0.02	0.28
REL_sup	−0.49**	−2.27	−0.13**	−2.28
REG_uni	0.52*	1.95	0.14**	1.96
SCHUMP	0.17	0.39	0.05	0.39
Log likelihood	−513.87			
Pseudo R²	0.17			

Notes: ** indicates 95% level of significance; * indicates 90% level.

Table A11.7 Dependent variable: *INNO*

	Coeff.	t-stat.	Slope	t-stat.
Constant	−1.33*	−1.79	−0.33*	−1.80
RESEARCH	17.00	1.54	4.24	1.54
TECHNIC	1.11*	1.81	0.28*	1.81
RD_inv	17.04**	6.98	4.25**	6.60
EMPL	1.14**	4.68	0.28**	4.54
EXPORT	0.41**	2.23	0.10**	2.24
REG_com	−0.69	−1.46	−0.17	−1.46
REG_cus	0.49	1.58	0.12	1.58
REL_sup	−0.44**	−1.97	−0.11**	−1.98
REG_uni	0.39	1.47	0.10	1.47
IMPORT	0.44*	1.90	0.11*	1.90
GROUP	0.11	0.94	0.03	0.95
Log likelihood	−445.42			
Pseudo R²	−0.24			

Notes: ** indicates 95% level of significance; * indicates 90% level.

Table A11.8 Three-variate probit for collaboration with universities with industry dummies for R&D and collaboration equations

	RD_dum	t-stat.	COL_uni	t-stat.	INNO	t-stat.
Constant	−1.28**	−15.24	−2.38**	−5.38	−1.00	−1.59
RESEARCH	23.93**	2.17	34.22**	2.33	21.85	1.22
TECHNIC	3.01**	6.01	2.35**	3.85	2.09**	3.20
RD_inv			−1.37	−0.60	3.53**	2.27
EMPL	1.43**	7.67	1.51**	7.65	1.22**	6.43

Table A11.8   Continued

	RD_dum	t-stat.	COL_uni	t-stat.	INNO	t-stat.
EXPORT	1.05**	6.01	1.03**	5.31	0.70**	3.81
REG_com					−0.73*	−1.68
REG_cus					0.36	1.19
REG_sup					−0.23	−1.01
REG_uni					0.09	0.35
IMPORT					0.49**	2.39
Food	0.29*	1.92	0.59	1.25		
Textiles			0.56	1.18		
Wood			0.40	0.84		
Paper	0.78**	2.07	0.94*	1.81		
Printing, publishing			0.20	0.39		
Oil, chemicals	0.45**	2.11	0.84	1.57		
Plastics, rubber	0.76**	4.40	0.72	1.49		
Non-metallic minerals	0.00	0.00	0.47	0.92		
Primary metals			1.10*	1.92		
Metal products	0.29**	2.32	0.70	1.51		
Machines, equipment	0.27**	2.15	0.74*	1.66		
Electronics			0.69	1.52		
Cars, vehicles	0.03	0.14	0.51	1.04		
Log likelihood	−1032.85					
R(01,02)	0.77**	15.58				
R(01,03)	0.83**	26.84				
R(02,03)	0.71**	14.21				

Note: A full set of dummies could not be used for all equations due to identification problems.

Notes

*   I am grateful for the comments by the participants of the TSER Workshop on Innovation and Economic Change at Delft University of Technology, the Netherlands, especially Pierre Mohnen, Chris Walters, and José M. Labeaga, and comments by seminar participants at INRA, Toulouse and Amos Tuck School, Dartmouth College. Steven Wolf provided valuable editing assistance. Remaining errors are mine alone. This research was funded by TEKES, the National Technology Agency of Finland. Statistics Finland compiled the data. I thank both for their support.

1.   However, Contractor and Lorange (1988) discuss in their introductory chapter both the benefits and costs of co-operative ventures.

2.   The traditional variables of industry concentration and market share were originally also included, but they did not capture statistically significantly the

aspects of competition in Finnish manufacturing, perhaps because of the too-high level of aggregation and the small open-economy environment.
3. The insignificance of the level of R&D holds even if one removes the *RESEARCH* variable, which is potentially endogenous, from the collaboration equation.

References

AUDRETSCH, D. B. (1995) *Innovation and Industry Evolution.* Cambridge, Mass.: MIT Press.
COHEN, W. M. and LEVINTHAL, D. A. (1989) 'Innovation and Learning: The Two Faces of R&D', *Economic Journal*, vol. 99, pp. 569–96.
COHEN, W. M. and LEVINTHAL, D. A. (1990) 'Absorptive Capacity: A New Perspective on Learning and Innovation', *Administrative Science Quarterly*, vol. 35, pp. 128–52.
CONTRACTOR, F. J. and LORANGE, P. (eds) (1988) *Cooperative Strategies in International Business*, Lexington, Mass.: Lexington Books.
FREEMAN, C. (1982) *The Economics of Industrial Innovation.* Cambridge, Mass.: MIT Press.
HAGEDOORN, J. (1993) 'Understanding the Rationale of Strategic Technology Partnering: Interorganizational Modes of Cooperation and Sectoral Differences', *Strategic Management Journal*, vol. 14, pp. 371–85.
HAGEDOORN, J. and SCHAKENRAAD, J. (1992) 'Leading Companies and Networks of Strategic Alliances in Information Technology', *Research Policy*, vol. 21, pp. 163–90.
HIPPEL, E. (1988) *The Sources of Innovation*, Oxford: Oxford University Press.
KLEVORICK, A. K., LEVIN, R. C., NELSON, R. R. and WINTER, S. G. (1995) 'On the Sources and Significance of Interindustry Differences in Technological Opportunities', *Research Policy*, vol. 24, pp. 185–205.
KLINE, S. J. and ROSENBERG, N. (1986) 'An Overview of Innovation', in R. Landau and N. Rosenberg (eds), *The Positive Sum Strategy: Harnessing Technology for Economic Growth*, Washington DC: National Academy Press, pp. 275–305.
LEIPONEN, A. (2000) 'Core Complementarities of the Corporation? Knowledge and the Organization of an Innovating Firm', in A. Leiponen, *Essays in the Economics of Knowledge: Innovation, Collaboration, and Organizational Complementarities*, Helsinki: Helsinki School of Economics and Business Administration doctoral dissertation A-175, pp. 11–33.
LEVIN, R. C., KLEVORICK, A. K., NELSON, R. R. and WINTER, S. G. (1987) 'Appropriating the Returns from Industrial Research and Development', *Brookings Papers on Economic Activity*, pp. 783–820.
LEVIN, R. R., COHEN, W. M. and MOWERY, D. C. (1985) 'R&D Appropriability, Opportunity, and Market Structure: New Evidence on Some Schumpeterian Hypotheses', *American Economic Review*, vol. 75, pp. 20–30.
MADDALA, G. S. (1983) *Limited-Dependent and Qualitative Variables in Econometrics.* New York: Cambridge University Press.
MALERBA, F. and ORSENIGO, L. (1993) 'Technological Regimes and Firm Behavior', *Industrial and Corporate Change*, vol. 2, pp. 45–71.

MOWERY, D. C. (1983) 'The Relationship between Intrafirm and Contractual Forms of Industrial Research in American Manufacturing, 1900–1940', *Explorations in Economic History*, vol. 20, pp. 351–74.

MOWERY, D. C. and ROSENBERG, N. (1989) *Technology and the Pursuit of Economic Growth*. New York: Cambridge University Press.

NELSON, R. R. and WINTER, S. G. (1982) *An Evolutionary Theory of Economic Change*. Cambridge, Mass.: Harvard University Press.

OXLEY, J. E. (1997) 'Appropriability Hazards and Governance in Strategic Alliances: A Transaction Cost Approach', *Journal of Law, Economics, and Organization*, vol. 13, pp. 389–409.

PAVITT, K. (1984) 'Sectoral Patterns of Technical Change: Towards a Taxonomy and a Theory', *Research Policy*, vol. 13, pp. 343–73.

PENROSE, E. (1959) *The Theory of the Growth of the Firm*. London: Basil Blackwell.

PISANO, G. P. (1989) 'Using Equity Participation to Support Exchange: Evidence from the Biotechnology Industry', *Journal of Law, Economics and Organization*, vol. 5, pp. 109–26.

POWELL, W. W., KOPUT, K. W. and SMITH-DOERR, L. (1996) 'Interorganizational Collaboration and the Locus of Innovation: Networks of learning in Biotechnology', *Administrative Science Quarterly*, vol. 41, pp. 116–45.

ROSENBERG, N. (1982) *Inside the Black Box: Technology and Economics*. Cambridge University Press.

ROTHWELL, R. (1994) 'Industrial Innovation: Success, Stragegy, Trends', in M. Dodgson and R. Rothwell (eds), *The Handbook of Industrial Innovation*. Aldershot: Edward Elgar, pp. 33–53.

ROTHWELL, R., FREEMAN, C., HORSLEY, A., JERVIS, V. T. P., ROBERTSON, A. B. and TOWNSEND, J. (1974) 'SAPPHO updated – Project SAPPHO phase II', *Research Policy*, vol. 3, pp. 258–91.

SCHMOOKLER, J. (1966) *Invention and Economic Growth*. Cambridge, Mass.: Harvard University Press.

TEECE, D. J. (1986) 'Profiting from Technological Innovation', *Research Policy*, vol. 15, pp. 285–306.

TEECE, D. J., PISANO, G. and SHUEN, A. (1997) 'Dynamic Capabilities and Strategic Management', *Strategic Management Journal*, vol. 18, pp. 509–33.

TUSHMAN, M. L. and ANDERSON, P. (1986) 'Technological Discontinuities and Organizational Environments', *Administrative Science Quarterly*, vol. 31, pp. 439–65.

WERNERFELT, B. (1984) 'Resource-Based View of the Firm', *Strategic Management Journal*, vol. 5, pp. 171–80.

WINTER, S. G. (1984), 'Schumpeterian Competition in Alternative Technological Regimes', *Journal of Economic Behavior and Organization*, vol. 5, pp. 287–320.

Part IV
Innovation and Export
Performance

12 Innovative Capabilities as Determinants of Export Performance and Behaviour: A Longitudinal Study of Manufacturing SMEs

*Elisabeth Lefebvre and Louis-André Lefebvre**

12.1 INTRODUCTION

Even though small and medium-sized enterprises' (SMEs) share of world trade still remains much lower than that of larger firms, numerous studies indicate that many SMEs are nevertheless very active abroad, and rely increasingly on the development of foreign markets to ensure corporate growth. For example, SMEs are 'directly producing about 20 per cent of OECD exports and about 35 per cent of Asia's exports' (OECD, 1997, p. 7). A report issued by the US Secretary of Trade and Commerce reveals that 70 per cent of all exporting firms were small firms with fewer than 100 employees (Prozak, 1993). SMEs are also the fastest-growing group of exporters in the USA (Axinn *et al.*, 1994, p. 49). A similar trend is observed in Canada, where the number of SMEs involved in export activities doubled in the six-year period from 1986 to 1992 (Industry Canada, 1996). In the future, SMEs are likely to be even more exposed to international competition (Reynold, 1997; OECD, 1997).

Considering the strategic role played by SMEs in industrialized economies, it appears essential to examine how they perform on international markets, and how they can improve their export performance. With this main objective, the specific focus of this chapter is to determine the role of firm-specific factors in export activities and, in particular, the relative importance of technological and commercial capabilities as determinants of export performance and behaviour, by analyzing empirical data from a longitudinal[1] survey of 3032 manufacturing SMEs over a three-year period.

12.2   THEORETICAL BACKGROUND

The chosen perspective is at the micro-business level, and the unit of analysis is the individual firm.

12.2.1   The Importance of Firm-specific Factors

This chapter focuses strictly on firm-specific factors related to export performance. There is now an established body of literature that points to the overwhelming importance of firm-specific factors, upon which competitive advantages are built (Amit and Schoemaker, 1993) and from which economic rents can be realized (Jacobson, 1988; Hansen and Wernerfelt, 1989). Several authors have found that firms differ widely within industries (Rumelt, 1991) with respect to either performance (Cool and Schendel, 1988), the enactment of technology policies and corporate strategies (Lefebvre *et al.*, 1997) or their use of technology (Davies, 1979; Baldwin and Rafiguzzaman, 1998). There is also convincing evidence that the firm-specificity of corporate applied R&D creates intra-industry differences (Helfat, 1994). The above studies are consistent with the resource-based view of the firm (Peteraf, 1993; Wernerfelt, 1984; Grant, 1991).

Within the theoretical perspective known as 'the resource-based view of the firm', we shall examine some firm-level determinants of export performance, and more specifically the role and importance of innovative capabilities. Capabilities refer here to a firm's ability to deploy resources, where resources are defined as 'stocks of available factors that are owned or controlled by a particular firm' (Amit and Schoemaker, 1993, p. 34). Capabilities are 'more broadly based (than core competencies) encompassing the entire value chain' of a particular firm (Stalk *et al.*, 1992, p. 62). Since innovation depends on technological capabilities as well as other 'critical capabilities in areas such as marketing and distribution' (Burgelman *et al.*, 1996, p. 8), innovative capabilities[2] will also include the commercial dimension.

12.2.2   Firms' Characteristics and Innovative Capabilities as Determinants of Export Performance and Behaviour

The literature on firm-level determinants of export performance and behaviour is extremely rich (see, for example, Chetty and Hamilton, 1993, for a thorough literature review on the subject), and covers a wide spectrum of issues, such as the relative importance of firms' demographics (Bonaccorsi, 1992; Wagner, 1995) or the relative impact of the beliefs, attitudes and perceptions of top management (Bijmolt and Zmart, 1994). We shall concentrate in this chapter on capabilities as determinants of export performance and behaviour, but this focus does not preclude the necessity to assess and control for the contribution of firms' characteristics to export entry and expansion.

Firms' Characteristics

Although the traditional assumption that in order 'to compete globally you have to be big' (Chandler, 1990) holds in several studies, a significant number of researchers have found no relationship, or a negative relationship, between *size* and exports (see, for example, Calof, 1993). These ambivalent results may partially be explained by the non-linear nature of this relationship (Lefebvre *et al.*, 1998). Furthermore, it is quite possible that, above a certain threshold, size no longer plays a significant role. Evidence from Australia, Denmark, Italy, Japan and Spain supports this observation: size is of considerable importance during the first stages of internationalization, but does not seem to be a significant factor afterwards (OECD, 1997). The overriding importance of relative size rather than absolute size may also explain these ambivalent results concerning the relationship between size and exports. Some smaller firms may well be important players in their own niche markets, whereas other SMEs find that they cannot compete with their larger rivals that occupy dominant market positions.

The relationship between *age* and exports may also produce conflicting results. On the one hand, more mature firms may have accumulated considerable knowledge stocks (Baldwin and Rafiquzzaman, 1998) and built strong core capabilities that allow them better to penetrate foreign markets. But on the other hand, core capabilities can become core rigidities or competence traps (Leonard-Barton, 1992) and younger firms may be more proactive, flexible and aggressive.

Larger, more mature manufacturers rely on domestic SMEs to provide them with components and subsystems that are inputs to their own products. It is therefore expected that contractors will realize more direct export sales than will subcontractors. *Manufacturing status* (contractor versus subcontractor) should thus be retained as a firm characteristic that must be controlled for.

Many SMEs are not unionized, but some are affiliated with various *trade unions*. Since it has been shown that strikes have a negative impact on trade performance (Greenhalgh *et al.*, 1994), the presence of trade union affiliations and their relation to export performance need to be investigated.

From the above arguments, Hypothesis 1 could be summarized as follows:

H1 – Firms' size, age, manufacturing status and presence of trade unions are characteristics that have to be controlled for when examining the relationships between capabilities and export performance, and behaviour in the context of SMEs.

Technological Capabilities

Technological capabilities refer to 'the firm's current ability and its future potential to apply firm-specific technology to solve technical problems and/or enhance the technical functioning of its production process and/or its finished products' (Nicholls-Nixon, 1995, p. 7). As competition is increasingly technology-based, it is expected that technological capabilities would play a major role in determining a firm's propensity to export. Kohn (1997, p. 50) suggests strongly that small exporters are able to compete on foreign markets because of their technological capabilities, but Sriram *et al.* (1989) observed a negative relationship between technology and exports, and Reid (1986) found no relationship. This warrants further investigation.

Among technological capabilities, in-house R&D not only generates innovations but also allows firms better to assimilate external technological knowledge. R&D is therefore viewed as one of the prime factors influencing export performance. The positive relationship between R&D and exports in small firms has been demonstrated by Ong and Pearson (1984). Moreover, SME exporters conduct more R&D (Baldwin *et al.*, 1994) and produce more patents (Moini, 1995).

The adoption of advanced manufacturing technologies has long been recognized as a key factor in the competitiveness of manufacturing firms (Naik and Chakravarty, 1992), as these technologies allow for increased productivity, improvements in product quality, or reductions in product rejection rates, all of which are essential on domestic and foreign markets. Benefits from automation increase both in scope and intensity, and employees' skills are enhanced, with increased technological penetration (Lefebvre *et al.*, 1995). In fact, the myth of deskilling following the adoption of new technologies has been contested strongly (Adler, 1986; Lefebvre *et al.*, 1996). An increased level of automation is thus viewed as an asset on foreign markets, and this assumption is supported by the fact that flexible manufacturing technologies have been related positively to exports (MacPherson, 1994). Similarly, modernization of machinery and equipment should also prove to be an asset if not an entry condition to operate on export markets.

Recognized quality norms and standards are often mandatory for an SME to qualify as a potential supplier (Ferguson, 1996). International norms such as ISO 9000 are in most cases a prerequisite for export activities (Chetty and Hamilton, 1996). National or sector-specific technical standards and norms, which are in certain cases more stringent and more comprehensive than international norms, carry less and less weight as they create artificial barriers between countries, regions and industries. In recent years, ISO has definitely increased its dominating influence on industrial buying behaviour, although one can argue that ISO 9000 certification as the only 'badge' of quality may in fact create market distortions. The relative impact of national and international quality norms on export performance will be examined.

One of the main downsides for SMEs is certainly the shortage of technological skills, as this was shown to be one of the strongest determinants of further advanced manufacturing technology adoption (Lefebvre *et al.*, 1996). This can hamper innovative capabilities seriously. The number of engineers, scientists and technicians reflects, to a great extent, a firm's stock of technological knowledge, and its technological knowledge intensity is expected to be related strongly to its export performance.

Small firms are responsible for a disproportionately large number of technological innovations in industrialized nations (Pavitt *et al.*, 1987; Rothwell, 1988), as well as in newly industrialized countries such as Korea (Lee, 1995). They also act as vital agents in the diffusion of technology, and their unique expertise is often based on the improvements they make to generic technologies developed elsewhere. This unique know-how should be a strong determinant of export performance.

As a result of the above discussion, Hypothesis 2 is proposed:

H2 – Technological capabilities, namely in-house R&D, level of automation, degree of modernization of equipment/machinery, technical knowledge intensity, unique expertise, and presence of quality norms, are all related positively to export performance and behaviour in the context of SMEs.

Commercial Capabilities

Market intelligence (Czinkota, 1982) and marketing capabilities (Haar and Ortiz-Buonafina, 1995) are shown to be prerequisites to export entry and expansion. In a sample of new high-technology firms, Fontes and

Coombs (1997) observed that small firms seem to be more able to overcome difficulties with technology than with the market. Since this sample was drawn from the information technology sector, there are some doubts as to whether the observation can be generalized. We will thus try to assess the relative contributions of a broader range of commercial capabilities to export performance, namely diversification, trademarks and/or proprietary products, networking in the form of commercial agreements with other firms, distribution access, manufacturing agents, and import activities.

Exports by SMEs based on a diversification strategy (range of products and diversity of product lines) have proven successful (Namiki, 1988) and are a major factor in export growth (Denis and Depelteau, 1985). If a firm operates in a number of industries, the knowledge and experiences acquired in one industry can be transferred to others, in particular with respect to commercial and competitive watch practices, which are highly related to export success (Christensen, 1991; Cafferata and Mensi, 1995). Diversification is thus assumed to contribute positively to SMEs' export performance, although this goes against the general tendency in recent years to reduce diversification and focus on core businesses (Markides, 1995), at least in the case of large firms.

Competitive advantages drawn from a unique product (Cooper and Kleinschmidt, 1985; Haar and Ortiz-Buonafina, 1995) or product specificity (Julien *et al.*, 1994) are linked positively to export performance. The presence of trademarks and, more often, of proprietary products should therefore be an asset for SMEs operating on foreign markets.

While showing dynamism and willingness to engage in international activities, SMEs face serious difficulties: under-capitalization (Buckley, 1997), imperfect information, and entry barriers erected by entrenched firms and by governments (Acs *et al.*, 1997) limit their international expansion. SMEs therefore turn to commercial agreements and strategic alliances with other domestic and foreign firms (networking) and rely on intermediaries (distributors and manufacturing agents) to enhance their export performance. The creation of marketing and distribution channels (Julien *et al.*, 1994) and an export entry based on intermediaries (Chetty and Hamilton, 1996) seem to sustain SMEs' international competitiveness.

Dealing beyond national frontiers is not limited to exports. In fact, import activities allow SMEs to experience cross-border activities with minimal risks. To what extent this first-hand knowledge of international activities influences the export performance of SMEs seems to be unknown, although there is an implicit assumption that it could be an advantage.

Hypothesis 3 is thus proposed:

H3 – Commercial capabilities, namely diversification, the presence of trademark and/or proprietary products, networking, distribution access, the use of a manufacturing agent and import activities, are all positively related to export performance and behaviour.

12.3 METHODOLOGY

12.3.1 Database and Procedures

The database used here is a subset of an existing database that is created and maintained for the purposes of offering contractors an inventory of available manufacturing capabilities within their region. It contains information on manufacturing firms acting as contractors or subcontractors, offering rich, valuable, detailed and up-to-date information on each firm.

In order to ensure adequate validity and reliability, the following four steps, first carried out in 1994 and repeated in 1997, were taken by the authors:

(i)   As 89 data fields exist on each firm, appropriate fields corresponding to the determinants identified previously were selected carefully;

(ii) Each field was validated and coded for each firm. Cross-validation within and between fields using computerized procedures was also carried out;

(iii) The data files were reprogrammed in order to be able to use multivariate data analysis methods; and

(iv) A hundred firms were randomly selected and data were cross-checked via a telephone survey. As the error rates were minimal (less than a tenth of 1 per cent for all fields for all firms), it was assumed that the database was very reliable.

In 1994, the database had information on 3289 manufacturing firms. In order to carry out a longitudinal analysis on exactly the same SMEs, two conditions were imposed:

(i)   Firms must have fewer than 500 employees in 1994, which corresponds to the definition of SMEs as accepted by organizations such as SBA (Small Business Administration) in the USA, the European Union, the OECD, or Statistics Canada and Industry Canada. The sample size dropped slightly to 3187 firms; and

(ii)   Firms identified in (i) must be present in both the 1994 and 199'
       databases. The sample size then fell again to 3032 firms. Some 15.
       firms therefore disappeared from the database in 1997, eithe
       because they went into bankruptcy or because they no longer wishe
       to be included in the database.

All subsequent analyses were performed on these 3032 firms.

12.3.2   Research Variables and their Operationalization

Table 12.1 displays more detailed information on the independent vari
ables namely firms' characteristics, technological capabilities and com
mercial capabilities. The database also provides factual information on
sales realized in the home province (Quebec) in other Canadian provinces
in the USA, in Europe and in other countries. In the case of non-exporters
it also allows the identification of those that would be interested in export
ing. The above data provide all the information needed to characterize
each particular firm by the following processes of internationalization: (i
non-exporters with no interest in exports; (ii) non-exporters with an inter
est in exports; (iii) domestic SMEs (with sales realized strictly in Canada)
(iv) North American SMEs (which are active in Canada and the USA
only); and (v) global SMEs (which generate sales in other foreign coun
tries). This five-stage internationalization process[3] builds on previous worl
by Cavusgil (1980), Christensen (1991), and Kleinschmidt and Coope
(1995).

12.3.3   Potential Biases and Strengths of the Chosen Research Strategy

The use of an industrial database as a source of empirical evidence create
some biases that must be discussed before presenting the results. First, the
database represents manufacturing firms engaged in subcontracting activities. Second, the firms in question have devoted time, effort and money to
ensure inclusion in this database: this represents an indication of an
emphasis on networking that is somewhat atypical of the smaller firms
These two points generate the following biases:

(i)   The firms are probably well-established, more mature, more innova-
       tive, and more 'networked';
(ii)   Some industrial sectors may be over-represented, while others could
       be under-represented; and

Table 12.1 Determinants of export performance and behaviour: firms' characteristics, technological and commercial capabilities

Determinants	Measures
Firms' characteristics	
Firm size	Annual sales; Number of full-time employees
Firm age	Number of years since the foundation of the firm
Manufacturing status	Subcontracting firms versus contractors
Trade unions	Existence of affiliation(s) with trade unions
Technological capabilities	
R&D	Presence or absence of R&D activities
Level of automation	Presence of CAD, CAM, CAE or any combination of these
Degree of modernization of equipment/machinery	Average age of the equipment/machinery (up to a maximum of 13 machines or pieces of equipment)
Knowledge intensity	Number of full-time engineers and scientists
Unique expertise	Presence or absence of a specific, unique type of expertise (mainly directed towards product and/or process innovations)
Quality norms	Presence or absence of the following quality norms (ISO 9001, 9002, 9003, 9004; Z299.1, Z299.2, Z299.3, Z299.4; MIL-Q-9858, MIL-I-4520; AQAP-1, AQAP-4, AQAP-9; AS1821, AS1822; DND 1015, 1016; BNQ 220, 210, 200)
Commercial capabilities	
Diversification	Number of different industrial sectors in which the firm operates (based on SIC codes)
Trademark/proprietary products	Presence or absence of trademark and/or proprietary products
Networking	Use of networks, alliances or other corporative agreements with other domestic or foreign firms
Distribution access	Presence or absence of distributor(s)
Manufacturing agent	Presence or absence of manufacturing agent
Import activities	Volume of imports realized by the firm

(iii)   The information contained in the database is useful for the allocation of subcontracting activities, and thus is highly directed towards standards, specifications and machinery. Table 12.1 shows, for example, that quality norms are well specified, whereas R&D activities are treated as just a bimodal variable, with no indication of the

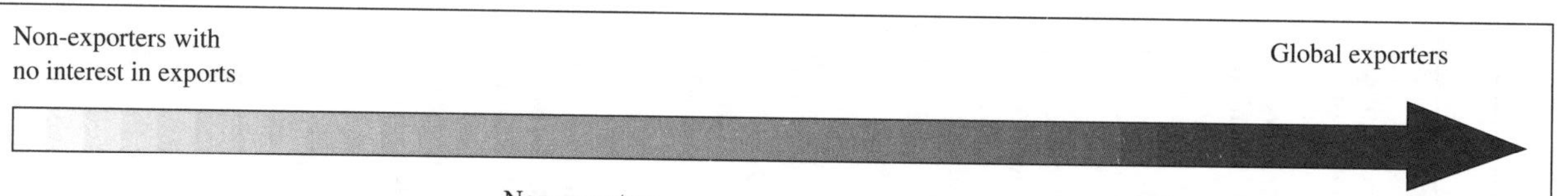

| | Non-exporters | | Active exporters | | |
	Non-exporters with no interest in exports	Non-exporters with an interest in exports	Exporters active in other Canadian provinces only	Exporters active in North-American markets only (USA and other Canadian provinces)	Exporters active beyond North-American markets
1994					
Number of firms	$n_1 = 382$	$n_2 = 1146$	$n_3 = 349$	$n_4 = 635$	$n_5 = 520$
Proportion of firms (%)	12.60	37.80	11.51	20.94	17.15
Average firm size (number of employees)	19	27	30	50	71
1997					
Number of firms	$n_1 = 331$	$n_2 = 621$	$n_3 = 446$	$n_4 = 907$	$n_5 = 727$
Proportion of firms (%)	10.92	20.48	14.71	29.91	23.98
Average firm size (number of employees)	20	31	36	69	140

Non-exporters with no interest in exports → Global exporters

Figure 12.1 SMEs and the process of internationalization

nature of or investment in such activities. The authors have no control over these variables, as is always the case with secondary sources of data.

Once the above biases have been taken into account, however, the database offers major strengths. First, it represents a unique source of longitudinal data based on a rather large sample size. With 3032 firms (for 1994 *and* 1997), almost 33 per cent of manufacturing SMEs of the province are represented. Second, the data are recent (1997). Third, the set of available variables displayed in Table 12.1 is rather exhaustive and some of the variables were not tested thoroughly in the literature.

12.4   RESULTS

12.4.1   Profile of SMEs and their Internationalization Process

As suspected, the database presents some biases with respect to sectorial and size representation. SMEs from the food, beverage and tobacco industries, the textiles and apparel industries, and petroleum and coal products were totally absent, whereas some sectors, such as metal products, were over-represented. Size representation is also slightly biased: medium-sized firms are more likely to be present. This should be taken into consideration when interpreting the results, and statistical analyses must take into account the industrial sector and firm size.

In 1994, more than half of SMEs were confined strictly to their local markets, but the vast majority of these non-exporters showed some interest in export activities (see Table 12.1). 11.51 per cent of SMEs generate some sales in other Canadian provinces. The remaining firms (which are 'true' exporters) were either active strictly in North American markets (20.94 per cent) or went beyond North America (17.15 per cent).

Between 1994 and 1997 there was a net change: the percentage of non-exporters decreased sharply from 50.1 to 31.4 per cent, and the same firms were much more active on foreign markets in 1997. In fact, in 1997, 1634 firms extended their sales beyond their domestic markets, compared to 1155 firms in 1994 (Table 12.1). There is no doubt that these SMEs became increasingly active on foreign markets during this three-year period.

However, Tables 12.2 and 12.3 show that the average volume of sales realized in the USA and foreign markets was rather modest in 1994 for all firms (8.01 per cent and 3.41 per cent, respectively – see Table 12.2), even for active exporters (16.16 per cent and 6.87 per cent respectively – Table 12.3). In 1997, these SMEs were much less dependent on their local markets, but most would not qualify as extensive or fully globalized SMEs, as defined by the OECD (1997).

12.4.2 Determinants of Export Performance and Behaviour

In order to assess the contribution and relative importance of the various determinants, multivariate analyses were conducted. Tobit and probit models allow us to assess, respectively: (i) the explanatory power of the independent variables towards export performance (that is, the percentage of sales realized by a particular firm on foreign markets); and (ii) the contribution of these independent variables to export behaviour (that is, the probability of a firm exporting). To begin with the interpretation of the outcomes, we shall start the discussion with those variables that turned out

Table 12.2 Mean percentage of sales realized by all SMEs in different markets, 1994 and 1997, percentages

	Average percentage of sales realized in:			
	Local markets (the province)	*Domestic markets (other Canadian provinces)*	*US markets*	*Other foreign markets*
1994 *n* = 3032	76.81	11.77	8.01	3.41
1997 *n* = 3032	67.77	15.72	12.97	3.54

Table 12.3 Mean percentage of sales realized by all exporters in different market, 1994 and 1997, percentages

	Average percentage of sales realized in:			
	Local markets (the province)	*Domestic markets (other Canadian provinces)*	*US markets*	*Other foreign markets*
1994 *n* = 1504	53.24	23.73	16.16	6.87
1997 *n* = 2080	53.01	22.92	18.90	5.16

to be non-determinants because they were removed from all subsequent analysis for the reason that they only introduce 'noise' and lengthen the presentation of statistical tables.

Independent Variables with No or Minimal Impact: Trade Unions, Technical Quality Norms and Degree of Modernization of Equipment

The fact that some variables are systematically not associated with any measure of export performance and behaviour is in itself a result. The existence of trade unions is not related to export performance or to the probability of exporting, whether in larger or smaller SMEs, in subcontracting firms or contractors, within all industrial sectors, or in 1994 versus 1997.[4] The existence of trade unions, which could raise the costs of production factors (mainly salaries), does not seem to hamper exports.

The presence of national or industry-specific technical norms such as Z2999, MIL, AQAP, AS, DND or BNQ gives ambivalent, but mostly positive, results. Although some of these norms are technically demanding, they remain related less significantly to export performance than does ISO 9000.[5] The adoption of the ISO 9000 series of standards by the major industrial nations, and the increasing reliance on ISO certification as a screening device for potential subcontractors contribute largely to the above results. In fact, between 1994 and 1997, the SMEs in this database adapted to this new reality and the number with ISO certification more than doubled. Furthermore, there is a strong relationship between adherence to a technical norm and ISO certification, resulting in some multicollinearity problems. The predominance of ISO 9000 over national, sectorial or subregional standards on international markets here receives additional empirical support. As a consequence of the above observations, only ISO certification will be included in the analyses.

The degree of modernization of equipment and machinery is not related to export performance.[6] In the context of SMEs, one would think that the presence of such important and capital-intensive physical assets would play a positive role on entering foreign markets. The operational measure of this particular variable (average age of all pieces of equipment) partially explains this surprising result: a firm with a large number of machines and pieces of equipment may be more penalized than a firm that has only recently invested in a few machines. Thus, the degree of modernization of equipment/machinery was also removed from the set of independent variables. As a result, 14 independent variables were retained for subsequent analyses.

Relative Importance of Each Determinants of Export Performance and Behaviour

Tobit and probit models are performed on the data obtained from the same 3032 manufacturing SMEs, first in 1994 and then in 1997 (see Table 12.4). With one exception, all independent variables are related positively to the dependent variables, both in 1994 and 1997 (Models 1, 2, 3 and 4). This reinforces our choice of innovative capabilities as determinants of export performance and behaviour. The only exception is diversification, which is related negatively to the percentage of sales realized on foreign markets in 1997 (Model 3) and non-significantly related to the dependent variable (Models 1, 2 and 4). Hence, diversification does not seem to be an asset on export markets, and SMEs, like larger firms, may do very well to concentrate on core products and core competencies.

Do Determinants of Export Performance and Behaviour Differ over the Three-year Period?

In 1994, the strongest determinants of export performance (Model 1 in Table 12.4) are in decreasing order: size, import activities, R&D, knowledge intensity, and distribution access. These five determinants are all significant at $p = 0.0000$. In 1997 (Model 3), the same five strongest determinants ($p = 0.0000$), are displayed, although size now plays a slightly less important role: this may be explained by the fact that an increasing number of the SMEs in our sample have increased in size and are more active on foreign markets.

The probability that SMEs will export is influenced significantly by two overriding factors, namely import activities and R & D (Models 2 and 4 in Table 12.4). Larger firms are also more likely to export, but size, once again, is less significant in 1997. The presence of manufacturing agents as well as knowledge intensity influence positively, and very significantly, the probability of exporting, both in 1994 and 1997.

Overall, we can observe an evolution in the relative importance of determinants of export performance and behaviour over the three-year period. With the exception of size and trademark, most determinants play a more significant and positive role in 1997:

(i)   This is particularly evident for the variables associated with the anticipated characteristics of firms conducting business in a knowledge-based and networked economy (Lefebvre *et al.*, 2001), namely knowledge intensity, level of automation, unique expertise and networking; and

Table 12.4 Determinants of export performance and behaviour, 1993 and 1997 ($n = 3032$)

Dependent variable	1993		1997	
	Percentage of sales realized on foreign markets Model 1 (tobit)	Probability of exporting Model 2 (probit)	Percentage of sales realized on foreign markets Model 3 (tobit)	Probability of exporting Model 4 (probit)
Constant	-49.98**** (-17.29)	-1.47**** (-20.45)	-31.83**** (-12.88)	-1.24**** (-13.82)
Firms' characteristics				
Firm size	0.14**** (8.87)	0.004**** (7.67)	0.02**** (5.91)	0.0004** (2.38)
Firm age	0.01 (0.24)	0.002* (1.36)	0.03 (0.87)	0.005*** (3.26)
Manufacturing status	0.83 (0.36)	0.03 (0.50)	8.67**** (4.72)	0.20** (2.65)
Technological capabilities				
R&D	18.16**** (8.18)	0.50**** (8.48)	14.55**** (8.16)	0.49**** (7.59)
Level of automation	0.76** (1.95)	0.03*** (2.58)	1.33**** (4.67)	0.01*** (2.91)
Knowledge intensity	0.83**** (5.98)	0.01*** (3.27)	0.82**** (6.89)	0.04*** (4.02)
Unique expertise	7.09*** (2.91)	0.21*** (2.88)	6.70**** (3.94)	0.21*** (3.05)
Quality norms	6.41* (1.58)	0.09 (0.71)	7.79*** (3.54)	0.24*** (2.51)

296

Table 12.4   Continued

Dependent variable	1993		1997	
	Percentage of sales realized on foreign markets Model 1 (tobit)	Probability of exporting Model 2(probit)	Percentage of sales realized on foreign markets Model 3 (tobit)	Probability of exporting Model 4 (probit)
Commercial capabilities				
Diversification	1.08	0.03	−0.51	0.06
	(1.20)	(0.57)	(−0.67)	(0.96)
Trademark	6.12***	0.15***	3.23**	0.14**
	(3.00)	(2.64)	(1.95)	(2.22)
Networking	2.22	0.08***	2.12*	0.05**
	(1.08)	(3.21)	(1.30)	(1.77)
Distribution access	7.52***	0.17***	8.25****	0.28****
	(3.52)	(2.76)	(4.90)	(4.12)
Manufacturing agent	7.14***	0.25****	7.80****	0.33****
	(3.21)	(3.97)	(4.52)	(4.72)
Import activities	17.72****	0.54****	14.86****	0.52****
	(8.44)	(9.52)	(9.23)	(8.72)
Log likelihood	−6784.72	−1627.33	8981.44	−1684.03
χ^2_{14}	748.54	775.96	863.10	816.79
Level of significance (χ^2)	p = 0.0000	p = 0.0000	p = 0.0000	p = 0.0000

Notes: * $p < 0.10$; ** $p < 0.05$; *** $p < 0.01$; **** $p < 0.0001$.

(ii)   Determinants related to the very practical down-to-earth issues encountered by SMEs are also stronger in 1997. This is the case for variables such as the access to distributors, the presence of manufacturing agents and the adherence to quality norms (that is, ISO 9000, which is being considered increasingly as the international badge on foreign markets).

Do Variables that Explain Export Intensity Differ from those Influencing the Probability of Exporting?

Surprisingly, the answer is negative: significant determinants appear to be identical, although if we place them in decreasing order of importance, the ranking is slightly different. The only exception is a firm's age, which is not related to export performance (Models 1 and 3 in Table 12.4) but influences significantly the probability of exporting (Models 2 and 4 in Table 12.4).

A firm's age may indeed indicate its stability, its maturity and the accumulation of knowledge stocks that are needed for first export activities, but age does not explain significantly the expansion of export activities.

Determinants of Export Performance in High-, Medium- and Low-knowledge Industries

In order to further investigate the relative importance of innovative capabilities, we have pooled the different industrial sectors into high-, medium- and low-knowledge industries. SMEs in low- and medium-knowledge industries share in 1997 the same five strongest determinants of export performance (import activities, R&D, knowledge intensity, distribution access, and size). These five determinants of export performance are also the five factors that influence positively and significantly the probability of exporting in the medium-knowledge industries. In low-knowledge industries, age (not size) seems significantly to predict the likelihood of a firm exporting. Table 12.5 clearly demonstrates the predominance of technological capabilities over the commercial capabilities as determinants of export performance and behaviour in SMEs from high-knowledge industries: all technological capabilities are significantly and positively related to both dependent variables (Models 5 and 6 in Table 12.5). Since high-technology exports have grown faster than other types of products/services (OECD, 1997), special attention should be paid to ensure that SMEs continue to build their technological capabilities.

Table 12.5 Determinants of export performance and behaviour in low-, medium- and high-knowledge industries, 1997 ($n = 3032$)[1]

Dependent variable	Low-knowledge industries $n_1 = 736$		Medium-knowledge industries $n_2 = 1724$		High-knowledge industries $n_3 = 376$	
	Percentage of sales realized on foreign markets Model 1 (tobit)	Probability of exporting Model 2 (probit)	Percentage of sales realized on foreign markets Model 3 (tobit)	Probability of exporting Model 4 (probit)	Percentage of sales realized on foreign markets Model 5 (tobit)	Probability of exporting Model 6 (probit)
Constant	−30.20****	−1.26****	−35.18****	−1.29****	−7.76	−0.89***
	(−5.55)	(−7.65)	(−11.31)	(−12.02)	(−1.08)	(−3.43)
Firms' characteristics						
Firm size	0.01***	0.08	0.03****	0.003****	0.04***	0.005***
	(2.65)	(0.23)	(5.64)	(5.91)	(2.40)	(2.67)
Firm age	0.14*	0.01***	0.06	0.003*	0.15**	0.001
	(1.58)	(3.42)	(1.28)	(1.63)	(1.71)	(0.34)
Manufacturing status	7.12**	0.20*	6.71***	0.04	−4.49	−0.07
	(1.69)	(1.46)	(2.76)	(0.43)	(−1.05)	(0.45)4
Technological capabilities						
R&D	13.56***	0.45****	16.84****	0.58****	8.33**	0.55***
	(3.57)	(3.95)	(7.51)	(7.50)	(1.94)	(3.51)
Level of automation	0.88*	0.05**	1.49****	0.04***	2.92****	0.06**
	(1.29)	(2.14)	(4.26)	(2.88)	(3.88)	(2.14)
Knowledge intensity	1.66***	0.05***	0.65****	0.008*	0.69**	0.03**
	(3.11)	(2.52)	(4.50)	(1.39)	(2.01)	(1.90)
Unique expertise	2.85	0.23*	5.73***	0.12*	12.27***	0.41***
	(0.65)	(1.61)	(2.73)	(1.53)	(2.87)	(2.48)

Quality norms	1.42	0.24	8.61***	0.06	11.51**	0.45**
	(0.23)	(1.06)	(3.32)	(0.54)	(2.12)	(1.84)
Commercial capabilities						
Diversification	−3.15**	−0.03	0.45	0.06**	−2.40	0.12*
	(−1.73)	(−0.52)	(0.49)	(1.69)	(−1.18)	(1.55)
Trademark	0.16	0.03	2.55	0.21***	−1.68	−0.12
	(0.05)	(0.29)	(1.22)	(2.77)	(−0.36)	(−0.74)
Networking	2.48	0.18**	2.06	0.05	7.65**	0.21
	(0.68)	(1.66)	(1.00)	(0.73)	(1.71)	(1.19)
Distribution access	10.03***	0.31***	8.19***	0.19**	5.59	0.12
	(2.80)	(2.75)	(3.65)	(2.14)	(1.10)	(0.69)
Manufacturing agent	8.20**	0.32***	7.82****	0.37****	6.68*	0.25*
	(2.17)	(2.58)	(3.51)	(4.12)	(1.46)	(1.42)
Import activities	21.61****	0.68****	12.59****	0.49****	3.56	0.11
	(6.11)	(6.32)	(6.21)	(6.66)	(0.83)	(0.69)
Log likelihood	−2073.26	−400.40	−4852.83	−911.94	−1377.63	−211.52
χ^2_{14}	176.99	209.73	566.26	520.31	84.98	85.16
Level of significance (χ^2)	$p = 0.0000$	$p = 0.0000$	$p = 0.0000$	$p = 0.0000$	$p = 0.0000$	$p = 0.0000$

Notes: 1. The groupings of industrial sectors are representative of Lee and Haas's (1996) classification. Similar results are obtained using OECD's classification (1997-b). * $p < 0.10$; ** $p < 0.05$; *** $p < 0.01$; **** $p < 0.0001$.

12.5 CONCLUSION

12.5.1 Brief Summary of Main Results

The results of the longitudinal survey of manufacturing SMEs reported on in this chapter have allowed us to examine the internationalization process of 3022 SMEs over a three-year period (1994–7) and the role of three categories of determinants of export performance and behaviour namely, firms' characteristics, technological capabilities, and commercial capabilities. Results demonstrate that most determinants in all three categories play a significant role. As a consequence, H1, H2 and H3 received overall strong support. Yet, out of the sixteen determinants, four did not show a positive relationship as had been hypothesized. These are:

(i)   The presence of trade unions, technical quality norms (with the exception of ISO 9000) and degree of modernization of equipment which were found to have no or minimal impact on exports; and
(ii) Diversification that is negatively related to export performance.

The strongest determinants are: import activities, R&D, distribution access, knowledge intensity, and size (the latter in the case of export performance). Determinants also vary according to the industrial sector. In high-knowledge industries, technological capabilities are the strongest while some commercial capabilities are more salient in low- and medium knowledge industries. In either low-, medium- or high-knowledge industries, R&D and knowledge intensity remain among the five strongest determinants of both export performance and behaviour. This suggests that international competition is indeed knowledge-based.

12.5.2 Implications

The focus of this chapter is on SMEs. This does not imply, however, that we play down the crucial role of larger firms. As a matter of fact, large dynamic firms have been, and are, responding to competitive (international) pressures by reducing organizational slack, retrenching on core competencies, and disposing of uncompetitive assets or operations. In doing so, they have received a bad press, especially as generators of jobs, but in reality they are contributing to the economic expansion of smaller firms, since SMEs are absorbing the results of the downsizing of large corporations. Furthermore, dynamic large firms and multinationals, in particular, often serve as international conduits for innovations of smaller firms (Acs *et al.*,

1997)[7] and definitely play a major direct and positive role in vertically integrated sectors. Let us simply state here that the lack of dynamic, competitive large firms could affect SMEs adversely, and that the reverse proposition is equally true.

Results have implications for academic researchers, CEOs, managers and practitioners as well as public policy-makers and, in some cases, they challenge certain widely accepted propositions. The following discussion is organized around some of the issues raised by the empirical evidence.

Issue 1: The Hidden Export Potential of SMEs

Despite an impressive and diversified literature on SMEs, gaps in our empirically-based knowledge seem to exist with respect to the export performance and behaviour of SMEs. In fact, 'very little is known about the process by which SMEs participate in the global economy' (Acs and Preston, 1997, p. 2). The empirical evidence presented in this chapter has demonstrated that many SMEs are indeed capable of facing international competition by building strong technological and commercial capabilities. According to the OECD, SMEs are not yet involved in the global economy to their full potential. Thus, we require:

(i)   A more accurate assessment of the current and future contribution of SMEs to the global economy. This assessment should include indirect exports (sales made to a domestic customer whose product is exported) and should focus not only on manufacturing firms but also on services;[8] and

(ii) The identification of SMEs with a strong export potential based on the most salient capabilities required on international markets, given that persistent real differences in capabilities have proven to constitute comparative advantages on export markets. Some encouraging facts emerge from the empirical evidence presented here: an increased number of SMEs are entering the international scene and, once they have started their export activities, they continue to progress to the more advanced stages of globalization. There is no sign of 'de-internationalization' or regression to the less advanced stages. The main purpose is to target the SMEs with the most potential, and to design policies and programmes accordingly.

Issue 2: The Positive Bias towards High-tech and High-knowledge-based Industries

Are we suffering from 'high-tech snobbery'?[9] There is a general tendency to focus on high-tech (OECD, 1997) and high-knowledge-based sectors

(Lee and Haas, 1996). Concerns with these sectors are omnipresent in the research community[10] as well as in public policy agencies.

Technological capabilities are powerful determinants of export performance and behaviour, but so are commercial capabilities and continuous efforts towards innovativeness in the non-technological dimensions. This suggests that building stronger technological and non-technological capabilities may be more important than operating in a particular high-knowledge-based sector. The following courses of action could be envisaged:

(i) Close monitoring of firms in the low- and medium-knowledge industries. Key to their competitiveness in foreign markets is the effectiveness with which they apply and use the full spectrum of their technological skills. Promotion of 'high-tech SMEs' within the low- and medium-knowledge industries could be one of the ways of ensuring visibility and creating 'a bandwagon effect' for other firms. The need to stimulate technological innovation is indeed greater than ever in all sectors, including the low- and medium-tech sectors.

(ii) Continued strong support for the international activities of SMEs in the low- and medium-knowledge industries. Empirical evidence shows that R&D and knowledge intensity are indeed strong determinants of export performance and behaviour in these industries: these firms tap into specialized skills and gain knowledge from these different foreign environments. During the internationalization process, organizational learning occurs, more advanced or specialized skills are sought, and firms become more knowledge-intensive.

Issue 3: The Neglected Role of Established SMEs

The literature displays a positive bias towards start-ups and spin-offs. There is an even stronger bias in favour of the new technology-based firms (this is obviously linked to Issue 2 above), especially in the biotechnology and information technology sectors (Hoffman *et al.*, 1998). As a result, we have gained considerable knowledge of these firms, but we know little about established SMEs, which have generally not been examined by researchers (for an exception, see North and Smallbone, 1996). In most countries, government assistance programmes, incentives and tax measures reflect similar biases.

Are government export assistance programmes more cost-effective[1] among established SMEs than among younger firms? Are the competitive advantages gained by established SMEs from their experience in foreign markets more sustainable? It would certainly be worthwhile to provide more definite answers to these questions.

Issue 4: Tailored Government Export Assistance Programmes

There is a general consensus that export assistance programmes should be tailored to the needs of SMEs. Barriers to entry in foreign markets are 'systematically higher for smaller firms than they are for larger firms' (Acs *et al.*, 1997): shortages of capital and management skills (Buckley, 1997), imperfect information (Acs *et al.*, 1997), and entry barriers errected by entrenched firms and governments. Although assistance programs do exist, they are still not known well enough and used by SMEs (Moini, 1998). Furthermore, they are not specifically designed to correspond to the needs of firms as they move along the different stages of the internationalization process. Increased attention could be paid to the continuous improvement of technological and commercial capabilities.

The four issues discussed above are very much interrelated. All four point to the same conclusion: exports by SMEs from all sectors of economic activity should be encouraged strongly, since they strengthen existing capabilities and contribute to the acquisition of new competencies and skills.

Notes

*   We wish to thank two annonymous referees for their insightful comments.
1.   Our research design qualifies as a longitudinal survey, since the same firms were observed twice over a period of time.
2.   This in line with the following: innovative capabilities can be defined as the comprehensive set of characteristics of an organization that facilitate and support innovation strategies (Burgelman *et al.*, 1996, p. 8).
3.   The degree of internationalization of a firm is a multifaceted concept (Ramanswamy *et al.*, 1996), and export performance represents only one dimension, albeit an important one, of this concept. Even when one limits oneself strictly to the dimension of export performance, numerous export development models exist (Leneidou and Katsikeas, 1996). Some are based on the successively greater commitment of resources to foreign markets (Johanson and Wiedersheim-Paul, 1975), the notion of psychological distance (Bilkey and Tesar, 1977), the notion of passive versus active exporters or reactive versus active exporters (Cavusgil, 1980, 1982) or the degree of control exercised by exporters in overseas operations (Wortzel and Wortzel, 1981). Other models are simply based on the level and frequency of export activities (Rao and Naidu, 1992) or of trade activities (OECD, 1997). For instance, Rao and Naidu (1992) consider that firms go through several stages

from non-exporters to failed exporters, first-time exporters, expanding exporters, and continuing exporters. An index of globalization ranging from 1 (domestic SMEs) to 10 (fully globalized SMEs) was proposed very recently by the OECD using the volume of traded inputs and outputs as well as the geographic coverage of these activities (OECD, 1997, p. 23). The five-stage internationalization process proposed here is simply based on the volume and destination of sales. Non-exporters (stages 1 and 2) are local SMEs whose sales are realized totally within one province. Domestic firms (third stage) have some extra-provincial sales, but no sales outside Canada: interstate or inter-provincial 'exports' are considered as a first and crucial step for SMEs before they engage in 'real' exports (Christensen, 1991, p. 52). Proximate export markets (third stage) are markets that are not too distant on geographical and/or psychological grounds: the USA, which historically has been by far Canada's largest trading partner, is considered as a proximate export market. Finally, exports realized in other foreign countries (fourth stage) are viewed as more demanding than the US markets and are a better indicator of the export performance of Canadian firms (Porter, 1991). Empirical evidence also shows that global markets require more substantial efforts than North American markets (Lefebvre *et al.*, 1998).

4. Some 54 tobit models and 54 probit models were performed and the level of significance for this variable never went below $p = 0.10$.

5. Tobit and probit models tested the relative importance of each technical norm (presence or absence of Z2999, MIL, AQAP, AS, DND and BNQ) for larger and smaller SMEs, subcontractors and contractors, within each industry, and in 1994 and 1997. As an alternative solution, the level of severity of all possible norms was introduced with less success than the simple presence or absence of ISO 9000.

6. It is insignificant in 97 models out of 108.

7. The authors make the following additional comment: 'Because of the greater scale and scope of multinational firms' global markets, the small innovative support firms can earn greater returns, and they do not even have to spend resources to overcome barriers against international expansion themselves!' (Acs *et al.*, 1997, p. 14).

8. The internationalization process for business service SMEs has received much less attention in the literature than manufacturing SMEs (for an exception, see O'Farrell *et al.*, 1998).

9. This expression was used by Van Hulst and Olds (1993) in their provocative analysis of the alleged exclusion of small countries from high-tech sectors.

10. For example, Hoffman and his co-authors arrive at the following conclusion based on their thorough literature survey of British work on SMEs and innovation during the 1990s: there is an 'over-concentration of the SME research community on a fairly narrow set of technology-intensive and new technology-based sectors, most notably biotechnology and, to a lesser extent, IT. (For example, 80% of the case studies with a high-technology focus in our review are concerned with these sectors)' (Hoffman *et al.* 1998, p. 41).

11. Contradictory evidence seems to exist. On the one hand, new firms show high exit rates (Kirchhoff and Greene, 1998) and, in many cases, a vast amount of effort, resources and capital is wasted. On the other hand, mature

firms seem to lose their ability to innovate, especially large, established firms (Leavey, 1997). Furthermore, in the case of subsidies for job creation, grants (capital grants, project grants, rent assistance) are 'more effective in small firms, but only those which are new or relatively young in age' (Wren, 1998, p. 279).

References

ACS, Z. J. and PRESTON, L. (1997) 'Small and Medium-sized Entreprises, Technology, and Globalization: Introduction to a Special Issue on Small and Medium-sized Entreprises in the Global Economy', *Small Business Economics*, vol. 9, pp. 1–6.

ACS, Z. J., MORK, R., SHAVER, J. J. and YOUNG, B. (1997) 'The Internationalization of Small and Medium-sized Enterprises: A Policy Perspective', *Small Business Economics*, vol. 9, pp. 7–20.

ADLER, P. S. (1986) 'New Technologies, New Skills', *California Management Review*, vol. 29, no. 1, pp. 9–28.

AMIT, R. and SCHOEMAKER, P. J. H. (1993) 'Strategic Assets and Organizational Rent', *Strategic Management Journal*, vol. 14, pp. 33–46.

AXINN, C. N., SAVITT, R., SINKULA, J. M. and THACH, S. V. (1994) 'Export Intention, Beliefs, and Behaviours in Smaller Industrial Firms', *Journal of Business Research*, vol. 32, pp. 49–55.

BALDWIN, J. R. and RAFIQUZZAMAN, M. (1998) 'The Determinants of the Adoption Lag for Advanced Manufacturing Technologies', in L. A. Lefebvre, R. Mason and T. Khalil (eds), *Management of Technology, Sustainable Development and Eco-Efficiency*, Amsterdam: Elsevier.

BALDWIN, J. R., CHANDLER, W., LE, C. and PAPAILIADIS, T. (1994) *Strategies for Success: A Profile of Growing Small and Medium-sized Enterprises (GSMEs) in Canada*. Ottawa, Canada: Business and Labor Market Analysis Division, Statistics Canada.

BIJMOLT, T. H. A. and ZWART, P. S. (1994) 'The Impact of Internal Factors on the Export Success of Dutch Small and Medium-Sized Firms', *Journal of Small Business Management* (April), pp. 69–83.

BILKEY, W. J. and TESAR, G. (1977) 'The Export Behavior of Smaller Wisconsin Manufacturing Firms', *Journal of International Business Studies*, vol. 8, no. 1, pp. 93–8.

BONACCORSI, A. (1992) 'On the Relationship Between Firm Size and Export Intensity', *Journal of International Business Studies*, vol. 23, no. 4, pp. 605–35.

BUCKLEY, P. J. (1997) 'International Technology Transfer by Small and Medium-sized Enterprises', *Small Business Economics*, vol. 9, pp. 67–78.

BURGELMAN, R. A., MAIDIQUE, M. A. and WHEELWRIGHT, S. C. (eds) (1996) *Strategic Management of Technology and Innovation* (2nd edn), Chicago, Ill.: Irwin.

CAFFERATA, R. and MENSI, R. (1995) 'The Role of Information in the Internationalization of SMEs: A Typological Approach', *International Small Business Journal*, vol. 13, no. 3, pp. 35–45.

CALOF, J. L. (1993) 'The Impact of Size on Internationalization', *Journal of Small Business Management*, vol. 31, no. 4, pp. 60–9.

CAVUSGIL, S. T. (1992) 'Some Observations on the Relevance of Critical Variables for Internationalization Stages', in M. R. Czinkota and G. Tesar (eds), *Export Management: An International Context*, New York: Praeger, pp. 276–85.

CAVUSGIL, S. T. (1980) 'On the Internationalization Process of Firms', *European Research*, vol. 9, pp. 273–81.

CHANDLER, A. D. (1990) 'The Enduring Logic of Industrial Success', *Harvard Business Review* (March–April), pp. 130–40.

CHETTY, S. K. and HAMILTON, R. T. (1993) 'Firm-Level Determinants of Export Performance: A Meta-analysis', *International Marketing Review*, vol. 10, pp. 26–34.

CHETTY, S. K. and HAMILTON, R. T. (1996) 'The Process of Exporting in Owner-controlled Firms', *International Small Business Journal*, vol. 14, no. 2, pp. 12–25.

CHRISTENSEN, P. R. (1991) 'The Small and Medium-sized Exporters Squeeze: Empirical Evidence and Model Reflection', *Entrepreneurship and Regional Development*, vol. 3, pp. 49–65.

COOL, K. and SCHENDEL, D. (1988) 'Performance Differences among Strategic Group Members', *Strategic Management Journal*, vol. 9, no. 3, pp. 207–24.

COOPER, R. G. and KLEINSCHMIDT, E. J. (1985) 'The Impact of Export Strategy on Export Sales Performance', *Journal of International Business Studies* (Spring), pp. 37–55.

CRAMER, J. S. (1991) *The Logit Model for Economists*. London: Edward Arnold.

CZINKOTA, M. R. (1982) *Export Development Strategies: U.S. Promotion Policy*. New York: Praeger.

DAVIES, S. (1979) *The Diffusion of Process Innovations*. Cambridge University Press.

DENIS, J. E. and DEPELTEAU, D. (1985) 'Market Knowledge, Diversification and Export Expansion', *Journal of International Business Studies* (Fall), pp. 68–89.

FERGUSON, W. (1996) 'Impact of ISO 9000 Series Standards on Industrial Marketing', *Industrial Marketing Management*, vol. 25, pp. 305–10.

FONTES, M. and COOMBS, R. (1997) 'The Coincidence of Technology and Market Objectives in the Internationalization of New Technology-based Firms', *International Small Business Journal*, vol. 15, no. 4, pp. 14–35.

GRANT, R. B. (1991) 'A Resource Based Theory of Competitive Advantage: Implications for Strategy Formulation', *California Management Review*, vol. 33, no. 3, pp. 114–35.

GREENE, W. H. (1997) *Econometric Analysis*, 3rd edn. Englewood Cliffs, NJ: Prentice-Hall.

GREENHALGH, C., TAYLOR, P. and WILSON, R. (1994) 'Innovation and Export Volumes and Prices: A Desegregated Study', *Oxford Economic Papers*, vol. 46, pp. 102–34.

HAAR, J. and ORTIZ-BUONAFINA, M. (1995) 'The Internationalization Process and Marketing Activities: The Case of Brazilian Export Firms', *Journal of Business Research*, vol. 32, pp. 175–81.

HAIR, J. F., ANDERSON, R. E., TATHAM, R. L. and BLACK, W. C. (1992) *Multivariate Analysis with Readings*. New York: Macmillan.

HANSEN, G. S. and WERNERFELT, B. (1989) 'Determinants of Firm Performance: The Relative Importance of Economic and Organizational Factors', *Strategic Management Journal*, vol. 10, pp. 399–411.

HELFAT, C. E. (1994) 'Firm-specificity in Corporate Applied R&D', *Organization Science*, vol. 5, no. 2, pp. 173–84.
HOFFMAN, K., PAREJO, M., BESSANT, J. and PERREN, L. (1998) 'Small Firms, R&D, Technology and Innovation in the UK: A Literature Review', *Technovation*, vol. 18, no. 1, pp. 39–55.
INDUSTRY CANADA (1996) *Small Business in Canada: A Statistical Overview*. Ottawa (Ca.): Research Publication Program.
JACOBSON, R. (1988) 'The Persistence of Abnormal Returns', *Strategic Management Journal*, vol. 9, pp. 41–58.
JOHANSON, J. and WIEDERSHEIM-PAUL, F. (1975) 'The Internationalization of the Firm: Four Swedish Cases', *Journal of Management Studies* (October), pp. 305–22.
JULIEN, P. A., JOYAL, A. and DESHAIES, L. (1994) 'SMEs and International Competion: Free Trade Agreement or Globalization?', *Journal of Small Business Management* (July), pp. 52–64.
KIRCHHOFF, B. A. and GREENE, P. G. (1998) 'Understanding the Theoretical and Empirical Content of Critiques of US Job Creation Research', *Small Business Economics*, vol. 10, pp. 153–69.
KLEINSCHMIDT, E. J. and COOPER, R. G. (1995) 'The Performance Impact of an International Orientation on Product Innovation', *European Journal of Marketing*, vol. 20, no. 10, pp. 56–71.
KOHN, T. O. (1997) 'Small Firms as International Players', *Small Business Economics*, vol. 9, pp. 45–51.
LEAVY, B. (1997) 'Innovation and the Established Organization', *Journal of General Management*, vol. 22, no. 3, pp. 38–62.
LEE, F. and HAAS, H. (1996) 'A Quantitative Assessment of High-Knowledge Industries versus Low-Knowledge Industries', in P. Howitt (ed.), *The Implications of Knowledge-Based Growth for Micro-economic Policies*. Calgary: University of Calgary Press, pp. 39–81.
LEE, J. (1995) 'Small Firms' Innovation in Two Technological Settings', *Research Policy*, vol. 24, pp. 391–401.
LEFEBVRE, E., LEFEBVRE, L. A. and BOURGAULT, M. (1998) 'R&D-related Capabilities as Determinants of Export Performance', *Small Business Economics*, vol. 10, pp. 365–77.
LEFEBVRE, L. A., LEFEBVRE, E. and HARVEY, J. (1996) 'Intangible Assets as Determinants of Advanced Manufacturing Technology Adoption in SME's: Towards an Evolutionary Model', *IEEE Transactions on Engineering Management*, vol. 43, no. 3, pp. 307–22.
LEFEBVRE L. A., LEFEBVRE, E. and MOHNEN, P. (eds) (2001) *Doing Business in the Knowledge-Based Economy: Facts and Policy Challenges*. forthcoming: Nowell, Mass.: Kluwer. (494 pages)
LEFEBVRE, E., LEFEBVRE, L. A. and ROY, M. J. (1995) 'Technological Penetration and Organizational Learning in SMEs: The Cumulative Effect', *Technovation*, vol. 15, no. 8, pp. 511–22.
LEFEBVRE, L. A., MASON, R. M. and LEFEBVRE, E. (1997) 'The Influence Prism in SMEs: The Power of CEOs' Perceptions on Technology Policy and its Organizational Impacts', *Management Science*, vol. 43, no. 6 (June), pp. 856–79.

LENEIDOU, L. C. and KATSIKES, C. S. (1996) 'The Export Development Process: An Integrative Review of Empirical Models', *Journal of International Business Studies* (third quarter).

LEONARD-BARTON, D. (1992) 'Core Capabilities and Core Rigidities: A Paradox in Product Development', *Strategic Management Journal*, vol. 13 (Summer), pp. 111–26.

MACPHERSON, A. D. (1994) 'Industrial Innovation among Small and Medium-sized Firms in a Declining Region', *Growth and Change*, vol. 25 (Spring), pp. 145–63.

MARKIDES, C. C. (1995) 'Diversification, Restructuring and Economic Performance', *Strategic Management Journal*, vol. 16, pp. 101–18.

MOINI, A. H. (1995) 'An Inquiry into Successful Exporting: An Empirical Investigation Using a Three-Stage Model', *Journal of Small Business Management* (July), pp. 9–25.

MOINI, A. H. (1998) 'Small Firms Exporting: How Effective Are Government Export Assistance Programs?', *Journal of Small Business Management* (January), pp. 1–15.

NAIK, B. and CHAKRAVARTY, A. K. (1992) 'Strategic Acquisition of New Manufacturing Technologies: A Review and Research Framework', *International Journal of Production Research*, vol. 30, no. 7, pp. 1575–601.

NAMIKI, N. (1988) 'Export Strategy for Small Business', *Journal of Small Business Management*, vol. 26, no. 2, pp. 33–37.

NICHOLLS-NIXON, C. (1995) 'Responding to Technological Change: Why Some Firms Do and Others Die', *The Journal of High Technology Management Research* (Spring), pp. 1–16.

NORTH, D. and SMALLBONE, D. (1996) 'The Role of Established SMEs in Regional and Local Economic Development: A Case of Neglect?', in R. Blackburn and P. Jennings (eds), *Small Firms: Contributions to Economic Regeneration*, London: Paul Chapman, pp. 87–98.

O'FARELL, P. N., WOOD, P. A. and ZHENG, J. (1998) 'Internationalisation by Business Service SMEs: An Inter-industry Analysis', *International Small Business Journal*, vol. 16, no. 2, pp. 13–33.

OECD (1997) *Globalization and Small and Medium Enterprises (SMEs)*, vol. 1 (Synthesis Report) and vol. 2 (Country Studies), Paris 1997.

ONG, C. H. and PEARSON, A. W. (1984) 'The impact of Technical Characteristics on Export Activity: A Study of Small and Medium-sized UK Electronics Firms; in: *R&D Management*, vol. 12, no. 4, pp. 189–96.

PAVITT, K., ROBSON, M. and TOWNSEND, J. (1987) 'The Size Distribution of Innovation Firms in the UK: 1945–1983', *Journal of Industrial Economics*, vol. 35, no. 3, pp. 297–317.

PETERAF, M. A. (1993) 'The Cornerstones of Competitive Advantage: A Resource-Based View', *Strategic Management Journal*, vol. 14, pp. 179–92.

PORTER, M. E. and the Monitor Company (1991) *Canada at the Crossroads: The Reality of a New Competitive Environment*, Ottawa (Ca.): Business Council of National Issues and Minister of Supply and Services.

PROZAK, S. L. (1993) 'Small Businesses are Exporting', *Business America*, vol. 114, no. 24, pp. 2–8.

RAMASWAMY, K., KROECK, K. G. and RENFORTH, W. (1996) 'Measuring the Degree of Internationalization of a Firm: A Comment', *Journal of International Business Studies* (first quarter), pp. 167–77.
RAO, T. R. and NAIDU, G. M. (1992) 'Are the Stages of Internationalization Empirically Supportable?', *Journal of Global Marketing*, vol. 6, no. 1–2, pp. 147–70.
REID, S. D. (1986) 'Is Technology Linked with Export Performance in Small Firms?', in H. Hubner (ed.), *The Art and Science of Innovation Management*, Amsterdam: Elsevier, pp. 273–83.
REYNOLD, P. D. (1997) 'New and Small Firms in Expanding Markets', *Small Business Economics*, vol. 9, pp. 78–84.
ROTHWELL, R. (1988) 'Small Firms, Innovation and Industrial Change', *Small Business Economics*, vol. 1, no. 1, pp. 51–64.
RUMELT, R. P. (1991) 'How Much Does Industry Matter?', *Strategic Management Journal*, vol. 12, no. 3, pp. 167–85.
SRIRAM, V., NEELANKAVIL, S. and MOORE, R. (1989) 'Export Policy and Strategy Implications for Small-to-Medium-sized Firms', *Journal of Global Marketing*, vol. 3, no. 2, pp. 43–60.
STALK, G., EVANS, P. and SHULMAN, L. E. (1992) 'Competing on Capabilities: The New Rules of Corporate Strategy', *Harvard Business Review* (March–April), pp. 57–69.
VAN HULST, N. and OLDS B. (1993) 'On High-Tech Snobbery', *Research Policy*, vol. 22, pp. 455–62.
WAGNER, J. (1995) 'Exports, Firm Size and Firm Dynamics', *Small Business Economics*, vol. 7, pp. 29–39.
WERNERFELT, B. (1984) 'A Resource-based View of the Firm', *Strategic Management Journal*, vol. 5, pp. 171–80.
WORTZEL, L. H. and WORTZEL, H. V. (1981) 'Export Marketing Strategies for NIC and LDC-Based Firms', *Columbia Journal of World Business* (Spring), pp. 51–60.
WREN, C. (1998) 'Subsidies for Job Creation: Is Small Best?', *Small Business Economics*, vol. 10, pp. 273–81.

13 R&D and Export Performance: Taking Account of Simultaneity

*Alfred Kleinknecht and Remco Oostendorp**

13.1 INTRODUCTION

While the Heckscher–Ohlin–Samuelson (HOS) theory explained international trade by differences in factor endowments (assuming that each country possesses the same technology), we saw during the 1980s a revival of interest in 'neo-technology' or 'technology gap' theories of international trade. While these theories go back to the seminal work by outsiders such as Posner (1961), Vernon (1966) and Hufbauer (1966), there are signs that they are becoming adopted by mainstream economists (see the survey by Siebert, 1991).

A number of empirical studies found a positive relationship between innovation and export performance. Examples are the work by Wolter (1977), Van Hulst and Soete (1989), Hirsch and Bijaoui (1985), and Hughes (1986). However, some studies raised doubts about this relationship (Hulsman-Vejsová and Koekkoek, 1980; Schlegelmilch and Crook 1988). Brouwer and Kleinknecht (1993) concluded that finding a relationship between indicators of innovation and export performance is dependent on the inclusion of adequate control variables. Moreover, the distinction between product and process innovation may add explanatory power.

In studies on innovation and exports, one important aspect has somehow been neglected. Many authors find a positive relationship between innovation and export, but the direction of causality is left open. Often it is assumed implicitly that R&D has a positive impact on export performance. However, it may well be that export success influences innovative investments. The rationale behind this is that R&D expenditures (and other innovation costs) tend to be fixed costs. As a consequence, expansion in export markets leads to declining unit costs of R&D that will enhance R&D investment. Hughes (1986) was the first to estimate a simultaneous model on sectoral export and R&D data, finding indications of a mutual relationship. A weakness of Hughes' approach is that sectors can be quite heterogeneous.

In this chapter, we estimate a simultaneous model using firm-level data. Section 13.2 presents the database and the model. In section 13.3 we present a summary of our estimates and some conclusions.

13.2 THE DATABASE AND THE MODEL

Our data are from the enterprise survey by OSA (Organization for Strategic Labour Market Research of the Netherlands). The data cover the year 1994. We have selected the 1773 firms that operate in the market sectors of the Dutch economy, including agriculture, manufacturing, construction, trade, transport, communications, and services. The survey is confined to firms that have five or more employees. Descriptive statistics on some key variables used in our estimates are listed in Appendix 13.1 (see page 318).

R&D efforts may influence a firm's export position positively, since it leads to new products and/or to achieving lower production costs. On the other hand, besides achieving economies of scale to R&D, expansion on foreign markets can increase the probability of a firm picking up foreign technology spillovers. It will also favour a quicker move along the learning curve. All this argues for formulation of a simultaneous equation model that allows a firm's R&D to influence exports, and exports to influence R&D efforts. We therefore estimate the following two-equation model:

$$R\&D = a_0 + a_1 \text{ export} + a_2 \text{ control variables} + \text{disturbance term}$$

$$\text{export} = b_0 + b_1 R\&D + b_2 \text{ control variables} + \text{disturbance term}.$$

As a measure of export performance, we use exports as a percentage of a firm's total sales. As measures of innovation, we use R&D expenditures (as a percentage of sales). We estimate our equations in two steps:

Step 1: A probit estimate that informs us about factors that influence the probability that a firm will have any R&D or any exports; and

Step 2: An OLS estimate that informs us about factors that influence a firm's R&D intensity or its export intensity, given that a firm has some R&D, or some exports.[1]

Since R&D and export performance are likely to be mutually dependent, we need to include in each of the two equations above at least one variable that is not included in the other equation, and which is safely exogenous. We decided to include the dummy variable 'the firm is strongly dependent on the mother company when taking decisions about innovation' in the R&D equation, but not in the export equation. The dummy variable 'the firm is located close the national borders' is included in the export equation, but not in the R&D equation. We assume that these are correct exclusion restrictions because:

- Dependence on the mother companies regarding decisions on innovation are likely to influence R&D, but not export;
- Location in a region close to the country's borders may imply that part of a firm's home market is abroad. In other words, part of a firm's local or regional sales may be counted formally as exports. In this case, exports are likely to have little to do with R&D performance. For the demarcation of regions we use the Dutch system of COROP regions which subdivides the country into 42 regions.

We estimate the Step 1 and Step 2 equations twice: (i) simple estimates that take no account of simultaneity; and (ii) an instrumented version, taking account of simultaneity between R&D and exports, and using the above exclusion restrictions.[2]

13.3   RESULTS

Tables 13.1–13.4 document a summary of our estimates. We document in each table two versions: one with, and one without, taking account of simultaneity. In Table 13.1 we find a significant impact of export intensity on the probability that a firm will have some R&D on both versions. This result is robust for our control for simultaneity. As expected, our instrumented variable ('firm is strongly dependent on its mother company regarding decisions on innovation') shows a significantly negative sign. Other control variables behave as expected: the probability of having some R&D activity is related positively to firm size and to education levels. However, it is not related to regions. In general, firms in service sectors have lower probabilities of performing any R&D than firms in manufacturing sectors.

Table 13.2 shows that the probability that a firm will be an exporter is influenced significantly by its R&D intensity, in both versions of our estimate. Our control variable ('firm is located close to the border') is also highly significant, while other regional dummies prove insignificant. Not surprisingly, the probability of being an exporter is influenced positively by firm size, underlining the importance of scale economies. As expected,

Table 13.1 Factors influencing the probability that a firm will have some R&D activities: summary of probit estimates (t-values in brackets)

	Model without instruments	Model with instruments
Continuous variables		
Export intensity	0.01 (3.75)	0.01 (4.27)
Firm size (log of employees)	0.18 (4.39)	0.18 (4.70)
Market share of 4 largest sellers in sector of principal activity	−0.05 (0.17)	−0.03 (0.11)
Share of employees with higher education	1.25 (3.56)	1.29 (3.89)
Share of employees with medium-level education	−0.15 (0.70)	−0.00 (0.02)
Dummy variables		
Firm is located in the country's semi-periphery*	−0.06 (0.51)	−0.11 (0.93)
Firm is located in the country's periphery*	−0.01 (0.07)	−0.05 (0.40)
Firm is a holding**	0.63 (2.68)	0.62 (2.86)
Firm is a daughter of a foreign group**	0.25 (1.24)	0.26 (1.38)
Firm is a daughter of a domestic group**	0.07 (0.46)	−0.02 (0.13)
Firm is a branch plant**	0.59 (2.39)	0.64 (2.51)
Firm belongs to a high technological opportunity manufacturing sector[@]	0.13 (0.79)	0.15 (0.98)
Construction and installation[@]	−0.40 (1.98)	−0.42 (2.18)
Trade, transport and communication[@]	−0.37 (1.95)	−0.35 (1.98)
Commercial services[@]	−0.29 (1.28)	−0.30 (1.39)
Firm produces for industrial clients	0.14 (1.29)	0.25 (2.13)
Firm is strongly dependent on mother company when taking decisions about innovation	−0.68 (4.47)	−0.76 (4.63)
Firm underwent a major restructuring (previous 2 years)	0.26 (2.30)	0.25 (2.28)
Constant term	−1.21 (5.40)	−1.31 (5.88)
Number of observations	833	833
prob > χ^2	0.00	0.00

Notes: * reference group: firms located in the Rim City (Randstad) and North Brabant (for details see Budil-Navornikova *et al.*, 1999); ** reference group: an independent firm; [@] reference group: low technological opportunity sectors; the latter are identical to Pavitt's (1984) 'supplier-dominated' sectors.

Table 13.2 Factors influencing the probability that a firm will be an exporter: summary of probit estimates (t-values in brackets)

	Model without instruments	Model with instruments
Continuous variables		
R&D intensity	0.05 (2.95)	0.05 (3.59)
Firm size (log of employees)	0.31 (6.76)	0.35 (7.79)
Market share of 4 largest sellers in sector of principal activity	−0.21 (0.67)	−0.25 (0.89)
Share of employees with higher education	0.67 (1.64)	0.45 (1.21)
Share of employees with medium-level education	−0.24 (1.00)	−0.53 (2.30)
Dummy variables		
Firm is located in the country's semi-periphery*	−0.01 (0.06)	−0.06 (0.45)
Firm is located in the country's periphery*	0.05 (0.34)	0.09 (0.66)
Firm is a holding**	0.37 (1.51)	0.37 (1.68)
Firm is a daughter of a foreign group**	0.60 (2.72)	0.68 (3.26)
Firm is a daughter of a domestic group**	0.06 (0.42)	0.12 (0.88)
Firm is a branch plant**	−0.03 (0.09)	−0.08 (0.30)
Firm belongs to a high technological opportunity manufacturing sector@	0.37 (2.02)	0.36 (2.27)
Construction and installation@	−1.25 (5.69)	−1.35 (6.19)
Trade, transport and communication@	−0.49 (2.50)	−0.47 (2.70)
Commercial services@	−1.13 (4.35)	−1.06 (4.37)
Firm produces for industrial clients	0.48 (3.67)	0.38 (3.01)
Firm is located close to the border	0.36 (3.06)	0.40 (3.66)
Firm underwent a major restructuring (previous 2 years)	0.06 (0.42)	0.05 (0.40)
Constant term	−1.59 (6.06)	−1.60 (6.28)
Numbers of observations	770	770
prob > χ^2	0.00	0.00

Notes: * reference group: firms located in the Rim City (Randstad) and North Brabant (for details see Budil-Navornikova *et al.*, 1999); ** reference group: an independent firm; @ reference group: low technological opportunity sectors; the latter are identical to Pavitt's (1984) 'supplier-dominated' sectors.

high technological opportunity sectors are more export-intensive than low technological opportunity (manufacturing) sectors, and the latter are in turn still more export-intensive than service industries.

Table 13.3 covers the OLS estimates of R&D intensities of those firms that have some R&D. The strong effect of export intensity on R&D intensity is again robust to the model choice. Our exogenous control variable ('firm is strongly dependent on its mother company regarding decisions on innovation') has the expected negative sign, and so do the various sector dummies. In general, it is not so easy to achieve a good explanation of inter-firm differences of R&D intensities, which is also obvious from our relatively low R-square of 0.10. For example, there is hardly any evidence of differences in R&D intensities that can be ascribed to regions, and this is consistent with earlier findings (using a different database on the Dutch economy) by Kleinknecht and Poot (1992). It is remarkable that firms in markets with a high degree of concentration (that is, a high market share of the four largest sellers) are not more R&D intensive than are firms in markets with low concentration levels. This supports Scherer's (1992) cautious conclusions about Schumpeter's famous market power hypothesis. Finally, the positive Heckman term underlines the necessity of correcting for selectivity.

Table 13.4 summarizes our OLS estimates of export intensities (given that a firm has some exports). To our surprise, a firm's R&D intensity appears to have no influence on its export intensity. In the model that takes no account of simultaneity (column 1), the R&D intensity is significant at the 10 per cent level. However, this effect seems to result from a simultaneity bias. Our exogenous control variable ('firm is located close to the border') has the expected ambiguous impact on exports: firms located close the border have a higher probability of having some exports (Table 13.2), but they do not have a significantly higher export intensity. In fact, they appear to have relatively low export intensities, but the effect is not significant (Table 13.4). Other regional dummies, again, do not matter, and the sector dummies behave as expected: service firms generally have lower export intensities than do manufacturing firms. Finally, it is interesting to note that there is less evidence than expected for scale effects: firm size has a positive influence only in the model that takes no account of simultaneity and the coefficient of market concentration is positive, but only weakly significant in both versions. Finally, it is interesting to note the positive impact on export intensity (in the simultaneous model) of the share of employees with higher education.

One could argue that inclusion of the higher education variable in the export equations (Tables 13.2 and 13.4) might influence the coefficients of R&D intensity, because of multicollinearity. It appeared, however, that this

316 *R&D and Export Performance*

Table 13.3 Factors influencing a firm's R&D intensity: summary of OLS estimates (t-values in brackets)

	Model without instruments	Model with instruments
Continuous variables		
Export intensity	0.06 (3.47)	0.10 (3.22)
Firm size (log of employees)	−0.03 (0.09)	0.44 (0.86)
Market share of 4 largest sellers in sector of principal activity	1.87 (0.97)	1.37 (0.72)
Share of employees with higher education	11.7 (4.52)	15.4 (3.95)
Share of employees wit medium-level education	−0.32 (0.20)	−0.29 (0.18)
Dummy variables		
Firm is located in the country's semi-periphery*	−0.72 (0.98)	−1.03 (1.37)
Firm is located in the country's periphery*	0.19 (0.24)	−0.25 (0.30)
Firm is a holding**	1.33 (0.97)	2.99 (1.41)
Firm is a daughter of a foreign group**	1.09 (0.91)	1.75 (1.43)
Firm is a daughter of a domestic group**	−1.17 (1.29)	−1.53 (1.59)
Firm is a branch plant**	4.28 (2.41)	6.10 (2.60)
Firm belongs to a high technological opportunity manufacturing sector@	2.08 (2.00)	2.27 (2.10)
Construction and installation@	−1.80 (1.16)	−2.94 (1.58)
Trade, transport & communication@	−2.61 (1.91)	−3.79 (2.19)
Commercial services@	−1.40 (0.85)	−1.94 (1.10)
Firm produces for industrial clients	−0.22 (0.31)	0.67 (0.75)
Firm is strongly dependent on mother company when taking decision about innovation	−4.75 (3.19)	−7.19 (3.21)
Firm underwent a major restructuring (previous 2 years)	1.09 (1.56)	1.26 (1.74)
Heckman term	8.97 (3.13)	14.8 (2.97)
Constant term	−4.08 (0.99)	−12.1 (1.73)
Number of observations	216	216
Adjusted R^2	0.12	0.10

Notes: * reference group: firms located in the Rim City (Randstad) and North Brabant (for details see Budil-Navornikova *et al.*, 1999); ** reference group: an independent firm; @ reference group: low technological opportunity sectors; the latter are identical to Pavitt's (1984) 'supplier-dominated' sectors.

effect is quite small. Tentative omission of the higher education variable led to only a modest increase of the coefficient of R&D intensity. By the same reasoning, one could argue that the higher education variable in the R&D equations of Tables 13.1 and 13.3 might be endogenous, and therefore

Table 13.4 Factors influencing a firm's export intensity: summary of OLS estimates (t-values in brackets)

	Model without instruments	Model with instruments
Continuous variables		
R&D intensity	0.95 (1.75)	−0.39 (0.26)
Firm size (log of employees)	4.90 (2.10)	2.45 (0.72)
Market share of 4 largest sellers in sector of principal activity	10.5 (0.98)	15.3 (1.32)
Share of employees with higher education	22.9 (1.73)	29.4 (1.94)
Share of employees with medium-level education	−0.19 (0.02)	4.39 (0.40)
Dummy variables		
Firm is located in the country's semi-periphery*	0.08 (0.02)	−0.26 (0.06)
Firm is located in the country's periphery*	7.70 (1.68)	7.56 (1.62)
Firm is a holding**	6.30 (0.72)	4.33 (0.49)
Firm is a daughter of a foreign group**	10.4 (1.69)	6.29 (0.83)
Firm is a daughter of a domestic group**	6.83 (1.40)	5.40 (1.04)
Firm is a branch plant**	−8.84 (1.03)	−8.85 (1.02)
Firm belongs to a high technological opportunity manufacturing sector@	1.42 (0.28)	0.39 (0.07)
Construction and installation@	−31.2 (2.94)	−20.6 (1.34)
Trade, transport and communication@	−5.91 (0.90)	−3.07 (0.41)
Commercial services@	−31.6 (3.79)	−24.2 (2.07)
Firm produces for industrial clients	5.28 (1.23)	2.52 (0.46)
Firm is located close to the border	−2.68 (0.64)	−4.88 (1.06)
Firm underwent a major restructuring (previous 2 years)	−4.62 (1.24)	−3.39 (0.85)
Heckman term	6.83 (0.65)	−7.69 (0.42)
Constant term	−1.23 (0.07)	21.2 (0.73)
Numbers of observations	282	282
Adjusted R^2	0.15	0.13

Notes: * reference group: firms located in the Rim City (Randstad) and North Brabant (for details see Budil-Navornikova *et al.*, 1999). ** reference group: an independent firm. @ reference group: low technological opportunity sectors; the latter are identical to Pavitt's (1984) 'supplier-dominated' sectors.

the coefficient of higher education might be upward-biased. However, given that the direct correlation between the share of highly-educated people and R&D intensity is only 0.08, we can assume that this upward bias is quite small.

13.4   CONCLUSIONS

From the above, we can conclude that:

- A firm's export intensity has a positive impact on its probability of having any R&D and on its R&D intensity; and
- A firm's R&D intensity has a positive impact on its probability of being an exporter. However, while a high R&D intensity acts as an entry ticket to export markets, it has no influence on export intensity (that is, on export sales as a percentage of total sales).

The latter finding does not confirm our expectations, and it is at odds with some of the findings quoted in our introduction. A possible explanation refers to the time lags in our model. We explain a firm's export intensity in 1994 with the firm's R&D intensity in 1992. This time lag is determined by data availability. It could well be that a longer time lag between undertaking R&D and export success would have been more appropriate.

Our results suggest there to be two options for government policy: (i) government may support R&D activities, since this will increase the probability that a firm will export; or (ii) government may support export activities, since this will enhance a firm's probability of undertaking some R&D, and export success may also enhance R&D intensities. Finally, education policies that increase the share of highly-educated people in the labour force may enhance both processes.

Appendix 13.1

Table A13.1   Description of variables and descriptive
statistics on some key variables

Variables	Mean	Stand. dev.
Export intensity (export sales as a percentage of total sales)	14.3	26.8
R&D intensity (R&D as a percentage of total sales)	1.6	3.7
Percentage shares of firms belonging to:		
agriculture	5.4	22.5
high technological opportunity manufacturing sectors	14.4	35.2
low technological opportunity manufacturing sectors	18.6	38.9
construction and installation	28.5	45.2
trade, transport and communication	21.3	41.0
Firm size (natural log of numbers of employees)	3.4	1.6
Share of personnel with higher education	10.5	16.3
Share of personnel with medium education	30.0	25.0
Firm products for industrial clients	84.0	48.1

Table A13.1 Continued

Variables:	Mean	Stand. dev.
Firm is located in the country's semi-periphery	21.9	41.4
Firm is located in the country's periphery	19.0	39.2
Average Market share of the 4 largest sellers	48.0	24.5
Firm is strongly dependent on mother company when taking decisions about innovation	19.1	39.3
Firm is located close to the border	33.4	47.1

Notes

* Our research was supported by OSA, the Organization for Strategic Labour Market Research. We thank the staff members of OSA, in particular Piet Allaart and Jean-Paul Vosse for valuable comments on an earlier version.

1. We also include a Heckman correction term from Step 1 to control for sample selection bias.

2. For the instrumented version, we used a 2-stage instrumental estimation procedure. In the first stage, we estimated a tobit regression to explain the R&D and export intensity of the firm, as a function of *all* exogenous variables (not reported). Here we found that the R&D intensity does not depend significantly on whether the firm is located close to the border, but it does depend significantly on whether the firm is strongly dependent on the mother company when taking decisions about innovation. The opposite is true for the export intensity. This confirms our choice of exclusion restrictions. In the second stage we used the predicted R&D intensity and export intensity as instruments for the observed R&D and export intensity. For the probit regression (Step 1), we used the predicted R&D and export intensities to form a non-linear 2SLS estimator (see Amemiya, 1985, pp. 245–9). For the OLS (Step 2), we used the predicted R&D and export intensity to form the 2SLS estimator.

References

AMEMIYA, T. (1985) *Advanced Econometrics*. Cambridge, Mass.: Harvard University Press.
BUDIL-NADVORNIKOVA, H., BROUWER, E. and KLEINKNECHT, A. (1999) 'Are Urban Agglomerations a Better Breeding Place for Product Innovation? An Analysis of New Product Announcements', *Regional Studies*, vol. 33, pp. 541–50.
GRUNERT, G. (1990) *Technologische Innovationen und Internationaler Handel*, thesis, University of Osnabrück, Germany.

HIRSCH, S. and BIJAOUI, I. (1985) 'R&D Intensity and Export Performance: A Micro View', *Weltschaftliches Archiv*, vol. 121, pp. 238–51.

HUFBAUER, G. C. (1966) *Synthetic Materials and the Theory of International Trade*, London: Duckworth.

HUGHES, K. (1986) *Exports and Technology*, Cambridge: University Press.

HULSMAN-VEJSOVÁ, M. and KOEKKOEK, K. A. (1980) 'Factor Proportions, Technology and Dutch Industries' International Trade Patterns', *Weltwirtschaftliches Archiv*, vol. 116, pp. 162–77.

KLEINKNECHT, A. and POOT, T. P. (1992) 'Do Regions Matter for R&D?', *Regional Studies*, vol. 26, pp. 221–32.

PAVITT, K. (1984): 'Sectoral Patterns of Technological Change. Towards a Taxonomy and a Theory', *Research Policy*, vol. 13, pp. 343–73.

POSNER, M. V. (1961) 'International Trade and Technical Change', *Oxford Economic Papers*, vol. 13, pp. 323–42.

SCHERER, F. M. (1992) 'Schumpeter and Plausible Capitalism', *Journal of Economic Literature*, vol. 30, pp. 1416–33.

SCHLEGELMILCH, B. B. and CROOK, J. N. (1988) 'Firm-level Determinants of Export Intensity', *Managerial and Decision Economics*, vol. 9, pp. 291–300.

SIEBERT, H. (1991) 'A Schumpeterian Model of Growth in the World Economy: Some Notes on a New Paradigm in International Economics', *Weltwirtschaftliches Archiv*, vol. 127, pp. 800–12.

TUYL, J. C. M. (1987) 'R&D en Concurrentievermogen', *Economisch Statistische Berichten*, vol. 72, pp. 140–3.

VAN HULST, N. and SOETE, L. (1989) 'Export en Technologische Ontwikkeling in de Industrie', *Proceedings of the Royal Dutch Economics Association*, Leiden: Stenfert-Kroese, pp. 63–86.

VERNON, R. (1966) 'International Investment and International Trade in the Product Cycle', *Quarterly Journal of Economics*, vol. 80, pp. 190–207.

WOLTER, F. (1977) 'Factor Proportions, Technology and West German Industry's International Trade Patterns', *Weltwirtschaftliches Archiv*, vol. 113, pp. 250–67.

Index

324 *Index*

Index